D1605397

Structured
VAX BASIC
A GOTO-less Approach

WILSON T. PRICE
RICHARD SPITZER California State University, Hayward

Structured
VAX BASIC
A GOTO-less Approach

Macmillan Publishing Company
NEW YORK
Collier Macmillan Publishers
LONDON

Copyright © 1988, Macmillan Publishing Company, a division of Macmillan, Inc.

Printed in the United States of America

Macmillan Publishing Company
866 Third Avenue, New York, New York 10022

Collier Macmillan Canada, Inc.

Library of Congress Cataloging in Publication Data.

Price, Wilson T.
  Structured VAX BASIC.

  Includes index.
    1. VAX computers—Programming. 2. BASIC (Computer program language) 3. Structured programming. I. Spitzer, Richard. II. Title.
QA76.8.V32P75 1988   005.2'45   87-11329
ISBN 0-02-396620-3

Printing: 1 2 3 4 5 6 7 8   Year: 8 9 0 1 2 3 4 5 6 7

PREFACE

During the 1970s important programming techniques (program modularization and structured methods) developed by computer scientists found their way into the world of commercial programming. Even though commonly used languages (such as Basic) were not especially compatible with the theory underlying these techniques, much success was achieved in implementing the theory in program design. The effect was very significant in improved program quality and programmer productivity. Languages that are specifically designed around structure theory, such as Pascal, allow a full implementation of the theory. On the other hand, most commonly used versions of Basic, with their heavy dependence on the GOTO, were very amendable to poor programming practices. The outstanding feature of Basic in the past was the great ease with which beginners could learn it, a feature for which fully structured languages have not been particularly noted. The very sophisticated versions of Basic now available, including VAX Basic, have placed the merits of Basic in a new perspective. In fact, VAX Basic includes features such as numerous control structures and block capabilities that are specifically oriented to take advantage of modern programming techniques and theory. The result is that the "kludges" previously used to achieve good structure are no longer necessary. Program code more readily follows from the program design, resulting in programs that are easier to understand, write, and maintain. VAX Basic is indeed a full production language with powerful structured capabilities and with its original ease of learning left intact.

As the title suggests, this book is written around the powerful features of VAX Basic. However, to consider it merely as a book on VAX Basic is to shortchange it, for this is a book on how to design good program solutions to problems using sound structured techniques (from a beginner's perspective). These solutions are implemented in VAX Basic as part of the learning process.

Important Features

Without doubt the most significant feature of this book is the extent to which structured theory is incorporated throughout. The powerful features of VAX Basic (such as numerous looping structures, block capabilities, and a case structure) allow broad implementation of structured techniques. Taking advantage of the rich language features, we introduce a simple form of the WHILE–NEXT in Chapter 3 (the second programming chapter). This gets the student doing repetitive processing using the looping structure almost immediately.

Although we place heavy emphasis on standardization and the use of structured techniques, we feel that is is not appropriate to be bound by total adherence to any standard if strict adherence results in clumsy code. For instance, we advocate using the EXIT statement (where appropriate) to force early exit from a controlled loop. Structured purists take a dim view of this. We consider such restricted transfers of control to be not only acceptable but highly desirable. If it does the job in a clear and understandable fashion, we use it. Our objective is good programs that utilize structured methods and are consistent with the many demands and complications of real-life tasks that the programmer encounters.

The subtitle of this book, "A GOTO-less Approach," really gets to the heart of what we are doing. (It is a slight misnomer, because we do describe the GOTO.) It is important to understand that programs in this book are *not* written with the intent of eliminating the GOTO. It is simply a case in which careful program design and use of the structured features of VAX Basic eliminate the need for the GOTO. As with most rules, there is an exception. The powerful error-trapping features of VAX Basic (ON ERROR statement) force a limited use of the GOTO in the version of VMS that was available to us when we began the book.

A glance at the table of contents will show you that we introduce the use of sequential files relatively early (Chapter 7). The student has little difficulty with this concept when it is approached from the viewpoint that getting data from a file is little different from getting it from a series of DATA statements or from the keyboard. With data input from files, much more meaningful programs can be introduced.

Much has been made of the evils of line numbers in Basic. Although it is possible to program VAX Basic using very few line numbers, example programs in the textbook use line numbers liberally. The reason is to provide the student with a tool that makes it easy to modify program statements without describing a separate editor. Instructors who wish to introduce an editor at an early stage can set a standard of minimizing line numbers in programs. To this end, the solutions to programming assignments in the Instructor's Manual contain a minimum of line numbers.

Another important aspect of our teaching philosophy relates to our handling of a complex new topic. That is, in many instances we introduce just enough for the student to use the material, but not all of the details. The WHILE–NEXT/EXIT combination is a good example. It is introduced with a use-it-because-it-works philosophy in Chapter 3. Conditional operations are described in Chapter 5, and the full complement of looping structures, in Chapter 8. Our experience has shown arrays to be the single topic that gives students the most difficulty. We have gone to considerable lengths to make this subject palatable.

About Our Usage of Terms

The word BASIC is an acronym for Beginner's All-purpose Symbolic Instruction Code. As such, it is normally written with all capital letters. However, we feel that with its broad usage, it has effectively become a word in itself. To that end, we have elected to capitalize only the first letter (Basic), thereby treating it as any other proper noun

Regarding the word *data*, we found ourselves in a quandary. In common usage the word *data* is treated as plural and *datum*, as singular. However, in data processing, *data* is commonly treated as singular. We interpret this usage as referring to a set, or collection of data values—hence, singular. Throughout this book we treat *data set* as singular and *data values* as plural.

Pedagogy

Students learn best by doing. This book is oriented to that end. Each chapter is opened with a statement of objectives and closed with a summary. In the first chapter, the student is given a simple program to enter into the computer and run, in order to become familiar with the overall process. Numerous examples are clearly stated and then solved. Several tools are used: hierarchy charts, flowcharts, and pseudocode. Numerous program solutions, some that are complete programs and others that are program segments, are presented. Important points are identified 1, 2, 3, ... In-chapter exercises are included for the student to answer before progressing further. Many of these relate to the subtleties of the example programs. Solutions to the exercises are given at the end of the chapter. Programming assignments at the end of the chapters have been selected to be both realistic and easy for the student to understand.

Programming Assignments

This book includes over 80 programming assignments. Great care has been taken to provide assignments in a variety of application areas. Also, the assignments for each chapter have been designed to reflect varying levels of difficulty. These assignment features provide maximum flexibility in making selections for a well-rounded course.

Instructor's Manual

The instructor's manual that accompanies this book includes:

1. Projection transparency masters of appropriate figures from the book.
2. For each programming assignment in the book:
   a. A listing of sample data file.
   b. A sample solution.
   c. A listing of sample output.

Furthermore, to simplify use of these materials, the sample solutions and data files, together with the example program solutions, are available on magnetic tape.

Acknowledgments

One of the advantages of being a teacher is the opportunity to work with a wide variety of people and to see so many different viewpoints. We have gained and learned from many others: students, colleagues, and fellow authors. We would like to express our special appreciation to the many individuals who made valuable contributions. The following four individuals deserve special thanks for their in-depth reviews and many helpful comments:

Ronald Dalla, Eastern Washington University
Ann Goodman, University of Massachusetts, Amherst
Cynthia Johnson, Bryant College
Larry Seiford, University of Massachusetts, Amherst

We thank Bob Mason for machine testing the example programs and program segments. In addition, we must give special thanks to Varda Schub for her care in typing the entire manuscript and in assisting with preparation of a multitude of materials. We sincerely appreciate the conscientious contributions of the staff at Macmillan in ensuring that this be a quality book: Mary Pickering (copy editor), Ronald Harris (college production), and David Johnstone (editor responsible for the project). To all who contributed, we offer our sincere thanks.

W. P.
R. S.

CONTENTS

1

Introduction to Computer Concepts

Chapter Outline

Preview

The purpose of this chapter is to introduce a broad range of subjects that will serve as the basis for learning to program in Basic. Important topics covered in this chapter are the following:

1. *The distinction between computer hardware and software.*
2. *The basic components of the computer: input/output, memory, control unit, arithmetic/logic unit, and auxiliary storage.*
3. *Characteristics of computer memory.*
4. *Computer software, including operating systems.*
5. *The nature of timesharing, whereby a single computer is shared by many users.*

6. *The principles of files, records, and fields.*
7. *The actions involved in preparing a problem for computer solution.*
8. *How to enter and run a program on the computer.*

Computer Hardware

Components of the Computer

A computer is an electronic device that can be used to process information and obtain results. The computing equipment itself is called *hardware*. The programs of instructions that make the computer work are called *software*. The combination of hardware and software is called a *computer system*. We shall learn more about software later in this chapter. For now, let us devote our attention to the hardware components that make up a computer.

For use within this book, we shall consider the functional components of the computer to be those illustrated schematically in Figure 1-1. The arrows show the possible directions of information flow. Following is a brief description of these components.

Input/Output. As the name implies, *input* units allow us to enter data into the computer for processing. Very often the only input device that many beginning students ever see is the keyboard that is attached to a computer *terminal*. However, there is a wide variety of other devices used for input, including machines that read data bar codes, such as those seen on items in the grocery store, magnetically encoded checks, and even handwritten documents.

Results of the machine computations are made available to us through *output* devices. The device that most students are familiar with is the terminal itself. Some terminals are much like typewriters and thus produce printed output. However, the most commonly encountered one is the CRT (meaning cathode-ray-tube) terminal.These units display the results on a television-like screen. The distinction between output to a printing terminal and that to a screen is important. Printer output is commonly called *hard copy* because it represents a permanent copy of the output. This is in contrast to the output to a screen, which is called *soft copy* because it is gone when the next screen is displayed.

Although printed output from terminals is convenient in some cases, it is relatively slow. For high-volume printing, printers that print full lines or even pages at a time are commonly used. There are many other types of output

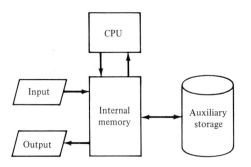

Figure 1-1. The logical components of a computer system.

devices, such as plotters that plot output in "picture" form and audio devices that speak to us.

Internal Memory. *Internal memory* is, in a sense, the information center of the computer. (Internal memory is also referred to as *primary memory* or *main memory*.) In general, information stored in memory falls into two broad categories: the instructions that comprise a program and the data upon which those instructions will operate. For instance, whenever a program (consisting of instructions telling the computer what to do) is to be run, that program must first be placed into memory (loaded). Then when the program is run, any *data to be processed by the program must be brought into memory* by the program instructions. Basic programs that we shall write in this book will allow us to bring data into memory, to manipulate the data, and to output the results. Special control commands will allow us to move programs into and out of memory.

The main memory of any computer is a highly organized storage area divided into individual storage units. For most commonly encountered computers, including the Digital Equipment Corporation VAX (the computer referred to in this book), the elementary unit of memory is called the *byte*. In a nutshell, the byte has the capacity for storing one character of information. Thus, in order to store the phrase

THIS IS A LINE.

the computer would use exactly 15 consecutive bytes of memory. Note that in addition to the letters, this line includes three spaces and a period; a space is a character that takes up one byte. Similarly, the Social Security number

336928111

would occupy 9 bytes, but if stored with "normal" punctuation, as

336-92-8111

it would occupy 11. Data quantities of this type are commonly called *alphanumeric* data because they can consist of letters of the alphabet, digits, or even special characters (such as the hyphen).

Whereas one byte is used for each character of an alphanumeric data item, numeric information is stored in quite a different way. That is, for numeric data, the system reserves two, four, or even eight consecutive bytes, depending on the type of numeric data it is. (We shall learn about the different data types in Chapter 6.)

There are two important and distinct concepts associated with each memory location: its *address* and its *contents*. In analogy, one can think of houses on a street; the addresses remain the same even though the occupants of any given house may change. The same is true of computer memory: the address of each position is permanent but the contents may change as a program is run. This change in the contents of a memory address is illustrated in Figure 1-2 for alphanumeric information. The Social Security number 336-92-8111 is

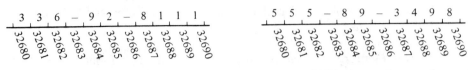

(a) When processing first person   (b) When processing second person

Figure 1-2.   Information in computer memory.

shown residing in 11 consecutive bytes of memory in Figure 1-2(a). During the course of processing, the number for one person could be replaced in that address by that of another, as shown in Figure 1-2(b); the most recent one is then replaced by the next one, and so on. Making the distinction between the address of a memory location and its contents is important, as we shall see in Chapter 2.

Central Processing Unit. The Central Processing Unit (CPU) is the computer's "control center." It includes two basic parts: the *control unit* and the *arithmetic/logic unit*. The task of directing operations within the computer is the function of the control unit. This portion of the computer can be considered analogous to a combination of traffic officer and automatic telephone switchboard. It obtains instructions from memory, interprets them, and makes certain that they are carried out as required. These functions require the opening and closing of appropriate circuits, starting and stopping of input/output devices, and, in general, directing the flow of information within the computer.

The arithmetic/logic unit contains the electronic switches and circuits necessary for computations. They provide the capability to perform, directly or indirectly, the operations of addition, subtraction, multiplication, and division. In addition to arithmetic, this portion of the computer performs *logical operations*. Herein lies the key to the versatility of the modern computer because logical operations provide "decision-making" capabilities. For instance, in a system to process credit card purchases, each time a new purchase is added to a customer account, it might be necessary to compare the customer balance to some maximum allowable amount.

Auxiliary Storage. When a program is to be run, it must first be placed into internal memory. After the program has run to completion, both the program and any data in memory from the program are replaced with something else, usually another program. During the course of a day, many hundreds of programs might be loaded into memory and run. If this is the case, then there is an obvious need for a storage area to keep programs that are not currently in use. Furthermore, it is important that the CPU be able to get programs (or data) from this storage area immediately as needed. Such a device is called *auxiliary storage* and is used for long-term retention of both programs and sets of data. Auxiliary storage can best be thought of as equivalent to a large file cabinet capable of storing huge quantities of information. As a rule, the capacities of auxiliary storage devices are many times those of internal memory units. Auxiliary storage is also called *mass storage* and *secondary storage*. The most commonly encountered types of auxiliary storage are *magnetic tape* and *magnetic disk*. The tape used in computer systems is similar to that used in ordinary home tape recorders. The most important characteristic of tape relates to its very nature. That is, the standard tape is 2400 feet long, and information is stored on it from one end to the other. Thus, if data values are required from a particular part of the tape, it may take some time (even for the computer) to get them since it takes time to wind and unwind the tape. In contrast, magnetic disk functions in an entirely different way. Many people have had some exposure to this medium because the common floppy disk used on home computers is, in fact, a magnetic disk storage medium. Without going into detail, magnetic disk provides very fast access to stored information regardless of where it is on the disk.

There is another very important difference between internal memory and auxiliary storage. That is, if the computer is shut down or power is lost even for an instant, the contents of internal memory are lost. In this respect, internal memory is said to be *volatile*. On the other hand, the computer can be completely shut down without affecting the information stored on auxiliary storage devices. In fact, many of the disk storage units in common use utilize removable disk "packs" that are stored in cabinets, in much the same way that we might store tape cassettes on a bookshelf.

In the computer field, the words *memory* and *storage* are commonly used interchangeably. However, in this book, *memory* will refer to internal memory, and *storage* will refer to auxiliary storage.

The Digital Equipment Corporation VAX

The computer around which this book is oriented is the Digital Equipment Corporation's (DEC) VAX. The VAX is a powerful extension of DEC's PDP-11 series of computers. The first generation of the VAX series includes several models of the VAX-11, including 11/725, 11/750, 11/780, and 11/785. Early in 1985, DEC began introducing its second-generation VAX computers, the VAX 8000 series.

Exercises

1-1. List the hardware components of a computer system and describe briefly the function of each component.

1-2. Explain the differences between primary memory and auxiliary storage.

Computer Software

On a broad basis, software is divided into two general types: *systems software* and *applications software*. The systems software can almost be thought of as an integral part of the machine. Without it, the computer has limited real value. Applications programs are of the kind we shall write in using this book. They describe the data we want the machine to process, the operations to be performed on the data, and the results we expect to receive.

Programming Languages

In this book, we shall learn how to program a computer using the Basic language, a system that was devised to make the power of the computer available to a computer nonexpert. Following is a set of Basic statements that instruct the computer to accept two numbers entered from the keyboard, add them together, and print the results.

```
INPUT A, B
C = A + B
PRINT C, A, B
```

We need not be a computer expert to guess the meaning of these statements. Computer languages in which the meaning of statements is practically self-evident and the statements can be used on many different types of computers are called *high-level* languages. However, instructions that actually control operation of the computer look nothing like the preceding readable forms. Before any Basic program statement to the computer can be carried out, it must be converted into *machine language*. For some statements, the conversion may result in only one machine-language instruction. For others, it will commonly result in many. Machine-language instructions are expressed in terms of the smallest memory unit in a computer, called a *bit* (*b*inary dig*it*). A bit can take on only the binary values 0 and 1. On the VAX, each byte is made up of eight bits. If we were to inspect the machine-language equivalent of one of our programs, we would see nothing but a series of binary values, 0s and 1s. Fortunately for us, we need not deal with these technical details when programming in Basic or any other high-level language.

A fundamental component of a Basic programming system is a special program called the *interpreter*. When a Basic program is run, the interpreter translates each Basic statement (as it is encountered) into equivalent machine-language instructions, then "gives them" to the computer to execute. It then proceeds to the next Basic statement and repeats the process.

Many Basic systems also include another program called a *compiler*. A compiler is different, in that it converts all of the statements of the Basic program into an equivalent machine-language program that can be run separate from the Basic system. The program written in Basic is commonly called the *source program*. The corresponding machine-language program resulting from the compiling operation is called the *object program*.

The focus on Basic in this book relates to using the interpreter. As we shall learn, it is an exceptionally convenient tool for programming. Furthermore, our studies in this book relate to using Version 2.0 of Basic for the DEC VAX computer; it is called VAX Extended Basic. It shall be called simply VAX Basic in this book. This version provides Basic with enhancements that make it a more powerful language than most of the commonly encountered versions of Basic.

The Operating System

Without a doubt, the single most significant set of software programs for any computer is the *operating system*. Simply stated, an operating system is a set of programs designed to manage the hardware resources of the computer. Some of the functions performed by various components of the operating system are

- Maintaining files of data and programs that are stored in auxiliary storage.
- Providing for automatic transition from job to job. (A *job* is a unit of work for a computer.)
- Allowing the computer to be shared by two or more programs that are in memory at the same time.
- Controlling the efficient operation of input and output devices.
- Supporting programming languages, such as Basic, that "remove" the programmer from the need for dealing with the computer at a machine-language level.

The key to the operating system and most modern computers is the *monitor* program (sometimes called a *supervisor* or *executive* program). The supervisor remains in memory at all times and maintains control, directly or indirectly, while the computer is in use (see Figure 1-3). In addition to supervising the operation of the computer, the operating system consists of programs for performing such chores as automatically maintaining records and keeping track of what is stored in auxiliary storage (the libraries), as well as ensuring that various other tasks are carried out properly.

The VAX operating system provided by DEC is called VAX/VMS, and the version available at the writing of this book was V3. The subject of this book is the writing and running of programs in Version 2.0 of the Basic language for the VAX computer running under Version V3 of the VMS operating system.

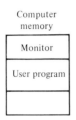

Figure 1-3. The monitor program in memory.

Timesharing Systems

Early computers were basically one-at-a-time machines. That is, at any given time, the computer would be running one job or one activity. As each activity finished, an operator would load the computer with the next, and it would be run. As computers became faster and more powerful, it was immediately obvious that this was a very inefficient way to use an expensive piece of equipment. Through the use of operating systems and special hardware features of the modern computer, the total amount of useful work performed (throughput) has been greatly increased over earlier systems. One way of making the computer more useful is to set it up so that many people can use it at the same time through terminals. One widely used technique for serving multiple users at the same time is called *timesharing*. Figure 1-4 illustrates the notion of a timesharing system. Each user has a communications terminal, a portion of

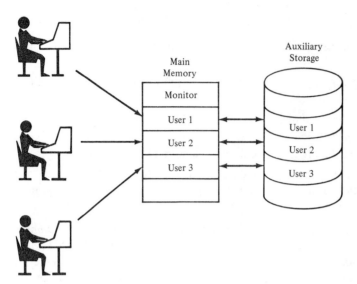

Figure 1-4. The principle of timesharing.

memory, and auxiliary storage. In timesharing, the underlying consideration is, in a sense, to maximize efficiency of each computer user and keep the user busy.

Technically speaking, timesharing refers to the allocation of computer resources in a time-dependent fashion to two or more users concurrently. The principal purpose of a timesharing system is to provide a large number of users with direct access to the computer to solve their individual problems. The different users' programs may be totally unrelated to one another, but they are in memory at the same time. Because of the speed at which the computer system operates, it appears to the users that the processor is serving them all simultaneously, but this is not the case. The CPU actually services only one user at a time, switching from one user to another on a scheduled basis. Each program will be allocated its slice of the processor time (commonly measured in fractions of a second) according to some predetermined scheduling basis, beginning with the first program and proceeding through the last. When the cycle is completed, it is begun again. Consecutive portions of a user's job thus alternate with consecutive portions of other users' jobs, independently of one another; this is called *interleaving*. The cycle time is so short on a human time scale that an individual user is usually aware that others are also using the computer only because of their visible presence at terminals in the same room.

The most significant feature of timesharing from the user point of view is that it is designed for *interactive programming*. That is, the programmer can enter a program or a segment of a program, run it, and get immediate feedback.

Computer systems that support timesharing are especially well suited to interactive processing because they tend to optimize both the processor and the multiuser efficiency. Timesharing is a feature of the VAX, which was designed for interactive use. Although timesharing and interactive processing are sometimes used interchangeably, they do not mean the same thing. Timesharing operating systems can support noninteractive as well as interactive processing. Furthermore, the notion of interactive processing should not be identified solely with that of timesharing. The modern personal computer allows you to process interactively on a machine that is dedicated completely to your own use.

Exercise

1-3. Explain the differences between a source program and an object program.

Principles of Processing Information

A Typical Information-Processing Problem

To gain some insight into how the computer is used to process information, let us consider a typical need of the Progressive Tool and Die Company, manufacturers of machine tools. One of the big problems they have is keeping track of the tools that they have in stock. Enough stock must be kept in the warehouse to satisfy orders as they come in. On the other hand, if the warehouse stock is too large, then the cost of the inventory becomes too high. The balance between shipping out sales and manufacturing replacements is a fine line. The method of record keeping used is illustrated by Example 1-1.

Example 1-1

The Progressive Tool and Die Company maintains a card file that includes one 5 × 7 card for each tool that they manufacture. The information on each card includes the following.

Tool stock number.

Tool type.

Quantity currently in stock in the warehouse.

Quantity currently in production.

Minimum allowable warehouse inventory quantity.

Manufacturing cost.

The principles of this card file are illustrated in Figure 1-5.

Now, what are some of the things that we should notice about this example? First of all, each card contains information *fields* about one machine tool. This collection of fields on each card is commonly called a *record*. The collection of all of the records is called a *file*. These are basic terms used in

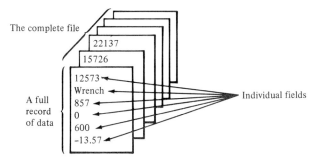

Figure 1-5. The inventory file of card records.

The complete file

A full record of data

22137
15726
12573
Wrench
857
0
600
-13.57

Individual fields

information processing; summarizing, we have the following:

Field. A basic unit of information (e.g., tool type, person's Social Security number, telephone number, street address).

Record. A group of related fields treated as a unit (e.g., inventory record, employee's payroll record).

File. The collection of all records of a given type (e.g., inventory file, company's payroll file).

It is important to understand that, whether the processing is done manually or by computer, the data set is organized into the same three components: fields, records, and files.

Processing All of the Data in the File

For any file such as this, there are always numerous processing operations that must be carried out. For example, a report might be required for tax purposes that would give the value of each inventory item in stock plus the total inventory value. The sequence of operations to carry this out would be as follows:

> Repeat the following sequence of steps for each card in the file:
> Get the next card.
> Multiply quantity on hand by cost, giving the item total.
> Write down the item total.
> Add the item total to the total cost subtotal.
>
> When finished, write down the total cost.

An important feature of this type of processing is that records are processed one after the other in the sequence in which they are stored in the file. This is commonly called *sequential processing*. A file that is arranged so that sequential processing is the only method that can be used is called a *sequential file*. (Files stored on magnetic tape must be processed sequentially because of the nature of the tape medium.)

Processing Only Selected Records

It is certainly easy to imagine a situation in which only one or two records (rather than the entire file) are to be processed. For instance, if an order comes in for an unusually large quantity of an item, it would be necessary to find the record for that particular item to determine if there is enough stock on hand. Another example is that the company might require that whenever a sale is made, the quantity-on-hand field be updated to reflect the reduced inventory. Processing of this type is called *direct processing* because any record of the file can be processed without having to process the preceding ones. (The nature of magnetic disk is such that files stored on disk can be processed either sequentially or directly.)

Batch and Transactional Processing

The preceding descriptions illustrate two very distinct types of information-processing methods that are commonly used with computers. They are called *batch processing* and *transactional processing*. In the first, a "batch" of data is generally collected and stored as a separate file. Periodically, the processing program is run and the original data file is processed sequentially, beginning with the first record and running through the last. This is sequential processing. Normally the processing, once begun, continues through its entire cycle without human intervention.

Transactional processing, on the other hand, involves processing each transaction as it comes in. For example, the preceding example in which the clerk enters the corrected amount into the inventory when the transaction is made illustrates transactional processing. Basic is a language that is well suited to preparing programs that handle transactional processing.

Exercise

1-4. State whether each of the following is most likely to be a field, record, or file:
  a. Address of a customer.
  b. Customer mailing list.
  c. Loan payment schedule for an individual.
  d. Payment due date.

An Example of a Simple Basic Program

Preparing and Running a Program

The focus in this book is learning how to program using the VAX Basic language. Programming problems in this book are clearly defined; there is not much guesswork regarding what is to be done. (*What* to do is generally straightforward; *how* to do it may be quite a different story with some of the problems.) This is not often the case for the professional programmer, who is frequently dealing with people who are not completely certain of what they want. In some working environments, it is the responsibility of the programmer to determine the *what* before thinking about beginning to write a program. Because the focus of beginning books is on learning the fundamentals of the language, programming assignments are clearly defined, and the beginning student need not be concerned with this phase of the operation. Once a problem has been clearly identified, the corrected program can then be put on the computer. The focus in this book will be the process of analyzing the nature of a problem, devising a solution to that problem, and preparing a computer solution. The overall process consists of the following four steps:

1. **Task:** Map out the solution to the problem.
   Activity: Study the problem and determine what must be done. Define the

procedures in ordinary English or in a graphic form called a *flowchart* (described in Chapter 3).

End result: A full understanding of what is to be done and how to do it.

2. **Task:** Write the program.

Activity: Write the computer program. This is called *coding*; it involves converting the English interpretation of our problem into instructions that tell the computer what to do to solve the problem. Note that this action is independent of the computer.

End result: A set of instructions (a program) telling the computer how to perform the steps to solve the problem. In Basic, these instructions are called *Basic statements* or simply *statements*. Thus, a Basic program is made up of individual statements.

3. **Task:** Enter the program into the computer.

Activity: The programmer types in the Basic program and saves it on auxiliary storage for later use. During the entering phase, the programmer interacts with the operating system. During this time, the computer is *not* performing the operations specified in the program (that is, the program is not being run). The computer is merely accepting the program. In addition to typing in the program itself, the programmer types instructions that tell the operating system what it should do with the program. These instructions to the operating system are called *system commands* or simply *commands*. They are *not* the same as statements.

End result: The program (of statements) now resides in the memory of the computer, ready to run. By execution of the proper command, it can be stored to disk storage.

4. **Task:** Run the program.

Activity: The programmer enters the command that directs the computer to run the program that has been entered. The computer carries out the action requested by each program statement (*executes* the statement) and produces the results that our program is designed to yield.

End result: The operations required by the program are carried out, usually giving results displayed on the screen or printed on a printer.

Because of the nature of interactive programming, the beginner often finds the distinctions between commands and statements and between entering and running a program confusing. You should study these steps carefully because these principles will be referred to in describing how to use Basic on the computer.

The rest of this chapter is devoted to some of the concepts of entering and running a program, steps 3 and 4 in the preceding series. The next example defines the nature of a problem and then includes a very simple solution. It is important to realize that we will use the program simply because it works. The intention here is to learn to interact with the computer. In Chapter 2, we shall learn the details of the Basic language illustrated by this program and how to write programs of our own. In other words, our sole interest in this chapter is to interact with the computer by way of the operating system.

Exercise

1-5. What is the difference between a statement and a command?

Example Definition

In order to illustrate to the owner of the tool company what can be done on the computer, we decide to set up the following simple example:

Example 1-2

A tool inventory file consisting of one record is to contain the following information:

Tool identification number.

Tool inventory (number on hand) at the beginning of the month.

Number of units manufactured during the month.

Number of units shipped for sale during the month.

Number of units lost or damaged during the month.

A program is required that will calculate the new amount on hand. Printed results must include the following information about the tool:

Tool identification number.

Tool inventory at the beginning of the month.

Updated inventory.

We can see that the operations are relatively simple: The processing sequence involves reading the data record, performing the calculations, then printing a line. The following data set will be the test case:

Tool number	12591
Tool description	Wrench
Old inventory	680
Manufactured	221
Shipped	419
Lost	3

The results that we can expect from the computer processing run are shown in Figure 1-6. A program to perform this task is shown in Figure 1-7. Again, we shall not be concerned with the specifics of Basic in this program in Chapter 1. Our sole interest here is to learn how to interact with the timesharing system by entering and running this program.

```
12591          Wrench              680                    479
```

Figure 1-6.   Expected output from Example 1-2.

```
100   READ T,T$,O,M,S,L
110   LET U = O + M - S - L
120   PRINT T,T$,O,U
130   DATA 12591, "Wrench", 680, 221, 419, 3
140   END
```

Figure 1-7. A program for Example 1-2.

Accessing the Timesharing System

The Terminal Keyboard

In using an interactive language such as Basic, the user "converses" with the computer via a terminal. The terminal may be a hard-copy device (printer), or it may be a soft-copy cathode-ray tube (CRT). In either case, input to the computer is via a typewriter-style keyboard such as that shown in Figure 1-8. As information is entered through the keyboard, it is transmitted to the computer and is also displayed on the screen for a CRT or printed by the terminal (hard-copy unit). We should note that in Figure 1-8, special attention is called to certain of the keys. These will be referred to throughout this chapter.

Logon

On a timesharing system, in which many users have access to the computer, some method is needed to keep order. For instance, programs that you enter and save to disk must not be confused with those that other programmers enter and store. Timesharing systems resolve this problem by assigning each user a separate account and an individual password for access to that account. To use the account, you must follow an exact procedure. The process of accessing the system from a terminal is called *logging on* (or logging in). To log on successfully, you must respond to system requests for your account (user) name and password *exactly* as these were assigned to you; successful logon establishes a *terminal session*. The process is illustrated and described in Figure 1-9.

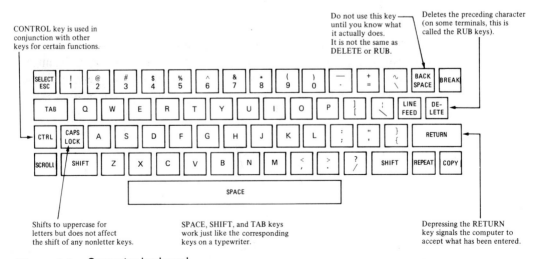

Figure 1-8. Computer keyboard.

```
Username: MICAL cr
Password:
    .

    .

    .
$>BASIC cr

VAX BASIC V2.0

Ready
```
                                    Figure 1-9. Logging on.

Within this book, certain symbols and conventions are used to illustrate interaction with the computer. These are explained here with reference to Figure 1-9.

Conventions Used to Distinguish Computer Output from User Entries*

Examples	Meaning
Password	Computer-printed illustrations that are shown in black printing represent information displayed by the computer.
RUN	Computer-printed illustrations that are shown in colored printing represent information typed from the keyboard by the user.
cr	Indicates the carriage return key, which must be depressed upon typing information into the computer.
∧	The *circumflex* is commonly used by the system to indicate depression of the control key while another key is struck. For instance, ∧U means to hold down the control key and concurrently depress the letter U. Note that this has nothing to do with the circumflex key itself (found on the 6 key of the keyboard). It is simply the way in which the system shows at the terminal that a control sequence has been entered.

*These conventions relate principally to Chapters 1 and 2.

The response you receive may vary somewhat from that of Figure 1-9, depending upon the version of the operating system that is on your computer. However, the essential elements will be as shown here. Note that the password you type in response to the computer *prompt* "Password" will *not* be displayed. (A prompt is a request by the computer for the user to respond with information, such as an instruction or a command.) The logon message on the next line of Figure 1-9 indicates the following:

1. The system has identified you as a valid user.
2. It has assigned to you a *work area* in memory.
3. You are at the operating-system (VMS) level.

The dollar sign that we see here is called the VMS *prompt*; whenever we see it, we know that control of the computer is under VMS. However, in this book we will primarily be using Basic with the computer at the Basic subsystem level. In order to get there, we must type in the command "BASIC" in response to the VMS prompt. This switches the computer to the Basic subsystem, which is indicated by the "Ready" prompt. Now the Basic subsystem is waiting for us to give a Basic command that will tell it what to do. The first thing that we shall consider is how to enter a Basic program.

Entering and Running a Program

Creating a New Program

The overall operation of entering the program is illustrated in Figure 1-10. The first thing to do is to enter the command NEW, which tells the system that we are ready to enter a new program. After we enter the command and press the Return key, the system responds with a prompt, asking for the program name (filename). You should choose a meaningful name in terms of what the program does. Choice of program names is limited as follows:

> Program name: May consist of from 1 to 9 characters, which may be any of the letters A through Z and digits 1 through 9.

This name may be entered as shown in Figure 1-10, or it may be entered on the same line as the NEW command, for instance:

    NEW INVEN

It is important to understand that the NEW command will erase anything that we have already entered into memory and start us with a clean slate. From here we proceed to enter the program, statement by statement, as if we were typing at a typewriter.

In order to become familiar with the computer, enter the program into your account exactly as shown in the steps of Figure 1-10. Remember that after you enter each statement, you must press the Return key. However, before depressing the Return, check the statement to make certain it was entered correctly. If it was not and you are using a CRT, you may simply depress the Delete key and back up the *cursor* (erasing as it goes) until the incorrect part is deleted. (A cursor is a movable marker on the screen that indicates the position where the next typed character will appear). Then resume entry of the remaining part of the statement. If you are using a hard-copy terminal, simply hold down the Control key and strike the letter U. Then reenter the statement.

It is of utmost importance to recognize that the computer does not perform the operations required by the program as the program is being entered. That is, after the entering task is finished (step 3 of the overall process), no calcu-

```
NEW
New file name--INVEN


Ready


100     READ T, T$, O, M, S, L
110     LET U = O + M - S - L
120     PRINT  T, T$, O, U
130     DATA 12591, "Wrench", 680, 221, 419, 3
140     END
```

Figure 1-10. Entering the program—Example 1-2.

lations of the new balance or anything else have been performed. These calculations are part of step 4 and are carried out only when the program is run. Upon completion of the entering operation, the program may be run.

Running the Program

Once the program has been entered, we can execute it using the RUN command, as illustrated in Figure 1-11. When execution of the program is complete (that is, when the data values have been processed), the system returns to the Ready state to await our next command. Notice in Figure 1-11 that the computer prints the program name, the time of day, and the date. This is called the *header line* and can be omitted by typing RUNNH instead of RUN. If your program output is not exactly the same as that shown here, then you have made a mistake somewhere. How to correct an error in a program is the topic of the next section.

```
Ready

RUN
INVEN     18-SEP-1987   16:40

12591          Wrench          680          479   ← Program output
Ready
```

Figure 1-11.   Running the program—Example 1-2.

Correcting a Program

Inserting and Deleting Lines

One of the useful features of Basic relates to the fact that the system always keeps statements in order according to line numbers. For instance, let us assume that we left out statement 120 when keying in the program. Upon noticing our error, we could simply key in the omitted statement, as illustrated in Figure

Entering this will produce ⎯⎯⎯⎯⎯⎯⎯⎯⎯→ this result

```
100   READ T, T$, O, M, S, L        100   READ T, T$, O, M, S, L
110   LET U = O + M - S - L         110   LET U = O + M - S - L
130   DATA ...                      120   PRINT T, T$, O, U
140   END                          130   DATA ...
120   PRINT T, T$, O, U            140   END
```

Note: The system will automatically insert
        statement 120 in its proper place (between
        110 and 130) regardless of when it is entered.

Figure 1-12.   Inserting a statement.

1-12. The system would automatically place the statement in its proper position between statements 110 and 130, regardless of when it was entered.

Sometimes we need to delete a statement from a program. This is easily done simply by typing only the line number and then hitting the Return key.

A rather subtle error is illustrated in Figure 1-13. Statement 110 has been misnumbered as 1100 and will end up someplace other than where it belongs. The remedy shown in Figure 1-13 involves deleting the incorrect line and adding the correct one. Note that typing a line number with no statement (1100 in this example) deletes any statement with that line number.

Entering this will produce ─────────────→ this result

```
100  READ T, T$, 0, M, S, L          100   READ T, T$, 0, M, S, L
1100 LET U = 0 + M - S - L                    .
        .                                      .
        .                                130   DATA ...
        .                                140   END
130  DATA ...                          1100  LET U = 0 + M - S - L
140  END
```

To correct must:
1. delete 1100
2. add 110

```
100  READ T, T$, 0, M, S, L          100   READ T, T$, 0, M, S, L
        .                            110   LET U = 0 + M - S - L
        .                                    .
        .                                    .
130  DATA ...                                .
1100 LET U = 0 + M - S - L           130   DATA ...
140  END                             140   END
```

```
1100                        delete 1100
110  LET U = 0 + M - S - L  add 110
```

Note: Typing a line number with no statement
       (1100 in this example) deletes any
       statement with that line number.

Figure 1-13. Deleting and inserting a statement.

Errors and Error Detection

Try as we might to eliminate errors, some will always creep into a program. In general, they can be classified in three broad categories: syntax errors, run-time errors, and logic errors. The Basic language consists of a very concise set of rules for writing statements. Any statement that does not follow those rules is said to have a *syntax* error. For instance, consider the following:

```
120 PRINT T, 0, U
130 DATA ...
```

entered incorrectly as

```
120 PRIND T, 0, U
130 NUMBERS ...
```

Entering this will produce ⟶   a result such as this

120   PRIND T, 0, U   ? Illegal verb at line 120

Ready

120   PRINT T, 0, U   120   PRINT T, 0, U

Ready

Figure 1-14.   Syntax errors.

In statement 120, PRINT is misspelled and, knowing the "rules" for writing statements, the system will respond with an error indication as soon as the statement is entered. Similarly, statement 130 should be DATA; we must use the exact forms defined in the language, not our own variations. The sequence of events of entering and correcting the error on line 120 is illustrated in Figure 1-14. If the line is reentered, the new one will replace the previous one with the same number. In some operating environments, the immediate diagnostic ability illustrated by Figure 1-14 is disabled. In such a case, inspection of the statements and display of appropriate error messages takes place at a later time. You should consult the system manager or instructor for your computer system regarding these details.

As a rule, the system is very helpful in detecting syntax errors. However, logic errors are a completely different story. For instance, if in the inventory problem we accidentally added the units sold rather than subtracted them, we would have

```
110    LET U = 0 + M + S - L
```

rather than the correct

```
110   LET U = 0 + M - S - L
```

Here we have an error in our *logic*, and the system has no way of recognizing that we mean something other than what we typed. It would be up to us to check everything carefully, including the output, and reenter a corrected version of the statement.

Exercise

1-6. What do you think would happen if you logged on, entered the Basic subsystem, and immediately typed in RUN (before entering a program)?

Listing a Program

Often when we are making corrections to a program, what we see typed at the terminal or printed on the screen is confusing. For example, after making the corrections shown in Figure 1-13 (lower left of the figure), it is usually convenient to see the program as it actually exists (lower right). This is easily done using the command LIST. That is, typing LIST (followed by depressing the Return key) will cause the latest form of the entire program on which we are working to be printed (or displayed) on the output device (terminal and/or printer). The command LISTNH displays the entire program without the program header. Selected lines of the program can also be displayed. The command

```
LIST   110,140
```

will display lines 110 *and* 140. The command

```
LIST   110-140
```

will display lines 110 *through* 140. The command

```
LIST   110-
```

will display line 110 through the last line in the program.

Exercises

1-7. You have just finished entering a complete program, and you realize that you forgot a statement that belongs between lines 150 and 160. How would you enter it and get the computer to put it in its proper place?

1-8. The following program to calculate and print the sum of two numbers has an error in it.

```
10     READ A,B
200    LET C = A + B
30     PRINT C
40     DATA 312,176
1000   END
```

The statement on line 200 has been misnumbered; it should have been number 20. Explain what is involved in correcting the error at the terminal.

Saving Programs

At this point, you can begin writing and entering programs of your own. Often, as you progress to more difficult problems, you will find that you cannot complete the entry and testing of a program in one terminal session. Thus, it will be necessary to save the program or portion of the program until your next session, which may be hours or days later. You may also want to save the program before using the command NEW in the middle of a terminal session. (Remember, the NEW command clears memory of everything you have entered.) To meet this need, some type of permanent storage capability must be provided.

Temporary and Permanent Program Storage

Whenever the user signs on to an account, a temporary work area is set up within the internal memory of the computer. This temporary area is initially empty. As a program (or anything else, for that matter) is entered, it is held in this temporary portion of memory. When the session is terminated (by logging off), everything in that temporary area is lost. It is somewhat analogous to "borrowing" the use of a desk. When we first sit down, the desk top is clean. When we leave, someone comes in and cleans it by discarding everything there. In other words, the desk top is a work and temporary storage area. Now let us carry this example one step further and assume that we have been provided a file cabinet for permanent storage of any work that we wish to save. Anything we wish to save must be placed in the file cabinet before we leave, or else it will be lost. If we must work on it at a later time, we can obtain it from the file and continue.

This is exactly the situation that exists in a timesharing system. Referring to Figure 1-1, the work space of internal memory corresponds to the desk top, and the disk storage corresponds to the file cabinet.

Saving a New Program

After we enter a new program, one of the first things we should do is to save it on disk. Most programmers have had the aggravating experience of entering

```
NEW
New file name--INVEN

100    READ T, T$, O, M, S, L
110    LET U = O + M - S - L
120    PRINT  T, T$, O, U
130    DATA ...
140    END

Ready

SAVE

Ready
```

Figure 1-15. Saving a program.

and correcting a large program and then forgetting to save it before signing off. A typical timesharing session is shown in Figure 1-15. Here a new program (INVEN) is entered; saved, using the SAVE command; and run. Note that when the SAVE command is executed, the system saves it under the name that was entered when the NEW command was entered. If you wish to save it under a different name, you can do so simply by entering the new name following the command word SAVE. For instance, the command

```
SAVE  INVENTORY
```

will save on disk the program currently in the work area and use the name INVENTORY regardless of the name previously used.

Ending a Terminal Session

Upon completing a session with the computer, you must *sign off* (or *log off*). This is especially important if you have your own account in the computer. If you simply walk away from the terminal, leaving it logged on, then someone else could use your account. They might change or destroy your programs or use up your allotted computer time (assuming your computer center limits the time you can have).

You logoff by first returning to the VMS level ($ prompt) and then logging off. Figure 1-16 illustrates EXITing from the Basic subsystem back to the VMS level and issuing the LOGOFF command.

```
Ready

exit
$>logoff
   MICAL       logged out at 25-AUG-1985 09:00:52.79
```

Figure 1-16. Logging off.

In Retrospect

The purpose of this chapter has been to present a broad introduction to the computer and its use. An intimate knowledge of how the computer works is hardly necessary to using one. However, a basic insight is helpful in coping with problems that arise when interfacing with the computer. The topics of entering, running, correcting, listing, and saving programs represent "utility" types of operations that are necessary to using Basic on the computer. Actual preparing of programs begins with the next chapter.

Answers to Preceding Exercises

1-1. Input: devices to enter information into the computer.

Output: devices onto which results from the computer are transferred.

Primary memory: the part of the computer in which information to be processed must reside.

Central Processing Unit: controls the operation of the entire computer system (control unit) and performs the arithmetic and logical operations (arithmetic/logic unit) specified by the program.

Auxiliary storage: devices used for long-term storage of programs and data; some of these may also be used for input and/or output.

1-2. Primary memory is part of the computer itself. Its contents are lost when the computer is turned off. Information must be in primary memory before the computer can process it. Auxiliary storage is on a separate device outside of the computer. (It is part of the computer *system*.) Its contents are stored even when the computer's power is turned off.

1-3. The program written in Basic is a source program. It is machine independent; that is, with minor modifications, it can be run on many types of computers. It must be converted to machine language before it can be run. An object program is one in machine language. It is understood by and specific to a given type of computer.

1-4. (a) field; (b) file; (c) record; (d) field.

1-5. Commands are used to tell the operating system what you wish to do, and are carried out when entered (they allow *you* to control the computer). Statements are used to form programs and are carried out only when your program is entered and run (they allow the *program* to control the computer).

1-6. The computer would have no program to run, so it would do nothing; try it on the terminal to see for yourself.

1-7. Give it a line number of 155; then key it in. The Basic system automatically places it in its proper position according to the line numbers.

1-8. The correction involves two steps:

a. Enter the statement with the correct line number:

    20   LET C = A + B

b. Delete line 200 by typing this line number followed by the Return key:

    200

Programming Problems

1-1. Enter and run the program of Figure 1-7.

1-2. List all system commands you entered in the terminal session of problem 1-1. State the function of each command. Identify those commands that are *necessary* to enter and run the program. If you have entered in your terminal session more commands than are necessary, repeat the session using only the necessary ones. Identify the additional system command that would have been necessary if you had saved the program on auxiliary storage before you ran it.

2

A Subset of Basic

Chapter Outline

Preview

The purpose of this chapter is to describe the fundamental principles of Basic and provide sufficient background to allow you to write some simple programs. Important topics covered in this chapter are the following:

1. *The concept of variables that allow for storing both numeric and alphabetic information in memory.*
2. *Line or statement numbers in Basic.*
3. *Remarks in the Basic program.*
4. *Basic expressions that specify arithmetic operations to be performed on information stored in memory.*
5. *The assignment statement, which stores the result of a calculation into a memory variable.*

6. *Input and output statements: using the READ to bring information into memory variables and the PRINT to get results out.*

7. *The use of commands for controlling the Basic system in handling of program files.*

8. *The Basic statements described in this chapter are*

   DATA
   END
   LET
   PRINT
   READ
   RESTORE

9. *The Basic commands described in this chapter are*

   DELETE
   EXIT
   LIST
   LISTNH
   NEW
   OLD
   RENAME
   REPLACE
   RUN
   RUNNH
   SAVE
   UNSAVE

Fundamental Concepts of Basic

The Program of Example 1-2 Revisited

Example 1-2 of Chapter 1 involves a simple program to process a data set for a machine tool company. This program was used to illustrate our interaction with the computer and the fundamental concept of commands in the Basic system. Although we did things with the program, we did not learn the information necessary to write one of our own. Now is the time to take a careful look at that program to begin our study of the Basic language itself. For the sake of convenient reference, Example 1-2 is restated here as Example 2-1.

Example 2-1

A machine tool company maintains a record of the following information for tools that it manufactures:

Tool identification number.

Tool description.

Tool inventory at the beginning of the month.

Units manufactured during the month.

Units shipped for sale during the month.

Units lost or damaged during the month.

The owner desires to computerize the record-keeping process. As an illustration of what can be done, one of the employees prepares a simple program to process the data for one particular tool manufactured by the company. This program is to print the following information about the tool:

Tool identification number.

Tool description.

Tool inventory at the beginning of the month.

Updated inventory.

The value for updated inventory is to be calculated as follows:

Updated inventory = old balance
+ units manufactured
− units shipped
− units lost and damaged

Most any task that we have to do can be broken down into a series of individual steps. For instance, if we were to perform the operations required in this example manually, the steps would be as follows:

1. Get the tool data set.
2. Perform calculations.
3. Print results.

This is what we would do manually; this is what the computer must be instructed to do in the program. The program that we entered and ran in Chapter 1 has been modified slightly and is included here as Figure 2-1. The important features illustrated by the program are

- Basic variables.
- String and numeric quantities.
- Line or statement numbers in Basic.
- Remarks in the Basic program.
- Basic expressions.
- Input and output capabilities.
- The LET statement.
- The END statement.

In the following sections of this chapter, we shall study each of these features and relate them to the fundamental concepts of Basic.

Principles of Variables

As just described, our sample program gets data values and operates on them. We know from Chapter 1 that whenever data values are brought into the computer, they are placed in memory. It is possible for the computer to store and

```
100   REM   EXAMPLE 2-1
110   REM   PROGRAM TO UPDATE AN INVENTORY
120   REM   INPUT VARIABLE NAMES ARE:
130   REM      TOOL.NUM   --   TOOL NUMBER
140   REM      TOOL.TYPE$  --   TOOL TYPE
150   REM      OLD.INV    --   OLD INVENTORY
160   REM      MANUFCT    --   UNITS MANUFACTURED
170   REM      SHIPD      --   UNITS SHIPPED
180   REM      LOST       --   UNITS LOST OR DAMAGED
190   REM   CALCULATED VARIABLE NAMES ARE:
200   REM      NEW.INV    --   UPDATED INVENTORY
300   REM
310   REM   PRINT THE HEADINGS
320       PRINT   "TOOL", "TOOL", "OLD", "UPDATED"
330       PRINT   "NUMBER", "TYPE", "INVENTORY", "INVENTORY"
340       PRINT
400   REM
410   REM   BEGINNING OF PROCESSING
420       READ TOOL.NUM, TOOL.TYPE$, OLD.INV, MANUFCT, SHIPD, LOST
430       LET NEW.INV = OLD.INV + MANUFCT - SHIPD - LOST
440       PRINT   TOOL.NUM, TOOL.TYPE$, OLD.INV, NEW.INV
500   REM   PRINT MESSAGE AND TERMINATE
510       PRINT
520       PRINT
530       PRINT "Processing complete"
800   REM
810   REM   **INPUT DATA**
820   DATA 12591, "Wrench", 680, 221, 419, 3
32767  END
```

Descriptive remarks to help make the program understandable to the user; the computer ignores them.

Print headings and one blank line.

Read data; calculate new inventory; print.

Tool inventory data to be processed (tool number, tool name, old inventory, manufactured, shipped, lost)

Figure 2-1. A program for Example 2-1.

retrieve information because each position of memory has an associated address. For us humans, keeping track of machine addresses would be a very big job; for the computer, it is relatively simple. To free us from these details, languages such as Basic allow us to use names of our choice, which are equated to memory addresses by the computer itself. These names are commonly called *variables*. The term *variable* (or *variable name*) has much the same meaning in Basic as in algebra; it is a symbolic name given to a quantity whose value can change during execution of a program. In Figure 2-1, we see the following variable names to represent the designated quantities:

Variable	Field
TOOL.NUM	Tool identification number
TOOL.TYPE$	Tool type
OLD.INV	Old inventory
MANUFCT	Number manufactured
SHIPD	Number shipped
LOST	Number lost
NEW.INV	Updated inventory

We shall learn the rules for selecting variable names in the next section.

Each variable encountered in a program will be assigned by the Basic system to some internal memory area in which a value can be stored. It is

Figure 2-2.   Contents of memory.

important not to confuse the variable name assigned to a memory area with its contents. The name relates to the address, which remains fixed during execution of the program. However, the contents of that memory area may change as the program is executed. Although we need not be concerned with the technical details of internal data representation, an overview of this topic helps in learning to program. Figure 2-2 illustrates this concept. As we learned in Chapter 1, the number of bytes reserved for each variable depends upon the type of information that it will contain. However, for the moment, we shall simply think of each variable being assigned to a memory "area." We see that the program of Figure 2-1 requires seven memory areas, one for each of the variables used. Each such memory area may contain one value at any given time. However, we can easily change the contents of a memory area by placing a new value in it. Prior to execution of any program, the VAX Basic system *initializes* all variables. (Later in this chapter, we shall see exactly what initializing means.) To gain insight into this process, let us consider the following data values:

Tool number	12591
Tool type	Wrench
Old inventory	680
Units manufactured	221
Units shipped	419
Units lost	3

In general, there are four ways in which variables in a Basic program can receive values:

1. From within the program itself by a READ statement.
2. From within the program itself by an assignment statement.
3. From a user at the terminal while the program is running.
4. From a file stored in auxiliary storage.

The first two methods are illustrated in Figure 2-3; we shall learn more of these in this chapter. The last two are described in Chapters 4 and 7.

Note that all except one of these quantities are numbers; the second field contains a word consisting of letters. As we might expect, these are handled differently by the computer. As in this example program, most programs read and process nonnumeric data as well as numeric data. When writing a program, it is imperative that we tell the computer what type of data it will be processing.

```
READ   T,T$,O,M,S,L
LET    N = O + M - S - L
```

Figure 2-3.   Two ways for Basic variables to receive values.

Although a rigorous definition of data types is postponed until later chapters, in a loose sense, data can be considered in two broad categories:

1. That upon which arithmetic can be performed.
2. That upon which arithmetic cannot be performed.

For instance, hours worked by an employee will be totalled and then multiplied by the pay rate. On the other hand, the employee name or even the employee Social Security *number* will not be involved in any arithmetic operations. Such data quantities, which may consist of letters, digits, or even special characters, are commonly referred to as *string data*. As we shall learn, the computer is able to process both numeric data and string data. As you might guess, it is important for the programmer to distinguish between the two. As we shall learn in the next section, we can set up a variable as being either a numeric variable or a string variable. String data can be read into a program in exactly the same way as numeric data.

Selecting Variable Names

In VAX Basic, the variable name can consist of from 1 to 31 characters, the first of which must be alphabetic (A through Z). The remaining characters can be any of the following:

Letter

Digit

Underscore (_)

Period (.)

Note that the space character is not included in this list. Thus, a variable name may not include a space (this is commonly referred to as an *embedded* space). Also, certain words have special meaning in Basic, such as LET, READ, and PRINT. These are called *reserved words* (also called *keywords*) and cannot be used as variable names. Appendix I contains a list of reserved words. The following are examples of valid and invalid choices for variable names:

Valid	Invalid	Reason
JR	2N	Letter must be first.
OLD.BALANCE	7	Cannot be a single digit.
WORK_3	WORK#3	The character # not allowed.
B8	LET	Reserved word.
COUNT	HOLD A	Spaces not allowed within a name.

When you are selecting names for program variables, the choice should always be made so that the name describes the quantity it represents. Note how well the names in lines 420–430 of Figure 2-1 document the program.

Variable	Field
TOOL.NUM	Tool identification number
TOOL.TYPE$	Tool type
OLD.INV	Old inventory
MANUFCT	Number manufactured
SHIPD	Number shipped
LOST	Number lost
NEW.INV	Updated inventory

Recall from Figure 1-10 that the sample program uses one-letter names for each of the variables. Although a single letter is just as acceptable to the computer as a long name, it is very poor documentation. The sole reason for using one-letter names in that example was to make the program as concise as possible while learning how to interact with the computer. Upon comparison of the two program segments in Figure 2-4, the value of long names for documentation becomes very obvious.

```
READ   T,T$,O,M,S,L
LET    N = O + M - S - L
PRINT T,T$,O,N
```

```
READ   TOOL.NUM, TOOL.TYPE$, OLD.INV, MANUFCT, SHIPD, LOST
LET    NEW.INV = OLD.INV + MANUFCT - SHIPD - LOST
PRINT TOOL.NUM, TOOL.TYPE$, OLD.INV, NEW.INV
```

Figure 2-4. Comparison of one-letter names and meaningful names.

Exercise

2-1. Which of the following variable names are invalid (give the reason)?

B	56	READ	SD_B
R8734	8E	R4	SHOP 7

The Distinction Between Numeric and String Variables

Perhaps by now you have noticed that the name for the tool type does not appear to follow the rules for naming variables because it includes a dollar sign ($). Actually, it is the presence or absence of a dollar sign that tells Basic whether a variable is numeric or string. For instance,

TOOL.TYPE$ is a string variable because the name ends with the dollar sign ($) character.

TOOL.NUM is a numeric variable because the name does not end with the dollar sign ($) character.

(We will learn in Chapter 6 that there is another way of defining a variable name as being string.) As we might expect, there are operations that can be done with string variables that cannot be done with numeric variables and vice versa. For instance, a data quantity that includes letters, digits, and special characters (such as the hyphen, period, or slash) can be placed in a string variable. In other words, virtually anything can be validly stored and processed as a string variable. On the other hand, the only quantity that we can place in a numeric variable is a number.

Another way in which the system distinguishes between the two is in the way it *initializes* numeric and string variables before it begins to execute the program: Numeric variables are set to the *value* zero, whereas string variables are set to zero *length*. In other words, the system initializes numeric variables by choosing the *contents* (zero) of the corresponding locations, but it initializes string variables by choosing the *number of memory units* (zero) for the corresponding locations. (What it means to reserve a location with zero memory units involves a rather subtle point, about which we shall learn more in later chapters.)

With these principles of variables and variable names, let us focus our attention on the program itself in Figure 2-1.

Principles of the Basic Language

Form of Basic Statements

Each line in the program of Figure 2-1 is called a *statement* and has a *statement number*, commonly called a *line number*, associated with it. (In Chapter 5, we shall learn about including statements without line numbers; however, for the present, example programs will include a line number for each statement.) A line number in VAX Basic must be an integer between 1 and 32767. Unless a Basic statement tells the computer to do otherwise, the computer will execute the statements in the order of increasing line numbers. Hence, these line numbers must be selected so that they fall in the order in which we want the computer to consider each statement. In general, consecutive line numbers are incremented by 10 or more, since this allows space to insert additional statements later if a program must be changed. Note that in the sample program of Figure 2-1, line 100 is followed by 110, which is followed by 120, and so on. However, as we see, line 200 is followed by line 300, and line 340 by line 400. In this example, the additional spacing (larger than 10) between line numbers serves as documentation for the user to identify different portions of the program. In general, these numbers may be chosen by the programmer; in Figure 2-1, they could as well have been 50, 100, 150, and so on.

Remarks in Basic

By placing REM at the beginning of the statement, the programmer may use that entire line for descriptive comments. Although the remarks line is ignored by Basic during running of the program, it will still be printed or displayed with the program. The remarks included in this program adequately describe the purpose of the program. Additional comments could be included to explain the purpose of each step. *The value of using extensive remarks in a program cannot be overemphasized.* Programmers commonly find that they must modify or expand an extensive program after completing it and progressing to another job. Even though programmers have written it themselves, much of the program can be very confusing unless remarks are used liberally.

In addition, VAX Basic allows use of the exclamation mark (!) to signal a remark, as shown in Figure 2-5. Note that the exclamation mark can be used to indicate that the entire line is a remark or that the remainder of a statement line contains a remark. For example, everything following the exclamation mark on lines 530–550 is treated as a remark, but the statement preceding it is not affected.

```
500   !
510   !   This portion of the program does
520   !   the rectangle calculations.
530   READ LEN, WIDTH            ! Read length and width
540   AREA = LEN * WIDTH         !    then calculate
550   PERIM = 2 * (LEN + WIDTH) !      area and perimeter
```

Figure 2-5. Using the exclamation mark to indicate a remark.

Exercises

2-2. State whether each of the following is valid or invalid when used as a line number in VAX Basic. For those that are invalid, give the reason.

a. 500
b. 55000
c. 0
d. 633
e. −550

2-3. How is a descriptive remark indicated in a Basic program?

2-4. Explain the nature of the logical error in Exercise 1-8 (the program is repeated here for convenience). What will be the output when this program is run?

```
10     READ A,B
200    LET C = A + B
20     PRINT C
40     DATA 312,176
1000   END
```

Input/Output of Data

The Nature of Input Operations

Conventional usage of the term *input/output* is generally related to the transfer of data between internal memory and external devices. For example, in an interactive program, a user might enter data directly into the computer through a keyboard. In other types of applications, the computer may read data from a data file stored on magnetic disk or tape. An inventory system such as that described in Example 2-1 would likely involve processing of an entire data file stored on an auxiliary storage device. As each record is to be processed, it is read from auxiliary storage into memory and perhaps written back to auxiliary storage. It is important to recognize that a data file and a program to process the file are usually two separate entities and are stored separately. Since the subject of file processing is somewhat above a beginning level, that topic is deferred until Chapter 7.

The DATA Statement

The Basic language has a feature that allows data for a program to be included as part of the program itself. Although use of this feature is not practical for most actual applications, it is very convenient for the beginner who is learning Basic. It involves a special statement called the DATA statement. As we see in the program of Figure 2-1, the DATA statement is included following the program statements. As we can see, it includes a line number. The keyword DATA is followed by a list of values that represent the input data to be processed. If we inspect these values, we see that they represent the inventory information for one tool type. In order for the computer to be able to distinguish one field from the next, they are separated by commas. If it makes things easier for us when checking over the values, they can be separated by one or more spaces. For instance, the following two DATA statements are equivalent.

```
200 DATA 12591,"Wrench",680,221,419,3
201 DATA 12591, "Wrench", 680, 221, 419, 3
```

Technically speaking, the DATA statement is classified as a *nonexecutable* statement. That is, it does not tell the computer to perform any processing. What does occur is the following: When the program, including all DATA statements, is brought into memory for a run, the fields from each DATA statement are placed, in order, into a *data pool*, one field after the other. It is important to understand that information can then be read into variables during execution of the program as if it were coming from a keyboard or a file. Whenever DATA statements are used in sample programs in this book, they will be included at the end of the program (immediately preceding the END statement). However, because of the way Basic treats the DATA statement, it can actually be placed anywhere in the program (beginning, middle, or end) without affecting execution of the program.

Next let us consider the READ statement, which allows information in the data pool to be placed into program variables.

The READ Statement

As defined earlier in this chapter, input/output refers to the transfer of data between internal memory and external devices. Technically speaking, that excludes the READ statement from being termed an input statement because the information it accesses is already in memory. However, we shall consider the READ as an input statement even though it does not follow the conventional definition.

When the READ statement is executed, data values stored in the data pool are copied into the named variables and thereby made available for processing. For example, the statement

```
420    READ TOOL.NUM, TOOL.TYPE$, OLD.INV, MANUFCT, SHIPD, LOST
```

will cause the computer to copy the six fields of data from the data pool into memory variables. The first field from the data pool will be placed in the memory area reserved for TOOL.NUM. The second field will be placed in the memory area reserved for TOOL.TYPE$, and so on. This procedure is illustrated in Figure 2-6. The important point to bear in mind is that *the numeric and string constants must appear in the* DATA *statement in the same sequence as the corresponding variables appear in the* READ *statement*. A program with a READ statement must have at least one DATA statement; otherwise, an error will be generated. If a READ is executed and there is not enough data, the program will be terminated automatically.

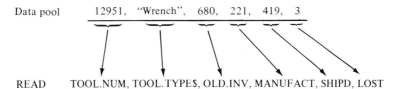

Figure 2-6.   Reading data from data pool into memory variables.

Exercise

2-5. The following DATA statement appears in a program:

```
900    DATA 267,58,391
```

What would be the difference between reading these values into A, B, and C (statement 300) and reading the data into X$, Y$, and Z$ (statement 400)?

```
300    READ A,B,C
400    READ X$,Y$,Z$
```

Restoring Access to Data in the DATA Statement

In some applications, a program requires that items in a DATA statement be processed two or more times. The RESTORE statement provides this capability. That is, execution of the RESTORE causes the data-pool pointer to be reset to the beginning of the data pool. Then the next READ executed after a RESTORE will read data from the first DATA statement in the program. The two sets of statements in Figure 2-7 illustrate the effect of using a RESTORE. Note that in both cases, the first two data values are read into A and B. In Figure 2-7(a), the READ of statement 30 reads the third and fourth data values into C and D. However, in Figure 2-7(b), the RESTORE moves the pointer back to the beginning of the data pool, and the first two values are reread by the READ of statement 30.

The PRINT Statement

The general form of the PRINT statement includes the word PRINT followed by a list of items, the *output list*, to be printed. Items in the output list are separated by *delimiters*, which can be commas or semicolons. The results of running the program of Figure 2-1 are shown in Figure 2-8. As we can see, the statement

        430   PRINT TOOL.NUM, TOOL.TYPE$, OLD.INV, UPD.INV

will cause the current values in memory areas reserved for the variables TOOL.NUM, TOOL.TYPE$, OLD.INV and UPD.INV to be printed. Whenever a variable name is listed in a PRINT statement, the current value of that variable will be printed. In addition, it is possible to print fixed information,

Data Pool

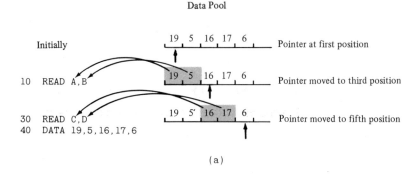

(a)

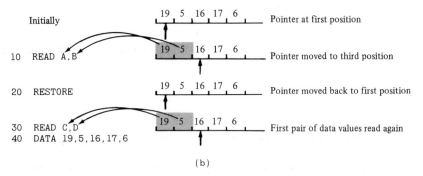

(b)

Figure 2-7. The RESTORE statement.

```
TOOL        TOOL          OLD           UPDATED
NUMBER      TYPE          INVENTORY     INVENTORY

12591       Wrench        680           479
```

Processing complete

Figure 2-8. Output from running the program of Figure 2-1.

such as headings. For instance, the statement

```
320    PRINT "TOOL", "TOOL", "OLD", "UPDATED"
```

causes the first line of the heading to be printed. Note that the information to be printed is enclosed in quotes (these are often referred to as *literals*). In other words, anything that is included in quotes will be printed exactly as quoted. It is important to understand that the Basic system does not even look at what is inside the quote marks. It simply prints exactly as quoted. Thus, the printed output of the following PRINT statements will be as shown.

Output of This Statement	Is This
PRINT "COST, IN DOLLARS"	COST, IN DOLLARS
PRINT "END"	END

Note that in the first case, a comma and spaces are included; commas normally separate fields. In the second case, a reserved word is printed.

Furthermore, variable values and fixed values can both be printed with a single PRINT statement, for instance:

Output of This Statement	Might Be This
PRINT "TOOL NUMBER",TOOL.NUM	TOOL NUMBER 12591

Whenever a PRINT statement has no output list, it results in a blank line (see Figure 2-8). This is very convenient for improving the readability of program output.

When the PRINT statement is used as it is in this example, the output will be printed according to a predetermined fixed format. A computer terminal line is divided into 14-character-wide *print zones*. A comma preceding the PRINT item causes that item to be printed in the next print zone. A print zone can be skipped by placing an extra comma between list elements. In this respect, we can think of the terminal as a typewriter with preset tab stops at positions 1, 15, 29, 43, and 57. Thus, the value for TOOL.NUM in statement 430 will be printed beginning in position 1. The comma separating TOOL.TYPE\$ from TOOL.NUM serves not only as a delimiter in the print list, but it also causes the terminal to tab over to position 15, where the value of TOOL.TYPE\$ will be printed, and so on. Each output field will be *left justified* (printed so that the leftmost character is output at the left print margin) beginning with the corresponding tab position. This is in contrast to normal data processing procedures, in which numeric fields are *right justified* (printed so that the rightmost character is output at the right margin) and alphanumeric fields are left justified. If the output number is negative, it will be preceded by a minus sign. If it is positive, it will be preceded by a space. (This is the reason the headings and the numeric results are not exactly aligned in Figure 2-8.) However, Basic includes other provisions for output to enhance the appearance of printed results. We will study some of these concepts next, others in a later chapter.

Exercise

2-6. The following PRINT statement is executed:

```
400 PRINT Q1, Q3, Q5
```

Where will each field be printed on the page?

Arithmetic Operations

Data Values and Constants in Basic

The program of Figure 2-1 uses simple whole-number values for each of the quantities processed. We know that Basic reserves an area in memory for each of the variables defined in a program. Now the question is "How large are these areas?" It is important to understand that the variables we have been working with are not limited to whole-number values. For instance, it is possible to store numbers with fractional parts, such as

625.573
0.0000674
− 1234.567

In computer terminology, these are called *real* numbers. (Chapter 5 includes a distinction between real numbers and *integer* numbers.) Within the computer, they are stored in four consecutive bytes in a form very similar to scientific notation form. Details of this are covered in Chapter 5. For now, we should simply be aware that they can consist of seven significant digits with a wide range for decimal-point positioning. Following are two additional examples of numbers that can be stored in a real variable.

12345670000000000.0
0.00000000001234567

When we are doing calculations in algebra, we commonly work with formulas. For instance, the following formulas represent the area of a circle and the perimeter of a rectangle:

$$A = 3.14r^2 \qquad \text{Circle}$$
$$P = 2(l + w) \qquad \text{Rectangle}$$

Note that these formulas are made up of fixed numbers, called *constants*, and variables. Furthermore, they are interrelated by virtue of arithmetic operations. For instance, the *l* and the *w* are related by the addition operation. Furthermore, this sum is related to the constant 2 by a multiplication operation that is implied by the general rules of algebra. As we shall learn in the next paragraph, many of these features carry over to Basic.

The Basic Expression

Computation with the computer in Basic involves (1) performing arithmetic operations on two or more quantities from memory and (2) saving the result in a preassigned area of memory. For example, if we assume that the length and width of a rectangle have been read into memory, then the following LET statement would calculate the perimeter and store it in PERIM:

```
LET PERIM = 2 * (LENGTH + WIDTH)
```

Let us first direct our attention to the *expression* located to the right of the equal sign. Note that it contains two variables, LENGTH and WIDTH, and the constant 2. (Constants can be used with the same range as those allowed for variables.) In Basic, the term *expression* has much the same meaning as it does in algebra. In essence, an arithmetic expression is any collection of variables and constants related by *arithmetic operators*. The five operations allowed by Basic and the corresponding operator symbols are

Addition	$+$
Subtraction	$-$
Multiplication	$*$
Division	$/$
Raising to a power (exponentiation)	$\wedge$ or $**$

Note that the first two symbols are identical to ordinary arithmetic; the asterisk (*) is used to denote multiplication. Since Basic requires that each operation be explicitly indicated, the computer form is slightly different from the equivalent algebraic form, as further illustrated by the following:

Discipline	Algebraic Expression	Computer Language
Business	$(1 + r)^y - 1$	(1 + R)**Y - 1
Mathematics	$b^2 - 4ac$	B**2 - 4*A*C
Physics	$\dfrac{mM}{m + M}$	M1*M2/(M1 + M2)

Whereas in algebra, multiplication is commonly implied (for instance, $4AC$ means 4 times A times C), in programming languages, the multiplication must be indicated explicitly by the operation symbol. (The computer would try to interpret 4AC as a variable name and would give an error message because the first character is not a letter.)

In general, the rules for performing the arithmetic operations (that is, *evaluating* an expression) are much the same as for evaluating an algebraic expression. That is,

1. All expressions within parentheses are evaluated first.
2. Raising to a power (exponentiation) is next.
3. Multiplications and divisions are then performed from left to right.
4. Additions and subtractions are performed last, from left to right.

The rule for the sequence in which arithmetic operations are performed (in the absence of parentheses) is commonly referred to as the *hierarchy of operations*. The hierarchy of arithmetic operators is

$\wedge$ Highest
* and /
+ and −   Lowest

As a simple illustration of this hierarchy rule, let us evaluate the expression

X − Y * Z

Given that values for X, Y, and Z are 88, 16, and 4 respectively, we have

$$88 - 16 * 4$$
$$88 - 64$$
$$24$$

With a hierarchy of operations, there are no ambiguities because the multiplication is performed *before* the addition.

The use of spaces in forming expressions is strictly up to the programmer. That is, spaces may be inserted for the purpose of clarity. Note that the preceding mathematics and physics expressions use spaces on each side of the addition and subtraction operators but not around the multiplication and division operators. This is done solely to clarify (to the programmer) the grouping of the various elements of the expression.

Exercises

2-7. Given the values A = 5, B = 14, and C = 7, evaluate each of the following:

a. A+B/C
b. 2*A+B/C
c. 2*(A+B/C)

2-8. Translate each of the following algebraic expressions into Basic expressions:

a. $a(b + c)$ e. $6.75ab$
b. $ax^2 + bx + c$ f. $x + a^y$

c. $\dfrac{x}{rs}$ g. $\dfrac{5}{9}(F - 32)$

d. $\dfrac{3.14}{4}d^2h$ h. $\dfrac{r}{1 - (1 + r)^{-n}}$

The Assignment Statement

As we saw earlier, the LET statement has much the form of the ordinary equation in algebra.

```
420    LET NEW.INV = OLD.INV + MANUFCT - SHIPD - LOST
```

However, the equal sign as used in the LET statement in Basic has a far different meaning than in algebra. In the LET statement, the equal sign says

1. Using the currently stored data values, evaluate the expression to the right of the equal sign,
2. Then place the result in the memory area indicated by the variable on the left.

Such a statement is called an *assignment statement* because it assigns a value to the variable on the left of the equal sign. The notion of an assignment statement is fundamental to all programming languages. The use of the word LET is specific to Basic. Most versions of Basic currently in use, including VAX Basic, allow the LET *statement* to be written with or without the *word* LET. Thus, statement 420 of Figure 2-1 could have been written in either of the following ways:

```
420    LET NEW.INV = OLD.INV + MANUFCT - SHIPD - LOST
420    NEW.INV = OLD.INV + MANUFCT - SHIPD - LOST
```

Example programs in chapters that follow omit the word LET.

Additional Features of the Basic Language

The END Statement

The END statement indicates to the Basic processor that no more statements follow. Its use is optional, but it is good programming practice to include it. Its line number must be larger than that of any other statement in the program. All programs in this book use 32767 (the largest allowable line number) for the END. Although this practice is not mandatory, it is a good one because it prevents the error of numbering a statement in the program larger than the END statement. If it is executed in a program, it terminates program execution. (It also closes all files that have been opened; the significance of this will become clear when we learn about file processing in Chapter 7.)

String and Numeric Quantities

As we know, a string value is indicated as such to the Basic system by enclosing it within quotes. In the example program we have seen, string values appear in two different places: the PRINT statement and the DATA statement. Virtually all versions of Basic indicate a string quantity by use of quotes. VAX Basic provides some flexibility in this respect. That is, *either* the single or the double quote can be used. For example, either of the following is acceptable with VAX Basic:

```
PRINT "This is a message."
PRINT 'This is a message.'
```

The only limitation is that the opening and closing quote for a given string quantity must be the same (either double or single). This provides the programmer a degree of latitude when forming messages; for example, consider the following:

```
PRINT "The record's format is:"
PRINT 'Press the "RETURN" key when ready.'
```

The two printed string quantities are

```
The record's format is:
Press the "RETURN" key when ready.
```

Note in the first example that the single quote is treated as part of the string quantity. In the second example, the double quotes are also treated as other characters, since the string is set off by single quotes.

Another thing to be aware of is that an error will result if an attempt is made to put a string quantity into a numeric variable. For example, the following READ and DATA combination would result in an error when the program is run:

```
500   READ A$, B$, C
900   DATA "First", "Second", "12345"
```

Even though the third field is a number, Basic considers it a string because it is enclosed within quotes. When the program attempts to place this string into the numeric variable C, it generates an error.

More on the DATA Statement

The program of Example 2-1 included exactly six data values in the DATA statement, which were read into six corresponding variables in the READ statement. This notion of an exact correspondence is consistent with the nature of the application. That is, we read one data record. It is important that we do not get the erroneous idea that the DATA statement is "record" oriented from our studies of Example 2-1 and examples in this chapter. The key to understanding how this statement works is that when the program is first loaded into memory, data values from *all* of the DATA statements are placed in the data pool. This is illustrated in Figure 2-6. Now, what if the following statement 820, from the program of Example 2-1, were replaced with the three statements 920–940?

```
820   DATA 12591, "Wrench", 680, 221, 419, 3
920   DATA 12591
930   DATA "Wrench"
940   DATA 680, 221, 419, 3
```

The answer is that the end result of these two forms is identical; the data pool contents will be exactly the same. If we wished to carry this to an extreme, we could include six DATA statements in this program, one for each of the quantities. In an example such as this, there is no reason to use more than one DATA statement. However, if the record being read contained many more fields, resulting in a very long line (wider than a terminal screen), it might be less confusing to use two or more DATA statements.

Another interesting aspect of data stored in the data pool relates to the manner in which it is obtained by the READ statement. That is, each READ obtains a number of fields from the data pool that corresponds to the number of variables in the list of the READ. If there is unused data, it will be available to the next READ in the program. For instance, statement 420 from Example 2-1 could be replaced by the corresponding statements 421 and 422.

```
420   READ TOOL.NUM, TOOL.TYPE$, OLD.INV, MANUFCT, SHIPD, LOST
421   READ TOOL.NUM, TOOL.TYPE$
422   READ OLD.INV, MANUFCT, SHIPD, LOST
```

Execution of this pair of READ statements is illustrated in Figure 2-9.

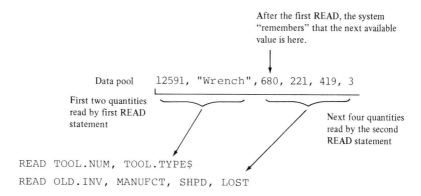

Figure 2-9. Execution of a pair of READ statements.

Exercises

2-9. The following program to calculate and print the sum of two numbers has an error in it. Explain what will happen during execution. Find the error and correct it.

```
10   READ A,B
20   C = A + B
300 PRINT C
40   DATA 312,176
100 END
```

2-10. Following is a sequence of READ and DATA statements. What will be read into the listed variables with execution of the following READ statements?

```
150  READ  A,B
160  READ  C,D
170  READ  E,F
180  READ  G,H
200  DATA  17,83
210  DATA  24,396,11,195,247
220  DATA  815
```

Using the Semicolon with the PRINT Statement

Remember from our earlier studies of the PRINT statement that every 14 positions serve as an effective tab stop and that results are printed according to this fixed format. However, it is possible to override the automatic tabbing operation by separating the variables in the list by semicolons rather than with commas. This has the effect of printing the quantities one after the other with no space between them. This is often confusing to the beginner because of the apparent difference between the output for numeric and string values. Let us consider string quantities first through the examples of Figure 2-10. Here we see that the comma tells the system to skip over to the beginning of the next print zone. However, the semicolon causes the second quantity to be printed without skipping any spaces beyond the last quantity.

To understand the effect on numeric output, we must know the exact form that the PRINT statement uses for numbers. This is illustrated in Figure 2-11, where we see that one position is reserved for the sign, whether the number is positive or negative. In addition, the PRINT statement tacks a space onto the end of the number. The effect of printing two numeric fields separated by a semicolon is illustrated opposite line 600.

Because of the manner in which printing works, the comma and semicolon provide us with an interesting (and useful) capability. Namely, a comma or a

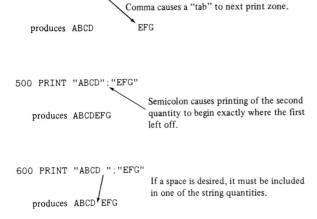

Figure 2-10. Using the semicolon to format string output.

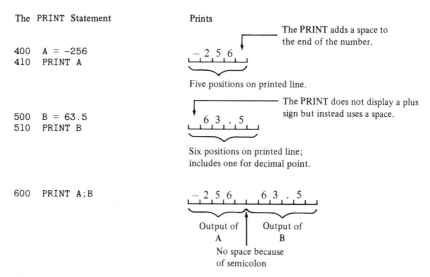

Figure 2-11.   Using the semicolon to format numeric output.

and 700–710 produce exactly the same results as statement 500.

```
500 PRINT A;B;C

600 PRINT A;
610 PRINT B;C

700 PRINT A;B;
710 PRINT C
```

semicolon after the last field will cause the cursor (or printing element) to maintain its current position for the next PRINT. The effect is that the next PRINT statement prints on the same line. Thus, the pairs of statements 600–610 In other words, if the last quantity to be printed (variable or literal) is followed by a semicolon, the next thing to be printed will immediately follow the last printed item. This is true regardless of where the next PRINT statement is located in the program.

The TAB Function

By itself, the semicolon has limited value. However, positioning of output is improved by combining use of the semicolon with the TAB *function*. (Note: This should not be confused with the TAB *key* on the terminal keyboard.) The typical terminal has 80 printing positions or columns (some have 132). These are numbered 0 through 79; thus, the first column would be identified by the system as position 0, the second as 1, and so on. Using the TAB function, we can specify in which column we wish a field to begin. The TAB function TAB(n) causes the cursor or printing element to move to the column specified by the value n. (Remember, column numbering starts with 0, not 1.) You can use more than one TAB function in the same PRINT statement; they should be separated by semicolons, not commas. This is illustrated in the example of Figure 2-12.

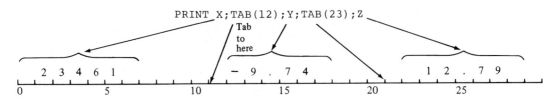

Assume the following values: x = 23461
                                     y = −9.74
                                     z = 12.79

Figure 2-12.   Using the TAB function.

Exercise

2-11. The following variables in a program have the values indicated:

X −296

Y 21.765

Z 3.518

Show how they will be printed by each of the following PRINT statements:

a. 100 PRINT X;Y;Z
b. 200 PRINT TAB(6);X;TAB(14);Z
c. 300 PRINT "X IS: ";X;TAB(15);"Z IS: ";Z

Additional Basic Commands

The DELETE Command

In earlier examples, whenever it was necessary to delete a line, we simply entered that line number and pressed the Return key. If several lines are to be deleted, then the DELETE command can be used. For instance, assume that we must delete lines 60, 85, 120, and 200. The following form of the DELETE statement would do this:

    DELETE   60,85,120,200

Actually, successive lines may be deleted, as illustrated by the following example:

    DELETE 40-70, 85, 90-250

In this case, lines 40 through 70 inclusive, line 85, and lines 90 through 250 inclusive will be deleted.

The DIR and TYPE Commands

As we learned in Chapter 1, the SAVE command saves a new program on auxiliary storage. The area in storage where it is saved is called your *library*. The system assigns a new version number each time a program with a given name is saved by SAVE. The first version is assigned 1, and consecutive version numbers increase by 1. You can get a listing of the *file directory* (*library directory*) of your account by typing the command DIR *at the* VMS *level*. (EXIT from Basic-system level, but remember that this clears your work area!)

An example listing of a file directory is shown in Figure 2-13. We see that four programs CUBE, PROB3, SALE, and MEAN are stored on the disk under this account. We should note that each source-program name is followed by .BAS;n. The suffix BAS, called the *extension*, is how the system distinguishes Basic programs from other types of files that may be stored. The integer *n* denotes the version.

You can also display the *contents* of a file, without bringing it into the work area, with the VMS-level command TYPE. For example,

```
TYPE INVEN.BAS;2
```

will display the specified program directly from your library.

The UNSAVE Command

Over a period of time, a large number of programs and different versions of the same program tend to accumulate on disk (in your *library* of programs). In most installations, the amount of disk space is limited, and users are expected to clear out unneeded programs and other files. The commands to delete library programs can be issued at either the VMS level or the Basic-system level. The UNSAVE command (Basic-system level) erases a particular version of a program from your library. For example, the command

```
UNSAVE  INVEN.BAS;3
```

erases the specified version of the file. If the version number (and the semicolon) are omitted, the latest version will be deleted. If the extension (and the period) are also omitted, the system assumes the BAS extension. (In other words, BAS is the *default* extension—a default is the option assumed by the

```
$DIR

Directory HSC001$DUA17:[BUCK]

CUBE.BAS;1        PROB3.BAS;1        SALE.BAS;1        MEAN.BAS;

Total of 4 files.

Ready
```

Figure 2-13. Getting a catalog listing of an account—the DIR command.

system when no option is specified by the user.) If no file is specified at all, the default is the library file that has the name of the program currently in memory. That is, the command

```
UNSAVE
```

erases from the library the source program whose version is currently in memory; it does not affect the copy in memory.

The OLD Command

With a timesharing system, it is common practice to work on a program over the course of several sessions at the terminal. For instance, we might have sufficient time today only to enter a program; however, we intend to come back tomorrow to test it and make necessary corrections. Obviously, we must save the program on completing the entry. When we wish to retrieve it from disk storage at a later date, we must use the command OLD. This command causes the system to get the selected program from disk and load it into memory so that we may continue just as if we had never left. For instance, let us assume that we entered and saved INVEN during a previous session. After checking a program *listing* (printout of the program), we discovered that the READ statement (420) was incorrect. After we sign in to our account, the correction procedure would be as shown in Figure 2-14. After the program has been corrected and saved, it may be run the same as if it had just been entered.

Note that correcting a program in your work area does *not* change the old version on disk. You still have to save the corrected version! Then you should get rid of the incorrect version on disk, as shown in Figure 2-14.

The RENAME and REPLACE Commands

To illustrate the RENAME command, let us assume that we must write a program that is very similar to one that we have on disk named SCAN. Since much of the code in SCAN can be used in the new program, it is senseless to reenter it. A better way is to load SCAN, *change the name*, make the necessary changes to the code, then save it back to disk. A typical sequence of events might be as follows:

```
OLD SCAN
RENAME SCAN2
```

(Make appropriate changes.)

```
SAVE
```

It is good practice to change the name immediately, since it is very easy to forget. Otherwise the confusing situation could occur in which different versions of a program are actually different programs. It is important to recognize that the RENAME only changes the name of the current program in memory. It does not change the name of the program on disk; this is done by the ensuing SAVE command.

```
OLD                          { Transfer the program version to be corrected
Old file name--INVEN.BAS;3   { from auxiliary storage into memory.

Ready
LIST
INVEN   12:43    03-Jan-84
100     REM EXAMPLE 1-1
          .
          .
          .
420     READ O, M, S, L  ◄────── Statement      Verify that this is the
430     LET N = O + M - S - L     in error       program to be corrected.
450     PRINT  T, T$, O, U
          .
          .
          .
32767   END

Ready

420    READ T, T$, O, M, S, L   Enter the corrected statement 420.

LIST
INVEN   12:43    03-Jan-84
100     REM EXAMPLE 1-1
          .
          .
          .
420     READ T, T$, O, M, S, L   Verify that the correction
430     LET N = O + M - S - L    has been entered properly.
450     PRINT  T, T$, O, U
          .
          .
          .
32767   END

Ready          Save the new version to
SAVE           auxiliary storage.

Ready

UNSAVE INVEN.BAS;3   Delete incorrect version
                     from auxiliary storage.
Ready
```

Figure 2-14. A typical terminal session.

In the preceding sequence, the SAVE command is used. VAX Basic also includes the REPLACE command. Its action is identical to that of the SAVE.

The VMS DELETE and PURGE Commands

All of the preceding commands are Basic level; they are executed from the Basic system. It is also possible to delete files from your library by using VMS DELETE. It is important not to become confused between the Basic DELETE and the VMS DELETE. In Basic, DELETE allows lines from the current program to be deleted. At the VMS level, DELETE performs much the same function as the Basic UNSAVE command; it erases files. For example, the following command will erase version 3 of INVEN.BAS:

```
DELETE  INVEN.BAS;3
```

One other VMS command that is very convenient is the PURGE, which will erase all versions of a program except the most recent. For instance, if the command

```
PURGE INVEN.BAS
```

is used in a program, then only the latest version will remain on disk.

Exercise

2-12. Explain the difference between the two commands in each of the following sets:

a. DELETE at Basic-system level and at VMS level.
b. UNSAVE and VMS-level DELETE.
c. LIST and TYPE.

In Retrospect

In the first two chapters, we have learned and used a variety of commands and statements. With the various types, it is easy to become confused; following is a brief summary.

Summary of Commands

VMS Commands. Following is a summary (in alphabetic order) of the VMS-level commands that we have studied in Chapters 1 and 2.

BASIC	Transfers control from VMS to Basic subsystem.
DELETE	Deletes specified version of program from user's library.
DIR	Lists the names, extensions, and versions of all files stored in user's library.
PURGE	Deletes all versions of a program except the latest from the user's library.
TYPE	Displays contents of specified file directly from user's library.

Basic-Subsystem-Level Commands. Following is a summary (in alphabetic order) of the Basic-subsystem-level commands that we have studied in Chapters 1 and 2.

DELETE	Deletes specified lines from program in work area.
EXIT	Clears work area and returns control to VMS.

LIST	Displays the program, or specified parts of it, that is currently in the working area of memory.
LISTNH	Same as LIST but without the program header.
NEW	Clears the work area of memory and prepares for the entry of a new program.
OLD	Copies a specified Basic program from the library into the work area.
RENAME	Changes the name of the program currently in the memory work area (*not* a program in the library).
REPLACE	Identical to SAVE.
RUN	Runs the program currently in the memory work area; if a program name is also specified, first loads that program from the library and then runs it.
RUNNH	Same as RUN but without the program header.
SAVE	Copies the program in the work area to the library and assigns a new version number to it.
UNSAVE	Deletes the named program from the library.

Interaction with the system can be speeded up in many cases by combining instructions to the system. This is illustrated by the following examples.

Short Form	Is Equivalent to
NEW INVEN	NEW New file name—INVEN
OLD INVEN	OLD Old file name—INVEN

Summary of Statements

Following is a summary (in alphabetic order) of the Basic statements that are described in this chapter.

DATA	Allows data values (to be processed by the READ) to be included directly in a program.
END	Indicates that no more statements follow. Must be the last statement in the program (suggested line number is 32767). Also terminates execution of the program.
LET	Assignment statement; causes the expression to right of equal sign to be evaluated, then stores the result in variable to left. (The word LET may be omitted.)
PRINT	Prints values of designated variables or constants to an output device (terminal and/or printer).
READ	Reads consecutive values from the DATA statements into variables listed in the READ statement.
REM	Allows descriptive remarks to be included in the program. These are ignored by the Basic system. REM can be replaced by the exclamation-mark character (!).
RESTORE	Resets the pointer to the beginning of the data pool.

Answers to Preceding Exercises

2-1. 56—first character not a letter.
READ—reserved word
8E—first character not a letter.
SHOP 7—embedded blank.

2-2. a. Valid.
b. Invalid, too large.
c. Invalid, zero not allowed.
d. Valid.
e. Invalid, negative numbers not allowed.

2-3. A descriptive remark is indicated by the keyword REM or an exclamation mark (!) following the line number. In VAX Basic, it is also possible to follow any statement with an exclamation mark and then a descriptive remark.

2-4. Because line 20 is misnumbered as line 200, the statement has been placed out of sequence: The PRINT statement will be executed before the value of C has been computed. Because Basic initializes all numeric variables to zero, the output for C will be 0 rather than the sum of A and B.

2-5. The three data values in statement 900 are numeric fields. In statement 300, they are read into the numeric fields A, B, C. As such, they can be involved in arithmetic operations. On the other hand, in statement 400, they are read into the string variables X\$, Y\$, Z\$. Within the computer, numeric and string data values are stored differently, even when they are the same numerals. The numbers stored in X\$, Y\$ and Z\$ cannot be involved in normal arithmetic operations. One important aspect of this exercise relates to defining data values that are to be read into string variables. In particular, notice that omitting quotes does *not* represent an error when using the DATA statement. Although examples in this book always enclose string data within quotes, the quotes are not required for an input quantity unless that quantity contains a delimiter such as a comma.

2-6. The values for Q1, Q3, and Q5 will begin in, respectively, printing positions 1, 15, and 29. (Remember, this corresponds to column numbers 0, 14, and 28.)

2-7. (a) 7; (b) 12; (c) 14

2-8. a. A*(B + C)
b. A*X**2 + B*X + C
c. X/(R*S)
d. (3.14/4)*H*D**2

e. 6.75*A*B
f. X + A**Y
g. (5/9)*(F − 32)
h. R/(1 − (1 + R)**(−N))

2-9. With the program as shown, the PRINT will not be executed, so there will be no output. The line number of END is not larger than those of all other statements in the program. The preferable fix is to change it to 32767. The program will then run as expected, even though the line number of PRINT is larger than that of DATA. Remember that the DATA statement can appear anywhere in the program before END. In keeping with the convention for DATA used in this book, it would be preferable to change the line number of PRINT to 30.

2-10. The values in the DATA statements are placed in the DATA pool in the sequence listed in lines 200, 210, and 220: from left to right in any given DATA statement and in increasing line numbers of multiple DATA statements. The following values are read with the variables on lines 150, 160, 170, and 180:

A	B	C	D	E	F	G	H
17	83	24	396	11	195	247	815

2-11 a. −296   21.765   3.518
    b.   −296   3.518
    c. X IS: −296   Z IS: 3.518

2-12. See the summary of commands that follows this exercise.

Programming Problems

2-1. Enter and run the program of Figure 2-1. After you get it running correctly, SAVE it. Next, modify it by deleting each of the following lines, one line at a time. Enter and run each of the modified programs. Explain the results in each case.

a. Line 420.
b. Line 430.
c. Line 440.
d. Line 820.

If you SAVE each modification, remember that the system will create a new version each time you SAVE. One way to deal with the system aspect of the problem is to use the OLD command to bring your SAVEd version of the *original* program (write down the version number when you SAVE it) into memory. Remember also that if you do not specify the version number with the OLD command, the system default is to the *latest* version.

2-2. A DATA statement includes the following employee payroll information:

Employee number.

Gross pay.

Tax withholding.

Other deductions.

Write a program that will calculate the net pay as follows:

Net pay = gross pay − tax withholding − other deductions

Print each of the input quantities and the calculated net pay. The following DATA statement represents a typical record:

```
1000  DATA  2365, 1463.80, 150, 92, 64.70
```

2-3. An instructor is testing a student exam-information system on the computer. Assume that there is one DATA statement with the following information:

Student ID.

First hour exam.

Second hour exam.

Third hour exam.

Final exam.

Write a program to calculate the total points earned as the sum of the scores of the three one-hour exams and twice the score on the final exam. A sample DATA statement for this program is

```
1000  DATA  634507968, 83, 92, 64, 96
```

2-4. A stock market investor keeps a record of all stocks that have been purchased and then resold. Assume that there is one DATA statement with the following information:

Stock ID number.

Number of shares of stock.

Total purchase price.

Total sale price.

Total commission paid to broker.

Write a program to calculate the profit (or loss). Print the stock ID number, the number of shares, and the profit.

```
1000  DATA  2678, 500, 3460.20, 3520.78, 103.81
```

2-5. The total resistance (R) of an electric circuit with three elements in parallel is given in terms of the individual resistances of the elements (1,2, and 3) by the following formula:

$$\frac{1}{R} = \frac{1}{R_1} + \frac{1}{R_2} + \frac{1}{R_3}$$

The DATA statement contains the following information.

$$R_1 \quad R_2 \quad R_3$$

Write a program to calculate the total resistance. Print this result and the input quantities.

```
1000   DATA 2.7, 4.0, 6.1
```

2-6. The solution of the linear system of equations

$$a_1x + b_1y = c_1$$
$$a_2x + b_2y = c_2$$

is given by

$$x = \frac{b_2c_1 - b_1c_2}{a_1b_2 - a_2b_1}$$
$$y = \frac{a_1c_2 - a_2c_1}{a_1b_2 - a_2b_1}$$

The DATA statement contains values (in order) for $a_1, b_1, c_1, a_2, b_2,$ and c_2. Write a program to compute x and y. Output should include

First line—input data.
Second line—values of x and y.
Third line—blank.

```
1000   DATA 3, 4, 7, 5, 2, 9
```

3

Program Loops

Chapter Outline

Preview

The purpose of this chapter is twofold: to provide a means for repeated execution of a sequence of statements and to lay the basis for an organized, efficient approach to programming. Important topics covered in this chapter are the following:

1. *The use of statement labels in place of line numbers.*
2. *Program modularization, whereby a program is broken into logically related parts.*
3. *The means to transfer control of program execution from one portion of the program to another and then back again (the GOSUB and RETURN).*
4. *The means to repeat the execution of a sequence of statements (the WHILE statement).*
5. *The nature of structured programming, whereby the three basic*

structures of sequence, looping, and selection form the basis for program logic.

6. *The use of pseudocode in problem solution, whereby a program solution begins with an English description of the required operations.*

The following new statements are introduced in this chapter:

EXIT
GOSUB
RETURN
STOP
WHILE–NEXT

Programming Tools

Fundamental Steps of Programming

Without a doubt, the single biggest mistake that the beginning programming student makes is wading into the programming of a problem without thoroughly understanding the nature of the problem. If we step back and think about it, to begin writing detailed instructions on how to do something without fully understanding how to do it simply does not make sense. However, this is what many programming students do. An organized approach to computer problem solving is essential. Following is a very straightforward set of steps to follow in preparing computer solutions.

1. *Define the desired results.* Analyze the problem to see what useful results, or output, are required. Decide on exactly what information is desired to come out of the computer.
2. *Analyze the input data.* Does the data set contain everything that you need to produce the desired output? If the needed data quantities are not there in exactly the desired form, can you combine some of the input fields to produce the desired output? A good way to find out (and a strongly recommended one) is to go through the steps manually to derive sample results. If the answer to one of these questions is yes, you can go ahead. However, if the answer to both questions is no, you do not have the necessary input data to produce the desired output.
3. *Devise an overall plan* (sometimes called an *algorithm*) for converting the input into the desired output. A number of techniques are commonly used for this purpose, including flowcharts and pseudocode (both of these are described later).
4. *Express the solution in a language that can be communicated to the computer.* This is called *coding* the program; this book deals with coding programs in the Basic language.

This overall process is called *programming*. As you can see, coding is only a part of programming. The first three steps are actually carried out, explicitly or implicitly, whether the processing is done manually or by computer. Only the fourth step is specific to processing by a computer.

The Concept of Modularizing a Program

In most any endeavor, if we are given a very large task to carry out, it is easy to become overwhelmed by the sheer magnitude of things. For example, building a house is not a job to be taken lightly. However, we would break the work down into smaller components, such as foundation work, framing, electrical work, plumbing, and so on. Each of these subtasks is more specialized and can be considered somewhat independently of the others. It is almost as if the sum of the complexity of the parts is less than the complexity of the overall project.

Much the same is true in programming. A single large program consisting of 30 or 40 pages of code can be rather staggering. However, if that same large programming task is broken down into relatively independent parts, then each can be considered separately. The important factor is that a person can much more easily comprehend many individual components of a program (and their interrelationship) than a single massive program entity. Even the simple program of Chapter 2 can be subdivided into three components, as shown in Figure 3-1. Here we see that the three parts have the following functions:

INITIALIZE: Print the report headings.
PROC.TOOLS: Process the data.
TERMINATE: Print the termination message.

We have broken the program into three *modules*, each designed to perform a particular function or group of functions. Modularization of programs in this fashion is the key to handling a large, complex task: Break it down into manageable parts.

```
2000 ! Initialization routine
2010    PRINT "TOOL",   "TOOL",     "OLD",        "UPDATED"
2020    PRINT "NUMBER", "TYPE", "INVENTORY",  "INVENTORY"
2030    PRINT
2050 ! End of initialization routine
2060 !
3000 ! Processing routine
3010    READ TOOL.NUM, TOOL.TYPE$, OLD.INV, MANUFCT, SHIPD, LOST
3020    NEW.INV = OLD.INV + MANUFCT - SHIPD - LOST
3030    PRINT TOOL.NUM, TOOL.TYPE$, OLD.INV, NEW.INV
3050 ! End of processing routine
3060 !
4000 ! Termination routine
4010    PRINT
4020    PRINT
4030    PRINT "Processing complete"
4050 ! End of termination routine
4060 !
8000 ! ** INPUT DATA **
8010    DATA 12591, "Wrench", 680, 221, 419, 3
32767  END
```

Figure 3-1. A simple program in component form.

Level of Operations

By taking the modularization concept one step further, it is possible to organize a program into two or more component modules that are controlled by a higher-level *control module* (also called *main module*). This is illustrated schematically by the diagram of Figure 3-2. Here we see the program represented by two levels of operations, wherein the first level oversees the components of the second level. Note that this does not tell us the order in which modules are executed; it simply illustrates the relationship between modules of the program. Needless to say, we do not yet have the programming tools to implement this organization. Let us now acquire these tools.

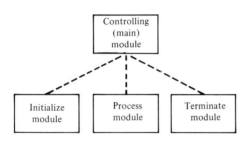

Figure 3-2. Module levels.

A Modularized Program

The modularized program of Figure 3-1 has been expanded in Figure 3-3. Here we clearly see four modules carefully identified: main, initialization, processing, and termination. Note that this new version is a two-level one (Figure 3-2), since it now includes a controlling module (the main module). As we shall learn, the main routine simply says

1. Perform the initialization routine.
2. Perform the process routine.
3. Perform the termination routine.

The three important Basic features that we shall use in organizing a program in this way are as follows:

1. The ability to execute statements in an order other than that of progressively increasing line numbers. In Chapter 2, we learned that this is the order in which the computer executes statements unless some statement tells it to do otherwise. Such a statement is said to *transfer control*.
2. The GOSUB statement, which provides the ability to transfer control to a separate module and to remember where this transfer originated.
3. Statement labels.

```
100    !     MODULARIZED EXAMPLE
110    !     PROGRAM TO UPDATE AN INVENTORY
120    !     INPUT VARIABLE NAMES ARE:
130    !        TOOL.NUM --   Tool inventory number
140    !        TOOL.TYPE$   --   Tool type
150    !        OLD.INV   --   Old inventory quantity
160    !        MANUFCT   --   Units manufactured
170    !        SHIPD     --   Units shipped
180    !        LOST      --   Units lost or damaged
190    !     CALCULATED VARIABLE NAMES ARE:
200    !        NEW.INV   --   Updated inventory quantity
210    !
1000  !  MAIN PROGRAM
1010     GOSUB INITIALIZE
1020        !
1030     GOSUB PROC.TOOLS
1040        !
1050     GOSUB TERMINATE
1060        !
1070     STOP   ! STOP EXECUTION
1080        !
1130  !  END OF MAIN PROGRAM
1140  !
1150  !
      INITIALIZE:
2000  !  INITIALIZATION ROUTINE
2010     PRINT "TOOL", "TOOL",    "OLD",         "UPDATED"
2020     PRINT "NUMBER", "TYPE", "INVENTORY", "INVENTORY"
2030     PRINT
2040     RETURN
2050  !  END OF INITIALIZATION ROUTINE
2060  !
      PROC.TOOLS:
3000  !  PROCESSING ROUTINE
3010     READ TOOL.NUM, TOOL.TYPE$, OLD.INV, MANUFCT, SHIPD, LOST
3020     NEW.INV = OLD.INV + MANUFCT - SHIPD - LOST
3030     PRINT TOOL.NUM, TOOL.TYPE$, OLD.INV, NEW.INV
3040     RETURN
3050  !  END OF PROCESSING ROUTINE
3060  !
      TERMINATE:
4000  !  TERMINATION ROUTINE
4010     PRINT
4020     PRINT
4030     PRINT "Processing complete"
4040     RETURN
4050  !  END OF TERMINATION ROUTINE
4060  !
8000  !  ** INPUT DATA **
8010     DATA 12591, "Wrench", 680, 221, 419, 3
32767  END
```

Figure 3-3. A modularized program.

Statement Labels

The forms illustrated in Figure 3-4 provide the means for executing one module under the control of another. As we shall learn in the following section, the GOSUB statement at line 1010 causes execution of the program to jump down

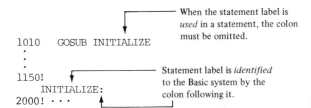

```
1010    GOSUB INITIALIZE
  .
  .
  .
1150!
     INITIALIZE:
2000! · · ·
```

When the statement label is
used in a statement, the colon
must be omitted.

Statement label is *identified*
to the Basic system by the
colon following it.

Figure 3-4. Statement labels.

to the portion of the program labeled INITIALIZE. We see that INITIALIZE
is defined between lines 1150 and 2000; it is called a *statement label*. In general,
a label is a name that is used to identify a place in a program to which control
is to be transferred. Any valid variable name can be used as a statement label.
A label is *defined* by the name followed by a colon (:) immediately preceding
a statement. The statement identified by the label can be on the same line as
the label or on the following line. In this program, we see that each of the
lower-level modules is preceded by a label. The other two are PROC.TOOLS
and TERMINATE.

It is important to realize that using a statement label is not the only way
of referring to another statement. In Chapter 1, we learned that line numbers
provide the means for the Basic system to place statements in their proper
order. They can also be used for transfer of control. In fact, most versions of
Basic do not allow the use of statement labels, and line numbers are the only
method by which a statement can be referenced. When transferring control,
VAX Basic allows the use of either statement labels or line numbers. But it is
clear that the statement on the left is much more meaningful to us when we
are examining the program than the equivalent form on the right.

GOSUB INITIALIZE   GOSUB 2000

In almost all examples in this book, labels are used because of their value
in documenting the nature of what is taking place. However, there are some
situations in VAX Basic in which a statement label cannot be used, so a statement number must be used. We shall learn about these situations in later
chapters.

The GOSUB and RETURN Statements

From the preceding discussion of statement labels, we see that the GOSUB
statement provides us with the means to transfer control from one module to
another. This is commonly called *calling* the submodule. The module that does
the calling (in this case, the main module) is called the *calling module*, and
the one to which control is transferred is referred to as the *called module*. In
addition to being able to transfer control to the called module, we need a means
for getting control back to the calling module. This is provided by the RETURN
statement. The action of the GOSUB is as follows:

1. Transfer execution of the program to the statement identified by the statement label.

2. "Remember" where in the calling program the transfer was initiated so that execution can be returned to that point when execution of the called module is completed.

The other half of the key to this operation is the RETURN statement, which transfers control back to the line following the GOSUB. The RETURN will clearly be the last statement executed in the called module, even though it need not be the last physical statement in that module.

These operations are illustrated in Figure 3-5. The sequence of events is as follows:

1. On encountering the GOSUB, control is immediately transferred to the named module (INITIALIZE).
2. Statements comprising this module are executed.
3. On encountering the RETURN statement, control is transferred back to the main program at the statement immediately following the module call. In this case, the return point is the remark at line 1020, so execution immediately falls through to the next GOSUB at line 1030.

The STOP Statement

One very important thing that we must keep in mind is the nature of the program when it is stored in the computer's memory. When we look at a program such as that in Figure 3-3, we see independent, logically related modules. We know that after the last module is executed (by the Termination Routine beginning line 4000), processing should terminate. However, the computer does not "see" these separate modules; it works with one statement at a time. Thus, after the execution of the last GOSUB at line 1050 and the return, execution would continue to the next statement. This is the reason for the STOP statement at line 1070. Its action is exactly as the word suggests; it suspends program execution. We might note that the program of Chapter 2 did not include a STOP. The reason is that there were no other executable statements between the last statement to be executed and the END statement. The END served the purpose of terminating execution of the program.

Each program must include one END statement, and it must be the last statement in the entire program. However, a program can have one or several STOP statements anywhere within the program. As a rule, techniques used in this book will involve only one STOP in a program.

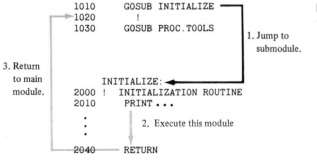

Figure 3-5. Execution of the GOSUB and RETURN statements.

Exercise

3-1. What do you think would happen during execution if the STOP statement of Figure 3-3 were omitted?

About Program Modularization

The most important thing about the program of Figure 3-3 is that logical components are isolated into individual modules. We see the main module, which is a simple, straightforward sequence of steps. The submodules themselves are simple, straightforward sequences of steps. Although this program is relatively short and simple, this approach to programming is very powerful. In particular, long and very complex problems can almost always be broken into relatively short and easy-to-handle modules. Then each module can be handled as being virtually independent of the others. Not only does it simplify the programming task, but it also simplifies later changes and corrections to the program (program maintenance).

The next topic is that of repeatedly executing a selected sequence of statements. However, before proceeding with this, let us detour for a moment and consider some programming theory that is basic to these principles.

Some Programming Theory

Structured Programming

In addition to the practice of modularizing programs, another development in modern computer programming arose in response to the changing views as to what constitutes high-quality software. In the past, the sole criterion was that the program produce the correct (that is, required) results. More recently, equal emphasis has been placed on the ease with which software can be thoroughly tested, modified, and otherwise maintained.

Within recent years, the technique known as *structured programming* has come into wide use to deal with these problems. This technique aims to reduce the complexity of programs and make them more readable. This is achieved by using only a limited set of well-defined control constructs. An overall goal of structured programming is to make the general flow of execution of a program proceed in a forward direction, except for specifically controlled program transfers. An important element of structured programming is the single-entry–single-exit concept. That is, each module has only one point to which control is transferred from the calling module, and each module has only one point from which control is returned to the calling module. Clearly, GOSUB refers to the entry point, and RETURN, to the exit point. Multiple RETURNs, which *are* valid in BASIC, violate the single-exit concept, but we live with them in the absence of better alternatives. Adherence to structured-programming concepts makes testing the program much simpler and provides a measure of self documentation. Experience has shown that use of structured techniques increases programmer efficiency very significantly.

In 1966, two computer scientists, Bohm and Jacopini, presented a paper in which they laid the basis for structured programming. In their paper, they showed that any computer program can be constructed using the following three programming structures:

1. *Simple sequence*—progression from one statement to the next one through sequential lines of code. This is the technique we have seen in the sample programs.
2. *Selection*—selection of one of two or more operations or groups of operations to be performed, depending upon a particular test condition.
3. *Repetition* or *looping*—repeated execution of one or more operations; looping may be one of two general types: The loop may continue either a specified number of times or be subject to a given condition.

These three fundamental structures are shown and described in Figure 3-6.

Most modern languages (such as Pascal, Algol, and PL/1) were designed as structured languages. That is, they support language constructs (statements) that correspond directly to the fundamental structures in Figure 3-6. Although VAX Basic has powerful features that come close to supporting a fully structured approach (much more so than most versions of Basic), it is not fully structured. In particular, as we shall learn, VAX Basic includes the GOTO statement, which is necessary to use in some instances. The GOTO provides for transfer of control from one point in a program to another without the "return" features of the GOSUB. In a fully structured language, any program can be written without the use of the GOTO statement. This is not the case

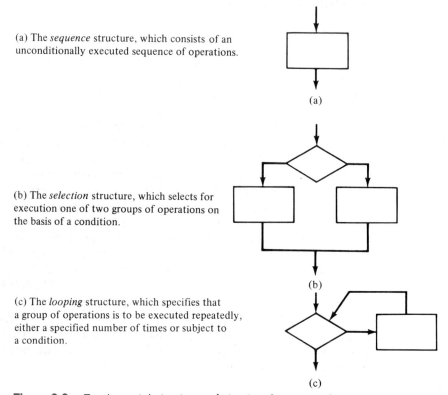

(a) The *sequence* structure, which consists of an unconditionally executed sequence of operations.

(a)

(b) The *selection* structure, which selects for execution one of two groups of operations on the basis of a condition.

(b)

(c) The *looping* structure, which specifies that a group of operations is to be executed repeatedly, either a specified number of times or subject to a condition.

(c)

Figure 3-6. Fundamental structures of structured programming.

with the languages most commonly used today (Cobol, Fortran, and most versions of Basic). VAX Basic, however, provides a full complement of constructs that directly parallel the fundamental control structures. In this sense, VAX Basic, in contrast to many other versions of Basic, includes features that very nearly place it in the category of being a fully structured language.

Repetitive Execution of a Sequence

Expanding Example 2-1 to Include Looping

A program to process one data record might be quite acceptable for illustrating basic principles, but it is totally inadequate for actual use. To this end, let us consider an expansion of Example 2-1 that involves processing an entire file of data.

Example 3-1

> The inventory processing of Example 2-1 is to be expanded to include processing an entire file of inventory records. The program is to include one DATA statement for each tool in stock. To indicate the end of the data, the last data set will be followed by a DATA statement with a value of 99999 for the inventory stock number. In view of the fact that arithmetic operations will never be performed on the stock number field, the decision has been made to treat it as a string field. The DATA statements to be used for this program, shown in Figure 3-7, reflect that change.

It is important to note that the there is one DATA statement for each set of data values. Also, the last DATA statement does *not* contain a set of data values to be processed. Its sole purpose is to serve as a *trailer* to mark the end of the data set. Note that it has ''dummy'' values for each of the six fields. This is essential because the READ statement will be expecting six values each time it is executed.

The program solution to Example 3-1, shown in Figure 3-8, is almost identical to that of Figure 3-3 to process a single data set. For convenience, the necessary additional statements are shaded. This program illustrates the following new Basic structures:

1. The combination of the WHILE and NEXT statements, which form one basis for looping, as described in the previous section on structured programming.
2. The EXIT statement, which provides for termination of execution of a program loop.

```
DATA "12591", "Wrench", 680, 221, 419, 3
DATA "13311", "Hammer", 512,   0, 186, 4
DATA "15118", "File",    82, 500, 160, 1
DATA "16881", "Pliers",   0, 201,   0, 0
DATA "99999", "EOF",      0,   0,   0, 0
```

Figure 3-7. The data values to be processed for Example 3-1.

```
100    !    EXAMPLE 3-1
110    !    PROGRAM TO UPDATE AN INVENTORY
120    !    INPUT VARIABLE NAMES ARE:
130    !       TOOL.NUM$   --  TOOL NUMBER
140    !       TOOL.TYPE$   --   TOOL TYPE
150    !       OLD.INV   --  OLD INVENTORY
160    !       MANUFCT   --  UNITS MANUFACTURED
170    !       SHIPD     --  UNITS SHIPPED
180    !       LOST      --  UNITS LOST OR DAMAGED
190    !    CALCULATED VARIABLE NAMES ARE:
200    !       NEW.INV   --  UPDATED INVENTORY
210    !
1000   !  MAIN PROGRAM
1010      GOSUB INITIALIZE
1020         !
1030      GOSUB PROC.TOOLS
1040         !
1050      GOSUB TERMINATE
1060         !
1070      STOP  ! STOP EXECUTION
1080         !
1130   !  END OF MAIN PROGRAM
1140   !
1150   !
     INITIALIZE:
2000   !  INITIALIZATION ROUTINE
2010      PRINT "TOOL", "TOOL",    "OLD",         "UPDATED"
2020      PRINT "NUMBER", "TYPE", "INVENTORY", "INVENTORY"
2030      PRINT
2040      RETURN
2050   !  END OF INITIALIZATION ROUTINE
2060   !
     PROC.TOOLS:
3000   !  PROCESSING ROUTINE
3002   !
          PROCESS.LOOP:
          WHILE -1
3010         READ TOOL.NUM$, TOOL.TYPE$, OLD.INV, MANUFCT, SHIPD, LOST
3015         EXIT PROCESS.LOOP IF TOOL.NUM$ = "99999"
3020         NEW.INV = OLD.INV + MANUFCT - SHIPD - LOST
3030         PRINT TOOL.NUM$, TOOL.TYPE$, OLD.INV, NEW.INV
3034      NEXT
3035      ! End of PROCESS.LOOP
3036      !
3040      RETURN
3050   !  END OF PROCESSING ROUTINE
3060   !
     TERMINATE:
4000   !  TERMINATION ROUTINE
4010      PRINT
4020      PRINT
4030      PRINT "Processing complete"
4040      RETURN
4050   !  END OF TERMINATION ROUTINE
4060   !
8000   !  ** INPUT DATA **
8010      DATA "12591", "Wrench", 680, 221, 419, 3
8020      DATA "13311", "Hammer", 512,   0, 186, 4
8030      DATA "15118", "File",    82, 500, 160, 1
8040      DATA "16881", "Pliers",   0, 201,   0, 0
8050      DATA "99999", "EOF",      0,   0,   0, 0
32767  END
```

Figure 3-8. Processing a data file—Example 3-1.

The WHILE and NEXT Statements

The looping structure of structured programming is commonly called the "Do While" form. The general meaning is "Do a set of operations while a given condition is true." In VAX Basic, there are several forms that provide the looping capability illustrated in Figure 3-6(c). Although details of exactly how these work are described in later chapters, we use one of them here, the WHILE statement, to provide the needed looping capability. If we are to define a group of statements to form a program loop, then some means is needed to identify the end of the loop. In VAX Basic, the beginning of the loop is marked with a WHILE statement and the end by a NEXT statement. These techniques are illustrated in Figure 3-9. Note that the keyword WHILE is followed by a minus one (-1). For reasons about which we shall learn in a later chapter, this causes the loop to execute indefinitely (without end). We shall also learn how the -1 value is normally replaced with a condition test that will yield the exact form illustrated in the structure form of Figure 3-6(c).

The EXIT Statement

A loop that executes indefinitely (has no logical end to it) is something to be avoided in any programming language. Of course, we know that the program will eventually stop because it will run out of data. However, attempting to read data values when there are no more represents an error condition that will cause the program to terminate (under an error) immediately. In this example, execution would "bomb" at the READ of line 3010 and execution of the Termination Routine would never occur. We obviously need a method to end execution of the loop upon encountering the "trailer record" containing 99999 in the first field (line 8050).

The EXIT statement of line 3015 (Figure 3-8) provides the means for ending the loop when the trailer record is read. The transfer of control out of the loop is realized only if a certain condition is satisfied. Details of this statement and its overall effect are shown in Figure 3-10. Actually, the effect of this statement is reasonably well described by the ordinary English of it. This is "The loop is to be exited when the value found in the variable TOOL.NUM is 99999." (Conditional statements of this kind are covered in detail in the next chapter.)

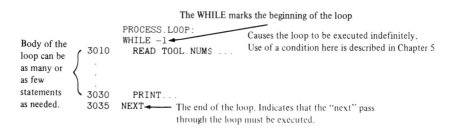

Figure 3-9. Principles of the WHILE/NEXT statements.

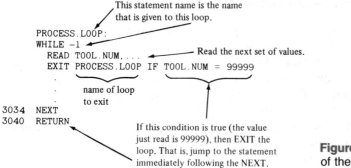

Figure 3-10. The effect of the EXIT statement.

The sequence of events when this program is executed will be as follows:

1. The INITIALIZE module is entered from statement 1010 of the main routine. Its execution causes headings to be printed; then control returns to the calling routine at line 1020.
2. The PROC.TOOLS module is entered from statement 1030 of the main routine. Its execution causes the following sequence of events to take place:
   a. The first data set is read; the value in TOOL.NUM$ is 12591 (not 99999), so the EXIT is ignored.
   b. The current data values are processed in lines 3020 and 3030.
   c. When the NEXT is encountered at line 3034, control is transferred back to the READ at the beginning of the loop.
   d. The preceding sequence is repeated for the data at lines 8020, 8030, and 8040.
   e. When the data values from line 8050 are read, the value in TOOL.NUM$ will be 99999. Thus, the EXIT at line 3015 will be executed, and program execution will transfer to the statement following the NEXT. Since this is a RETURN, control returns to the main module at line 1040.
3. The TERMINATE module is entered from statement 1050 of the main routine. Its execution causes the termination message to be printed. Control is then returned to the main module at line 1060.
4. The STOP statement at line 1070 terminates execution of the program.

The printed results from running this program are shown in Figure 3-11. Note that there is one line for each data line of the program except for the trailer value, which is not printed.

LINE NUMBER	TOOL NUMBER	TOOL TYPE	OLD INVENTORY	UPDATED INVENTORY
1	12591	Wrench	680	479
2	13311	Hammer	512	322
3	15118	File	82_	421
4	16881	Pliers	0	201

PROCESSING COMPLETE

Figure 3-11. Sample output—Example 3-1.

Exercises

3-2. How many times will the READ statement at line 3010 in Figure 3-8 be executed using the data values in lines 8010–8050? How many times will the PRINT statement at line 3030 be executed?

3-3. What would happen in the program of Figure 3-8 if there were no data (if lines 8010–8040 were omitted) and only line 8050 were present?

3-4. Which of the three fundamental programming structures have been used in the programs of each of the following figures?

a. Figure 2-1.
b. Figure 2-7(b).
c. Figure 3-3.
d. Figure 3-8.

Calculating Summary Totals

The Concept of Accumulating

The printed report of Figure 3-11 provides a convenient summary. However, it lacks one item that is commonly required in many types of applications: totals. For instance, the warehouse manager would probably be interested in the total number of tools shipped, lost, and so on. The concept of computing a total in a computer program is very similar to the way we would total a column of figures with a pocket calculator. For instance, as each number is entered through the keypad, it is added to the value in the calculator display. (It is *accumulated* in an *accumulator*.) Thus, when we are finished, the accumulator contains the final sum. In computing, the need to accumulate values is very common to both business and scientific computer applications. For example, consider a situation in which the average of the following set of numbers is to be determined:

85 65 75 92 88 83 90 65 69 74 96 62

The process would be

1. Add up all of the numbers in the sequence.
2. Count them to determine how many there are.
3. Divide the total by the count to get the average.

If these values were stored in the computer and a program were required to do the computation, then an accumulation process would be involved just like the one illustrated with the pocket calculator.

To illustrate how this would be done in the program, let us assume that the preceding sequence of data values is to be read one after the other into the variable AMOUNT. Furthermore, as they are being read, their total is to be accumulated in the variable TOTAL. Figure 3-12(a) illustrates this concept after the first three values have been read. Here we see that TOTAL contains 225. The process of reading and accumulating the next value is shown in Figure 3-12(b), where the assignment statement is the key to the process. Here it is very important that we remember how this statement functions.

1. The expression to the right of the equal sign is evaluated (without any consideration of what is on the left).
2. The result of the evaluation (a number) is stored in the variable listed on the left of the equal sign. Note that this is done without any consideration of the variables from which the number was calculated.

In this case, the value 92 from AMOUNT will be added to the value 225 in the variable TOTAL, giving a result of 317. This quantity then replaces the previous value in TOTAL.

One important consideration in using an accumulator relates to its initial value. For instance, assume that we are using a desk calculator to total several columns of numbers. Upon finishing with one column, the first thing we would do before beginning on the next is to get rid of the previous value from the memory of the calculator. That is, we would *initialize* the accumulator to zero. We can anticipate that the accumulator of Figure 3-12 (TOTAL) must have contained zero before the accumulation process was started.

Using an Accumulator in a Program

Let us now consider an expansion of Example 3-1 that involves using an accumulator in the program.

Example 3-2

Example 3-1 is to be expanded to include the following additions to the output report:

1. The detail lines must be numbered (with a line number) beginning at 1 and progressing to 2, 3, and so on.
2. After the entire data set has been processed, the total number of tools currently in stock must be printed.

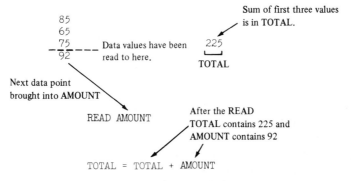

Figure 3-12. The concept of accumulating.

If we think about it, we will see that these additions to the problem do not change the overall logic of the Example 3-1 program. In fact, it illustrates a very important feature of modularizing programs: Changes can usually be pinpointed to one or more individual modules. Of the four modules in this program (main and three second-level), we can immediately see that the Processing Routine and Termination Routine will need at least the following changes:

1. Processing Routine: Each time a data set is processed, the new inventory value will have to be added into the total.
2. Termination Routine: Statements to print the total quantity for the inventory must be added.

Perhaps not quite as obvious is that the Initialization Routine will require appropriate statements to ensure that accumulator initialization is done properly.

These relatively simple modifications are shaded in the program of Figure 3-13(a); the result of running the program is shown in Figure 3-13(b). Following are important points that we should focus on in this program.

1. Two accumulators are used: CNT and TOT.INV.
2. Both accumulators are set to zero in the Initialization Routine (lines 2034 and 2036). Technically speaking, this is not necessary because Basic sets all numeric variables to zero when the program is first executed. However, it is a good idea to get in the habit of zeroing an accumulator for two reasons. First, most other languages do not zero variables. Second, sometimes an accumulator must be set back to zero within the program. Hence, it is good practice simply to be in the habit of always zeroing accumulators.
3. The accumulator CNT, which maintains the line count, is incremented by 1 with each execution (line 3024). We can see the result in the first column of the printed output in Figure 3-13(b).
4. The total number of tools in stock will be stored in the accumulator TOT.INV.

As with the modification in progressing from the program of Example 2-1 to that of Example 3-1, we were able to isolate the particular module (or modules) requiring modification in order to change the program. For a large program in real life, such isolation is critical. A programmer does not want a change in one part of a program to cause problems in another totally unrelated area.

Exercises

3-5. The use of accumulators (such as CNT and TOT.INV in Figure 3-13) is based on a very important assumption regarding the initial values of CNT and TOT.INV. What is it? What would the consequences be if it were not true?

3-6. What would be printed from the program of Figure 3-13 if the data records (lines 8010–8040) were omitted and only the trailer record (line 8050) were included?

```
100    !     EXAMPLE 3-2
110    !     PROGRAM TO UPDATE AN INVENTORY
120    !     INPUT VARIABLE NAMES ARE:
130    !       TOOL.NUM$ --  Tool inventory number
140    !       TOOL.TYPE$    --  Tool type
150    !       OLD.INV   --  Old inventory quantity
160    !       MANUFCT   --  Units manufactured
170    !       SHIPD     --  Units shipped
180    !       LOST      --  Units lost or damaged
190    !     CALCULATED VARIABLE NAMES ARE:
200    !       NEW.INV   --  Udated inventory quantity
204    !       TOT.INV   --  Total updated inventory quantity
206    !       CNT       --  Counter
210    !
1000 !  MAIN PROGRAM
1010     GOSUB INITIALIZE
1020       !
1030     GOSUB PROC.TOOLS
1040       !
1050     GOSUB TERMINATE
1060       !
1070     STOP  ! STOP EXECUTION
1080       !
1130 !  END OF MAIN PROGRAM
1140 !
1150 !
     INITIALIZE:
2000 !  INITIALIZATION ROUTINE
2010     PRINT "LINE",    "TOOL", "TOOL",    "OLD",       "UPDATED"
2020     PRINT "NUMBER", "TYPE", "NUMBER", "INVENTORY", "INVENTORY"
2030     PRINT
2034     CNT = 0
2036     TOT.INV = 0
2040     RETURN
2050 !  END OF INITIALIZATION ROUTINE
2060 !
     PROC.TOOLS:
3000 !  PROCESSING ROUTINE
3002 !
         PROCESS.LOOP:
         WHILE -1
3010       READ TOOL.NUM$, TOOL.TYPE$, OLD.INV, MANUFCT, SHIPD, LOST
3015       EXIT PROCESS.LOOP IF TOOL.NUM$ = "99999"
3020       NEW.INV = OLD.INV + MANUFCT -.SHIPD - LOST
3024       CNT = CNT + 1
3026       TOT.INV = TOT.INV + NEW.INV
3030       PRINT CNT, TOOL.NUM$, TYPE$, OLD.INV, NEW.INV
3034     NEXT
3035     ! End of PROCESS.LOOP
3036     !
3040     RETURN
3050 !  END OF PROCESSING ROUTINE
3060 !
     TERMINATE:
4000 !  TERMINATION ROUTINE
4002     PRINT
4004     PRINT
4006     PRINT "Number of inventory items processed:"; CNT
4008     PRINT "Total updated inventory quantity is:"; TOT.INV
4010     PRINT
4020     PRINT
4030     PRINT "PROCESSING COMPLETE"
4040     RETURN
4050 !  END OF TERMINATION ROUTINE
4060 !
8000 !    ** INPUT DATA **
8010     DATA "12591", "Wrench", 680, 221, 419, 3
8020     DATA "13311", "Hammer", 512,   0, 186, 4
8030     DATA "15118", "File",    82, 500, 160, 1
8040     DATA "16881", "Pliers",   0, 201,   0, 0
8050     DATA "99999", "EOF",      0,   0,   0, 0
32767  END
```

(a)

Figure 3-13(a). Using accumulators—Example 3-2 program.

LINE NUMBER	TOOL NUMBER	TOOL TYPE	OLD INVENTORY	UPDATED INVENTORY
1	12591	Wrench	680	479
2	13311	Hammer	512	322
3	15118	File	82	421
4	16881	Pliers	0	201

Number of inventory items processed: 4
Total updated inventory quantity: 1423

PROCESSING COMPLETE

(b)

Figure 3-13(b). Using accumulators—Example 3-2 Output.

Exercises

3-7. What would be the effect of incrementing the counter CNT immediately following the READ (say as line 3011) instead of on line 3024?

3-8. Explain whether each of the following is valid or invalid as an algebraic equation and as a Basic statement.

a. $A/B = C$

b. $C + D = E + F$

c. $C = C + 1$

d. $P = Q + 3$

More Programming Theory

Program Evolution

The original program of Example 2-1 has now undergone the following sequence of modifications:

1. Modularization.
2. Modularization with looping.
3. Modularization with looping and accumulating.

This sequence of repeatedly modifying the program to meet changing needs was done in order to demonstrate new concepts. However, it bears a striking resemblance to the way in which programs evolve in an actual programming environment. The ideal way to program a given application is to obtain all of the facts before beginning. This normally involves studying the needs of the application and interviewing others in order to gain insight and to clearly define what is to be done. Thus, when we lay out the initial program planning, we know what is to be done. Actually, things do not always work this way. Very often users do not know exactly what they desire. Also, needs of an application have a way of changing because of changing circumstances. Hence, the sequence of continually modifying a program, as illustrated by the preceding examples, is not unlike the way things happen in the real world. Because of such facts of life, it is critical that program planning be done with great care and that all of the analysis and programming tools available be used, as appropriate. Let us expand some of the preceding program theory concepts and consider other tools that can be of value.

Top–Down Development

The principle of breaking a large program into manageable components, modularization, lies at the core of good programming practices. As illustrated by Example 3-2, modularization produces a *hierarchy of levels* of modules. Modules at a lower level of the hierarchy are said to be *subordinate* to the modules at higher levels, from which they derive. At the highest level, a main (master) program whose only function is to invoke subordinate modules is not only acceptable but actually highly desirable. This is clearly illustrated by the *hierarchy chart* (also called a *structure chart*) of Figure 3-14. Note that the structure chart shows the modules in the program and the relationship between them. If this program were very large, then each module of the chart would be subdivided into smaller modules until a given module dealt with a problem of easily manageable size. This approach, where the components of a problem are developed to successively lower levels of the hierarchy, is called *top–down development*.

In using this technique, it is important for us to understand that we do not simply chop a problem into a series of smaller parts. Indeed, a great deal of analysis is involved in this phase. Each component must perform a clearly defined function or set of related functions. A module is defined by specifying what data it will be operating on and what results it will produce: its input and output. For instance, a program might require a module for calculating the mean and standard deviation of a data set. For this module, we would have

Input: Set of data values.

Output: Mean and standard deviation of the input data.

The function of this module would be to calculate the mean and standard deviation. Defining what goes in and what comes out essentially defines for us *what* the module is to do. It is important to understand that in breaking a problem into modules such as this, the main concern is to first define *what* is

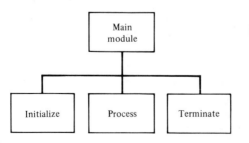

Figure 3-14. Hierarchy chart for Example 3-2.

to be done. The *logic* of the module, that is, *how* the specified output is produced from the given input, is deferred to a later stage of program development.

There is no hard rule as to how large a module should be—too many small modules is almost as bad as modules that are too large and complex. A rough guide is that the code of a given module should fit on a single page.

Preparing and Testing Modularized Programs

Another important aspect of this overall approach is that it is possible to test each program module independently of the others. When developing your program, you should code only one module at a time and use skeletal forms of the other modules. *Skeletal form* of a module means that representative values of the outputs of that module are generated using minimal logic, for example, by ignoring the input values and writing suitable assignment statements. These representative values need not be equal to any of the actual values that will be produced by the program in its final form. Such skeletal forms of modules are sometimes called *stub programs*.

In general, stub programs should demonstrate that they were reached by displaying the input values they received and the output values they generated. This allows you to treat stub programs as fully functional for purposes of checking program logic. When a fully coded module has been tested and found to work correctly, you can repeat this procedure by expanding the other modules, *one at a time*. By confining your changes in this manner, you minimize the possibility of problems arising in any part of the program other than the one you are currently changing. A great deal of development time can be saved by localizing potential errors this way. Such an approach is called *stepwise refinement*.

We can see how different features of a program can be brought in separately from others in connection with the program of Figure 3-13. As the first stub program we would have the complete main program and TERMINATE routine. The other routines would be stubs. INITIALIZE would print the headings and initialize the two counters to some arbitrary *nonzero* values. PROC.TOOL would READ and PRINT *one* record. By printing something from each subroutine, this first stub would show that each routine was reached and exited properly. We would also see that the values of the two counters are being transmitted correctly. For the second stub, we could initialize the counters to zero on lines 2034 and 2036. We would also include the three assignment statements on lines 3020, 3024, and 3026. At this stage, we would check the computations by hand to verify that the arithmetic was being done correctly. INITIALIZE would now be complete. For the final version, we would implement PROC.LOOP in PROC.TOOLS. Although this development departs somewhat from our guideline to modify only one module at a time, we nonetheless see that at any given stage we would be dealing with a minimal set of potential errors.

When stepwise refinement is combined with top–down development, the programmer begins with the main program, using stub programs for any subordinate modules. When the logic of the main program and its communication with its stub programs have been tested and found to work correctly, the next step is to progress to lower levels. Completing and testing of the lowest levels means that the entire program is completed.

Modularization, top–down development, and stepwise refinement have proved highly effective in producing more easily coded and maintained programs. These techniques have become even more critical in the development of very large programs, which involve teams of professional programmers. On such large projects, writing and testing of the individual modules is not done in series, one at a time. Rather, it is done in parallel, by dividing work on the different modules among different team members. The input and output specifications for the modules define the tasks of the individual programmers. Each team member uses stub programs for the other members' modules. The self-contained nature of each module is thus decisive. The modules are combined at the end to form a complete program.

The Use of Flowcharts

The saying ''A picture is worth a thousand words'' relates as well to programming as it does to many other areas of human endeavor. For instance, the three basic constructs of structured programming are clearly illustrated by the block representations of Figure 3-6. The first, repeated here as Figure 3-15, represents the progression from one action to the next. This represents the action of our program in Figure 3-1: progression from one statement to the next without interruption. On the other hand, the third form, repeated here in Figure 3-16, illustrates the action of repeatedly executing a given sequence. We learned how to do this with the WHILE statement of Figure 3-8. The second of these three structures relates to selection, a topic covered in the next chapter.

Now let us contrast the hierarchy chart block representation of these structure forms and the block representation of these structure forms. The hierarchy chart illustrates the component breakdown of a program and designates *what* is to be done. By contrast, the structured forms illustrate the *logic* of *how* things

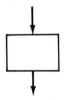

The *sequence* structure, which consists of an unconditionally executed sequence of operations.

Figure 3-15. The sequence structure.

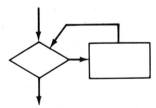

The *looping* structure, which specifies that a group of operations is to be executed repeatedly, either a specified number of times or subject to a condition.

Figure 3-16. The looping structure.

are to be done. Solving a problem generally involves first breaking the problem into its individual components (determining the *what*), and then determining the logic of each component. One of the tools used to define the logic is called a *flowchart* and has the form of the structure components in Figure 3-6. In a nutshell, a flowchart is a pictorial representation of the logic of a program solution. The modules of Example 3-2 are flowcharted in Figure 3-17, in which meanings of the various shapes are included.

With the advent of modern programming techniques, the use of flowcharts has attracted some criticism. However, in some situations, they are very helpful in laying out the logic of a solution. Each of us thinks in a different way. Some find experimenting with blocks of a flowchart to be very productive in arriving at a good solution. Others do not. You should use those development tools that you find comfortable and that produce results for you.

Pseudocode

Another technique that has been shown to be very useful in programming is called *pseudocode*. This method involves defining the ''what is to be done'' of each program module through English descriptions of the task. The action is first described in very general terms. The next step, in what amounts to a stepwise refinement process, is to expand the detail of the actions to be carried out. The end product is an English description that is a virtual copy of the computer language program itself. One of the important advantages of pseudocode is that a pseudocode development is commonly done with a word processor. It is a simple matter to include some level of the pseudocode solution at the beginning of the module as remarks for the sake of program documentation.

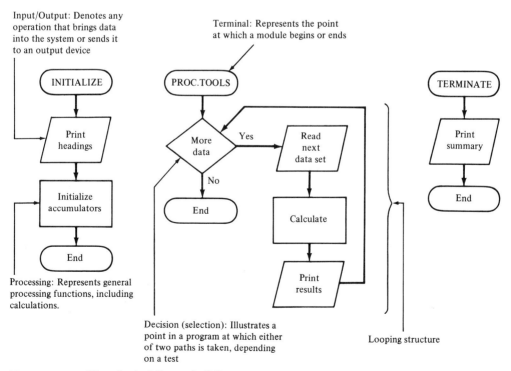

Figure 3-17. Flowchart of Example 3-2.

At this stage of our studies, it is difficult to give a good example to illustrate all the aspects of pseudocode, but the following pseudocode solution for the process-tools module of Example 3-2 will give you an insight to this approach. The first step would be

While there are data values remaining, process the tool information

The next step in refinement would be

While there are data values remaining
  Get the next data set
  Calculate the new inventory
  Add calculated amount to subtotal
  Increment the counter
  Print the results

Note that this is the ideal form. In view of the fact that Basic does not include all of the features required to conform exactly to the structured forms, we must modify the logic slightly to lead to our solution.

Repeat the following sequence
  Get the next data set
  Exit this loop if end of data detected
  Calculate the new inventory
  Add calculated amount to subtotal
  Increment the counter
  Print the results

The first reaction of many experienced programmers to pseudocode is often negative. On the other hand, most agree that, when used appropriately, it is a valuable tool, especially when used in conjunction with program modularization.

In Retrospect

In a first programming course, the student must struggle with learning two things: the rules of the programming language and the techniques of computer problem solving. By and large, the rules of the language are relatively mechanical. Once mastered, they become automatic, much like our use of the English language for ordinary communication. However, the technique of computer problem solving is quite another story. Over the past several years, the computer scientist has provided the programmer with valuable guidelines for good programming practice. The first step in achieving a computer solution to a large task is to break it down into smaller, relatively independent components, or *modules*. Once the task is modularized, program solutions for each of the parts can be developed independently of one another. Modularization is implemented in Basic through use of the GOSUB-RETURN pair of statements. The basis for writing good programs is the three constructs of structured programming: sequence, looping, and selection. Looping is implemented in this chapter with the WHILE statement; in Chapter 5, we will learn how to implement selection with the IF statement.

In struggling with some of the more complex forms of Basic statements or a complicated problem, the beginner tends to let good programming techniques drift into the background in favor of something that might appear to be expeditious at first glance. Do not fall into this trap. Always think through a problem solution carefully and completely, using the techniques of this chapter. At first it may appear to impede progress, but it pays large dividends in the long run.

Answers to Preceding Exercises

3-1. After returning from the Termination Routine, execution would fall through the remark lines (1080–2000) and execute the statement at line 2010. Note that this is the first statement of what we know as the Initialization Routine. When the RETURN at line 2040 was encountered, an error would occur because the computer would have no GOSUB just executed to which it could relate this RETURN.

3-2. READ will be executed five times; PRINT, four times.

3-3. The trailer record would be read the first time READ is executed, and no values would be printed after the column headings.

3-4. a. Sequence.
b. Sequence.
c. Sequence; GOSUB does not cause either selection or looping; although it transfers control to a line *number* that is out of sequence, it involves neither a choice of one of two statements to execute nor repeated execution of a group of statements.
d. Sequence and looping.

3-5. The initial value of accumulators is assumed to be zero. If we begin with any nonzero value in an accumulator, the final sum will be incorrect.

3-6. The headings would be printed, followed by total lines with values zero. No detail lines would be printed.

3-7. The trailer record would be counted incorrectly as a data record.

3-8. a. and b. Both are valid algebraic equations. They are invalid Basic expressions because the assignment statement can have only a single variable on the left-hand side of the equal sign.
c. Valid Basic expression. The value of C on the right-hand side of the equal sign is that *before* execution of the statement, the

value on the left-hand side is that *after* execution. However, this is *not* a valid algebraic equation because there can be no single value of C for which this equation is true.

d. Valid both as an algebraic equation and as a Basic expression.

Programming Problems

3-1. Carry through the three-stage development (two stubs and one final version) of the program in Figure 3-13 that was described in the text. At each stage, enter, run, and debug the program.

3-2. The payroll for the Fibonacci Reproduction Company includes the following calculations for each employee:

• Net pay = gross pay − deductions − 15 × number of dependents

• Gross pay = hours worked × pay rate

The output report is to include

• Appropriate descriptive headings.

• One detail line for each employee; the line is to include the employee number, gross pay, and net pay.

• Summary lines—appropriately labeled—that display the number of employees processed and the total gross amount paid out.

The following is a typical data set.

Employee Number	Hours Worked	Pay Rate	Deductions	Dependents
30157	38	9.16	32.56	3
32409	40	12.56	32.72	4
36750	45	8.11	29.11	1
56791	40	14.53	51.37	2

The trailer record contains 99999 in the employee-number field.

3-3. The Hardware Consulting Company needs a computerized mailing system. The address labels will be used for mailing literature. Each label is six lines in height (can hold six lines). Thus, for each record, a total of six lines (including blanks) must be printed. The output requirements are

• One header label with the job description.

• One label to be printed for each data record as follows:
  Name
  Address
  City and ZIP

• Last label to include a summary line with the number of labels printed.

In the following sample data set, the first record contains only one field: the job description.

Job Description: Tinkerer

Name	Address	City	ZIP
Al Zweistein	112 Madonna	Grass Valley	56390
Henry Fermi	863 Florence	Modoc	53960
Vern leisburg	1361 Mesquite	Eureka	59630
Wolf Pauli	23 Milton	Tundra	59360

The trailer record contains EOF in the name field.

3-4. Write a program to compute the sum of consecutive integers, starting with 1. Terminate the computation when the sum becomes greater then 2000. Print the final sum and the number of integers that were added. Output should be appropriately labeled.

3-5. In his spare time away from running his Reproduction Company, Mr. Fibonacci investigates properties of numbers. He has come up with the series

0, 1, 1, 2, 3, 5, 8, 13, 21, 34, . . . ,

known as Fibonacci's series. The first two terms of the series are 0 and 1. Each succeeding number is the sum of the two preceding ones. ($2 = 1 + 1$, $5 = 2 + 3$, $21 = 8 + 13$, and so on.) Write a program to print all terms of the Fibonacci series that are smaller than 1000 and the number of such terms. Label the output.

4

Interactive Processing and Output Formatting

CHAPTER OUTLINE

Preview

The purpose of this chapter is to introduce interactive input and techniques for producing formatted output. Important topics covered in this chapter are the following:

1. The distinction between batch and interactive processing.
2. The nature of the INPUT statement, which allows data to be entered into a program through the keyboard.
3. The PRINT USING statement, which allows the programmer to produce output that has been well formatted. The features include column alignment of both numeric and string data.

Interactive Data Input

Batch and Interactive Processing

As mentioned in Chapter 2, conventional usage of the term *input/output* is generally related to the transfer of data between internal memory and external devices. In this sense, the READ-DATA combination that we have used to get data into our programs does not truly give us an input capability. However, it *does* illustrate the technique of processing data called *batch processing*. We shall learn how this limited ability for batch processing that we have with the READ-DATA is made practical using data files, as described in Chapter 7. In a batch-processing environment, data quantities are accumulated over a period of time, then processed in batches. In the early days of data processing, operations were almost exclusively batch. Today many types of applications continue to be well suited to batch processing (for example, the common business data-processing application of payroll).

However, there is a broad range of applications for which batch processing is simply not practical. For instance, in the inventory example of Chapters 2 and 3, it might be totally impractical to wait until the inventory run is made in a "few days" in order to get updated information. The extreme case of an inventory system requiring constantly updated information is an airline reservation system. (Remember, an airline reservation system effectively maintains an inventory of seats in aircraft.) In a case such as this, up-to-the-minute information is essential. A customer purchasing a ticket cannot wait until the inventory run is made tomorrow in order to find out if a seat is available for a requested flight.

What is needed is a system whereby data can be entered into the computer and processed immediately upon receipt. That is, when an airline customer requests a reservation for two on the January 7 Flight 270 to Dallas, a sequence of events such as the following would take place.

1. An inquiry is made to determine if space for two is available on the requested flight.
2. If space is available, then the reservation is made and the number of available seats is reduced by two (the inventory is updated).

Processing of this type is commonly referred to as *interactive processing* or *transactional processing*. Actually, interactive processing is nothing new to you. Since Chapter 1, you have interacted with the computer via the Basic system in entering and running your programs. Through the use of commands, you have been able to direct the computer to load, save, and run your programs. If you keyed in an incorrect command, the computer has immediately responded with an error message, and you have been allowed to reenter the command. The key element of working in this way is *interactivity*; you interact with the computer directly. This is precisely what the airline reservation clerk is doing in making your airline reservations: interacting with the computer. More specifically, the clerk is interacting with the airline reservation system program. This type of processing is widely used. Computers such as the VAX-11 were designed for interactive use. Let us consider how we can write programs that allow for user interaction.

The INPUT Statement

In the preceding chapter, we learned how variables can receive values by the READ–DATA combination. The READ statement allows us to do batch processing. On the other hand, the INPUT statement allows for interactive

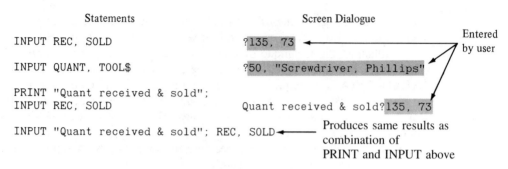

Figure 4-1 The INPUT statement.

processing by accepting values from the terminal keyboard while the program is running. The form of the INPUT statement is virtually identical to that of the READ; that is, the keyword INPUT is followed by a list of variables in which data will be stored. We see four examples of its use in Figure 4-1. Whenever an INPUT statement is executed, execution stops, the computer displays a question-mark (?) prompt, and awaits input from the user. Upon entering the required data, the user must strike the Return key to signal the computer to accept the data and continue. The first two examples involve only the INPUT statement.

Consider a long program containing INPUT statements at several different places. We run it and suddenly execution stops, displaying the following on the screen.

?

What do we do now? Is this the result of an INPUT statement to read several data values or one that is expecting a Yes/No response? To avoid this type of confusion, it is important that the INPUT be accompanied by a "verbal" prompt that tells the user what information is expected from the keyboard. The third example in Figure 4-1 includes a PRINT statement to display a meaningful prompt prior to the INPUT. By following the message with the semicolon character, the cursor remains on the same line as the prompt in progressing to the INPUT statement. We see this in the screen dialogue of the third example in Figure 4-1.

This prompt feature can conveniently be incorporated directly into the INPUT statement itself, as shown in the fourth example. Note that this form includes the keyword INPUT, followed by a literal, followed by the list of variables into which data is to be input.

Exercises

4-1. Summarize the similarities and differences between the form of the INPUT statement as used here and the READ statement.

4-2. What would happen if, in response to the first INPUT in Figure 4-1, a nonnumeric quantity were entered for either the amount received or sold? The answer is not in the text; experimentation at the terminal will be required.

4-3. What would occur if the tool type

```
Screwdriver, Phillips
```

were entered without the quotes used in Figure 4-1?

An Interactive Program Loop

In the programs of preceding chapters, the process of terminating the program used the principle of checking for a "never-occurring" value as a trailer. With interactive programming, a number of methods can be used, each suitable to the particular requirements of an application. To illustrate one such approach, let us consider the following example.

Example 4-1

A schoolteacher desires a program that will accept two numbers from the keyboard, then calculate and print their sum and product. The program is to be designed so that the student can repeat the process as many times as desired.

For this program, let us break this task down into two modules: The first is to display a set of instructions to the user, and the second is to perform the required processing.

1. Display an announcement screen with a set of instructions to the user regarding what the program does and how to interact with it. Upon reading the instructions, the user should be allowed to terminate if there is no interest in continuing.
2. Repeatedly accept two numbers from the user, calculate and display their sum and product, and display the result.

At this point, a question arises: How is the loop terminated? For this example, let us use the same technique that we used with input from the READ-DATA combination: a trailer value of -9999 for the value of the first number entered. In order to simplify matters for the user, we will also design the program so that a separate INPUT statement is used for each of the two numbers. Then the verbal description, or pseudocode solution, of the second module is as follows:

Repeat the following sequence
    Accept the first number from the keyboard
    If the value entered is -9999, then exit this sequence
    Accept the second number from the keyboard
    Calculate the sum and product
    Print the results

The program in Figure 4-2 reflects the logic of the preceding pseudocode directly. Actually, the program involves no new principles; it is simply a com-

```
100  ! EXAMPLE 4-1
110  ! Calculate the sum and product of
120  ! two numbers entered from the keyboard.
130  !
140  !
1000 !  MAIN PROGRAM
1010    GOSUB INITIALIZE
1020       !
1030    GOSUB PROCESS
1040       !
1050    STOP  ! STOP EXECUTION
1060       !
1070 !  END OF MAIN PROGRAM
1080 !
     INITIALIZE:
2000 !  INITIALIZATION ROUTINE
2010  PRINT 'This program calculates the sum and product of pairs'
2020  PRINT 'of numbers entered from the keyboard.  After being'
2030  PRINT 'asked for the first number, you must enter it then'
2040  PRINT 'strike the Return key.  You will then be asked for'
2050  PRINT 'the second number.  If you do not wish to continue'
2060  PRINT 'then enter a value of 0 for the first number and the'
2070  PRINT 'program will be terminated.'
2080  PRINT
2090  PRINT 'Press the Return key to continue '; DUMMY$
2100 !  END OF INITIALIZATION ROUTINE
2110 !
2120 !
     PROCESS:
3000 !  PROCESSING ROUTINE
3010 !
     PROCESS.LOOP:
     WHILE -1
3030    PRINT
3040    INPUT 'Please enter the first number <0 if finished> '; A
3050    EXIT PROCESS.LOOP IF A = 0
3060    INPUT 'Please enter the second number '; B
3070    PRINT
3080    PRINT 'The sum is:     '; A+B
3090    PRINT 'The product is:'; A*B
3100    PRINT
3110  NEXT
3120  ! End of PROCESS.LOOP
3130  !
3140  RETURN
3150 !  END OF PROCESSING ROUTINE
32767 END
```

Figure 4-2   Program for Example 4-1.

bination of Basic concepts that we have already used. Figure 4-3 is a typical interactive session with this program. Points to note in this program are as follows:

1. An introductory screen is displayed from the Initialization routine, and execution of the program is halted at the INPUT statement of line 3060. Entering a number and striking the Return key causes the program to continue. As we can see, entering −9999 causes the program to terminate.

```
Please enter the first number <0 if finished> 25
Please enter the second number 150
The sum is:      175
The product is:  3750
Please enter the first number <0 if finished> 140
Please enter the second number 95
The sum is:      235
The product is:  13300
Please enter the first number <0 if finished> 0
```

Figure 4-3 Typical interactive session—Example 4-1.

2. The program involves a loop that is identical in principle to that of the inventory problem of Example 3-2.
3. Exit from the loop is via a value of -9999 entered for the first number (see the prompt at line 3040). The exit test is performed at line 3050.

Exercise

4-4. What would happen if a person keyed in -9999 in response to the INPUT in line 3060 of Figure 4-2?

Improving the Appearance of Output

Introduction

The crude appearance of output in Chapter 2, using the predefined zones, was improved somewhat by using the semicolon and TAB function. However, columns of numbers remained aligned on the left rather than the right. For instance, our printed results are as displayed in the left column of the following; that to the right is much better.

1254	1254
34	34
610	610
0	0
21156	21156

Although the example program did not use decimal quantities, the problem with them is even worse than that above. For instance, assume that we are printing a column that consists of a money amount (dollars and cents). The following column to the left is typical output that we might obtain using methods of Chapter 3, and the column to the right is what we would prefer.

35.62	35.62
1.374	1.37
226.81	227.81
6.8	6.80

The preferred form can be obtained using the PRINT USING statement to format the output.

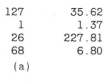

```
127        35.62
  1         1.37
 26       227.81
 68         6.80
```
(a)

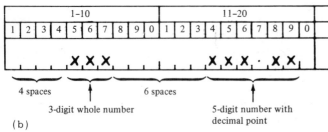

(b)

Figure 4-4   (a) Desired output form. (b) Print layout.

Simple Form of PRINT USING

As an illustration, let us assume that we wish to print two columns of numbers resulting from some calculations. We desire the output to be in the form shown in Figure 4-4(a). Before beginning the program, the first thing we would do would be to lay out the format of the printed output that we desire. The results of the planning session might be as shown in Figure 4-4(b).

What we really need is a means to describe the exact form in which the number is to be printed out: some code form that is equivalent to the layout of Figure 4-4(b). In programming, such a device is commonly referred to as a *format image*. The formatting is done through special characters called *format characters*. These format characters are placed in the image to specify the form of the number when it is printed. The Basic language includes a special form of the PRINT statement called the PRINT USING, which allows for the inclusion of a format image. Its general form is

PRINT USING *image, output list*

In essence, this statement says, "PRINT the indicated quantities USING a designated image." For instance, Figure 4-5(a) is a PRINT USING to print the variables A and B; it includes an image matching the layout form of Figure 4-4(b). Typical output resulting from repeated execution of this statement is shown in Figure 4-5(b). Things to notice about this example and about numeric image specification in general are

1. Each pound sign reserves one place for a digit position. An additional pound sign is required if a negative sign is to be printed.
2. The fields from the list of the PRINT statement are matched in the order in which they appear to items of the format definition.
3. Apart from a possible decimal point and negative sign, the only place that the computer inserts information in the format image is where # signs are replaced by values from the corresponding variables. Note that spaces in the image are left exactly as quoted in the image.
4. The layout in Figure 4-4(a) and the format image in the print statement are virtually identical.

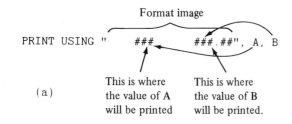

(a)

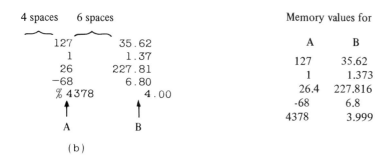

(b)

Figure 4-5   A PRINT USING statement and corresponding output.

5. If the fractional part of a number (digits to the right of the decimal) is to be printed, the decimal point is included in the format image in exactly the position in which it is to be printed. (The decimal point serves as *both* format character and print character.)

6. If the fractional part of a number takes up more spaces than are reserved by the image to the right of the decimal, the number is rounded.

7. If an integer field takes up fewer spaces than its image specification, the number will be printed right justified with spaces to the left.

8. If an integer field or the integer portion of a real field (digits to the left of the decimal) takes up more spaces than allowed for by the image, the entire field will be printed. A percent sign (%) will be printed to the left of the field as a warning. Thus, printing overrides the image specification in this case.

Exercise

4-5. Give the output resulting from execution of

```
PRINT USING "####     ####.##", AMOUNT1,AMOUNT2
```

for each of the following values of AMOUNT1 and AMOUNT2: (Note: There are five spaces between the two field definitions.)

	AMOUNT1	AMOUNT2
a.	123	9876.5
b.	1234	987.65
c.	1234.6	−987.65
d.	12345	9876.543
e.	−123	−9876.54
f.	1	6.543

PRINT USING for Strings

To illustrate editing string fields, consider a description field SAMPLE$ that will never be more than nine positions. Figure 4-6 shows four different edit images and their corresponding uses. The starting positions of string data in the respective image areas depend on which format characters (L, R, C, or E) are specified. For all but the E specification, strings that are longer than their images are truncated. The following relates to editing string fields.

1. The string field is identified in the image by a single apostrophe ('), which also reserves a place for one character. If there are no additional format characters in the image specification, the image is that for a one-character field; that is, only the first (leftmost) character of the string will be printed, and all following characters will be *truncated* (omitted).

```
(a) 600 PRINT USING "'LLLLLLLL", SAMPLE$
(b) 700 PRINT USING "'RRRRRRRR", SAMPLE$
(c) 800 PRINT USING "'CCCCCCCC", SAMPLE$
(d) 900 PRINT USING "'E", SAMPLE$
```

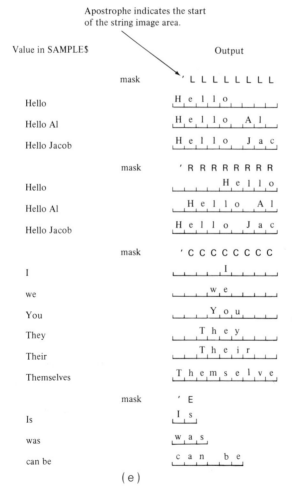

Figure 4-6   String-field edit masks. (a) Image using L specification. (b) Image using R specification. (c) Image using C specification. (d) Image using E specification. (e) Additional examples.

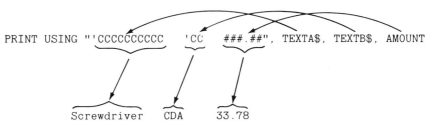

Figure 4-7 Numeric and string quantities in a format image.

2. The apostrophe may be followed by a series of format characters. All of the format characters following the apostrophe must be of the same kind until a new string or numeric field is identified. The possible format characters include L to *left justify*, R to *right justify*, and C to *center* the string. (If the string cannot be centered exactly, it is printed one character off center to the left.) An additional format character, E, is used to *expand* the field. We will learn the meaning of this in item 5, following.
3. Each format character L, R, and C reserves place for one character.
4. If a string to be printed is shorter than the image specification, the string is padded with spaces.
5. For L, R, and C specifications, if the string to be printed is longer than the image, the string is left justified and truncated on the right to fit the image. For the E specification, the string is left justified, and the output is expanded to print the entire string.

As might be expected, numeric and string definitions can be combined to form a needed format image, as illustrated by the example of Figure 4-7.

Defining Format Images as Separate Strings

The preceding examples of format images give us a basic insight into their use in obtaining output. However, if an image is very long, then including the definition as part of the PRINT USING statement can be clumsy. Another way of handling this is to define the image as a separate string variable. The combination of statements in Figure 4-8 is exactly equivalent to the statement of Figure 4-7. Here we see that the format image is placed into the variable FORMAT$. Then, when the PRINT USING is executed, the system uses the value in FORMAT$ to define the output format.

The value of this technique for aligning column headings with data becomes obvious the first time you use it. For instance, the output of the report program of Figure 3-13 can easily be set up using format string definitions. Appropriate statements have been included in Figure 4-9 to illustrate this technique. Note that by grouping all of the format-image defining strings together, it is a simple matter to make certain that everything is properly aligned.

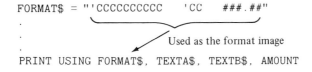

```
FORMAT$ = "'CCCCCCCCCC    'CC    ###.##"
 .
 .                          Used as the format image
 .
PRINT USING FORMAT$, TEXTA$, TEXTB$, AMOUNT
```

Figure 4-8 Specifying the format image by a string variable.

```
2002   H1$ = "             TOOL INVENTORY SUMMARY"
2003   H2$ = "LINE    TOOL    TOOL           OLD       UPDATED"
2004   H3$ = "NUMBER  NUMBER  TYPE           INVENTORY INVENTORY"
2005   F$  = " ##     'LLLL   'LLLLLLLLLLLLLLL   ###       ###"
2006   PRINT H1$  ! Print main heading
2007   PRINT
2010   PRINT H2$  ! Print first line of column heading
2020   PRINT H3$  ! Print second line of column heading
   .
   .
   .
3030   PRINT USING F$, CNT, TOOL.NUM, TOOL.TYPE$, OLD.INV, NEW.INV
```

Figure 4-9   Formatting the output of Example 3-1.

Exercise

4-6. What would be the output of the following program?

```
200   PRINT USING "'LLLLLL","1234"
210   PRINT USING "'LLLL", "123"
220   PRINT USING "'LLLLL","12345678"
300   RIGHT.JUSTIFY$ = "'RRRRR"
310   PRINT USING RIGHT.JUSTIFY$, "ABCD"
320   PRINT USING RIGHT.JUSTIFY$, "AB"
330   PRINT USING RIGHT.JUSTIFY$, "ABCDEFGH"
400   CENTER$ = "'CCCC"
410   PRINT USING CENTER$, "A"
420   PRINT USING CENTER$, "AB"
430   PRINT USING CENTER$, "ABC"
440   PRINT USING CENTER$, "ABCD"
450   PRINT USING CENTER$, "ABCDE"
32767 END
```

More on PRINT USING

Additional features that enhance formatting and edited output, both numeric and string, are available with PRINT USING. For example, a leading dollar sign may be called for, leading spaces are often replaced by asterisks on printed checks, commas are normally inserted to the left of the decimal point in large numbers, and minus signs are occasionally printed to the right of a number rather than to the left. VAX Basic provides format characters for all these needs.

Commas in Numeric Fields

To improve readability, numeric quantities greater than 999 are conventionally written with commas. For example, 7358912 is normally written as 7,358,912. The format image to print a comma every third significant digit to the left of the decimal point includes a *single* comma *anywhere* to the left of the decimal point and to the right of the leftmost pound sign. The comma must also be to the right of the rightmost dollar sign or asterisk (whose descriptions follow). These features are illustrated in Figure 4-10.

Statement	Value of AMOUNT	Output
PRINT USING "#,######.##", AMOUNT	2468024.13	2,468,024.13
PRINT USING "#######,.##", AMOUNT	2468024.13	2,468,024.13
	2468.1	2,468.10
	2.13	2.13

Figure 4-10   Inserting commas in numeric fields.

Floating Dollar Sign

In many applications, it is important that a printed dollar sign be made to *float*, that is, printed immediately to the left of the most significant digit. This is achieved by two format dollar signs ($$) immediately to the left of the pound signs in the image. These format characters reserve one space for a printed dollar sign and one space for a digit, as shown in Figure 4-11.

Edited Negative Numbers

In some applications, it is customary to print negative numbers with the minus sign to the *right* of the field. This is achieved by including a minus sign as the

Statement	Value of AMOUNT	Output
PRINT USING "$$##.##", AMOUNT *Allows for printing three digits*	246.13	$246.13
	2.13	$2.13
	0.05	$0.05
PRINT USING "$$###,#.##", AMOUNT *Allows for printing five digits*	24680.10	$24,680.10
	24.13	$24.13
PRINT USING "$$##.##-", AMOUNT	−24.13	$24.13 −
	24.13	$24.13

Figure 4-11   Printing a dollar sign.

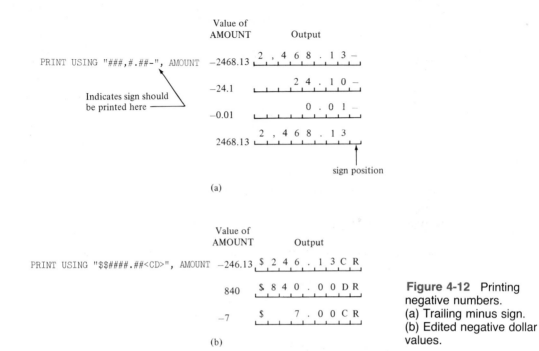

Figure 4-12 Printing negative numbers. (a) Trailing minus sign. (b) Edited negative dollar values.

last format character in the image, as illustrated in Figure 4-12(a). Note that if both a minus sign and a dollar sign are to be printed, the minus sign *must* be printed on the right.

An alternative method of differentiating between positive and negative dollar values is to use credit and debit notation. To do this, you place <CD> (credit/debit) at the end of the image. This causes printing of CR (credit record) after negative numbers and DR (debit record) after positive numbers, as shown in Figure 4-12(b).

Asterisk Fill

An alternative to using a floating dollar sign for check protection is to fill in leading blanks in the output with printed asterisks. As illustrated in Figure 4-13, this is achieved with two consecutive asterisks to the left of the pound signs in the edit mask. Note that one *or both* of the format asterisk characters will be replaced by digits if the field is large enough.

Exercises

4-7. Using the edit mask

#####.#.##

how would each of the following be printed?

2468.1   24680.13   0.02857   2468013

VAX Basic provides many additional formatting and editing features with PRINT USING, for which the reader is referred to the VAX manuals.

4-8. Repeat Exercise 4-7 for the following edit mask:

$$#,######.##

4-9. Using the edit mask

$$###,#.##−

how would each of the following be printed?

−24680.13
246.13
−2468.1

4-10. Repeat Exercise 4-9 for the following edit mask:

**##,#.##

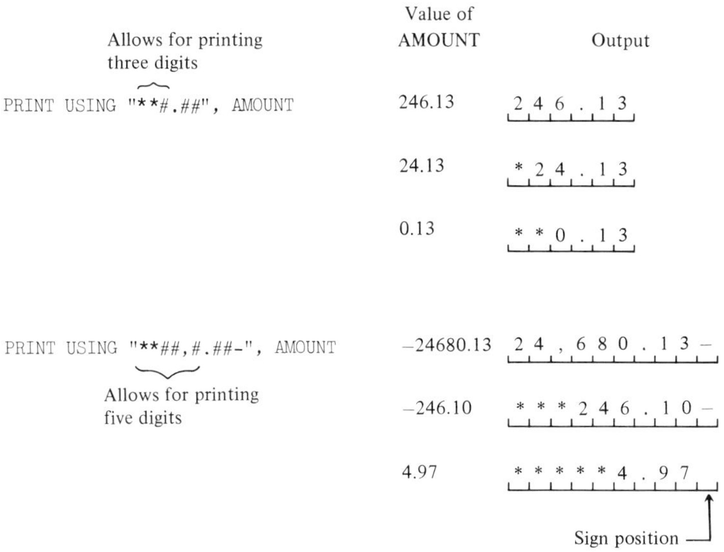

Figure 4-13 Asterisk fill.

In Retrospect

This chapter has focused on two topics: interactive programs and improving the appearance of output. The INPUT statement provides the means for entering data into the computer from the keyboard during execution of the program. At the other side of the processing picture, PRINT USING provides a broad range of features for improving the appearance of printed output. Following is a summary of the PRINT USING formatting characters from this chapter.

Numeric Field Editing

\#   Replaced with a digit or a space for leading zeros.

.   Indicates the position of the decimal point; unchanged by editing operation.

,   A single comma in the edit image causes commas to be placed in the numeric field every three digits, progressing to the left from the decimal point (conventional comma positioning for large numbers).

*   When the asterisk is the first character in the edit image, it causes leading zeroes to be replaced with the asterisk character.

\$ A single dollar sign positioned to the left in the image causes each leading zero to be replaced with a dollar sign. Two consecutive dollar signs cause a single dollar sign to be placed to the immediate left of the first nonzero digit.

−   Indicates that the minus sign for a negative number is to be to the right of the number. The minus sign must be the rightmost character of the edit image.

CR   Serves the same function as the minus sign.

String Field Editing

'   The single quote alone is used to indicate a one-character string field. For fields longer than one character, the single quote serves as the first position of the edit image, followed by one of the codes L, R, C, or E.

L   Each L character is replaced by one character of the field; the field is positioned to the left in the edit image, and unused positions to the right are filled with spaces.

R   Each R character is replaced by one character of the field; the field is positioned to the right in the edit image, and unused positions to the left are filled with spaces.

C   Each C character is replaced by one character of the field; the field is centered in the edit image, and unused positions on either side are filled with spaces.

E   Each E character is replaced by one character of the field; if the field is longer than the edit image, the image is expanded in length to hold the entire field.

Answers to Preceding Exercises

4-1. Both statements result in variables receiving values. The values for READ come from inside the program, from the DATA statement; these values are determined *before* the program is executed. The INPUT statement causes the program to stop during execution and prompt for data input by the user from the keyboard, data whose values can be decided *during* execution.

4-2. If a numeric variable is named in an INPUT statement, numeric data must be entered. If a nonnumeric value is entered for a numeric variable, Basic signals "illegal number" (ERR = 52).

4-3. If a string variable is named in an INPUT statement, Basic treats any data typed in response, including numeric data, as a string. However, if the string contains a comma, the string must be enclosed in quotation marks. Otherwise, Basic treats the comma as a delimiter. In the specific case of this exercise, only *Screwdriver* would be assigned to the tool type.

4-4. The program would treat this as a value of the variable B to be added to and multiplied by that of A.

4-5. a. 123   9876.50
     b. 1234   987.65
     c. 1235   −987.65
     d. % 12345   9876.54
     e. −123   % −9876.54
     f.   1   6.54

4-6. 1234
     123
     123456
       ABCD
          AB
     ABCDEF
       A
      AB
       ABC
     ABCD
     ABCDE

4-7.   2,468.10
       24,680.13
             0.03
       % 2468013

4-8. $2,468.10
         $24,680.13
               $0.03
       $2,468,013.00

4-9. $24,680.13−
        $246.13
       $2,468.10−

4-10. 24,680.13−
       ***246.13
       *2,468.10−

Programming Problems

Note: All interactive programs must include appropriate descriptive prompts.

4-1. This program is designed to prepare a monthly report of all customers who have exceeded their allowable charge limit. Data records are to be input from the keyboard. Each record includes the following information, subject to the indicated restrictions:

Account number: always 4 digits (treat as a string).

Customer name: maximum of 22 positions.

Maximum charge: less than $10,000.00.

Credit limit: less than $10,000.00.

Main headings and column headings should appear as follows:

```
                     OVER-LIMIT REPORT
                 CUSTOMER ACCOUNT SYSTEM
ACCT              CUST                    MAX        CREDIT
NUM               NAME                  CHARGE        LIMIT
```

The output report is to include one detail line for each customer and a summary line. Numeric quantities in the detail line should be edited to include the comma and decimal point, as appropriate. The summary line is to include the number of customers processed for this report and the total by which the customers exceeded their credit limits, including dollar sign.

4-2. The total capital P on an initial investment I compounded yearly at an interest rate r (decimal) is given by

$$P = I(1 + r)^n$$

where n is the number of years. Write an interactive program to input the rate *in percent*, the initial investment, and the number of years from the keyboard. The program should continue processing input data until the user enters a negative number for the initial investment. Output should include the input data and the principal P, all suitably identified.

4-3. The amount A in a savings account at the *end* of a month is given by

$$A = B(1 + r)$$

where B is the amount at the *beginning* of the month and r is the *monthly* interest rate in decimal. The depositor wants to deposit a fixed amount at the beginning of each month, so that the capital will grow both because of the interest and because of the monthly deposits. Write an interactive program that will tell a depositor how much is in the account T months after it is opened, for a given set of input data. The *yearly* rate in percent, the amount deposited each month, and the number of months are to be input from the keyboard. The program is to query the depositor whether to repeat the calculation for another set of input data. It should continue as long as the reply is "Y" and stop for any other reply.

4-4. A credit-card company assesses a monthly service charge of 1.5 percent on the balance due. The input quantities for each customer are subject to the following restrictions:

Account number: 5 digits.

Customer name: maximum of 25 positions.

Balance due (dollars and cents): less than $10,000.00.

Write an interactive program to calculate the service charge; print all input quantities, service charge, and total amount (balance due plus service charge). Include appropriate main and column headings. (See the example of Problem 4-1.) Edit all numeric quantities as appropriate.

4-5. If the quoted yearly interest rate on an investment is compounded semiannually, the *effective* yearly rate is higher than the quoted one. In general, the effective rate e is expressed in terms of the quoted rate r by

$$e = (1 + r/n)^n - 1$$

where n is the number of conversions per year. Write a program to compute the effective rate for a specified quoted yearly rate and number of conversions. Data values are to be entered interactively, and the program is to continue processing until a negative value is entered for the rate. In addition, after each calculation for a given quoted rate and conversion number, the program is to query the user whether the calculation should be repeated for the *same* quoted rate but for *daily* conversion ($n = 365$). Output is to include an appropriate main heading and three column headings.

```
QUOTED      NUMBER OF       EFFECTIVE
RATE        CONVERSIONS     RATE
```

The printed rates are to be expressed in percent, and all numeric quantities are to be properly aligned.

5

Conditional Operations

CHAPTER OUTLINE

Preview

In Chapter 3, we learned about the three fundamental constructs of structured programming: sequence, selection, and looping. The examples of that chapter illustrate the process of looping, or iteration. *The statements (WHILE and NEXT) that allow these repetitive operations to be performed are referred to as* control statements (*or* control structures). *The logic of conditional loops and tests is known as the* control logic *of programs. Control structures are essentially the heart of programming logic. VAX Basic provides a very comprehensive set of control statements. These include statements to perform operations on a conditional basis, the third of the program structures: selection. The types of operations that we shall learn about in this chapter are those illustrated by the two selection structures of Figure*

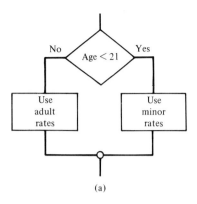
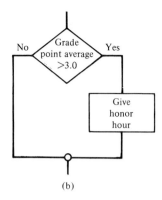

Figure 5-1 Selection structures.

5-1. In some cases, the conditional action to be taken might consist of only a single statement. For instance, the action of Figure 5-1(b) might be

> *If GPA greater than 3.0*
>   *then add 1 to total hours*

In many other situations, the action to be taken may consist of several statements, for example:

> *If taxable income greater than 20000*
>   *then special exemption = 300*
>   *special tax = .04 times (20000 − regular exemption)*
>   *regular tax = .15 times taxable income*

Here we have a situation in which a group of instructions is treated as a **block.** *The entire block is executed if the taxable income is greater than 20000 and ignored if it is not.*

From this chapter you will learn to use a wide variety of conditional forms. These include the following:

- *The IF statement and its component relational expression that provides the criterion for determining whether or not an action is to be taken.*
- *More extensive capability of the WHILE statement.*

Statements, Text Lines, and Program Lines

Introduction

Conditional operations require the ability for a group of statements to be treated as a statement block. Before beginning our study of the IF statement, let us learn more about the form that VAX Basic statements can assume. These forms will be essential in implementing the selection structure.

Until now, the terms *statement* and *line* have been used interchangeably. However, VAX Basic does not require that a line number be associated with each statement; it allows

1. A single statement on one line of text.
2. A single statement continued over several lines of text.
3. Multiple statements on one line of text.
4. Multiple statements continued over several lines of text.

Programs in the preceding chapters have used only the first case. To make use of the other cases, we must clearly understand the difference between a *statement*, a *text line*, and a *program line*.

Line-to-Line Statement Continuation

Each statement in example programs to this point has been written on a single line. However, VAX Basic provides the capability to continue a statement on one or more additional lines. This is obviously convenient for a very long statement that will not fit on a single line. It also allows us to format statements to improve the readability of the program. To indicate that a single statement is continued on the next line, type an ampersand (&) at the end of the current line and then press the Return key. Note that the Return key must be pressed *immediately* after the ampersand; nothing can follow the ampersand, not even a space. This method is illustrated in statement 431 of Figure 5-2(a). Note that this program statement covers four lines and that each is ended with a carriage return (by striking the Return key). It is important to recognize that this is a single statement in the same sense that its corresponding single-line form in 430 is a statement. Do *not* become confused and feel that a number must be associated with each of the three lines that follow. Remember, the number is a *statement* number and is associated with the statement, not the individual lines.

```
430   NEW.INV = OLD.INV + MANUFCT - SHIPD - LOST

431   NEW.INV = OLD.INV         &
                +MANUFCT         &
                -SHIPD           &
                -LOST
(a)


*VALID*
200   PRINT "Smallest input value is"; A,   &
            "Largest input value is"; B
300   NEW.BAL = OLD.BAL + RECEIVED    &
                  - SOLD - LOST

*INVALID*
200   PRINT "Smallest input    &
            value is"; A,       &
            "Largest input value is"; B
300   NEW.BAL = OLD.          &
                BAL + RECEIVED   &
                  - SOLD - LOST

(b)
```

Figure 5-2 Multiple lines per statement.

Where statement continuation is used, it must not split a string literal or a reserved word. For instance, Figure 5-2(b) shows two valid and correspondingly invalid forms. There is no limit to the number of continuation lines that may be used with a statement.

The lines themselves are called *text lines*. A text line may contain

1. One complete statement, as illustrated in statement 430.
2. A portion of a statement, as illustrated in statement 431.
3. Two or more statements separated by the backslash (\) character (described in the next section).

Eliminating Line Numbers

So far, every one of our statements in a program has had a line number. Even statement 431 of Figure 5-2, which is comprised of four text lines, includes one statement number. However, VAX Basic does *not* require that each statement have a statement number. In fact, technically speaking, only the first statement in a program must have a number; however, this theoretical case is not always practical. This concept is illustrated in Figure 5-3 with the first version of the inventory program from Chapter 1. If we were to enter this program and then type

```
LIST 100
```

three lines would be displayed upon the screen (the READ, LET, and PRINT statements). That is, all three of these statements are associated with the number 100. Thus, a *program line* consists of all statements from a given line number to the next line number. As we have learned, line numbers are very convenient for placing statements in the correct sequence and for making corrections. If we were to make an error in the LET statement of Figure 5-3, it would be necessary to reenter the entire group of three statements or else get out of Basic and use an *editor*. (An editor is a utility program that allows you to enter, modify, delete, and format text.)

```
100   READ T,T$,O,M,S,L            ⎫  All of these statements are
      LET U = O + M - S - L        ⎬  associated with line 100.
      PRINT T,T$,O,U               ⎭
800   DATA 12591,"Wrench",680,221,419,3
32676 END
```

Figure 5-3 Several statements associated with one line number.

```
100 REM This program updates a
        single inventory record.
    READ T,T$,O,M,S,L
    LET U = O + M - S - L
    PRINT T,T$,O,U
    DATA 12591,"Wrench",680,221,419,3
32767  END
```

> All of this is associated with line 100 and hence becomes a remark.

(a)

```
100  ! This program updates a
110  ! single inventory record.
    READ T,T$,O,M,S,L
    LET U = O + M - S - L
    PRINT T,T$,O,U
    DATA 12591,"Wrench",680,221,419,3
32767  END
```

(b)   **Figure 5-4** An error situation.

Also, there are some potential booby traps when line numbers are eliminated. For example, consider the example of Figure 5-4(a), where the line number is associated with a REM statement. Everything is just fine for the second line because it is considered to be a continuation of the REM on the first line. However, trouble develops with the third line (consisting of the READ statement) because Basic considers it to be a continuation of the REM at line 100. Thus, the program is nothing but one long remark to the Basic system. In contrast, a remark line indicated by ! is terminated by a carriage return; hence, the form of Figure 5-4(b) is valid. A series of DATA statements can also be included without line numbers. However, the first DATA statement should have a line number, and the statement following the last DATA statement *must* have a line number. If it does not, it will be considered part of the preceding DATA statement.

To summarize these points of caution, the REM and DATA statements begin with the respective words REM and DATA and end with the next line number. Hence, to avoid having the Basic processor ignore text that we do not want to be ignored, any statement following a REM or a DATA statement must have a line number.

In the preceding section, it was pointed out that two or more statements separated by the backslash (\) character can be included on a single text line. This technique is used only sparingly in this book because it tends to detract from the documentation value of the program. However, in some cases it is convenient to use. For example, assume that our program must print three blank lines. This can be done with either of the following two forms:

```
500 PRINT
    PRINT
    PRINT

510 PRINT \ PRINT \ PRINT
```

The backslash character can be used to separate any two unconditional statements on a single text line.

Exercise

5-1. For each of the following that represents invalid line continuation forms, state the error.

```
200   PRINT "This is supposed to be a literal spread "; &
            "over two lines."

300   PRINT "This is also supposed to be a literal spread &
            over two lines."

400   GOSUB        &
          PROC.TOOLS

500   GO
          SUB 500  &
```

Conditional Statements

The Concept of the IF

The emphasis in the first three chapters has been on the mechanics of Basic and on writing relatively simple programs; from a structured programming viewpoint, we have studied the two structures of sequence and looping. Let us now consider the selection structure; the abstract Basic form of that statement is

> IF (particular condition is true)
>   THEN (take an action)
>   ELSE (take another action)

Following is a typical example that we might encounter in programming.

> IF an employee has been with the company more than 10 years
>   THEN the employee is to receive a $500 bonus
>   ELSE the employee is to receive a $300 bonus

A special case of the conditional situation is that in which an action is taken if a given condition is true; otherwise, no action is taken.

> IF a student earned a B average or higher for the current semester
>   THEN award the student an honor hour

These are commonly called *conditional operations* and are the subject of this chapter. Overall, conditional operations increase the complexity of the program; this in turn increases the need for careful planning of the program logic.

Relational Operators and Expressions

The part of the IF statement that forms the test basis is called the *relational expression*. In general, a relational expression involves two quantities (often

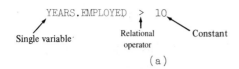

(a)

```
If  YEARS.EMPLOYED contains 7
      then the expression says 7 > 10 which is false

If  YEARS.EMPLOYED contains 12
      then the expression says 12 > 10 which is true.
```

(b)

Figure 5-5   A relational expression.

each is a single variable or constant) and a *relational operator*. The general form[*] is

$$(expression) \quad (relational\ operator) \quad (expression)$$

Note that the term *expression* can mean a single variable or constant as well as a complete Basic expression. For instance, the preceding employee/bonus example would involve the relational expression shown in Figure 5-5(a). Here we see that the expression states "YEARS.EMPLOYED is greater than 10." (The symbol $>$ is a mathematical symbol meaning *greater than*.) Note that this statement (relational expression) can be either *true* or *false*, as shown explicitly in Figure 5-5(b).

If the criterion for determining whether or not employees are eligible involves calculations, that is not a problem. It is simply a case of choosing the appropriate expression and creating a relational expression, as shown in Figure 5-6. Here the computer will take the following action:

1. Add the value stored in the variable YEARS.EMPLOYED to the value stored in the variable VACATION.TIME.
2. Add 5 to the value stored in the variable CUTOFF.
3. Compare the two sums to determine if the the relational expression is true or false.

It is important to realize that during the arithmetic operations, none of the variable values in the expressions will be changed. In general, when evaluating a relational expression, the computer performs any necessary calculations and then makes the designated comparisons. The expression is determined to be either true or false.

The examples of Figures 5-5 and 5-6 involve the "greater than" operator ($>$). The complete set of relational operators available in VAX Basic is summarized in Table 5-1.

```
YEARS.EMPLOYED + VACATION.TIME > CUTOFF + 5
      Add YEARS.EMPLOYED and VACATION.TIME
      Add CUTOFF and 5
      Compare the two sums to determine if true or false
```

Figure 5-6   Evaluating a relational expression.

---

[*] The conventions used for describing the general form of Basic statements (together with a summary of all statements) are included in Appendix III.

Table 5-1 Numeric Relational Operators

Symbol	Meaning	Expression	Value
>	Greater than	50 > 100	False
		100 > 100	False
		150 > 100	True
=	Equal to	50 = 100	False
		100 = 100	True
		150 = 100	False
<	Less than	50 < 100	True
		100 < 100	False
		150 < 100	False
>= or =>	Greater than or equal to	50 >= 100	False
		100 >= 100	True
		150 >= 100	True
<= or =<	Less than or equal to	50 <= 100	True
		100 <= 100	True
		150 <= 100	False
<> or ><	Not equal to	50 <> 100	True
		100 <> 100	False
		150 <> 100	True
==	Approximately equal to[*]	H == Y	

* Because of the manner in which computers store numbers, the value stored internally may not be exactly the number expected. The "approximately equal to" operator takes this into account and compares numbers only to the first six significant digits. The result *true* or *false* is returned on the basis of this comparison.

It should be noted that the equal sign is used in Basic to mean two totally different things. For instance, the LET statement, with or without the word LET, assigns a new value to a variable. For example,

```
400   LET AMOUNT = CALCULATED + 20
```

directs the computer to do the following:

1. Add the 20 to the value in the variable CALCULATED.
2. Store the result of that calculation in the variable AMOUNT.

However, if this same form

```
AMOUNT = CALCULATED + 20
```

is used in an IF statement as the relational expression, the following action takes place:

1. Add the 20 to the value in the variable CALCULATED.
2. Compare this sum to the value in AMOUNT. If they are equal, then the expression is true; if they are not equal, then the expression is false. As

with all relational expressions, *none of the variables is changed when the comparison is made.*

As we can see, the computer knows how to treat the equal sign based on the context in which it is used.

Comparing String Quantities

All of the preceding examples involve comparing numeric quantities; however, string quantities can be compared as well. For instance, the relational expression

```
TOOL.DESCR$ = "EOF"
```

is just as valid as the numeric relational expression

```
NEW.INV = 400
```

However, there are two important points in this connection. First, the expressions must be of the same type on the two sides of the relational operator. For instance, *the following would be invalid as a relational expression*:

```
TOOL.NUM$ <> 99999
```

The second point relates to the concept of *greater* and *less than* for string quantities. If two string quantities are the same (for instance, TOOL.DESCR$ in the preceding example contains EOF), then the equal condition results and this expression is true. Otherwise, they are not equal and the expression is false. But what determines whether one string quantity is greater than or less than another? The answer to this relates to the actual binary code used for each character. The computer orders characters in increasing sequence according to this code. We shall learn about this in detail in Chapter 11. For now, our needs will be served with the following simple rules:

1. String comparison for alphabetic characters can be considered to be based on an alphabetic sequencing. For instance, the names in a telephone directory, which are arranged alphabetically, progress from the "smallest" to the "largest." The following examples illustrate this:

Comparison	Relational Value
"SMITH" > "JOHNSON"	True
"SMITH" = "JOHNSON"	False
"SMITH" < "JOHNSON"	False
"SMITH" = "SMITH"	True

The fact that SMITH consists of more letters than JOHNSON has nothing to do with the comparison. It is merely a matter of alphabetic sequencing.

2. Uppercase and lowercase letters are *not* the same: lowercase letters are *all* "larger than" uppercase letters. This principle is illustrated by the following examples:

Comparison	Relational Value
"SMITH" <> "Smith"	True
"SMITH" < "Smith"	True
"SMITH" > "johnson"	False

3. Digits are smaller than letters.
4. Space is smaller than either digits or letters.
5. If two strings are identical up to the last character in the shorter string, Basic pads the shorter string with spaces to generate strings of equal length. It then compares the remaining characters in the longer string against these spaces.

When a comparison is made, Basic compares strings character by character, left to right, until it finds a difference or reaches the end of the string. When two corresponding characters are found to be different, the greater-than or less-than relationship is determined. If all corresponding characters are the same, the strings are deemed equal.

Exercises

5-2. Consider the following IF statement:

IF 4.5 * DEP >= 18 THEN *statement*

a. Identify the relational expression.
b. Find the "value" of the expression when

```
DEP = -6;
DEP = 4;
DEP = 10.
```

5-3. In each of the following, determine whether A$ and B$ are equal or, if they are unequal, which is larger. (The symbol b̶ represents a space character.)

	A$	B$
a.	SANDY	SAND
b.	SAND	SANDb̶b̶b̶
c.	Mb̶QUAN	Db̶QUAN
d.	QUAN	BATTERSBY
e.	BATS	BAT7
f.	TRACYb̶	b̶TRACY
g.	CARBON	CARBON

5-4. The relational operator = = , when applied to two strings, checks whether these two strings are identical in composition *and* length without padding. (Note that this operator has a different meaning when applied to strings than when applied to numbers. We shall learn more in Chapter 6 about such different meanings of a given operator applied to different types of data.) Determine which of A\$ and B\$ in Exercise 5-3 yields the relational value "true" when compared by this operator.

The IF–THEN Statement

Now that we have gained insight into the nature of relational expressions, let us consider how they are used in the simple form of the IF statement, which has the following general form:

IF *relational expression* THEN *statement*

Execution of the IF statement involves first evaluating the relational expression to determine whether it is true or false. If it is true, execution of the statement following THEN is carried out; if it is false, execution continues to the next sequential statement. To illustrate this statement, let us consider the newly founded IB Monarchy, which has just discovered the notion of taxation.

Example 5-1

The IB Monarchy has a new plan for taxation of its citizens that it wishes to computerize. One of the routines is to calculate certain taxes; following are the input to and output from the routine.

Input:	Gross income (GROSS)
Output:	Taxable income (TAXABLE)
	Total tax due (TAX)
	Net income (NET)

The tax is to be calculated based on taxable income, which is calculated as

Taxable income = Gross income − 2000

Total tax due is calculated according to the following:

IF taxable income > 10000
    THEN Tax due = 0.15 × Taxable income

Note that if the taxable income is not greater than 10000, then no tax is due. Net income is to be calculated as follows:

Net income = Gross income − Tax due

A program segment to perform these operations and the corresponding flowchart segment are shown in Figures 5-7(a) and (b). Here we see that the specific form of line 440 corresponds almost exactly to the general form of the IF statement described earlier. The components of the IF are described in Figure 5-7(c).

The form illustrated here is the standard IF format, which is common to almost all versions of Basic. Most versions of Basic, including VAX Basic, allow the programmer to include more than one statement on the IF statement

```
400  ! Example 5-1
410  !
420  TAX = 0
430  TAXABLE = GROSS - 2000
440  IF TAXABLE > 10000 THEN TAX = 0.15*TAXABLE
450  NET = GROSS - TAX
```

(a)

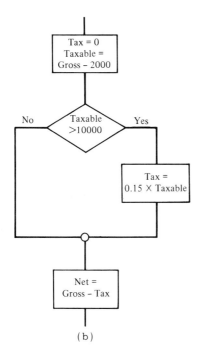

(b)

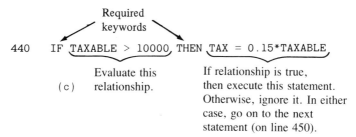

(c)

Figure 5-7 A simple IF—Example 5-1.

line for conditional execution. However, this usually results in a program that is confusing to read and that has limited documentation value. In this respect, VAX Basic has a very useful feature that allows an IF statement to occupy two or more lines without the use of ampersands. One of the allowable forms is

```
400   ! Example 5-1
410   !
420    TAX = 0
430    TAXABLE = GROSS - 2000
440    IF TAXABLE > 10000
          THEN TAX = 0.15*TAXABLE
450    NET = GROSS - TAX
              (a)
```

Press Return key
to end this line.

```
440    IF TAXABLE > 10000
          THEN TAX = 0.15*TAXABLE
```

At least one space
is required to begin
this line.   (b)

Statement to be executed
if condition is true.

Keyword THEN must
begin this line. Note
that it must *not* include
a line number.

Figure 5-8   An alternative form of the IF.

shown in Figure 5-8. Here we see that the keyword IF and the relational
expression are on one line, and the keyword THEN and the action to be taken
are on the next line. It is important that the line containing THEN begin with
at least one space and that it *not* include a line number. Execution of this form
is exactly the same as that of Figure 5-7. The advantage of the two-line version
is that we can see the IF at a glance when looking at a sequence of statements.

A third form is shown in Figure 5-9. Here we see that the statement to be
executed conditionally is entered on a third line. In the examples of Figures
5-8 and 5-9, it is important that the statements following the last line of the IF
include a statement number. A later example illustrates the reason for this.

Exercise

5-5. For each of the following values of RECEIPTS, show what will
be printed by the PRINT statements.

```
200   PRINT "THE SHOW WILL ";
210   IF RECEIPTS <= 1000
         THEN PRINT "NOT ";
220   PRINT "GO ON"

a.   RECEIPTS = 500
b.   RECEIPTS = 1000
c.   RECEIPTS = 1500
```

The IF–THEN–ELSE Statement

Example 5-1 illustrates a case of either taking a given action or not taking it.
Actually, this is a special case of the selection structure. Let us consider the
more general case in which either of two actions will be taken.

```
400   ! Example 5-1
410   !
420    TAX = 0
430    TAXABLE = GROSS - 2000
440    IF TAXABLE > 10000
       THEN
           TAX = 0.15*TAXABLE
450    NET = GROSS - TAX
         (a)
```

440   IF TAXABLE > 10000 ◄─────────────────┐ Press Return key to
       THEN ◄────────────────────────────────┘ end each of these lines.
           ╱   TAX = 0.15*TAXABLE ◄────── Statement to be executed if
       Keyword   condition is true is on a separate line.

         (b)

Figure 5-9   Another form of the IF.

Example 5-2

The costs of running the government of the IB Monarchy of Example 5-1 have soared. The solution is to tax everyone. Hence the tax calculation is to be modified as follows:

IF taxable income $>$ 10000
     THEN tax due $= 0.15 \times$ taxable income
     ELSE tax due $= 0.11 \times$ taxable income

The difference in logic between Examples 5-1 and 5-2 is illustrated by the flowcharts of Figure 5-10. In Figure 5-10(a) (which corresponds to Example 5-1) an action either is or is not taken, depending on the result of the test. In Figure 5-10(b) (which corresponds to Example 5-2) either of two actions is taken, depending on the result of the test.

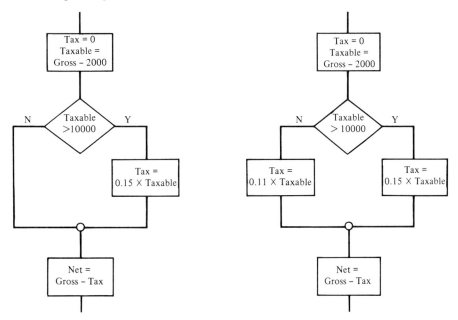

Figure 5-10   Flowchart representations.

```
400  ! Example 5-2
410  !
420  TAX = 0
430  TAXABLE = GROSS - 2000
440  IF TAXABLE > 10000
         THEN TAX = 0.15*TAXABLE
         ELSE TAX = 0.11*TAXABLE
450  NET = GROSS - TAX
```

(a)

```
440     IF TAXABLE > 10000              ⎫ One complete
          THEN TAX = 0.15*TAXABLE       ⎬ IF statement
          ELSE TAX = 0.11*TAXABLE       ⎭
```

Keywords THEN and ELSE
used on new lines

Figure 5-11 The
If–Then–Else form—Example
5-2.

(b)

The general form of the IF–THEN–ELSE is

IF *relational expression* THEN *statement* ELSE *statement*

The required operations for Example 5-2 are performed by the program segment of Figure 5-11. Actually, the IF statement of line 440 has a form that is virtually identical to the form of the example statement. We see that one of the two tax calculations will always be performed. Whichever occurs, execution will then continue to statement 450. As with the example of Figure 5-9, Basic interprets line 440 as a single statement because it recognizes the keywords THEN and ELSE as part of the IF statement.

Note how indentation is used to show us at a glance that statements are to be executed conditionally. These features enhance program readability and highlight its structure. Such stylistic techniques become even more important when applied later to statement blocks in the IF statement.

Blocks of Statements

Blocks of Statements in the IF

The ability to execute a statement on a conditional basis, as provided by the IF statement, is a powerful tool. However, more often than not, the programmer is faced with the problem of executing several consecutive statements on a conditional basis. VAX Basic includes the capability to execute an entire *block* of statements conditionally. To illustrate this, let us consider a slight modification to Example 5-1.

Example 5-3

The government of the IB Monarchy has found itself faced with an undesirably high birth rate. In order to discourage large families, they enact an extra tax increment based on the number of children in the family. The tax is to be calculated as follows:

IF taxable income > 10000
      THEN Regular tax $= 0.15 \times$ taxable income
               Child penalty $= 25 \times$ number of children

END IF
Net pay $=$ Gross pay $-$ regular tax $-$ child penalty

A program segment to perform this operation is shown in Figure 5-12. It clearly illustrates the nature of the block IF; the following commentary explicitly spells out the technique.

1. The IF keyword itself marks the beginning of the block IF; the END IF statement terminates the IF statement.
2. Corresponding to the simple IF–THEN form, the THEN clause marks the beginning of actions to be taken.
3. All of the statements between the THEN and the END IF will be executed if the test condition is true. If it is false, then the entire block is skipped.
4. Each statement that makes up the conditional block is indented to indicate clearly the beginning and end.

```
                    400   ! Example 5-3
                    410   !
                    420    TAX = 0
Marks the           430    TAXABLE = GROSS - 2000
beginning           440    IF TAXABLE > 10000
of the block ————————————> THEN
                              TAX = 0.15*TAXABLE
                              C.TAX = 25*CHILDREN
Marks the   ————————————> END IF
end of              450    NET = GROSS - TAX - C.TAX
the block
```

Figure 5-12 The block IF—Example 5-3.

Concerning the first item of the preceding commentary, in this example the IF statement is terminated by END IF. Though the END IF is not required, it is highly recommended, both to provide good documentation (it identifies explicitly where the IF ends) and to avoid possible coding mistakes. Without the END IF, the Basic processor looks for the next line number to terminate the IF. If a line number is inadvertently left out, then one or more statements following the intended IF block will be treated as part of the IF block.

Regarding statement 440, it is important to understand that if we were to type

```
LIST 440
```

the system would display everything from line 440 through the END IF statement. Remember from the earlier discussion that when line numbers are omitted, then any statement with no number is associated with the numbered state-

```
                                   400   ! Example 5-3
                                   410   !
                                   420   TAX = 0
                                   430   TAXABLE = GROSS - 2000
Beware:                            440   IF TAXABLE > 10000
Statements of                            THEN
the block must          →444                TAX = 0.15*TAXABLE
not be numbered.        →446                C.TAX = 25*CHILDREN
                                         ENDIF
                                   450   NET = GROSS - TAX - C.TAX
```

Figure 5-13   Invalid numbering of the statements in a block IF.

ment preceding it. This creates a problem when modifying or debugging a program in which statements must be changed. For instance, if the formula for C.TAX must be changed, then the entire statement 440 must be reentered or else an editor must be used. *Beware:* It is *not* possible to get around this by using line numbers on each statement between the THEN and END IF, as shown in Figure 5-13. Also, note that the THEN and the END IF *must not be numbered.*

In all examples of this book, the block IF will always be terminated by an END IF statement. However, it is important to know that the END IF is not necessary. (You may encounter it in programs written by others, or you may forget to include an END IF in a program.) The example of Figure 5-14 illustrates this. Upon finding no END IF that corresponds to the THEN, the system automatically searches for the first statement with a line number and uses it to terminate the block of the preceding IF. Not only is this poor documentation, but it is simply too prone to errors. Again, all examples used in this book include the END IF.

```
        400   ! Example 5-3
        410   !
        420   TAX = 0
        430   TAXABLE = GROSS - 2000
        440   IF TAXABLE > 10000
              THEN
                     TAX = 0.15*TAXABLE
                     C.TAX = 25*CHILDREN
      → 450   NET = GROSS - TAX - C.TAX
```

Next statement with
a line number marks
the end of the block

Figure 5-14   Terminating an IF blocking with a numbered line.

The IF–THEN–ELSE Block

The final modification to Example 5-1 will serve to illustrate the IF–THEN–ELSE block form.

Example 5-4

The final attempt by the IB Monarchy to increase tax revenue and reduce population growth involves expanding the tax calculation as follows:

IF Taxable income > 10000
    THEN Regular tax = 0.15 × taxable income
           Child penalty = 25 × number of children
           Luxury tax = 50
    ELSE Regular tax = 0.11 × taxable income
           Child penalty = 14 × number of children
END IF
Net pay = Gross pay − Regular tax − Child penalty − Luxury tax

The form of Figure 5-15 does not require much comment. We can see that it is a logical extension of the forms of Figures 5-11 and 5-12.

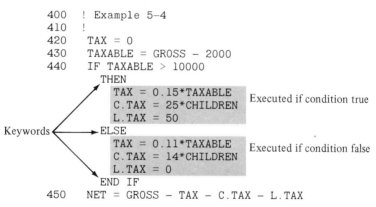

```
400    ! Example 5-4
410    !
420    TAX = 0
430    TAXABLE = GROSS - 2000
440    IF TAXABLE > 10000
          THEN
            TAX = 0.15*TAXABLE      Executed if condition true
            C.TAX = 25*CHILDREN
            L.TAX = 50
Keywords    ELSE
            TAX = 0.11*TAXABLE      Executed if condition false
            C.TAX = 14*CHILDREN
            L.TAX = 0
          END IF
450    NET = GROSS - TAX - C.TAX - L.TAX
```

Figure 5-15   The block IF–THEN–ELSE—Example 5-4.

Exercises

5-6. What is the main difference between the IF–THEN and IF–THEN–ELSE statements?

5-7. When the statement on the next page is executed, some of the variables in it change values; others do not.

```
IF A = B + 1
THEN
     B = C
     C = A
ELSE
     B = A - 1
     C = B + 1
END IF
```

What are the final values of the variables A, B, and C for each of the following sets of initial values?

a. A = 4, B = 3, C = 7
b. A = 3, B = 4, C = 2

Tests Consisting of Multiple Conditions

Some Elementary Concepts of Logic

Often it is necessary to combine several tests to determine whether or not a particular action is to be taken. For instance, the IB Monarchy might change their tax test condition to the following:

Taxable income $>$ 10000
and Tax code $=$ 9

In this case, both conditions must be true in order for the combined condition to be true. The possible combinations are represented by the following table:

Income	Code	Income AND Code
True	True	True
True	False	False
False	True	False
False	False	False

The student of logic will recognize this as a *logical* AND. Another way to look at this is to think of these conditions as representing switches in an electrical circuit, as shown in Figure 5-16. Note that this type of representation is commonly called a *boolean* circuit.

The current flows from point 1 to 2 only if both *I* and *C* are switched on (that is, are true). This is equivalent to the logical AND.

Figure 5-16   Representing the AND by a series circuit.

On the other hand, the IB Monarchy might give their senior citizens a special tax break, yielding the following condition:

Taxable income $>$ 10000
or Age $<$ 65

In this case, only one of the conditions need be true in order for the combined condition to be true. The possible combinations are represented by the following table:

Income	Age	Income OR Age
True	True	True
True	False	True
False	True	True
False	False	False

The boolean circuit representation for the logical OR is shown in Figure 5-17.

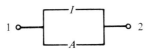

The current flows from point 1 to 2 if either *I* or *A* is switched on (that is, is true). This is equivalent to the logical OR.

Figure 5-17 Representing the OR by a parallel circuit.

The final variation of these test conditions is the somewhat more complex condition involving both the AND and OR, that is

Taxable income > 10000 or Age < 65
and Tax code = 9

Great care must be used in dealing with problems of this type to ensure that program execution corresponds to the action or group of actions called for in the problem. For instance, what if the problem were stated as

Taxable income > 10000 or Age < 65 and Tax code = 9

The question here is "Should the *or* or the *and* be considered first?" That is, should the condition be evaluated as

(Taxable income > 10000 or Age < 65) and Tax code = 9

or as

Taxable income > 10000 or (Age < 65 and Tax code = 9)

It is important to recognize that the two produce very different results. For instance, consider the following set of values:

Taxable income:	12000	(yields true)
Age:	50	(yields true)
Tax code:	8	(yields false)

(Taxable income > 10000 or Age < 65) and Tax code = 9

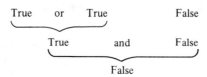

Taxable income > 10000 or (Age < 65 and Tax code = 9)

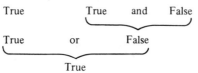

Figure 5-18 Evaluation of AND and OR combinations.

The result of evaluating both of these forms is illustrated in Figure 5-18. In the first, we see that the combined condition is false, whereas in the second, it is true. It is clearly important that the exact relationships be defined unambiguously.

The Logical AND and OR in Basic

From the earlier sections of this chapter, we learned that relational operators are used to compare two quantities. The result is either true or false. (Quantities that can take on only two values are called *logical* or *boolean* quantities.) In addition to relational operators (such as > and =), Basic also includes the *logical operators* AND and OR. They are so called because they operate on logical quantities. Logical operators allow us to build complex test conditions (also called *compound conditions*) for use in control logic. In general, we have

<relational expression> <logical operator> <relational expression>

The Basic form of logical expressions takes virtually the same form as the English expressions for the tax conditions, for instance:

```
TAXABLE > 10000 AND CODE = 9
TAXABLE > 10000 OR AGE < 65
```

To illustrate the compound condition, let us consider a clearly defined statement of the problem.

Example 5-5

Tax is to be calculated as in Example 5-4, except that the test condition is to be

(Taxable income > 10000 OR Age < 65)
AND Tax code = 9

```
400   ! Example 5-5
410   !
420     TAX = 0
430     TAXABLE = GROSS - 2000
440     IF (TAXABLE > 10000 OR AGE < 65) AND CODE = 9
          THEN
            TAX = 0.15*TAXABLE
            C.TAX = 25*CHILDREN
            L.TAX = 50
          ELSE
            TAX = 0.11*TAXABLE
            C.TAX = 14*CHILDREN
            L.TAX = 0
          END IF
450     NET = GROSS - TAX - C.TAX - L.TAX
```

Figure 5-19 Multiple conditions in an IF.

The program segment is shown in Figure 5-19. Note that parentheses are included in order to ensure the proper sequence of evaluation. Whenever a complex test form consisting of ANDs and ORs without parentheses is evaluated, the ANDs are done first and the ORs next. This is analogous to evaluating an arithmetic expression where multiplication is done before addition. As with evaluation of arithmetic expressions, logical expressions within parentheses are evaluated as the first step. This principle is illustrated in Figure 5-18. In the case of Example 5-5, the parentheses are necessary or else the evaluation would be in the wrong sequence. However, much confusion can be avoided by always using parentheses with compound expressions. This serves as good documentation and avoids confusion.

The NOT Logical Operator

There is one other logical operator that is convenient to use in some situations: NOT. (It is especially useful with logical variables, one of the topics of the next chapter.) To illustrate it, consider the expression

```
TAXABLE > 10000 OR AGE < 65
```

Let us assume that we wish to take some action only if this expression is *not* true. However, we know that when this expression is included in an IF statement, the action occurs if it is true. Needless to say, the condition can be rewritten to handle this. However, it might be somewhat confusing and also poor documentation of what we are doing. Here is where we can use the NOT:

```
NOT (TAXABLE > 10000 OR AGE < 65)
```

If the compound condition inside the parentheses is not true, then the overall is true. That is,

NOT (true) is false

NOT (false) is true

An IF statement might then take the form

```
IF NOT (TAXABLE > 10000 OR AGE < 65)
THEN
    (statements to be executed)
```

Here the statements to be executed will be executed only if the expression inside the parentheses is not true. The NOT operator is commonly referred to as the *negation* or the *logical complement*.

In the absence of parentheses, the order in which logical operators are handled (their hierarchy of operations) is as follows:

1. NOT (logical complement).
2. AND (logical and).
3. OR (inclusive or).

When the various *types* of operators (arithmetic, relational, and logical) are combined in an expression, the normal sequence of evaluation is

1. Arithmetic operators (evaluated first, according to their hierarchy rules).
2. Relational operators.
3. Logical operators (evaluated last, according to their hierarchy rules).

Again, Basic evaluates expressions inside parentheses first.

About Program Planning

In the progression of Examples 5-1 through 5-5, we saw a very simple tax system grow in complexity by simple steps. This is actually a way of life for the programmer. It is quite common for a relatively simple program to grow, step by step, until it becomes very complex. Programs that are not carefully structured and modularized (and well documented) can end up being very difficult to modify. Time spent in initial planning is time well invested.

Exercise

5-8. Given the values

$$A = 0,$$
$$B = -1$$
$$C = 1$$

find the *relational value* of each of the following compound relational expressions.

a. A < 0 AND B < 0
b. A < 0 OR B < 0
c. A = 0 OR (C > 0 AND B > 0)
d. A = 0 AND (C < 0 OR B > 0)
e. NOT (A <> 0 AND B > 0)
f. (NOT A <> 0) AND B > 0

Use of Conditionals in Loop Control

In Chapter 3 (Example 3-2), we learned to use the WHILE statment for looping and a combination of the EXIT and IF statements to terminate a loop. At that point, the thinking was "do it because it works." Let us consider both of these in more detail here.

Conditional Execution of a Statement

Line 3015 from Figure 3-8 is as follows:

```
3015  EXIT PROCESS.LOOP IF TOOL.NUMBER$ = "99999"
```

This statement actually consists of one complete statement modified by another. As we learned in Chapter 3, the EXIT provides the means for terminating execution of a loop and proceeding to the statement following the NEXT statement (the last statement in the loop). The EXIT has the following general form:

```
EXIT label
```

Here *label* is a statement label for the statement block. Thus, the form

```
EXIT PROCESS.LOOP
```

would cause execution to exit from the loop name PROCESS.LOOP the moment the statement is encountered. One of the features of VAX Basic is that any statement, including the EXIT, can be executed on a conditional basis. This is done by *following* the statement with an ordinary IF of the type we have learned to use in this chapter. For instance, consider the following PRINT statement:

```
PRINT "This is an example" IF AMOUNT > LIMIT
```

When used in this manner without the THEN, the IF is called a *statement modifier*. The overall effect of this statement is the same as if it were written

```
IF AMOUNT > LIMIT THEN PRINT "This is an example"
```

In either the statement-modifier form or the equivalent IF-THEN form, the statement will be executed only if the IF condition is true. An IF-modified statement *cannot contain* a THEN or ELSE clause, but such a statement *can be part of* a THEN or ELSE clause. The use of such a construct is left as an exercise.

Now the nature of the EXIT statement that we have been using should be apparent. That is, the EXIT statement of line 3015 will be executed if the condition

```
TOOL.NUMBER$ = "99999"
```

is true.

Exercises

5-9. Division by zero causes an error when a program executes. Rewrite the statement

```
500   Z = (X + Y)/(P + Q)
```

so that Z is computed only if $(P + Q)$ is not zero.

5-10. In the following IF–THEN–ELSE statement, each of the IF statement modifiers applies *only* to the PRINT statement immediately preceding it.

```
100   IF A = B
      THEN
         PRINT A IF A > 7
      ELSE
         PRINT B IF B < 0
      END IF
```

What will be printed by this statement for each of the following values of A and B?

a. A = 4, B = 4
b. A = 8, B = 8
c. A = 7, B = 4
d. A = 7, B = −5

The WHILE Statement

The WHILE statement in Figure 3-8 has the form

WHILE − 1

This results in a loop that is repeated endlessly. As we shall learn in the next chapter, the value − 1 is interpreted as true. The complete form of the WHILE is as follows:

WHILE (*condition*)

So long as the condition is true, the loop defined by the WHILE and its corresponding NEXT will continue to be executed. This concept is illustrated by the example of Figure 5-20. Here the condition that controls the loop is

CNT < 10

This is commonly called a *counted loop* because it uses a counter and is executed a predetermined number of times. The following commentary describes this example:

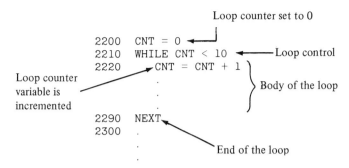

Figure 5-20 A counted loop.

1. Prior to entering the loop at line 2210, the variable CNT is given a value of 0.
2. The first time line 2210 (the entry point to the loop) is executed, the condition will be true (0 is less than 10). Thus, the statements making up the loop will be executed.
3. Within the loop, the loop counter variable CNT is incremented by 1; the value in CNT is now 1.
4. Upon encountering the NEXT, control will return to the WHILE at line 2210. Since 1 is less than 10, the sequence will be repeated again.
5. This will continue until CNT contains a value of 10. At that point, the loop will be exited, and execution will continue at statement 2300.

It is important to recognize that the condition test in the WHILE can be any valid relational or logical expression. Thus, the test can be compound, consisting of ANDs and ORs, as needed in a particular application.

Exercises

5-11. How many times will the body of the program in Figure 5-20 be executed if the counter is initialized to 7; that is, line 2200 is replaced by

```
2200   CNT = 7
```

5-12. What are the three essential operations that must be performed on a counter used for loop control? How is each of these three operations done when a counter is used with the WHILE statement?

5-13. Name two primary functions of conditional statements.

Data Verification

Perhaps the biggest single task in writing interactive programs is verifying that the data quantities entered are valid. For example, if a program required that the user enter a two-letter state abbreviation, then the program should check to

```
3040   INPUT 'Please enter the first number <-9999 if finished>'; A
3044   IF A = -9999
           THEN INPUT 'Are you certain you are finished'; QUERY
       END IF
3050   IF QUERY = 'Y' OR QUERY = 'y'
           THEN EXIT PROCESS.LOOP
           ELSE INPUT 'Reenter the first number'; A
       END IF
```

Figure 5-21 Confirming a user response.

ensure that the entry is indeed valid. This is especially important when building data files, since it is very important to have accurate data stored in files. It is also critical to avoid having the program crash. For instance, assume that you had someone write a program to compile the results of a survey. After an hour of data entry, you accidentally entered some letters instead of a number and the program crashed—goodbye to your hour of hard work; hello to some harsh words to the programmer.

The program of Figure 4-2 is not very *user friendly*, in that if the student intends to key in, for example, 9999 as the first number and accidentally keys in −9999, the program terminates. If we were to replace statement 3050 with those of Figure 5-21, then the student would be asked to confirm whether or not the program is to be terminated. User friendliness is further increased (in a small way) when the user is asked for a Y or N answer regarding continuing. Note that the test includes checking for either the uppercase or lowercase letter Y. Testing for an uppercase letter only would mean that the program would terminate if the student forgot to hold down the shift key when entering the response.

On the other hand, this program is not as friendly as it might be. For instance, what if the student misses the Y key and strikes the U? The answer is that a Y (uppercase or lowercase) is the only response that will allow the program to continue. Anything else will cause it to terminate. This problem is resolved by the statements of Figure 5-22, in which the only valid responses are Y, y, N, and n. Anything else will cause a screen prompt with a request for the response to be reentered.

This example of data verification on input might seem to be a nuisance and take up a lot of valuable programming effort. However, program code such

```
3040   INPUT 'Please enter the first number <-9999 if finished>'; A
3044   IF A = -9999
           THEN INPUT 'Are you certain you are finished'; QUERY
       END IF
3047   WHILE QUERY <> 'Y' AND QUERY <> 'y' AND QUERY <> 'N'    &
                              AND QUERY <> 'n'
3048       INPUT 'Please enter Y or N -- try again'; QUERY
3049   THEN
3050   IF QUERY = 'Y' OR QUERY = 'y'
           THEN EXIT PROCESS.LOOP
           ELSE INPUT 'Reenter the first number'; A
       END IF
```

Figure 5-22 Checking a user response.

as this is essential. It is extremely important to identify all possible ways in which the user who knows nothing about the program can go astray. A program that crashes or gives nonsense whenever a user makes a mistake will not be a problem for long. The program will quickly find its way to the trash container where it belongs.

Use of Immediate Mode

Statements in Immediate Mode

The subject of this chapter is control structures. Overall, if a program is carefully planned and modularized, problems associated with getting it running can be minimized. However, loops and conditional statements do tend to cause problems, especially for the beginner. One of the features that is sometimes helpful in debugging a program is the immediate-mode facility of VAX Basic. As we have learned, one distinction between commands and statements is that commands are executed immediately, while statements are not executed until the program containing them is executed. This is not exactly true, since many of the statements can be entered at the terminal *without* any preceding line number, thus causing them to be executed immediately, as if they were commands; hence the term *immediate mode*. (Because a leading space or tab implies a continuation line, immediate-mode statements must begin in the first column, with no leading spaces or tabs.) For instance, let us consider the following scenario: We have entered and run a program that crashes and displays the following message:

Division by zero at line 2430

Upon typing the command

    LIST 2430

the computer displays the statement

    2430 HOLD = 25*A/B + C/(X - Y + 2)

Inspecting this, we see that the problem is in either of two areas:

1. The value in B is zero.
2. The expression (X − Y + 2) is zero.

One of the important features of Basic is that when execution of a program is terminated, the values of all variables remain at their last values. Using the immediate mode, we can take advantage of this and inspect the values of appropriate variables of the program. A typical dialogue with the computer is as shown in Figure 5-23. Upon examination, we see that the expression is zero. We can now look at other portions of the program and print the current values of variables used in calculating X and Y (if appropriate).

It is important to recognize that Basic retains the current values of all variables when program execution is terminated by either an error condition or

```
PRINT  B
 63
Ready
PRINT  X - Y + 2
 0
Ready
```

Figure 5-23   Using the immediate mode.

a STOP statement. This gives us a very powerful debugging tool since we can either inspect values after an error termination or insert a STOP at *any* point in the program to inspect variables. For instance, assume that our program is using a loop (with loop-control variable J) to calculate the mean of a data set, and the body of the loop contains the statements

```
510   READ N$, Q, AMNT
520   next statement
```

Furthermore, the program has terminated on an error condition at statement 810. We are suspicious of the data quantities and the loop variable J the instant after the READ is executed. To find out what is occurring, we could insert the statement

```
515   STOP
```

and rerun the program. Now on each pass through the loop, the computer will suspend execution when it encounters line 515 and print the following:

```
STOP AT LINE 515
```

We can then use the following immediate-mode PRINT (beginning in the first column!) to get the desired values printed at the terminal:

```
PRINT  "J = "; J, "N$ = "; N, "Q = "; Q, "AMNT = "; AMNT
```

We resume program execution after each pass through the loop by typing the system command

```
CONTINUE
```

The process can then be repeated, provided we do not make changes in our program, until we find the input quantities that caused the error. Once the debugging session is finished, the STOP statements that were inserted solely for debugging purposes need to be removed.

The possibility of interrupting program execution, examining program variables (and even changing their values), and then resuming program execution at the point of interruption is a powerful feature of immediate mode. Some care has to be exercised in using this feature because not all Basic statements are valid in immediate mode. For example, the DATA statement is invalid because it makes no sense in the context of a single line.

```
I = 7 \ PRINT I, I**2, I**3, I**4
 7         49        343          2401
```
Figure 5-24 Using calculator mode.

The preceding example illustrates immediate-mode debugging of a program that terminates on an error condition by stopping execution *from within* this program, by means of a STOP statement. Occasionally, bad program logic will cause a program to lock into a loop that does not terminate, called an *infinite loop*. In that case, we would want to be able to stop program execution *from the keyboard*. This is done by holding down the Control key and striking the letter C (called a *Control C*). We shall learn more about its use in Chapter 8.

Calculator Mode

Actually, immediate-mode statements need not be used in conjunction with a program. That is, the computer can be used as if it were a very powerful calculator with most of the features of the Basic language available. When used this way, immediate-mode statements are sometimes referred to as being in *calculator mode*, because they let you use Basic much like a calculator.

For example, calculator-mode statements can be used to compute powers of a number, as shown in Figure 5-24. We see that immediate-mode statements have two different roles:

1. As a tool in debugging a program.
2. To perform calculations independent of the current program.

The first of these is extremely valuable and is best appreciated by a programmer who has worked only with compiler (noninteractive) languages. However, it is no substitute for careful program planning with the philosphy of preparing programs that are relatively free of errors.

Exercise

5-14. Write a calculator-mode statement to compute and print the value of $[(7)(3) - (2)(8)]^2 + (4)(8)/[(9)(5) - 2^3]$

In Retrospect

We now have the Basic tools for implementing sequence, selection, and looping, the three fundamental constructs of structured programming. The WHILE provides the control structure for looping, and the IF, for selection. The key to the VAX Basic IF as a structured programming tool is the ability to define blocks of statements for conditional execution by use of the END-IF.

The basis for conditional operations is the *relational expression*, which has the form

(expression) *(relational operator)* *(expression)*

Examples:

```
WORK > 44.6
SAVE < 0
3*HOLD - 25 >= CHECK
LINE.CNT = 60
```

Relational operators are:

Symbol	Meaning
>	Greater than
=	Equal to
<	Less than
>= or =>	Greater than or equal to
<= or =<	Less than or equal to
<> or ><	Not equal to
==	Approximately equal to

The expressions to be compared can be simple constants, variables, or complex expressions. Conditional operations are further enhanced by the inclusion of the logical operators AND, OR, and NOT, which allow for more complex conditional forms. They can be used in the following form:

(*relational expression*)   (*logical operator*)   (*relational expression*)

Examples:

```
AGE > 60   AND   LEAVE >= MINIMUM
AGE > 60   OR   SEN > 25
(AGE > 60   OR SEN > 25) AND   LEAVE >= MINIMUM
HOLD = 0 AND AMOUNT < UPPER.LIMIT
```

The NOT is called the negation and is used in the usual English sense. For instance, if

```
AMOUNT < UPPER.LIMIT
```

is true, then

```
NOT (AMOUNT < UPPER.LIMIT)
```

is false.

The relational expression, which forms the basis of the IF statement, is also used as the evaluation condition for control of the WHILE looping statement. That is, the WHILE has the general form

```
WHILE (test condition)
  .
  .
  .
NEXT
```

Note that the test condition can be any relational or logical expression.

The conditional capabilities described in this chapter provide the programmer with a complete set of tools for implementing structured programming techniques in VAX Basic. In later chapters, additional conditional features that fit a variety of situations will be introduced. However, the structures of this chapter are sufficient to implement structured techniques to the fullest extent.

Answers to Preceding Exercises

5-1. Statement 300; cannot break a string constant.
Statement 500; GOSUB is a single keyword and cannot be broken.

5-2. a. 4.5 * DEP >= 18
   b. DEP = -6; false
      DEP = 4; true
      DEP = 10; true

5-3. In (b) and (g), A$ and B$ are equal; in all others, A$ is larger (occurs later in the ordering sequence).

5-4. The relation A$ = = B$ is true only in (g). In (b), the two strings have different lengths before padding.

5-5. a. THE SHOW WILL NOT GO ON
   b. THE SHOW WILL NOT GO ON
   c. THE SHOW WILL GO ON

5-6. In the IF–THEN selection structure, a statement (or group of statements) is executed only if the relational expression is true; if it is false, control transfers to the statement after the IF-THEN without any additional statements being executed. In the IF-THEN-ELSE structure, one statement block is executed if the relational expression is true, and another statement block is executed if the condition is false.

5-7. a. A = 4, B = 7, C = 4
   b. A = 3, B = 2, C = 3

5-8. a. False, because A < 0 is false.
   b. True, because B < 0 is true.
   c. True, because A = 0 is true.
   d. False, because (C < 0 OR B > 0) is false.
   e. True, because (A <> 0 AND B > 0) is false.
   f. False, because B > 0 is false.

5-9. 500   Z = (X + Y)/(P + Q) IF (P + Q) <> 0

or

500   IF (P + Q) <> 0 THEN Z = (X + Y)/(P + Q)

5-10. a. Nothing; the THEN clause applies, but A is printed only if its value is greater than 7.

b. 8.

c. Nothing; the ELSE clause applies, but B is printed only if it is negative.

d. −5.

5-11. Three times.

5-12. It must be initialized *outside* of the loop, incremented *inside* the loop, and its value tested *inside* the loop. When it is used as part of the condition in a WHILE statement, the initialization and incrementation are done *explicitly* with assignment statements; the testing is done *implicitly* (no separate Basic statement) by the WHILE statement.

5-13. They underlie selection and facilitate loop control.

5-14. PRINT (7*3 − 2*8)**2 + 4*8/(9*5 − 2**3) starting in the first column.

Programming Problems

5-1. Each record contains three fields, P, Q, and R. Write a program to find the largest value of each set of P, Q, and R and place it in the variable X. Print the input quantities and the value of X. Use READ/DATA statements to read in the values. Terminate execution by reading −99 for all three fields.

5-2. Write a program for the data set of Problem 5-1 that will rearrange the values for each set of P, Q, and R so that P contains the smallest value, Q the next, and R the largest. In this problem, it will be necessary to interchange values between variables, which will require a temporary storage variable. For instance, M and N would be interchanged by the following subroutine:

```
SWAP:
100   T = M    ! save M
110   M = N    ! place value of N in M
120   N = T    ! place value of M saved in T into N
```

5-3. Expand the requirements of Problem 4-1 as follows: The data set to be processed now includes *all* customers, not only those who have exceeded their credit.

Account number.

Customer name.

Balance at beginning of month.

Total charges during month.

Total credits during month.

Credit limit.

Write an interactive program to calculate the new balance (add charges to beginning balance and subtract credits) and compare the new balance to the credit limit. Only for those accounts that exceed the credit limit, print the following:

Account number.

Customer name.

New balance.

Credit limit.

The new balance will never exceed $10,000. The summary line should contain the number of customers processed, the number who exceeded their credit limit, and the total by which the credit limits have been exceeded.

5-4. Expand the requirements of Problem 4-4 so that the monthly service charge is 1.5 percent on the first $1,000.00 of the balance due and 1.2 percent on the balance due in excess of $1,000.00.

5-5. Write an interactive program to input the cost of an item (not more than $20) for which the customer tenders $20, and then compute the amount owed to the customer. Also calculate the *least* number of bills and coins of each denomination that should be given to the customer. Do *not* use two-dollar bills or half dollars. Note that the number of five- and ten-dollar bills can be at most 1. The same is true of nickels. Output is to consist of the cost of the item and the results of the calculation.

5-6. Consider a sequence of numbers, such as

2 7 11 9 15 23 26 13 21 19 27 27 31 46

A segment of the sequence in nondecreasing order is called a *pass*. For the preceding example, the passes are

2 7 11
9 15 23 26
13 21
19 27 27 31 46

Note that the end of each pass, except the last one, is signalled by a larger value followed by a smaller one. Write a program to read a sequence of numbers (one number per DATA statement) and print each pass on a separate line. Trailer is indicated by -9999.

5-7. Modify the requirements of problem 4-3 so that it will accept only Y and N as responses to the query to continue. Any other answer should result in a message to the user that the only acceptable reply is Y or N.

5-8. A utility company computes the electrical bills for its customers according to the following rates:

Kilowatt-hrs (kwh)	Cost per kwh (in $)
0–100	.093
101–400	.075
401 and over	.063

There is also an additional service charge of $6.50 per month. Write an interactive program to input the kwh consumed (less than 10,000) and compute the bill. Input the following seven values for the consumed electricity (kwh): 50, 145, 305, 530, 5003, 70, 495. Appropriately labeled output is to include account number (exactly 6 digits), kwh consumed, and amount due. A summary line is to print the two totals for all customers.

5-9. Write an interactive program to enter a sequence of positive numbers and output the largest and smallest numbers. You can start by setting two variables, LARGEST and SMALLEST, to the first number entered. Process approximately 15 numbers in the range 0–500. Terminate execution by entering any negative number.

6

Data Types, Operations, and Predefined Functions

Preview

From our studies in previous chapters, we have learned that data can be considered as either of two general types: numeric or string. Actually, VAX Basic includes five data-type classifications. We shall study three of them in this chapter: One is string (as we used in preceding chapters), and the other two are numeric, as follows:

> *Integer (whole numbers only)*
> *Real (numbers with fractional parts)*

This chapter focuses on the principle of data types; from it you will learn about the following topics.

1. *How to designate to the Basic system that a given variable is integer or real.*
2. *The use of integer variables as logical (true/false) variables.*

3. *The nature of integer division, whereby the remainder is discarded.*
4. *The nature of functions for performing common operations.*
   Mathematical functions described include

   a. *Absolute value.*
   b. *Converting real to integer.*
   c. *Trigonometric functions.*
   d. *Square root.*
   e. *Raising to a power.*
   f. *Logarithm.*
   g. *Random number generation.*

   String functions described include

   a. *Extracting substrings from strings.*
   b. *Obtaining length of a string.*

5. *The combination of two or more strings into a single string (string concatenation).*
6. *Processing using random numbers.*

The Integer Data Type

One of the first topics in this book relates to the storage of information in memory and the distinction between numeric and string data. Figure 2-4 illustrates the concept that each numeric variable in a program causes the Basic system to set aside one numeric storage area. Actually, the descriptions relating to this figure are really an understatement of what occurs and how numeric quantities are handled in memory. Each type of number is stored and handled differently. We will begin by considering integers.

Integer Numbers

Let us assume that we are preparing an inventory control program in which the variable CASES contains the number of cases of tools that we have in stock. Since each case contains 24 tools, we can calculate the total tool count as

```
2200    TOOLS = 24*CASES
```

The expression to the right consists of the *constant* 24 and the *variable* CASES. Constants are handled by the system in much the same way as variables in evaluating expressions. One important aspect of this example is that the "things" with which we are dealing are whole numbers. That is, we will be dealing with, for instance, 150 cases (and correspondingly 3600 tools) and not with 6.738 cases.

As we shall learn, there are three classes of integers; for the moment we shall concentrate on the default class. For each one of these, the computer reserves two consecutive bytes of memory. The memory requirements for the elements of the preceding statement 2200 are illustrated in Figure 6-1. (Note

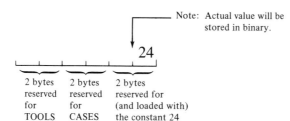

Figure 6-1   Single-word integer quantities in memory.

that in an actual program with many other variables and constants, these quantities would probably not be next to each other within memory.) In the VAX family of computers, two consecutive bytes of memory are called a *word*. The word size (16 bits for the VAX) is an important characterisic of any computer. As we shall learn in the next section, real numbers (those with fractional parts) require more memory than one-word integers.

Designating the Integer Data Type by Its Name

Now the question arises, "How does the computer know whether a quantity is intended to be integer?" The answer is that we must tell it. As we already know, string variables are distinguished from numeric variables by appending the dollar sign character ($) to the name. For example, SSN$ is a string variable, whereas AMOUNT is a numeric variable.

Similarly, a percent-sign character (%) is used to indicate that a quantity is to be treated as integer. Thus, Basic will recognize COUNTER% as an integer variable, but not TOTAL. Thus, the earlier statement 2200 might be written as follows:

```
2200    TOOLS% = 24*CASES%
```

Note that the constant need not include an appended % sign (although a % sign is allowed). Basic automatically treats it as an integer because it is written without a decimal point.

Types of Integers

Unless we say otherwise in a program, all integer quantities will default to one word (two bytes) in size. In addition to word integers, two other sizes are available to meet the needs of a given program. These are summarized in Table 6-1.

Table 6-1 Integer Data Types

Type	Size (Bytes)	Range
BYTE	1	−128 to +127
WORD	2	−32768 to +32767
LONG	4	−2147483648 to +2147483647

Here we see that the default WORD integer can range in size from -32768 to $+32767$. In a later section, we shall learn how to incorporate BYTE and LONG integers into a program.

The Real Data Type

Real Numbers

In contrast to the preceding integer calculations, in a payroll application, we might calculate overtime pay rate as 1.5 times the regular pay rate:

```
2210    OT.RATE = 1.5*REG.RATE
```

Here 1.5 is obviously not a whole number. Furthermore, REG.RATE and OT.RATE will likely contain quantities that are not whole numbers, for instance, 8.32. In Basic, numbers of this type are called *real*. (This definition is slightly different from the mathematical definition, in which the reals include the integers.) For each one of these, the computer reserves four consecutive bytes of memory. The memory requirements for the elements of the preceding statement 2210 are illustrated in Figure 6-2.

As with integers, we might question how the system knows that a variable is intended to be real. Unless it is otherwise overridden, the absence of a suffix ($ or %) specifies to the system to store a quantity as real. Thus, in statement 2210, as well as in all of the sample programs of previous chapters, all variables have defaulted to real.

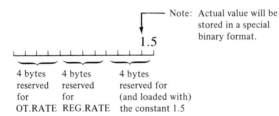

Note: Actual value will be stored in a special binary format.

1.5

4 bytes reserved for OT.RATE　　4 bytes reserved for REG.RATE　　4 bytes reserved for (and loaded with) the constant 1.5

Figure 6-2 Four-byte real quantities in memory.

Types of Reals

Unless we say otherwise in a program, all real quantities will default to two words (four bytes) in size. In addition to four-byte size, three other sizes are available to meet the needs of a given program. These are summarized in Table 6-2.

Here we see that the size of reals is defined by two entities: *range* and *precision*. The range refers to the overall magnitude that the quantity can have. (Note that the limits given in Table 6-2 are rather substantial.) The precision refers to the number of significant digits that can be stored. For instance, a *single-precision* variable (SINGLE) could store numbers such as

953.224

0.000644482

7622190000. (Trailing zeros are not significant.)

Table 6-2 Real Data Types

Type	Size (Bytes)	Range	Precision (Decimal Digits)
SINGLE	4	$.29 \times 10^{-38}$ to $.19 \times 10^{39}$	6
DOUBLE	8	$.29 \times 10^{-38}$ to $.19 \times 10^{39}$	16
GFLOAT	8	$.56 \times 10^{-308}$ to $.9 \times 10^{308}$	15
HFLOAT	16	$.84 \times 10^{-4932}$ to $.59 \times 10^{4932}$	33

On the other hand, a *double-precision* variable (DOUBLE) could store numbers such as

> 953.2241134584638
>
> 0.0006444827749037539 (Leading zeros are not significant.)
>
> 76221955295.9926

For most applications, the default single precision is quite adequate. In a later section, we shall learn how to incorporate DOUBLE, GFLOAT, and HFLOAT quantities into a program.

Floating-Point Format for Real Quantities

The term *floating point* is often used in referring to numbers with fractional parts. The term comes from the way these numbers are handled within the computer. Whenever a number is entered into the computer or a new one is calculated, it is automatically placed in a form similar to scientific notation. This representation is standardized by moving the decimal point to the left of the first nonzero digit of the number and then multiplying by 10, raised to the appropriate power. For example, the number

> 253.28

can be represented as

> .25328 × 1000,

which can in turn be represented as

> $.25328 \times 10^3$

This is the basis of the floating-point form. Additional examples of floating-point quantities are given here.

Decimal Number	Floating-Point Representation
123.456	0.123456×10^3
0.009703	0.9703×10^{-2}
0.1	0.1×10^0
2501.	0.2501×10^4
-386.2	-0.3862×10^3

Exercise

6-1. Represent each of the following products in standard floating-point representation:

a. 3 × 4
b. .2 × .3
c. 7 × .3

Using the E Format for Output of Real Quantities

From Table 6-2 we know that real numbers can consist of six decimal digits (for type SINGLE) to thirty-three digits (for type HFLOAT). When printing floating-point numbers with the PRINT statement, the format of the output will depend on the size of the number. Usually in a program, we will print the number in our "standard" form, for example,

    3.67891

However, for very large and very small numbers, this is not very practical. For instance, numbers such as the following would simply take too much room on the printed line (and be too clumsy to read).

    36789100000000000000000000   0.000000000000367891

VAX Basic gives us the ability to print the result in a form that is virtually identical to the floating-point format. For instance, the preceding numbers could be printed as

    .367891E 24   .367891E-12

This form is called E *format* (or *exponential format*); it specifies the power of 10 (24 and -12, in these cases) by which the decimal numbers to the left of E must be multiplied.

To print in E format with PRINT USING, place four of the circumflex characters(five for HFLOAT) at the far right of the format field. This is illustrated in lines 100, 110, 120, following. Output is left justified in the format field, and the exponent compensates for this adjustment.

```
100   PRINT USING "###.##^^^^", 7
110   PRINT USING "###.##^^^^", 7000
120   PRINT USING ".##^^^^", 7
```

will print

    700.00E − 02
    700.00E + 01
    .70E + 01

Exercise

6-2. Write each of the following numbers using the E format. Standardize by placing the decimal point to the left of the leftmost nonzero digit.

a. 75649
b. 0.00567
c. 2.9467

More About Numeric Types

The DECLARE Statement

Earlier in the chapter, we saw how the system determines the variable type by looking at the name. That is, an appended % indicates integer, $ indicates string, and the absence of either special character indicates real. This is called implicit typing because the type is implied by the name. Data types can also be assigned explicitly to either variables or constants by the DECLARE statement. This statement is not executable; it must precede any reference within the program to the declared quantities. The examples in Figure 6-3 illustrate the format of the DECLARE statement.

The following comments about these examples should clarify features of the VAX Basic DECLARE statement:

1. All valid data types may be declared explicitly. Statements 100-120 declare integers, 200-230 declare reals, and 300 declares a string.
2. More than one data item (variable or constant) may be listed for a given type. For instance, in line 110, we see that the variables LEVEL and TOT.COUNT are both declared as WORD integer quantities.
3. More than one variable type may be named in one DECLARE. For instance, line 400 defines ID, SCOPE, and LEVEL as BYTE integers and NAMES as a STRING. However, for the sake of documentation, a separate DECLARE for each type is recommended.

```
100   DECLARE BYTE CNT
110   DECLARE WORD LEVEL, TOT.COUNT
120   DECLARE LONG POPLTN, INCOME

200   DECLARE SINGLE WAGES
210   DECLARE DOUBLE AMOUNT, CREDIT
220   DECLARE GFLOAT NUM.ATOMS
230   DECLARE HFLOAT NUM.QUARKS

300   DECLARE STRING EMPLOYEE, TITLE

400   DECLARE BYTE ID, SCOPE, LEVEL, STRING NAMES

500   DECLARE INTEGER LINE.COUNT
600   DECLARE WORD CONSTANT TOTAL = 456
610   DECLARE SINGLE CONSTANT PERCENT = 46.35
```

Figure 6-3 Examples of the DECLARE statement.

4. Declared variable and constant names *must not* end with a percent sign (%) or a dollar sign ($). Types specified in a DECLARE statement override any default or implicit specification.

5. Use of REAL or INTEGER in DECLARE specifies the default subtype. For example, if the system default for INTEGER is WORD, then LINE.COUNT on line 500 is a WORD integer.

6. Numeric variables in a DECLARE statement are initialized to zero; string variables, to null.

7. Constants can be declared in a DECLARE-CONSTANT statement in which the value of the constant is specified. The value of the declared constant cannot be changed during program execution. Technically speaking, the equal sign in lines 600 and 610 is not interpreted as an assignment symbol. Once a constant value is set in a DECLARE statement, it may not be assigned a new value in the program.

8. Only one *constant type* can be specified in a DECLARE-CONSTANT statement. To declare a constant of a different type, you must use a separate DECLARE.

9. The value assigned to the named constant must be in the allowable range of the data subtype being declared. If the value is outside this range, you will get an error message.

There are two definite advantages to using a mnemonic name for a numeric constant rather than its literal value within the body of programs. First, a well-chosen constant name makes the program easier to read. Although a few constant values, such as the mathematical pi, can be identified fairly easily, this is not true for most constants. For example, use of INTEREST.RATE rather than 0.14 makes it easier to interpret statements in which this constant is used.

To illustrate the second advantage, assume that a program uses the value 3.1416 for the mathematical constant pi. Furthermore, this constant is used in numerous places in the program. Unfortunately, testing of the program shows that more digits are necessary and that 3.1415926536 must be used to ensure the desired accuracy. In the program segment of Figure 6-4(a), each literal value would have to be located and changed separately. However, in the Figure 6-4(b) version, which uses a constant definition, the only change necessary would be to replace the constant declaration of line 100 with the corresponding DECLARE of Figure 6-4(c).

However, the preceding two advantages can be achieved just as well by using a suitably initialized variable. For instance, the constant declaration for PI in Figure 6-4(b) could be replaced with the assignment statement

```
100  PI = 3.1416
```

The main reason for using a declared constant rather than an initialized variable has to do with the meaning of a constant in a program: a quantity that does not change during program execution. If an initialized variable were used, the programmer might inadvertently change its value by an assignment statement in the body of a program, with unintended consequences. If an attempt is made to change the value of a declared constant by an assignment statement, an error message is given.

```
2200   AREA = 3.1416*R*R
  .
  .
  .
3310   A2 = (A+B+C-3.1416)*R**2

       (a)

100    DECLARE SINGLE CONSTANT PI = 3.1416
  .
  .
  .
2200   AREA = PI*R*R
  .
  .
  .
3310   A2 = (A+B+C-PI)*R**2

       (b)

100    DECLARE DOUBLE CONSTANT PI = 3.1415926536

       (c)
```

Figure 6-4   Making use of tne DECLARE CONSTANT in a program. (a) Using a literal. (b) substituting a constant declaration. (c) Changing the value of the constant.

Exercises

6-3. Declare variable names for the following, using types that are consistent with the data:

a. A page counter.
b. A Social Security number.
c. A national sales total (maximum value: $14 million).
d. Hourly pay rate.

6-4. The following program prints a table of positive and negative powers of 2:

```
1000   DECLARE BYTE I, DOUBLE X, Y
1100   I = 0
1110   WHILE I < 20
          X = 2**I
          Y = 2**(-I)
          PRINT I, X, Y
          I = I + 1
       NEXT
32767 END
```

However, the PRINT statement only displays up to six digits of precision for floating-point numbers. This corresponds to the precision of the SINGLE data type. Hence, for the larger values of I in the program, the calculated numbers X and Y will be stored in memory with more precision than when they are printed. The advantage of declaring X and Y to be double precision is thereby lost. To print the extra digits in DOUBLE (and GFLOAT or HFLOAT) numbers, we must resort to the PRINT USING statement.

Rewrite the program to print up to 10 decimal digits of precision for the calculated numbers. Use a separate string to define the format image.

Choosing Among Different Numeric Data Types

With the broad variety of data types and subtypes illustrated in Figure 6-3, we might wonder when we select what. If our computations are to involve fractional quantities, then we would obviously use real. In view of the limited capabilities of integers, we might wonder why we should use them at all. There are actually two considerations: speed and memory needs. Arithmetic operations involving integer quantities are much faster and more efficient than those with floating point or a combination of the two. In many cases, the power of floating point is simply not required. For instance, several example programs in preceding chapters have involved counters that begin at 0 and are incremented by 1 for each execution. This concept is expanded further in Chapter 8, concerning counters used for loop control. In cases such as this, the use of integers is quite appropriate and preferable.

Regarding memory needs, the default WORD integers occupy only two bytes of memory, whereas the default SINGLE reals occupy four bytes. This can be critical if large arrays of data are to be processed. (Arrays are described in Chapter 9.)

The choice between using integer and real arithmetic is usually obvious. But the beginner often wonders when to use what precision; for instance, when should DOUBLE be used instead of SINGLE? The higher the precision, the more memory required, which may be an important factor for a very large program. Also, the higher the precision, the longer it takes the computer to perform the calculations. As a rule, in business programming (which is more oriented toward input/output than internal computations), the speed consideration is not as important as it is in scientific and engineering applications. Since business programming commonly deals with dollars and cents (sometimes tenths of cents), single precision is usually not adequate. That is, the best accuracy we can expect is 9999.99, which is less than $10,000. Thus, for most business programming, double precision should be used (or the decimal type, which is not described in this book). Even then, accuracy problems may occur, as illustrated by programming assignment 8-7. For scientific applications, one must usually strike a careful balance between precision and speed.

Exercises

6-5. Rewrite the program segment of Figure 5-20 with the loop-control variable declared as a WORD subtype.

6-6. a. How do the INTEGER, REAL, and STRING data types differ?
   b. How do BYTE, WORD, and LONG differ from one another?
   c. How do SINGLE, DOUBLE, GFLOAT, and HFLOAT differ from one another?

Integers as Logical Variables

Frequently in programming, the need arises to save yes-or-no type information. As we learned in Chapter 5, quantities that take on only one of two values (yes or no, true or false) are called *logical* or *boolean* quantities. VAX Basic does not provide explicitly for this data type; however, we can use integer variables to represent logical quantities. A variant of the interactive arithmetic drill-and-practice program of Example 4-1 can benefit from using this concept. Remember that this program calculates the sum and product of the two numbers entered at the keyboard. The appropriate section of code from the program of Figure 4-2 is shown here in Figure 6-5. Note that the process loop is terminated by entering a specific negative number.

By contrast, suppose that we wish the loop to terminate if the sum is greater than some specified number. The program segment of Figure 6-6 uses the variable CONTINUE, which is defined in line 200 as a one-byte integer variable. In line 3020, it is given a value of −1; in line 3105, its value is changed to 0. Any time an integer quantity is encountered as the test condition, the system treats it as a logical quantity, with the following results:

False if the quantity is zero.

True if the quantity is not zero.

```
      PROCESS.LOOP:
         WHILE  −1
3030        PRINT
3040        INPUT 'Please enter the first number, −9999 if finished ';A
3050        EXIT PROCESS.LOOP IF A = −9999
3060        INPUT 'Please enter the second number ';B
3070        PRINT
3080        PRINT 'The sum is:     '; A + B
3090        PRINT 'The product is:   '; A * B
3100        PRINT
3110     NEXT
```

Figure 6-5   Program segment from Example 4-6.

```
200   DECLARE BYTE CONTINUE
210   DECLARE SINGLE CONSTANT MAX.VALUE = 1000
  .
  .
  .
3020  CONTINUE = −1
      PROCESS.LOOP:
         WHILE CONTINUE
  .
  .
  .
3100        PRINT
3105        CONTINUE = 0   IF A + B > MAX.VALUE
3110     NEXT
```

Figure 6-6   Using an integer as a logical variable.

Thus, in the program segment of Figure 6-6, the value -1 assigned to CONTINUE causes it to be interpreted as true when it is evaluated in the WHILE statement for the first time. Upon being changed to 0 in line 3105, it will be evaluated as false. When integer variables are used in this fashion, they are sometimes referred to as *logical* variables. Although -1 is used to indicate true in examples throughout this book, *any* nonzero quantity is treated as true when an integer variable is evaluated as a logical. However, if a nonzero quantity other than -1 is used with the NOT operator, troubles arise because of the way in which these quantities are handled internally. Hence, always use a -1 for the false case. Then the NOT operator can be used in conjunction with these forms, as illustrated in Figure 6-7 (a variation of Figure 6-6) because of the following:

GETOUT	NOT GETOUT
T	F
F	T

Again, this is reliable only if -1 is used for true.

This concept of logical quantities provides the reason that the WHILE of earlier chapters works. For instance, our first looping program (Figure 3-8) used the looping structure shown here in Figure 6-8. In this case, the integer constant -1 is also used as the condition to be tested, though in connection with a trailer record rather than a computed value. In this context, it is treated as a logical quantity and is consequently true. The result is that the loop is repeated endlessly until action within the loop terminates it.

More on Arithmetic Operations

Integer Arithmetic

In general, integer addition, subtraction, and multiplication give identical results to those using floating-point arithmetic for these operations with whole

```
200    DECLARE BYTE GETOUT
  .
  .
  .
3020   GETOUT = 0
       PROCESS.LOOP:
          WHILE NOT GETOUT
  .
  .
  .
3105          GETOUT = -1 IF A + B > MAX.VALUE
3110      NEXT
```

Figure 6-7 Using the NOT operator
with a logical variable.

"Condition" to be tested. The value -1
is treated as a logical value that is true.

```
3005  WHILE -1
3010     READ TOOL.NUM, ...
3015     EXIT PROCESS.LOOP IF TOOL.NUM = 99999
 .
 .
 .
3034  NEXT
```
Figure 6-8 Controlling a loop.

numbers. Integer division, however, differs in an important way from floating-point division. This is the case because, whereas the result of adding, subtracting, and multiplying whole numbers is always a whole number, the result of dividing two whole numbers is not generally a whole number. Integer division always gives an integer result, with the remainder being discarded; such a result is said to be *truncated* (not rounded). This is illustrated in Figure 6-9. The results produced by lines 150–170 are a bit subtle and demonstrate the importance of hierarchy of operations.

```
50      DECLARE INTEGER A, B, C, X1, X2, X3, X4, X5, REMAINDER
100     A = 5
110     B = 13
120     C = 8
130     X1 = B/A                ! RESULT IS 2  (REMAINDER OF 3 IS LOST)
140     X2 = A/B                ! RESULT IS 0
150     X3 = A/B*C              ! RESULT IS 0  (A/B GIVES 0, TIMES C)
160     X4 = A*C/B              ! RESULT IS 3
170     X5 = A/B + C/B          ! RESULT IS 0  (0 + 0)
180     REMAINDER = B - A*(B/A) ! RESULT IS 3 (REMAINDER OF 13/5)
```
Figure 6-9 Integer arithmetic.

Exercise

6-7. What will be stored in each of the variables P1-P5 by the following statements?

```
50      DECLARE INTEGER  X,Y,Z,P1,P2,P3,P4,P5
100     X = 12
110     Y = 18
120     Z = 7
130     P1 = Y/Z
140     P2 = (Z + 11)/Y
150     P3 = X/Y*2*Z
160     P4 = Y/X + Y/Z
170     P5 = Y/(X+Z)
```

Mixing Data Types

Now we might wonder what occurs if an expression contains operands of different data types. These are called *mixed-mode* expressions. Basic automatically converts all operands to a common data type before evaluating mixed-mode expressions. With one exception, this conversion is done in such a way that none of the operands in the expression loses any range or precision when the conversion is made. Suppose, for example, we have the following variables:

Variable	Data Type
I.CNT	INTEGER
D.TOTAL	DOUBLE
TRANS	SINGLE
HOLD	SINGLE
I.HOLD	INTEGER
SOLTN1	DOUBLE
SOLTN2	DOUBLE
INCREMENT	GFLOAT

Then, in the expression

```
3.2*I.CNT/(D.TOTAL + TRANS)
```

we have each of the three types INTEGER, DOUBLE, and SINGLE. During execution, this expression will be evaluated, with the values of I.CNT and TRANS converted to equivalent double-precision values. The result will be double precision.

A slight variation of this procedure occurs when the operands are DOUBLE and GFLOAT, for example,

```
(SOLTN1 - SOLTN2)/INCREMENT
```

In this case, all three variables are converted to HFLOAT, and the result is in HFLOAT. The reason the calculation is not done in either DOUBLE or GFLOAT is that, although a DOUBLE value is more precise than a GFLOAT value, it cannot contain the largest possible GFLOAT value. Hence, Basic converts to HFLOAT, a data type that can hold the largest and most precise value of *either* operand.

The exception just referred to occurs when an operation involves SINGLE (real) and LONG (integer) data types. In this case, Basic converts LONG to SINGLE rather than to DOUBLE, and the result is SINGLE.

The Effect on the Assignment Statement

The concept of mixed mode relates to expressions used in an assignment statement, in forming a condition test or wherever. If they are used in an assignment statement, what occurs if the variable to the left (the assignment variable) is of a different type than the computed result? The answer to this is simple: The result will be stored according to the type of receiving variable. If the result of the expression is double precision and the receiving field is also double precision, then the result is obvious. Using the earlier double-precision expression, let us consider the following:

```
HOLD = 3.2*I.CNT/(D.TOTAL + TRANS)
```

Since HOLD is single precision, the double-precision result will be rounded before being stored in the variable HOLD. If the receiving field is integer, for instance,

```
I.HOLD = 3.2*I.CNT/(D.TOTAL + TRANS)
```

the result is truncated before being placed in I.HOLD. If the number falls outside the allowable integer range, then an overflow error occurs.

Exercise

6-8. In the preceding example, what is stored in I.HOLD for the following sets of values?

a. I.CNT = 5   D.TOTAL = 5.863   TRANS = 4.137
b. I.CNT = 1   D.TOTAL = 5.863   TRANS = 4.137

System Functions

The Concept of the Function

In programming, many operations are required that are general in nature and commonly performed. These include such basic operations as calculating the square root or the trignometric sine of a number. Basic includes no specific arithmetic operators beyond the primitive ones $+$, $-$, $*$, $/$, and $**$ ($^\wedge$). Other operations must be obtained by programming means. Basic provides for combining specific sequences of primitive operations into *functions* that are easy to use. The user simply specifies one or more *arguments* of the function, the system carries out the combination of operations that defines the function, and the result is returned to the system as the *function value*. This value is then used directly in, for example, an assignment statement. More generally, a function is a procedure that returns a specific value, which need *not* be numeric. Fortunately for the user, many of the common operations are preprogrammed by the system and available to the user as *system functions*. These are also called *predefined, built-in, internal,* or *library* functions. Basic also allows users to define their own functions; these are called *user-defined functions*. Both system and user-defined functions may be either numeric or string. In this chapter, we discuss only system functions; user-defined functions are covered in Chapter 12.

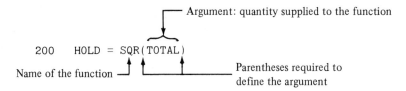

Figure 6-10   The nature of the function.

Using Functions in Expressions

To illustrate the use of functions, consider statement 200 in Figure 6-10, which calculates the square root of TOTAL and places the value in HOLD. During execution of the program, the computer will

1. Obtain the value for the argument (TOTAL in this case).
2. Give this value to a special routine named SQR (included as part of the Basic system), which will calculate the square root of TOTAL.
3. Assign the result to the variable HOLD by virtue of the assignment statement.

   It is important to recognize that, once the function is evaluated, its value is included in the evaluation of an expression as if the function name were an ordinary variable. The main difference between the role of a system function and an ordinary variable in an expression is that the program itself supplies the value of the variable, whereas the *value of the function* is computed by the system. However, as we see in the example of Figure 6-11, the program supplies the *value of the argument*.

```
                            ┌──────────┐ ⎰ Variable values
                            │          ⎱ supplied by program.
300    HOLD2 = 7.5*SQR(TOTAL)  +  INCR
                      └──────────┐ ⎰ Function value
                                 ⎱ supplied by system.
```

Figure 6-11   Using a Basic system function.

   Versatility of the function is further enhanced by the fact that the argument may be any acceptable expression. For instance, the statements in Figure 6-12 give the results indicated at the bottom of the figure.

```
400   X = 10
420   Z = 3*SQR(2*X + 16)
```
First evaluate this, giving 36.

Then take the square root, giving 6.

3*SQR

Then multiply the resulting square root (6) by 3, giving 18.

Figure 6-12   Using an expression as a function argument.

Predefined Mathematical Functions

The various mathematical functions available in VAX Basic follow:

Function Name	Value Returned by Function	Examples
ABS(X)	Absolute value of X.	ABS(-10)$=10$ ABS(10)$=10$.
SGN(X)	-1 for X $<$ 0 0 for X $=$ 0 $+1$ for X $>$ 0.	SGN(-27)$= -1$ SGN(0)$=0$ SGN(23)$= +1$
INT(X)*	Greatest integer that is less than or equal to X.	INT(23)$=23$ INT(23.7)$=23$ INT(-26.8)$= -27$
FIX(X)*	Truncated value of X.	FIX(23.7)$=23$ FIX(23)$=23$ FIX(-26.8)$= -26$
COS(X)	Cosine of X (X in radians).	
SIN(X)	Sine of X (X in radians).	
TAN(X)	Tangent of X (X in radians).	
ATN(X)	Angle (in radians) whose tangent is X.	
SQR(X)	Square root of X. If X is negative, an error condition will occur.	
EXP(X)	Value of the natural logarithm base e raised to the X power.	
LOG(X)	Natural logarithm of X.	
LOG10(X)	Logarithm to the base 10 of X.	
RND	Pseudorandom number between 0 and 1.	

* Note the difference between FIX and INT when dealing with negative numbers.

Since the argument of a mathematical function can be any arithmetic expression, it is possible to use another function as an argument. For instance,

```
200     X = SQR(ABS(Y))
```

is equivalent to

```
300     A = ABS(Y)
310     X = SQR(A)
```

It is only necessary to take care in matching opening and closing parentheses.

Exercise

6-9. A common use of the mathematical function INT is to round a value. For instance, 26.2 would round to 26 but 26.5 and 26.7 would round to 27. For positive numbers, adding 0.5, then truncating achieves the desired result. Using the appropriate mathematical functions, write a simple, one-line statement to round the positive value in the variable QUANT.

String Functions

In Chapter 5, we learned about *comparing* operations with string fields. Basic also provides programmed operations for *manipulating* strings. These are called *string functions*. String operations find many applications, including *text editing* and *word processing*. We shall see the meaning of these terms in later chapters. Note that a string function may return either a numeric value or a string; in the latter case, it is sometimes called a string-*valued* function. Thus, system *functions* themselves may be typed by an appropriate suffix, in addition to the implicit or explicit typing of their *arguments*. In general, string functions leave unchanged the string on which they operate.

Extracting Substrings

Programmers in business data processing commonly deal with Social Security numbers. For instance, a program might include the string variable SSN$ for this purpose. When the number is read into the computer and stored, it commonly consists of the nine digits without punctuation. A number such as 532242005 is adequate for internal operations in the computer, but it leaves something to be desired for printed reports. As we know, Social Security numbers are grouped by the first three, the next two, and the last four digits. In other words, the preceding number should be printed as 532-24-2005. There are four functions provided by VAX Basic to extract substrings from strings: LEFT$, MID$, RIGHT$, and SEG$. These are illustrated in Figure 6-13. Note that the second argument of LEFT$ specifies the actual *number* of characters to be extracted, whereas that of RIGHT$ specifies the starting *position* of the substring to be extracted. The MID$ function specifies the number of characters to be extracted (third argument) and the starting position of the substring (second argument). The SEG$ function provides an alternative to all three of the preceding functions. Note that, whereas the MID$ function specifies the substring's starting position and length, the SEG$ function specifies the starting and ending position.

By use of these functions, the value of SSN$ (532242005) will be printed as shown by either of the statements that follow. Note that the function may be used directly in the PRINT statement itself, yielding exactly the same output as the SSN1$, SSN2$, SSN3$ form.

```
532-24-2005

PRINT  SSN1$; "-"; SSN2$; "-"; SSN3$
PRINT  LEFT(SSN$,3); "-"; MID(SSN$,4,2); "-"; RIGHT(SSN$,6)
```

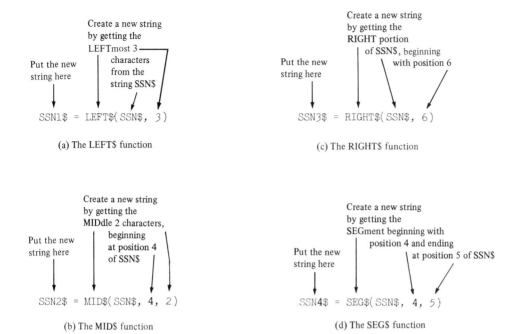

Figure 6-13   Substring functions.

Exercise

6-10. If the value stored in A$ is ABC123456, show what will be in B$
after each of the following statements:

a. B$ = LEFT$(A$,2)
b. B$ = MID$(A$,1,2)
c. B$ = MID$(A$,3,5)
d. B$ = RIGHT$(A$,7)
e. B$ = RIGHT$(A$,9)
f. B$ = MID$(A$,9,1)
g. B$ = RIGHT$(A$,12)
h. B$ = SEG$(A$,1,4)
i. B$ = SEG$(A$,3,6)
j. B$ = SEG$(A$,5,9)

The LEN Function

In many applications, it is necessary to know the length of a string. For instance, in checking Social Security numbers being entered, the string should
always have a length of 9. This is done with the LEN function, which returns
the length of a string field. Its use is illustrated by the following statement:

```
500    Y = LEN(SSN$)
```

The length (number of characters) in SSN$ will be placed in the numeric
variable Y. For instance, if SSN$ contains a valid Social Security number,

then Y will be given a value of 9. Note that LEN returns a number, not a string. The following example illustrates using the length function as part of an IF.

Example 6-1

> A program to accept and edit employee information from a keyboard is required. The Social Security number must be checked for the proper length of 9.

The program segment in Figure 6-14 accepts a Social Security number from the keyboard. If the length is not equal to 9 (see statement 520), then the WHILE loop is executed repeatedly until a value of correct length is entered.

```
500 !  SOCIAL SECURITY LENGTH CHECK
510        INPUT "SOCIAL SECURITY NUMBER"; SSN$
520        WHILE LEN(SSN$) <> 9
530          PRINT "SSN MUST BE 9 DIGITS."
540          PRINT "PLEASE REENTER IT."
550          PRINT
560          INPUT "Social security number"; SSN$
570        NEXT
         .
         .
         .
```

Figure 6-14 Length check of Social Security number.

Exercise

> **6-11.** Write a program segment to verify that a 9-character string is numeric. In other words, each character must be between 0 and 9. This segment can be used to verify that a Social Security number that has passed the length test is numeric. Use a WHILE loop to scan the string to check each character.

Concatenation of Strings

A very common operation in working with string fields is to combine two or more to form another by joining one string to the end of another. This operation, called *concatenation,* is done with an assignment statement and the operator +. (The plus sign is an example of an operator symbol that specifies two completely different operations, according to the data types on which it operates.) For instance, in the preceding section, the Social Security number was broken into three parts—SSN1$, SSN2$, and SSN3$—and then printed with inserted hyphens. Let us assume that we have a program in which the Social Security number is printed in a number of different places. In such a case, it would be convenient to build a copy of it that includes the hyphens. This is easily done by either of the following statements:

```
SSNH$ = SSN1$ + "-" + SSN2$ + "-" + SSN3$
SSNH$ = LEFT$(SSN$,3) + "-" + MID$(SSN$,4,2) + "-" + RIGHT$(SSN$,6)
```

Of course, the first example assumes that SSN1$, SSN2$, and SSN3$ have been previously extracted from SSN$. Thus, if SSN$ contained 532242005 (length of 9), the statement

```
PRINT  SSNH$
```

would print the following:

```
532-24-2005
```

Note that the string components have been tacked onto one another in the order indicated by the assignment statement. Of course, the length of the result (SSNH$ in this case) is the sum of the lengths of the components (11).

Exercises

6-12. Rewrite the expression for SSNH$ by using the SEG$ function to operate on SSN$ three times.

6-13. What will be the output of the following program?

```
1000   Q$ = "0123456789"
1010   PRINT LEN(Q$)
1020   Q$ = " AB" + "   " + "XY "
1030   PRINT LEN(Q$)
1040   Q$ = ""
1050   PRINT LEN(Q$)
32767 END
```

6-14. What are the operations produced by the operator + in the following program segment?

```
1000 DECLARE BYTE A,B,P, STRING C,D,Q
2000 P = A + B
2010 Q = C + D
```

The DATE$ and TIME$ Functions

In addition to the preceding mathematical and string functions, VAX Basic includes a wide variety of other functions. Some of these are described at appropriate places in later chapters. We shall use two of them here in order to enhance our reports.

Heading lines printed at the top of the computer-generated page tell which report is printed. In addition to the name of the report, other information should also be printed. For instance, most reports include a date, which may be the date the report was run or even some past or future date. For example, a budget status report might be printed on June 5 for all transactions through June 1. In addition to the date, it is sometimes convenient to know the time of day the report was run. For instance, was the run made at the start of the day or after the day's activities were recorded? For this need, VAX Basic includes two functions: DATE$ to give a date and TIME$ to give the time. Their use is

```
200     PRINT "SUMMARY REPORT DATED "; DATE$(0)
300     PRINT "UPDATE COMPLETED AT "; TIME$(0); DATE$(0)
```

(a)

```
SUMMARY REPORT DATED 21-FEB-84
UPDATE COMPLETED AT 11:29 AM  21-FEB-84
```

(b)

Figure 6-15 Using the DATE$ and TIME$ functions.

illustrated in Figure 6-15. Note that the argument used to obtain the current date and time is 0 for both functions. Other values of the argument provide other date and time information. The dating of program output is a common and useful practice.

Principles of Random Numbers

Random Number Generation

Many actual phenomena that cannot be solved by ordinary mathematical methods can be solved by simulation techniques. The key to simulation is the use of numbers that are selected (over a given range) to approximate the statistical properties of random numbers. The generation of such pseudorandom numbers, which will be referred to as random numbers, is done with the RND random number function. It returns a random number greater than or equal to 0 and less than 1.

Unlike most of the other functions, RND does not involve an argument (if one is included, it is ignored). The generation of 20 random numbers is illustrated by the simple program of Figure 6-16. By inspecting the results, we see that the two different runs produced exactly the same sequence. This reflects the fact that pseudorandom numbers are computed by a specific sequence of computations, generally carried out on a starting value called the *seed*. There are many different algorithms for computing pseudorandom numbers. The number returned depends on the particular algorithm used to generate it and the value of the seed. Different values are obtained for the numbers within the sequence because the random-number generator uses the most recently calculated number as the seed for the next number to be calculated. For example, the seed for .229581 in Figure 6-16 is .204935, that for .533074 is .229581, and so on. The seed for the first number, .204935 in Figure 6-16, is a system default. Hence, different runs will produce identical sequences unless the initial seed for the sequence is somehow varied.

This can be accomplished with the RANDOMIZE statement shown in Figure 6-17. This statement should be used only once in a program and must precede any reference to the RND function. As a general rule, programs using

```
LISTNH
10 !   RANDOM NUMBER DEMO
20       I% = 0
30 !   PROCESSING LOOP
40       WHILE I% < 20
50         R = RND                ! NOTE:  Statements 50 and 60 could
60         PRINT R,               !        be replaced with PRINT RND
70         I% = I% + 1
80       NEXT
32767  END


RUNNH
   .204935      .229581      .533074      .132211      .995602
   .783713      .741854      .397713      .709588      .67811
   .682372      .991239      .806084      .915352      .237358
   .185981      .979664      .204159.     .40798       .610446

Ready

RUNNH
   .204935      .229581      .533074      .132211      .995602
   .783713      .741854      .397713      .709588      .67811
   .682372      .991239      .806084      .915352      .237358
   .185981      .979664      .204159      .40798       .610446

Ready
```

Figure 6-16   Random number generation.

```
LISTNH
10 !   RANDOM NUMBER DEMO
15        RANDOMIZE
20        I% = 0
30 !   PROCESSING LOOP
40        WHILE I% < 20
50          R = RND              ! NOTE: Statement 50 and 60 could
60          PRINT R,             !       be replaced with PRINT RND
70          I% = I% + 1
80        NEXT
32767  END

Ready

RUNNH
  .457144      .7428        .342504      .369828      .13643
  .490131      .712917      .866321      .78167       .893137
  .32379       .904507      .51293       .937015      .57157E-2
  .601162      .555531      .922726      .53658       .914946

Ready

RUNNH
  .842705      .559781E-1   .751522      .532917E-2   .268276
  .561695      .955686      .678855      .471959      .72206
  .847283E-1   .983073E-2   .296429      .6901        .472736
  .625513      .498457      .361124      .68063       .83367

Ready
```

Figure 6-17   Random number generation; using the RANDOMIZE statement.

random numbers are written and tested without the RANDOMIZE statement, so that the results are predictable and the programmer can determine whether or not the program is correct. However, when the program is ready for use, a different sequence of random numbers is usually desired each time it is to be generated. Therefore, once the program is debugged, the RANDOMIZE statement is inserted.

One thing to notice about the preceding descriptions is that the generated random numbers are always between 0 and 1. However, we often want numbers in a different range, for example, between 0 and 99. This can be done by some simple arithmetic procedures; for instance, consider the following statement:

```
3010   A = INT(100*RND)
```

Since RND produces numbers equal to or greater than 0 and less than 1, 100*RND will produce numbers equal to or greater than 0 but less than 100. The INT function will then convert the resulting value to a whole number. Typical values from the preceding statement 3010 might be as follows:

RND	100*RND	INT(100*RND)
.204935	20.4935	20
.999999	99.9999	99
.0847283	8.47283	8
.0068234	0.68234	0

The form of statement 3010 can be generalized to give numbers in any desired range. For instance, if we wish random numbers between A and B, with $A < B$, we would use the following general form:

```
(B - A)*RND + A
```

If the desired numbers must be integer, then it is simply a matter of applying the INT function to this expression.

Exercise

6-15. Write a statement that assigns to a variable a random integer in the range -100 to $+100$.

Problem Definition

As a final example in this chapter, let us consider one that will not only illustrate using random numbers but will also bring together many of the concepts of preceding chapters. In particular, this example will illustrate how a programmer approaches a problem, from clarifying the needs of the user to planning the solution. To this end, let us assume that the imagination of the teacher in Example 4-1 has been stimulated to more creative uses of the computer. Requirements for the new program are defined by the following:

Example 6-2

An arithmetic drill and practice program is required that will allow a student to practice the simple addition of pairs of numbers between 0 and 99. The program is to operate as follows:

1. The student must be presented with two numbers between 0 and 99, generated at random, and asked to add them.
2. If the response is correct, the student must be informed.
3. If the response is incorrect, the student must be informed and given another chance. After three incorrect responses, the answer must be displayed.
4. The student must be asked whether the lesson should continue with another pair of numbers.
5. If the student does not wish to continue, execution must be terminated and a count of the number of drill problems and the number of correct answers must be displayed.

Designing the Solution

This is the most complex problem that we have encountered thus far; it includes a variety of features. However, it appears that it will consist of three basic components:

1. Initialize (announce the program and initialize counters).
2. Process (interact with the student with drill and practice).
3. Terminate (print a summary of results).

Let us begin by stating the logic of the process module.

Generate two numbers.

Increment the problem counter.

Interact with the student.

Ask whether to continue with another pair of numbers.

The key to this program is the third step, "Interact with the student," since it involves both decision making and looping. If the student gives the correct answer, we simply go on. However, an incorrect answer involves allowing for another attempt. One way to handle this is to set up a loop that is terminated under *two* conditions: a correct answer entered or three passes through the loop. The logic of this portion of the program then becomes

Display the two numbers.
WHILE less than three attempts and no correct answer
    Accept user response for their sum
    IF user response is correct
        THEN Take "correct" action
        ELSE Take "incorrect" action
    END IF
Endwhile

In a real programming environment in which a program is being prepared for someone else, it is imperative that the programmer work closely with the person requesting the program. With this in mind, let us assume that we have taken our evaluation of the problem to the teacher. After some discussion, we arrive at the following form of the interaction with the student:

Display the two numbers.
WHILE less than three attempts and no correct answer
  Accept user response for their sum
  IF user response is correct
    THEN Display the message to the student
        Count the correct answer
    ELSE IF answer too large
        THEN Display "Too large" error message
        ELSE Display "Too small" error message
    END IF
    IF not the third attempt
      THEN Display message to try again
      ELSE Display error message and correct answer
    END IF
  END IF
END WHILE

With the amount of testing in this module, things are beginning to become a bit complicated. Often the practice of flowcharting extensive logic of this type can help clarify it. To that end, the task that we have before us has been flowcharted in Figure 6-18. If this adds to your understanding of the program needs, then fine—use it. If not, then concentrate on the pseudocode solution.

In either case, combining this logic with the overall needs of the process module, we might arrive at the following detailed pseudocode solution.

Generate two numbers
Increment the problem counter
Set the "try" counter to 0
Set the "incorrect" indicator to true
Display the two numbers
WHILE less than three trys and "incorrect" indicator is true
  Accept user response for the sum
  IF user response is correct
    THEN Display that message to the student
        Increment the "correct" counter
        Set the "incorrect" indicator to false
    ELSE IF answer too large
        THEN Display "Too large" error message
        ELSE Display "Too small" error message
    END IF
    IF not the third try
      THEN Display message to try again
      ELSE Display error message and correct answer
    END IF
  END IF
  Ask whether or not to continue with another pair of numbers
END WHILE

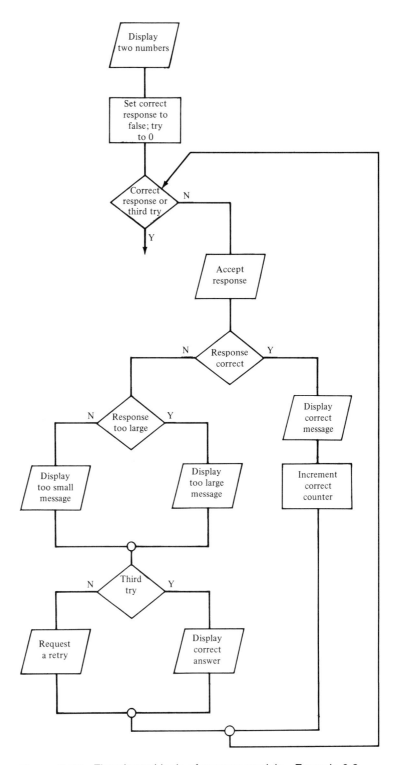

Figure 6-18 Flowcharted logic of process module—Example 6-2.

161

```
100    ! Drill and practice for arithmetic
110    !
1000   ! Main program
1010   GOSUB INITIALIZE
1020   GOSUB PROCESS WHILE CONT = 'Y' OR CONT = 'y'
1030   GOSUB TERMINATE
1040   STOP
1050   !
2000   ! Initialization routine
       INITIALIZE:
       PRINT 'Welcome to addition drill & practice.'
2020   PRINT 'You will be presented with two numbers.'
2030   PRINT 'You are to add them together and enter'
2040   PRINT 'Their sum.'
2100   DECLARE STRING CONT                                    &
            BYTE, TRY, INCORRECT, COUNT, CORRECT.COUNT
2200   INPUT 'Do you wish to try this <Enter Y or N>'; CONT
2210   COUNT = 0    ! Initialize count of drill problems
2220   CORRECT.COUNT = 0  ! Initialize count of correct answers
2230   RANDOMIZE
2240   RETURN
2300   !
3000   ! Process routine
       PROCESS:
       A = INT(100*RND)    ! Generate random number for addition
3020   B = INT(100*RND)
3030   TRY = 0    ! Initialize count of number of attempts
3040   COUNT = COUNT + 1
3050   INCORRECT = -1  ! initialize flag to allow loop entry
3060   WHILE TRY < 3 AND INCORRECT
3070     TRY = TRY - 1
3080     PRINT 'The two numbers are ';A;'and ';B
3090     INPUT 'What is their sum '; C
3100     IF C = A + B
         THEN
             INCORRECT = 0
             PRINT 'Congratulations, that is correct'
             CORRECT.COUNT = CORRECT.COUNT + 1
         ELSE
             PRINT 'Sorry, but your answer is too ';
             IF C > A + B
               THEN PRINT 'large'
               ELSE PRINT 'small'
             END IF
             IF TRY < 3
               THEN PRINT 'Please try again'
               ELSE PRINT 'The correct answer is '; A + B
             END IF
         END IF
3200     NEXT
3210     PRINT
3220     INPUT 'Do you wish to try another pair of numbers <Y/N>';CONT
3230     RETURN
       TERMINATE:
4000   PRINT 'NUMBER OF DRILL PROBLEMS  =';COUNT
4010   PRINT 'NUMBER OF CORRECT ANSWERS =';CORRECT.COUNT
4020   RETURN
32767  END
```

Figure 6-19   Program solution—Example 6-2.

162

A Program Solution—Example 6-2

One of the convenient features of developing a program solution with pseudocode is that this English form can be discussed with a nonprogrammer who requested the job. Once all of the details are ironed out, the pseudocode can be converted almost directly to corresponding computer-language statements. We can see this by inspecting the program solution of Figure 6-19. Other than a few details that were not explicitly discussed in the preceding section, we do not see any surprises in the code. One important item that is different about this program relates to the repeated execution of the process routine. In all previous programs, this routine had been executed by a statement such as

```
GOSUB PROCESS
```

Repeated execution was accomplished by a WHILE statement within that routine. However, the routine was only called once from within the main calling routine.

On the other hand, main loop control for this example is accomplished from the main calling routine by the statement

```
GOSUB PROCESS WHILE CONT = 'Y' OR CONT = 'y'
```

In this case, the GOSUB is executed repeatedly so long as the specified condition is true. Each call to the PROCESS routine causes it to be executed one time.

The question might arise, "Which approach is the best?" The answer is that it depends upon the circumstances. It might be argued that the approach

```
Do you wish to try this <Enter Y or N>? Y
The two numbers are 12 and 45
What is their sum? 57
Congratulations, that is correct
Do you wish to try another pair of numbers <Y/N>? Y
The two numbers are 7 and 6
What is their sum? 15
Sorry, but your answer is too large
Please try again
The two numbers are 7 and 6
What is their sum? 13
Congratulations, that is correct
Do you wish to try another pair of number <Y/N>? Y
The two numbers are 67 and 78
What is their sum? 133
Sorry, but your answer is too small
Please try again
The two numbers are 67 and 78
What is their sum? 143
Sorry, but your answer is too small
Please try again
The two numbers are 67 and 78
What is their sum? 155
Sorry, but your answer is too large
The correct answer is 145
Do you wish to try another pair of numbers <Y/N>? N
NUMBER OF DRILL PROBLEMS   = 3
NUMBER OF CORRECT ANSWERS  = 2
```

Figure 6-20   A user/computer dialogue for Example 6-2.

of Figure 6-19 provides us with better insight into the overall program when we can look at the main routine and see that the PROCESS routine will be executed repeatedly. In any case, whichever technique gives the simplest and most straightforward solution is usually the best.

A typical dialogue with the computer is shown on the preceding page in Figure 6-20.

In Retrospect

This chapter contains a broad range of topics and presents a seemingly endless variety of data types from which to select. With regard to integer and real, usually the simple single-word (two bytes) integers and single-precision floating point are adequate. The others would be used only if data to be processed dictated it.

The availability of standard functions greatly simplifies many of the common operations; functions described in this chapter are

Mathematical
ABS
SGN
INT
FIX
COS
SIN
TAN
ATN
SQR
EXP
LOG
LOG10
RND

String
LEFT$
MID$
RIGHT$
SEG$
LEN

Other
DATE$
TIME$

Answers to Preceding Exercises

6-1. a. 0.12×10^2
   b. 0.6×10^{-1}
   c. 0.21×10^1

After the answer is put in scientific notation, the decimal point is "floated" to put the result in standard form.

6-2. a. .75649E 05
   b. .567E − 02
   c. .29467E 01

6-3. a. DECLARE WORD PAGE.COUNT
   b. DECLARE STRING SSN
   c. DECLARE LONG SLS.TOT
   d. DECLARE SINGLE PAY.RATE

6-4. Add the two lines

```
1010   FORM1$ = "    #.#########^^^^"
1020   FORM2$ = "###" + FORM1$ + FORM1$
```

and replace the PRINT statement by

```
PRINT USING FORM2$, I, X, Y
```

6-5. Add the statement

```
1000   DECLARE WORD CNT
```

6-6. a. The different data types are represented differently in memory and handled using different operators.
   b. The different INTEGER subtypes differ in the number of bytes each occupies in memory and consequently in the range of numbers each can hold.
   c. The different REAL subtypes differ in the number of bytes each occupies in memory and in the range and precision of each.

6-7. P1 = 2; P2 = 1; P3 = 0; P4 = 3; P5 = 0

6-8. a. Evaluation of the expression gives 1.6, which is truncated to 1 in I.HOLD.
   b. Evaluation of the expression gives 0.32, which is truncated to 0 in I.HOLD.

6-9. RQUANT = INT(QUANT + 0.5)   or
   RQUANT = FIX(QUANT + 0.5)

These give the same result when dealing with positive numbers. The situation is somewhat different with negative numbers. If rounding of negative numbers is defined as adjusting to the nearest integer, then the adjustment must be −0.5. Furthermore, the FIX and INT functions do not give the same result when dealing with negative numbers.

6-10. a. AB
   b. AB
   c. C1234
   d. 456
   e. 6

      f. 6

      g. null string; A$ contains only 9 characters

      h. ABC1

      i. C123

      j. 23456

6-11.
```
600   ! Check for digits
610     I = 1
        CHECK.DIG:
          WHILE  I <= 9
            SSDIG$ = MID(SSN$,I,1)
            IF SSDIG$ < "0" OR SSDIG$ > "9"
              THEN
                PRINT 'This SSN contains non-digits'
                EXIT CHECK.DIG
            END IF
            I = I + 1
          NEXT
```

6-12.
```
SSNH$ = SEG$(SSN$,1,3) + "-" + SEG$(SSN$,4,5) + "-" +
SEG$(SSN$,6,9)
```

6-13. 10

    8

    0

The length of a string includes leading, imbedded, and trailing blanks.

6-14. 2000 : addition of two numbers

    2010 : concatenation of two strings

6-15.
```
1000  RAND.NUM = INT(200*RND) - 100
```

Programming Problems

6-1. Write a program that will allow a number of seconds to be entered from the keyboard into an integer variable. Using integer arithmetic, calculate the number of hours, minutes, and seconds. For each entry, print the input, followed by the hours, minutes, and seconds. Allow for program termination by entering -1 for the seconds. Use an appropriate prompt at the terminal and headings for output. Declare the appropriate constants for this problem.

6-2. Using integer arithmetic (and some ingenuity), it is possible to strip any desired digit from an integer quantity. Write a program that will accept an integer of up to six digits; then strip out and print each digit. For instance, the dialog might appear as follows:

```
INTEGER VALUE?   475912

DIGIT 1    4
DIGIT 2    7
DIGIT 3    5
DIGIT 4    9
DIGIT 5    1
DIGIT 6    2
```

6-3. The greatest common divisor (GCD) of two positive integers A and B is defined to be the largest positive integer that divides into *both* A and B with zero remainder. For example, the GCD of 42 and 24 is 6. Euclid's algorithm for calculating the GCD involves a sequence of divisions, continuing until the remainder is zero. The last nonzero remainder is then the GCD. Let A denote the *larger* of the two integers, Q_i the quotient at step i, and R_i the remainder at step i. The divisors and dividends at each step are conveniently described by the following schematic:

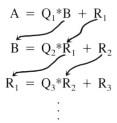

$$A = Q_1{*}B + R_1$$
$$B = Q_2{*}R_1 + R_2$$
$$R_1 = Q_3{*}R_2 + R_3$$
$$\vdots$$

When we find a remainder that is zero, then the preceding remainder is the GCD. Write a program to input two positive integers from the keyboard and find the GCD. Note that each quotient can be found with the system function INT: $Q_1 = \text{INT}(A/B)$. Furthermore, we then have $R_1 = A - B{*}\text{INT}(A/B)$, and so on. Output should include the two integers and the GCD. Terminate processing by entering a value of zero for one of the integers.

6-4. In trigonometry, the law of cosines relates the sides of a triangle and one of the angles. If A, B, and C represent the lengths of the three sides and a is the angle opposite the side A, then the law can be written as

$$A = \sqrt{B^2 + C^2 - 2BC \cos(a)}$$

Write a program that will accept B, C, and a from the keyboard (with suitable prompts) and calculate A. Output is to include the input quantities and the area, all appropriately labeled. Allow for the value of a to be entered in degrees; check to ensure that it is greater than 0 and less than 90. Declare a constant to handle the conversion from degrees to radians; 1 rad $=$ 57.29578 deg. Allow for termination of the program by entering a value of 0.

6-5. The area of a triangle can be expressed in terms of the lengths A, B, C of its sides by the formula

$$\text{Area} = \sqrt{S(S - A)(S - B)(S - C)}$$

where $S = (A + B + C)/2$. Write a program that will accept A, B and C from the keyboard and calculate the area. Output should include the lengths of the three sides and the area. Note that in order for the three lengths to represent the sides of a triangle, they must satisfy specific inequalities ($A + B > C$, and so on). The program is to test whether all the inequalities are satisfied and to print a message when they are not.

6-6. Modify problem 4-5 so that the effective yearly rate for $N = 365$ (daily conversion) is replaced by the effective yearly rate for *continuous* conversion. This means that we need the limit $N \rightarrow \infty$ of the expression given in problem 4-5 for E. Fortunately, we do not have to do this part of the calculation, as this limit is a known function. It is given by

$$E(\infty) = e^R - 1$$

where e is the base of the natural logarithm. Thus, $E(\infty)$ can be evaluated in terms of the system function EXP(R). Printed answers should be *rounded* to four decimal points. Output should also include the following heading:

EFFECTIVE–RATE TABLE PROGRAMMED BY your name ON system date

6-7. This problem illustrates use of the random-number generator for simulation. A rat sits in a square enclosure with a single door that leads to food. The door is not visibly different from the rest of the walls. Contact with any part of the wall other than the door gives the rat a mild electrical shock, enough to impress on him that this is not the way to go. To get an idea of how quickly the rat learns where the door is if he is repeatedly put into the same enclosure, we must know the probability that he would reach the door if he walked in random directions. To approximate such random behavior, we make use of random numbers and of the following diagrammatic representation of the enclosure:

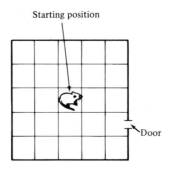

Starting position

Door

Write a program to simulate the rat's movement from square to square in the enclosure. The rat moves only one square at a time, in either of the two horizontal or two vertical directions. A random number between 0 and 4 is used to decide the direction in which the rat takes his step. Use two variables (row and column) to track his movement. Starting position is always the center square. The random walk ends when the rat reaches a square that borders one of the sides. Compute the fraction of walks on which the rat reaches the door for 100, 1000, and 10,000 walks. Print suitably labeled results.

6-8. Write a program to check that a Social Security number entered at the keyboard has nine characters and, if it does, that they are all numeric. In effect, this is a combination of the two program segments in Figure 6-14 and Exercise 6-11. Use a separate subroutine for each of the two checks. Declare all data types explicitly. Note that this problem will take some care to insure that all pieces fit properly.

6-9. Write a program to print mailing labels. Each record contains the following six fields:

Number of labels to be printed for this person.

Name (last name, a space, first name).

Social Security number.

Street address.

City and state.

ZIP (treat it as a string quantity).

Note that none of the fields includes a comma character. For instance, a sample record and the first label are illustrated here.

```
DATA   4,WATSON CARL,246813579,2467 ELM STREET,VENICE CA,97512

      246-81-3579          ←——Note:  hyphens

                           ←——        Two blank lines
      CARL WATSON          ←——        First name first
      2467 ELM STREET
      VENICE CA 97512
```

One of the program requirements is that the order of the first and last names be reversed. Note that the number of labels printed for each person will depend on the value of the first field in that record. Also, skip three lines between each label. Terminate processing upon detecting a value of zero for the number of labels.

6-10. Each record in a DATA statement contains one long string of characters (no punctuation). Write a program that will read each string, form a new string, and print the new string. Operations to be performed on the input string are as follows:

a. Eliminate all leading spaces (spaces at the front of the string).
b. Eliminate all trailing spaces (spaces at the end).

6-11. Expand problem 6-10 to perform one more operation. Reduce all multiple occurrences of a blank *within* the string to one space. For example, if two words are separated by five spaces in the DATA statement, they will be separated by only one space when printed.

7

Sequential Files and Error Handling

Preview

One of the most important topics in all of programming is that of files. Everything stored on disk storage is stored as a file. (In simple terms, a file is defined as a set of related records.) This means, technically speaking, that each Basic program stored in an account is a file. In any timesharing system, a wide variety of types of files will be stored. For instance, a given user might have Basic program files, Fortran program files, special system files, data files, and so on. From this chapter you will learn the following concepts relating to disk files and their processing:

1. The nature of terminal-format files, in which information is stored in much the same manner as that entered from the keyboard.

171

2. *The concept of preparing a file (which is not part of the program) for use by the program. This is called* **opening the file.** *Existing files containing data to be processed can be opened, and new files can be created (opened) to which output can be written.*

3. *The INPUT# statement, which is similar to the INPUT statement. It allows information to be read from a file and placed in listed variables.*

4. *The PRINT# statement, which is similar to the PRINT statement. It allows information to be written to a file.*

5. *The nature of the ON ERROR statement, which provides the basis for error handling. Errors result from actions such as division by zero and detection of the end of a data file. A variety of techniques for handling errors is illustrated.*

Fundamental Concepts of Files

VAX Basic supports several types of files. On a broad basis, they can be placed into two categories: *sequential* and *random*. In working with files, it is important to distinguish between file *organization* and file *access*. File organization has to do with the method by which the data quantities are stored on the physical medium (magnetic tape or disk). File access relates to the way in which the data quantities stored in a disk file are read (and processed). It is important to understand that file access is related to file organization. As we shall learn in later chapters, it is not possible to use all of the different access methods on all of the different file organizations.

In this chapter, our focus will be on processing data from sequential files. The first type of file we will learn about is a particular sequential type, called a *terminal-format* file. Reading data from files of this type is almost identical to accepting input from the keyboard; hence the name terminal format. Technically, terminal-format files are sequential files made up of variable-length records; that is, different records in the file may have different lengths. We shall learn more about this point, as well as organization and access methods, in Chapter 13.

The Nature of Sequential Files

In a sequentially *organized* file, the records are stored in the sequence in which they were written. That is, the first one entered into the file becomes the first physical record in the file, the second entered becomes the second in the file and so on. Furthermore, there is no special indication of where any given record has been stored. Although this might appear to be the only way to store records in a file, it is not, as we shall learn in Chapter 13.

Generally speaking, such a file can only be *accessed* (that is, records read from the file) sequentially. In other words, prior to processing the twenty-fifth record, the twenty-four records preceding it must be read. As a general rule, sequential files are processed by beginning with the first record and proceeding, record by record, until the entire file has been processed.

The Filename, Extension, and Version

In VAX Basic, files are identified by a filename, an extension (also called type), and a version. They must conform to the following restrictions:

Filenames can be up to nine letters or digits.

Extensions can be up to three letters or digits.

A period is used to separate the filename and extension.

Versions are decimal numbers assigned by the system.

Either a semicolon or a period is used to separate extension and version.

If we refer to the directory listing for Figure 2-13 (repeated here as Figure 7-1), we see that Basic programs have the extension BAS (for example, CUBE.BAS and MEAN.BAS). When the NEW and OLD commands are used, the Basic system automatically adds on the .BAS to the designated filename. For all other files, the user must specify the filename *and* the extension. For standardization, certain types of files have predetermined extensions (for example, Basic programs use BAS). Otherwise, selection of the extension is up to the user; for instance,

INVEN.DAT;1 A data file for an inventory control system.
STOCK.OUT;3 A report output file for a stock market summary program.

As we learned in Chapter 2, in many situations it is not necessary to provide the entire file specification. For example, when one is dealing with a program that has been automatically assigned the .BAS extension, only the filename need be specified, and the system supplies the default values of the extension and version.

```
$DIR

Directory HSC001$DUA17:[BUCK]

CUBE.BAS;1      PROB3.BAS;1      SALE.BAS;1      MEAN.BAS;

Total of 4 files.

Ready
```

Figure 7-1   A directory listing of files on the disk.

Exercise

7-1. Indicate which of the following would be invalid for use as a file identification and give the reason.

a. A3.BAS
b. A3.BASIC
c. CAMOUFLAGE.A4
d. WAREHOUSE.3
e. CAM.1.2
f. 8;RUN

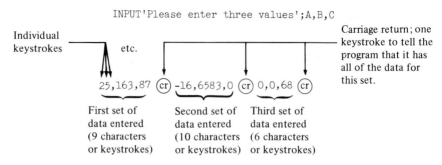

Figure 7-2 Information entered from the terminal.

About the Information Stored in a File

To understand how information is stored in a terminal-format file, let us refresh our memories regarding what actually takes place when we enter data from the keyboard. Figure 7-2 illustrates a sequence of values entered from the keyboard in response to the repeated execution of an INPUT statement. Here we see that each set of values consists of three numbers. Individual numbers are separated from one another by a comma. Sets of three numbers are "separated" by the carriage-return operation. Note that each set must consist of three numbers; this is required by the INPUT statement because it contains the names of three variables in its list.

Interestingly, the form of Figure 7-2 is almost identical to the form that each data record takes when stored on disk as a terminal-format file. A number of features of this type of file are illustrated in Figure 7-3. Note that within the file the separate sets of values are separated by a special code, commonly called an *end-of-line* code. (We shall learn in Chapter 11 that this code actually represents two special characters: the *carriage return* and the *line feed*.) Each set of values is commonly called a *line* or a *record*. Individual values that make up the record are called *fields*. The end of the entire file is marked by still another code called the *end-of-file*, or *eof*.

In a normal processing environment, each record must consist of the same number of fields. For instance, if records from this file are read by an INPUT statement similar to that in Figure 7-2 (which includes three variables in the list), then each record must consist of three fields.

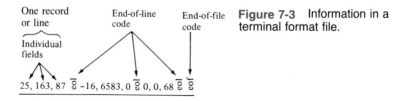

Figure 7-3 Information in a terminal format file.

Exercise

7-2. How can we inspect the contents of a file stored on disk?

A File-Processing Example

Many example programs in the remainder of this book will use input data files and will write the results to output files. Such output files can then be printed on a printer. To illustrate file processing, let us consider the following variation of Example 3-1:

Example 7-1

> The inventory control program of Example 3-1 is to be modified to process data stored in an input file named INVEN.DAT. Each record of this file contains the tool type, old inventory, units received, units shipped, and units lost. Following the last data record is the trailer with EOF in place of the tool type. A new file named INVEN.OUT is to be created and all calculated results written to this file.

A complete program to perform these operations using input and output files is shown in Figure 7-4. Let us consider each of the new statements introduced in this program.

Preparing a File for Use

The OPEN Statement

Because files are separately stored and are completely independent of the program, each program must designate which file is to be used. This action is called *opening* the file. It is carried out by the OPEN statement, which names the file to be processed and opens a channel of communication between the program and the data file. Each file to be processed in a program must include its own OPEN statement. The OPENs from the program of Figure 7-4 are illustrated in Figure 7-5. As we shall learn in later descriptions, the OPEN statement allows several options.

Opening for Input. The designation FOR INPUT tells the system to search the directory for an existing file. Note that, contrary to the implied connotation, the FOR INPUT clause does *not* specify how the program can *use* the file. If the named file is not found, then an error occurs and the program is terminated. Thus, we should take care to ensure that the filename is spelled correctly. Line 2004 of Figure 7-4 designates the input data file INVEN.DAT as the input file in this example.

Opening for Output. Most timesharing computer systems include a high-speed printer for printing program results (output). Although it is possible to set up a system to allow printing directly to the printer, that is not usually done. The reason relates simply to efficiency: The printer must serve many users. As a result, most programs create a new file (an *output* file), then write all program output to that file. Other capabilities are normally provided for automatically sending completed output files to the printer for fast and efficient printing.

```
100   !      EXAMPLE 7-1
110   !      PROGRAM TO UPDATE AN INVENTORY
120   !      INPUT VARIABLE NAMES ARE:
130   !        TOOL.NUM  --   TOOL NUMBER
140   !        TOOL.TYPE$  --   TOOL TYPE
150   !        OLD.INV   --   OLD INVENTORY
160   !        MANUFCT   --   UNITS MANUFACTURED
170   !        SHIPD     --   UNITS SHIPPED
180   !        LOST      --   UNITS LOST OR DAMAGED
190   !      CALCULATED VARIABLE NAMES ARE:
200   !        NEW.INV   --   UPDATED INVENTORY
210   !        C         --   LINE COUNT
220   !
1000  !   MAIN PROGRAM
1010      GOSUB 2000
1020        !   PRINT HEADINGS
1030        !
1040      GOSUB 3000 UNTIL TOOL TYPE$="EOF"
1050        !   REPEATEDLY PROCESS UNTIL NO MORE DATA
1060        !
1070      GOSUB 4000
1080        !   PERFORM TERMINATION OPERATIONS
1090        !
1100      STOP
1110        ! TERMINATE PROCESSING
1120        !
1130  !   END OF MAIN PROGRAM
1140  !
1150  !
2000  !   INITIALIZATION ROUTINE
2004      OPEN "INVEN.DAT" FOR INPUT AS FILE #1
2005      OPEN "INVEN.OUT" FOR OUTPUT AS FILE #2
2006        ! OPEN FILES
2008      PRINT "INVENTORY PROCESSING BEGUN"
2010      PRINT #2, "LINE", "TOOL", "TOOL", "OLD", "UPDATED"
2020      PRINT #2, "NUMBER", "TYPE", "NUMBER", "INVENTORY", "INVENTORY"
2030      PRINT #2
2040      INPUT #1, TOOL.NUM, TOOL.TYPE$, OLD.INV, NEW.INV, MANUFCT, SHIPD, LOST
2050  !   END OF INITIALIZATION ROUTINE
2060  !
3000  !   PROCESSING ROUTINE
3010      NEW.INV = OLD.INV + MANUFCT - SHIPD - LOST
3020      C = C + 1
3030      PRINT #2, C, TOOL.NUM, TOOL.TYPE$, OLD.INV, NEW.INV
3040      INPUT #1, TOOL.NUM, TOOL.TYPE$, OLD.INV, MANUFCT, SHIPD, LOST
3050      RETURN
3060  !   END OF PROCESSING ROUTINE
3070  !
4000  !   TERMINATION ROUTINE
4010      PRINT #2
4020      PRINT #2
4030      PRINT #2, "PROCESSING COMPLETE"
4032      CLOSE #1,#2
4033        ! CLOSE FILES
4038      PRINT "INVENTORY PROCESSING COMPLETE"
4040      RETURN
4050  !   END OF TERMINATION ROUTINE
4060  !
32767  END
```

Figure 7-4   Program for Example 7-1

```
2004    OPEN    "INVEN.DAT"    FOR INPUT     AS FILE #1
```

Figure 7-5 The OPEN
statement.

```
2005    OPEN    "INVEN.OUT"    FOR OUTPUT    AS FILE #2
```

The OPEN statement of line 2005 in Figure 7-4 (and 7-5) includes the option

```
FOR OUTPUT
```

When this statement is executed, the processor checks if a file by that name exists. If one does not exist, then it is created. Now what happens if there is already a file on the disk by that name? The answer to this involves a very convenient feature of VAX Basic. Rather than destroying the old one or simply terminating with an error message, it uses a version-numbering scheme. That is, if the output file opened in line 2005 (INVEN.OUT) did not exist prior to running the program, then one would be created as INVEN.OUT, version 1, or, in VMS notation, INVEN.OUT;1.

However, if version 1 already existed on disk, then the newly created file would be version 2, or INVEN.OUT;2. Note that when creating an output file, the system will always use a version number one higher than the last one on the disk. In any case, the newly created file will be empty, since nothing will yet have been written to it.

Opening Without Input or Output. Although minimal use will be made of it in this book, it is possible to open a file using the following form.

```
200   OPEN "ABC.XYZ" AS FILE #2
```

This form, without FOR INPUT or FOR OUTPUT, causes the system to search for an existing data file (ABC.XYZ in this case). If found, it will be opened. If no file ABC.XYZ exists, then one will be created.

Exercise

7-3. A program is to open a file TEST.DAT to serve as the input data file. A lazy programmer does an OPEN without the FOR INPUT option, assuming that the program, upon finding the file, will open it for input regardless. What is the flaw in this thinking?

Designating a Channel

Another thing that the OPEN statement does is to establish a channel of communication between the program and the data file. The data filename refers to a data file that is *external* to the program. That is, each file is a separate, independent entity that has meaning to the operating system but not to the program. On the other hand, the *channel number* (also called the *filenumber*) is the means by which the file is referenced *within* the program. Thus, the channel number is called an *internal* reference, whereas the filename is an *external* reference. The OPEN statement ties the internal channel number to the external name. The AS FILE portion of the OPEN (see Figure 7-5) defines this internal channel. The channel specification provides the means for letting the system know that the input will be coming from a source that is external to the program. Thus, in Figure 7-4 INVEN.DAT is associated with channel 1, and INVEN.OUT is associated with channel 2. VAX Basic allows the use of 99 channels numbered 1 through 99. Thus, the OPEN statements could as well have been

```
2004  OPEN "INVEN.DAT" FOR INPUT AS FILE #9
2005  OPEN "INVEN.OUT" FOR OUTPUT AS FILE #27
```

The channel number defined in the OPEN must be used for all program references to the designated file.

If a file is opened on a channel already associated with an open file, the open file will be closed and a new one will be opened.

Exercise

7-4. Write an OPEN statement for a terminal-format file named WAREHOUSE.DAT on channel 3 for each of the following cases:

a. The file does not exist, and output is to be written to it.
b. The file exists, and data values are to be read from it.

File Input and Output

The INPUT# Statement

We have by now learned three different ways in which variables can receive values. In two of these, the assignment and READ statements, the variables get their values from inside the program. The third, the plain INPUT statement, involves interactive input from the keyboard. The INPUT# statement, which we have used in the program of Figure 7-4, is another form of the INPUT; it involves input from a file stored on disk. Although INPUT# uses the same reserved word as INPUT, there is an important difference between them. Whereas INPUT causes the computer to stop and wait for the user to enter data and strike the Return, INPUT# gets data from the file without user intervention. Each time INPUT# is executed, the next set of values is brought into the program and assigned to the listed variables in the sequence in which they appear in the list. The number and types (for example, string and integer) of the variables in the list must correspond exactly to the number and types of fields in the record.

In order for the system to know which file is to be accessed (a program may have one or more input files open), the corresponding channel number must be specified. A detailed explanation of the INPUT# is shown in Figure 7-6.

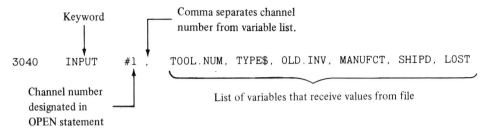

Figure 7-6 The INPUT# statement.

The PRINT# Statement

When writing to a file, exactly the same information is required as for INPUT#. Thus, the keyword PRINT# is followed by the channel-number information and then the list of variables. Following is the PRINT# statement from the program of Figure 7-4.

```
3030  PRINT #2, C, TOOL.NUM, TYPE$, OLD.INV, NEW.INV
```

Each time the PRINT# statement is executed, a new line will be written to the end of the output file whose specified channel number was assigned in the OPEN statement. Any output list allowed with the PRINT statement can be used with the PRINT# form of the statement. Because each record (line) is stored on the file exactly as it would have appeared if it had been printed on the terminal, the output will appear as if it had been written directly to the terminal. For instance,

```
1200 PRINT "RADIUS:", R, "VOLUME:", V
```

will cause the output to be displayed on the terminal. The form

```
1200 PRINT #9, "RADIUS:", R, "VOLUME:",V
```

will cause the exact same line of output to be written to the file associated with channel 9.

A word of caution is appropriate here. Special procedures must be followed in printing to a file if that file is to be used later as an input file with a program. We shall learn more about this in Chapter 13.

Exercises

7-5. Following is the skeleton of a program prepared by a student.

```
100   !   MAIN PROGRAM
110          GOSUB 1000
120          GOSUB 2000 WHILE A<>0
130          GOSUB 3000
140          STOP
1000  !   INITIAL ROUTINE
1010         OPEN "TEST.DAT" FOR INPUT AS FILE #2
1020         OPEN "TEST.OUT" FOR OUTPUT AS FILE #3
1030         INPUT #2, A,B
1040         RETURN
2000  !   PROCESSING ROUTINE
2010         C = 2*A + 2*B
2020         D = A*B
2030         PRINT #2, A,B,C,D
2040         INPUT #2, A,B
2050         RETURN
3000  !   TERMINATION ROUTINE
3010         CLOSE #2,#3
3020         RETURN
32767  END
```

The results of running the program were very strange—the file
TEST.OUT did not contain anything. What is wrong with the
program?

7-6. Find the error in the following program and correct it:

```
1000  OPEN STUD.DAT FOR INPUT AS FILE #2
1010  OPEN STUD.OUT FOR OUTPUT AS FILE #2
2000  INPUT #2 STUD.NAME$, STUD.SSN$
2010  PRINT #2 STUD.NAME$, STUD.SSN$
32767 END
```

Closing a File

All files that are opened in a program, both input and output, should be closed
before terminating execution of the program. If an output file is left open at
the end of a program, then part of the output will probably be lost. On one
hand, each OPEN statement must specify the external file name, the channel
number, and normally INPUT or OUTPUT. Furthermore, each OPEN can be
used to open only one file. On the other hand, the CLOSE must designate only
the channel number and can be used to close one or more files. In other words,
the following statement 800 is equivalent to 900 and 910:

```
800   CLOSE #1, #2

900   CLOSE #1
910   CLOSE #2
```

Actually, there is one other way to cause files to be closed: by execution of the END statement. If the END statement is executed in a program, then it causes the system to close all open files before terminating execution of the program. This is in contrast to the STOP statement, which does *not* close files. Although the technique for closing files and terminating execution by sending control of the program to the END statement is not uncommon, it is better practice to close all files explicitly with the CLOSE statement.

Opening Devices as Files

The practice of writing output to a file and then sending that file to a printer is a clumsy procedure at best. However, this is not the only way of handling printed output. For instance, if the computer system includes a separate printer that is directly available to the program, then you can output directly to the printer. This is done by first *allocating* it and then using the allocated name in the OPEN statement. For example, let us assume that LP: is the *device name* that designates the line printer and KB: is the one that designates the keyboard. Then we assign those devices for our program use before starting file operations by the *commands* (recognize that they are commands, *not* statements)

```
$ ALLOCATE LP:
$ ALLOCATE KB:
```

Note that this operation is done at the operating-system level, not the program level. We should also notice that device names include the colon character. You can then refer to these device names in the appropriate Basic statements. A simple program to calculate and print the perimeter of rectangles for lengths and widths entered at the terminal is shown in Figure 7-7. The terminal and printer are opened in statements 200 and 210 respectively.

```
100 !  USING THE KEYBOARD AND
110 !  LINE PRINTER AS FILES
200       OPEN "KB:" AS FILE #1
210       OPEN "LP:" AS FILE #2
220 !  PROCESSING LOOP
225      WHILE -1
230        INPUT #1, "ENTER LENGTH & WIDTH:  "; L, W
240        P = 2*L + 2*W
250        PRINT #2, L, W, P
260      NEXT
32767  END
```

Figure 7-7   Using device names.

Exercise

7-7. The program of Figure 7-7 does not provide for terminating the loop. This is a very bad feature, which should always be avoided. Rewrite this program to provide for terminating the loop by suitable input from the keyboard.

The GOTO Statement

Thus far, all of our programming has revolved around the three constructs of structured programming (Figure 3-6). It has been the powerful block structures of VAX Basic that have allowed us to do this. Actually, many of the commonly used versions of Basic do not include these structures and consequently must rely on a statement that sends execution from one point to another in a program. It is called the GOTO statement. It shares with GOSUB the feature that it transfers control, but it differs from GOSUB fundamentally in that there is no return associated with it, as there is with GOSUB. Because of this difference, GOSUB is an acceptable construct in structured programming, and GOTO is not. However, there are times when it is necessary to supplement the structured capabilities of VAX Basic with a GOTO.

To illustrate how it is commonly used, let us consider a simple example of how we would write a Basic program using a Basic that does not have all the features of VAX Basic. For instance, let us assume that our Basic does not include either the WHILE statement or the block structure that represents the backbone of our studies. Then a simple program to process a set of inventory values might appear as shown in Figure 7-8. Note that the looping function is controlled by a GOTO on line 140 that sends execution back to the first statement of the program. Termination is accomplished by a GOTO on line 110 that is executed only if the trailer record is sensed. It is this loop-termination role of the GOTO that was replaced by the EXIT statement in structured programs. Although the two statements serve identical functions *in this case*, they nonetheless differ fundamentally. EXIT can provide transfer of control only under *specific* conditions to a *specific* location. GOTO can be used to transfer control under *any* conditions to *any* location. Programs using an excessive numbers of GOTOs are usually confusing, difficult to debug, and even worse to modify. The block structure and other features allow us to dispense with the GOTO almost completely.

Our primary use of the GOTO will relate to error handling, where it is essential in version V3 of VMS. Programmers should attempt to limit the use of this statement to situations such as those illustrated in this book. Its overuse can create real problems.

```
100    READ TOOL.NUM, TOOL.TYPE$, OLD.INV, MANUFCT, SHIPD, LOST
110    IF TOOL.TYPE$ = "EOF"   THEN GOTO 150
120    NEW.INV = OLD.INV + MANUFCT - SHIPD - LOST
140    PRINT TOOL.NUM, TOOL.TYPE$, OLD.INV, NEW.INV
140    GOTO   100
150    PRINT "Processing complete"
160    DATA 12591, "Wrench", 680, 221, 419, 3
170    DATA 13311, "Hammer", 512,   0, 186, 4
180    DATA 15118, "File",    82, 500, 160, 1
190    DATA 16881, "Pliers",   0, 201,   0, 0
200    DATA 99999, "EOF",      0,   0,   0, 0
32767  END
```

Figure 7-8   Using the GOTO statement in a program.

Error-Handling Capabilities

About Errors

Without a doubt, the reader has encountered numerous error messages by this time. Overall, errors can be placed in three broad categories: *syntax* errors, *logic* errors (which we learned about in an earlier chapter), and *run-time* errors. Syntax errors are the result of not following the rules for writing program statements (note that this is a broader interpretation than that made in the VAX manuals). A typical error of this type may involve improper use of an ELSE clause in an IF statement, in which case the monitor displays

```
ELSIMPCON
```

These errors are normally detected when the program is first entered. When a line is entered, the system scans it. If an error is detected, the programmer must reenter the corrected version of the line.

By contrast, run-time errors normally occur because the program tells the computer to do something that cannot be done. For example, a program might say to READ from the DATA pool after the last value has already been read or to divide A by B when B is zero (division by zero). Typical messages of this type are

```
OUTOF_DAT
DIVBY_ZER
```

Appendix VI is a summary of selected run-time error messages and their meanings. Some of these errors cause termination of execution (*unrecoverable* errors), while others allow the programmer to include code to detect and recover from these errors (*recoverable* errors).

The section of code that handles the response to an error is called an *error handler*. A user-written error handler may allow the program to keep running. When a user-written error handler takes control to avoid the system's normal response to an error, the error is said to *trap*. If such an error handler is not part of the program, the Basic error handler usually terminates execution.

The ON ERROR Statement

Transfer to a user-written error handler is accomplished by use of the ON ERROR statement, the general form of which is

ON ERROR GOTO *line number or label*

Execution of this statement must precede the lines on which errors are expected to occur; in essence, it says to the system: If an error occurs at any point in the program after execution of ON ERROR statement, then execution should GOTO the specified line number or label reference. In effect, this amounts to a "delayed GOTO"—one that is executed *only* if an error occurs. Presumably, the statement to which control is transferred is the first statement of the error

```
100   READ TOOL.NUM, TOOL.TYPE$, OLD.INV, MANUFCT, SHIPD, LOST
120   NEW.INV = OLD.INV + MANUFCT - SHIPD - LOST
130   PRINT TOOL.NUM, TOOL.TYPE$, OLD.INV, NEW.INV
140   GOTO  100
150   PRINT "Processing complete"
160   DATA 12591, "Wrench", 680, 221, 419, 3
170   DATA 13311, "Hammer", 512,   0, 186, 4
180   DATA 15118, "File",    82, 500, 160, 1
190   DATA 16881, "Pliers",   0, 201,   0, 0
200   DATA 99999, "EOF",      0,   0,   0, 0
32767  END
```

Figure 7-9 A program with an infinite loop.

handler. (If the line number is 0, however, error trapping is disabled, and control is transferred back to the Basic error handler.)

For a very simple illustration of using the ON ERROR statement, let us consider the problem of what happens if the IF statement is removed from the program of Figure 7-8 (see Figure 7-9). In theory, the loop will be repeated indefinitely, since nothing in the program indicates that the program is to stop. A loop such as this is called an *infinite loop*. However, we do know that after the last set of data is read, executing the READ at line 100 will cause an error to occur, and the program will immediately be terminated by the system. As a consequence, the PRINT statement at line 150 will not be executed.

On the other hand, the program shown in Figure 7-10 includes an ON ERROR statement. Here we are telling the system what to do in the event that

```
50    ON ERROR GOTO 150
100   READ TOOL.NUM, TOOL.TYPE$, OLD.INV, MANUFCT, SHIPD, LOST
120   NEW.INV = OLD.INV + MANUFCT - SHIPD - LOST
130   PRINT TOOL.NUM, TOOL.TYPE$, OLD.INV, NEW.INV
140   GOTO  100
150   PRINT "Processing complete"
160   DATA 12591, "Wrench", 680, 221, 419, 3
170   DATA 13311, "Hammer", 512,   0, 186, 4
180   DATA 15118, "File",    82, 500, 160, 1
190   DATA 16881, "Pliers",   0, 201,   0, 0
200   DATA 99999, "EOF",      0,   0,   0, 0
32767 END
```

Figure 7-10 Using the ON ERROR statement.

an error occurs. We are basically saying, "If an error occurs, do not cancel this program but rather transfer control to statement 150." We now no longer have an infinite loop. When the attempt to read beyond the available data triggers an error, execution will now automatically transfer to statement 150.

We see that the function of the GOTO in the ON ERROR statement is similar to that of EXIT in loop termination: transfer of control to a *specific* location when a particular condition occurs.

Exercises

7-8. The use of GOTO on line 50 of the program in Figure 7-10 is essential for error trapping. However, using a GOTO at line 140 is *not* necessary. Rewrite this program so that looping is controlled without the GOTO.

7-9. The program given here is to print the message "Processing Complete" when the program reads past the end of file. However, the message does not print. Explain.

```
100  OPEN 'INVEN.DAT' FOR INPUT AS FILE #1
110  INPUT #1, TOOL.NUM, TYPE$, OLD.INV
120  PRINT TOOL.NUM, TYPE$, OLD.INV
130  GOTO 110
140  ON ERROR GOTO 150
150  PRINT 'Processing Complete'
32767  END
```

Automatic End-of-File Detection

The program of Figure 7-10 uses the fact that an error results when an attempt is made to read past the end of the data pool. Virtually the same technique can be used with a data file. Whenever a sequential file is created, the system marks the end with a special end-of-file (EOF) code. If the program attempts to read data and encounters this EOF, then an error occurs. Referring to Figure 7-11, we see that the file version of the program of Figure 7-10 takes on the same form as that for the READ–DATA version.

```
20    OPEN 'INVEN.DAT' FOR INPUT AS FILE #1
50    ON ERROR GOTO 150
100   INPUT #1, TOOL.NUM, TOOL.TYPE$, OLD.INV, MANUFCT, SHIPD, LOST
120   NEW.INV = OLD.INV + MANUFCT - SHIPD - LOST
130   PRINT TOOL.NUM, TOOL.TYPE$, OLD.INV, NEW.INV
140   GOTO  100
150   PRINT 'Processing complete'
32767 END
```

Figure 7-11   End of file detection.

These two examples illustrate a very simple use of the ON ERROR: a case in which program execution is terminated. More often, the GOTO statement begins some type of error-recovery routine. Once corrective action has taken place, then execution of the main program commonly continues. This is achieved with the RESUME statement.

The RESUME Statement

The RESUME statement, which is used in conjunction with the ON ERROR, is similar to the RETURN statement. Remember that the RETURN transfers control of the program back to the statement immediately following the corresponding GOSUB. Similarly, the RESUME returns control to a specified point in the program after an error transfer has occurred. Unfortunately, situations in which the ON ERROR and RESUME are most useful are far too complex to use for illustrating how the RESUME works. In the interest of keeping this description simple, the following example is somewhat contrived. In considering it, recognize that a simple IF test could be made prior to the calculation to achieve the same result. Focus on how the RESUME is used here, not on the fact that the task could be done more simply without the ON ERROR and RESUME.

Example 7-2

A program includes several different instances in which an expression is divided by the variable CALC. Unfortunately, the value of CALC might be zero in some cases. An error-recovery routine is required that will handle each division by zero condition as follows:

1. Set the value of CALC to 1.
2. Increment the value of ERRORCOUNT by 1.
3. Resume processing.

An error-recovery routine is shown in Figure 7-12(a). Regardless of which statement is in error, 320 or 560, control will be transferred to the error-recovery routine beginning on line 1000 if division by 0 occurs. As with the RETURN, the system remembers the statement that caused the error branch.

```
100   ON ERROR GOTO 1000
  .
  .
  .
320   HOLD = (A + B)/ CALC
  .
  .
  .
560   AMOUNT = 1/CALC
  .
  .
  .
1000 ! Error recovery routine
1010   ERRORCOUNT = ERRORCOUNT + 1
1020   CALC = 1
1030   RESUME

      (a)
```

Figure 7-12 An error recovery routine—Example 7-2.

```
310   INPUT CALC \ HOLD = (A + B)/CALC
  .
  .           Resumes at first statement of this line
  .           (relates to line number)
  .
1030  RESUME

      (b)
```

Hence, when the RESUME statement at line 1030 is executed, control continues at the statement that was in error.

If the error-causing statement is one of a multiple-statement line, then control is returned to the *first* statement following the line number (or statement label). This is illustrated in Figure 7-12(b). Use caution in situations such as this to ensure that the recovery routine does what you want it to do.

As another illustration, let us assume that we have a program that asks the user the name of the data file to be opened. Upon entering the desired filename and extension, the program opens the file and proceeds with processing. However, what occurs if the file to be processed is PAYROL.DTA and the user keys in PAYROL.DAT (which does not exist)? The answer is that error number 5 occurs; the terminal displays the following message (''cannot find file''):

```
CANFINFIL
```

Execution then terminates. The user must rerun the program and key in the correct name this time. Let us consider an error routine to handle this problem.

Example 7-3

An error-recovery routine is required to respond to a filename of a file that does not exist. The user is to be given an error message and asked to reenter the name.

Through use of an ON ERROR and corresponding RESUME, the user is ''given another chance'' in the program segment of Figure 7-13. Here we see the error

```
400    ON ERROR GOTO 900
410    INPUT "What is the filename & ext of the data file";F$
430    OPEN F$ FOR INPUT AS FILE #1
  .
  .

  .
900 ! FILE OPEN ERROR TRAP
910      PRINT "Could not open file";F$
920      INPUT "Filename & extension";F$
940      RESUME
950 ! END OF FILE OPEN TRAP
```

Figure 7-13 An error recovery routine—Example 7-3.

''switch'' set at line 400. The filename of a nonexistent file causes an error at line 430, which in turn executes a GOTO statement 900. Upon execution of that sequence, the RESUME statement causes a return to the statement that caused the error. In general, every error-checking routine *must* contain a RESUME, since any detected error effectively disables the ON ERROR capabilities until the RESUME is executed. (An exception to the requirement for RESUME involves subprograms, the subject of Chapter 11.) To illustrate the effect of not using a RESUME, let us assume that line 940 is replaced with the following:

```
940    GOTO 430
```

If a nonexistent file name is entered, then execution will be transferred to the recovery routine at line 900 (as designated by the ON-ERROR statement). At this point, the ON ERROR is effectively disabled by virtue of the error at line 430. Now if another nonexistent file name is entered, then another OPEN failure would occur when line 430 is executed for the second time. However, because a RESUME was not executed, this error will be treated as if statement 400 did not even exist, and execution will be terminated.

The second form of the RESUME involves the use of a statement number for the return. In many instances, the programmer wishes to resume at some statement other than the one that caused the error. To illustrate this, let us consider a situation in which a file is to be opened for output. For this operation, we must remember that if a file with the selected name already exists, the open-for-output creates a new version of that file. This may not be what is wanted. To illustrate further the use of error-recovery routines, let us consider the following example:

Example 7-4

A routine is required that will allow the user to enter the name of a file to be created. If there is already a file by that name, the user is to be warned.

From past programs, we know how to perform a variety of tests within a program. However, how can we tell from a program whether or not a particular file exists on disk? A relatively simple approach is to attempt to open the file for input. If an open failure occurs, then a file of the name entered does not exist. However, if there is no error upon attempting to open, that means that the file has been opened and that it indeed exists. This technique is illustrated in the program segment of Figure 7-14. Here we see that the RESUME statement includes a statement number. Furthermore, note that the RESUME must not be executed if no error occurred. (If you do a RESUME *without* an error having occurred, you *generate* an error.) This is a rather subtle program. To get its full impact, it is helpful to step through it for various possibilities. This is left as an exercise.

```
500    ON ERROR GOTO 600
510    LOOP = -1
       ASK!
         WHILE LOOP
520        INPUT "Filename & extension for the output file"; F$
530        OPEN F$ FOR INPUT AS FILE #3
540        CLOSE #3
550        PRINT "File "; F$; "already exists"
560        INPUT "Do you wish to open another version for output <Y or N>"; Q$
570        LOOP = 0 IF LEFT$(Q$,1) = "Y" OR LEFT$(Q$,1) = "y"
580      NEXT
600  ! Error recovery branch-to point
610    IF LOOP THEN RESUME 620
620    OPEN F$ FOR OUTPUT AS FILE #3
630    ON ERROR GOTO 0      ! Disable further error trapping
```

Figure 7-14   An error recovery routine—Example 7-4.

This example also illustrates disabling the error-trapping capability by the statement at line 630. This prevents subsequent errors from trapping to statement 600 (in this example) and will return error handling to the system as if statement 500 never existed.

Exercises

7-10. Modify the program segment of Figure 7-13 so that the error trap still responds properly to a reference to a nonexistent file, but with statement 920 eliminated.

7-11. List the line numbers in sequence, starting with 520, of the statements executed when the program of Figure 7-14 is run for each of the following three scenarios. For each line number, indicate what happens when the statement executes.

a. Filename ABC is entered at line 520. It exists, and you want to open another version for output.
b. Filename XYZ is entered at line 520. It does not exist.
c. Filename ABC is entered at line 520. It exists, but you do not want to open another version of an existing file for output. Rather, you want to open XYZ, which does not exist, for output.

The ERR and ERL Variables

The preceding examples illustrate a variety of techniques for performing error checks. However, one very important facet of the problem has been overlooked: the fact that different actions may be required for different errors. Furthermore, the action for a given error might be one thing if the error occurred in one part of the program and something else if it appeared in a different part of the program. In other words, the action taken in an error routine might depend on the type of error that occurred *and* the line at which it happened. VAX Basic includes two keyword variables, ERR and ERL, that provide this information. When an error occurs, ERR is loaded with the error number, and ERL is loaded with the statement number of the offending statement.

To illustrate this concept, let us consider an expansion of the file-open check of Figure 7-14.

Example 7-5

A program segment is required that queries the user for a desired input file for opening. If the file exists and is available, then it should be opened. Provide for the following three possible error conditions:

2	ILLFILNAM	Illegal file name.
5	CANFINFIL	Can't find file or account.
10	PROVIO	Protection violation.

In this example, the variable ERR will be tested for a value of 2, 5, or 10, and the appropriate message will be printed. The program segment of Figure 7-15(a) performs these tests through a series of IF statements. Furthermore, if the error was not one of the three, then an error message is printed identifying the error number (ERR) and the line at which the error occurred (ERL). Some sample dialogues are shown in Figure 7-15(b).

```
500     ON ERROR GOTO 2000
510     INPUT 'What is the filename & extension of the input file'; F$
520     OPEN F$ FOR INPUT AS FILE #1
  .
  .
  .
2000 !
2010 ! File open error trap
2020       IF ERR = 2
           THEN
             PRINT F$; ' is a bad filename'
           ELSE
             IF ERR = 5
             THEN
                 PRINT 'File '; F$;' does not exist'
             ELSE
                IF ERR = 10
                THEN
                   PRINT 'You are not authorized to use ';F$
                ELSE
                   PRINT 'Unexpected error'
                   PRINT 'Error = '; ERR
                   PRINT 'Error line = '; ERL
                   PRINT 'Terminating processing'
                   CLOSE #I FOR I = 1 TO 12
                    STOP
                END IF
             END IF
           END IF
2200 !
2210 ! Return point
2220    INPUT 'Do you wish to try again <Y or N>'; Q$
2230    IF LEFT(Q$,1) <> 'Y' OR LEFT$(Q$,1) <> 'y'
        THEN
             CLOSE #I FOR I = 1 TO 12
             STOP
        END IF
2240    PRINT
2250    RESUME 520
2260 !
32767 END
```

(a)

```
What is the filename & extension of the input file?  PAY.MAS
You are not authorized to use PAY.MAS
Do you wish to try again? Yes
What is the filename & extension of the input file? PAY.DAT
```

(b)

Figure 7-15   Checking error codes—Example 7-5.

More About EOF Processing

We learned from the program segment of Figure 7-11 that the ON ERROR capability can be used in conjunction with detecting the end of a data file. Whenever a program attempts to read this EOF code as a data value, error number 11 occurs:

ENDFILDEV

Although the termination of Figure 7-11 does allow for an orderly termination of the program, it includes no provision for the fact that the error might have been caused by something other than detection of the EOF. To this end, the example of Figure 7-11 has been expanded in Figure 7-16. Important principles illustrated by this example are as follows:

```
20    OPEN 'INVEN.DAT' FOR INPUT AS FILE #1
50    ON ERROR GOTO 145
100   INPUT #1, TOOL.NUM, TOOL.TYPE$, OLD.INV, MANUFCT, SHIPD, LOST
120   NEW.INV = OLD.INV + MANUFCT - SHIPD - LOST
130   PRINT TOOL.NUM, TOOL.TYPE$, OLD.INV, NEW.INV
140   GOTO 100
145 ! Print message and terminate
147   IF ERR <> 11 THEN ON ERROR GOTO 0
150   PRINT 'Processing complete'
32767  END
```

Figure 7-16   Using ON ERROR to detect the end of a data file.

1. When an error occurs, the error number of the occurring error (see Appendix VI) is stored in the predefined variable ERR. Since the end-of-file error is 11, line 147 tests for this value.
2. In some instances, the programmer may wish to trap only certain types of errors and let the system handle others. This is possible by including ON ERROR GOTO 0 within the error routine itself. We see that if ERR<>11, then the error switch is reset to zero. This effectively cancels the original error switch setting (line 50) retroactively and causes the system to handle the error as if line 50 never existed. The end result is that the system will print the error code and line number, then terminate processing. However, if the error is an 11, then processing is handled by the error routine.

In Retrospect

This chapter has focused on two major topics. The first is file processing, one of the most important topics in programming. The second is error handling and the special provisions for it that are included in Basic.

Answers to Preceding Exercises

7-1. The invalid identifiers are

A3.BASIC	Extension cannot be more than three characters.
CAMOUFLAGE.A4	Filename cannot be more than nine characters.
CAM.1.2	The period indicates the beginning of the extension; there can be only one period.
8;RUN	Filename and extension must be separated by a period.

7-2. As we learned in Chapter 2, the contents of a file can be displayed directly from the user's library by the VMS-level TYPE command followed by the filename.

7-3. If, for some reason, the file TEST.DAT does not exist, the OPEN will be executed to create a new (empty) file. This will lead to erroneous results.

7-4. a. 3000 OPEN 'WAREHOUSE.DAT' FOR OUTPUT AS FILE #3
b. 3000 OPEN 'WAREHOUSE.DAT' FOR INPUT AS FILE #3

7-5. The channel number in the PRINT statement, #2, does not match the one on which the output file is opened, #3.

7-6. The same channel number cannot be assigned to more than one file. Replace the channel number on lines 1010 and 2010 by #3 (or any valid channel number other than #2).

7-7. Add the line

```
218  CONTINUE$ = 'Y'
```

and replace lines 220 and 225 by

```
PROC.PERIM:
  WHILE CONTINUE$ = 'Y'
    INPUT 'Do you wish to continue <Y/N>; CONTINUE$
    EXIT IF CONTINUE$ = 'N'
```

7-8. Insert the line

```
90  WHILE -1
```

and replace line 140 by

```
140  NEXT
```

7-9. The ON ERROR GOTO statement must *precede* the lines on which errors are to trap to the error handler. Hence, change line number 140 to 90.

7-10. Eliminate statement 920 and change 940 to

```
940   RESUME 410
```

7-11. a. 520   filename ABC is entered
     530   existing file ABC is opened; no error generated
     540   opened file is closed
     550   message
     560   input indicates that another version of ABC is to be opened
     570   LOOP is set to false
     580   the loop is terminated and control transfers to 600
     610   because LOOP is false, RESUME is *not* executed
     620   another version of ABC is opened
     630   error trapping is disabled

   b. 520   filename XYZ is entered
     530   attempt to open nonexisting file generates an error; control transfers to line 600 because of ON ERROR statement
     610   because LOOP is true, RESUME *is* executed
     620   file XYZ is opened for output; new file XYZ is created
     630   error trapping is disabled

   c. 520   filename ABC is entered
     530   existing file ABC is opened; no error generated
     540   opened file is closed
     550   message
     560   input indicates that another version of ABC is *not* to be opened
     570   LOOP is left as true
     580   looping continues
     520   filename XYZ is entered
     530   attempt to open nonexisting file generates an error; control transfers to line 600 because of ON ERROR statement
     610   because LOOP is true, RESUME *is* executed
     620   file XYZ is opened for output; new file XYZ is created
     630   error trapping is disabled

Programming Problems

7-1. Write a program to compute gross pay of employees and company totals. Each record in the input file includes the following data:

Employee number

Hourly pay rate

Hours worked: Monday
                 Tuesday
                 Wednesday
                 Thursday
                 Friday

For each employee, calculate regular hours, overtime hours (anything over 40 hours per week), and gross pay. Pay at the rate of 1.5 times the hourly rate for all overtime hours. Accumulate regular hours, overtime hours, and gross pay for all the employees. Output for each employee must include appropriate headings and the following:

Employee number.

Regular hours.

Overtime hours.

Hourly rate.

Gross pay.

After processing the last record, print a summary line for accumulated values of regular hours, overtime hours, and gross pay.

7-2. Modify problem 7-1 to calculate overtime hours as all hours worked in excess of 9 hours in any given day or 40 in the entire week; use whichever criterion yields the maximum overtime. For instance, if an employee works 12, 8, 8, 8, and 8 hours, there are 40 regular hours and 4 overtime hours (based on 44 hours for the week). However, an employee who worked 12, 8, 8, 8, and 6 hours is credited with 39 regular hours and 3 overtime hours (based on 12 hours for Monday).

7-3. Each record in a salesperson file is to include the following information:

Salesperson name.

Units sold.

Unit commission.

Base pay.

Bonus point.

Bonus.

Write a program to *create* this file by input from the keyboard and writing to disk. Terminate the creation part by input of a zero-length string for the name. When the creation part is finished, close the file and then reopen it. In the second part of the program, calculate the commission (units sold times unit commission) and determine the gross pay for each salesperson as follows:

$$
\text{Gross pay} = \begin{cases} \text{Base pay} & \text{If commission less than base pay} \\ \text{Commission} & \text{If commission between base pay and bonus point} \\ \text{Commission} + \text{bonus} & \text{If commission greater than bonus point} \end{cases}
$$

As output, print the salesperson's name, commission, and gross pay.

7-4. Using a file of registered voters as a source, write a program that will produce a listing of the names of Libertarians who are married and have an annual income of at least $35,000. The registered-voter records contain the following data:

Name

Street address

City, state, ZIP code

Annual income (dollars)

Party of registration: R = Republican
D = Democrat
L = Libertarian

Marital status: 1 = Married
2 = Not married

7-5. A file contains examination score information for each student as follows:

Examination group number (four-digit integer).

Student number.

Examination score.

The file has been sorted such that the records in the file are grouped by their examination group number. (For instance, all students in examination group 17 will be together in the file, followed by all students in group 18, and so on.) The file is ended with a trailer 9999 for the examination group number.

Write a program that will calculate the average for each group and print the group number and average.

Also, keep a subtotal in order to calculate the overall average of all the scores. Upon completion, print the number of groups processed and the overall average. To detect the end of each group, use a similar technique to that used in problem 5-6.

8

Advanced Control Structures

CHAPTER OUTLINE

Preview

Most of the sample programs in this book involve the repeated execution of statement blocks. This chapter deals with loop constructs of VAX Basic in a general way. We will study several looping structures, one or another of which may be better suited for implementing the various techniques that we have been using to control looping. Topics that you will study in this chapter include the following:

1. *The ITERATE statement, which allows execution to skip to the end of the looping structure.*
2. *The FOR–NEXT, designed to execute a loop a specified number of times, as controlled by a counter-type variable that is automatically incremented and tested by the statement.*
3. *The principle of nested loops, whereby one or more loops are included entirely within another loop.*

4. The use of statement structures (such as IF and WHILE) as statement modifiers that provide a convenient feature for conditional execution of single statements.

5. The SELECT–CASE statement, which provides a multiple selection capability in a single statement.

More About Loop Structures

Introduction

Example programs of preceding chapters have used different techniques to control continued execution of a loop. One involves a loop terminated by detection of a trailer record. In another, the value of the condition that controls the loop is changed, for example, from true to false, within the body of the loop. In both of these formats, the number of times the body of the loop is to be executed is unspecified when looping begins. In the third method, the body of the loop is executed a predetermined number of times. These three techniques are illustrated in the three example loops of Figure 8-1.

```
(a) WHILE -1  ◄───────────────────────────        Infinite loop on WHILE,
        READ TOOL.NUM,...                          but EXIT here on true.
        EXIT PROCESS.LOOP IF TOOL.NUM = 99999 ◄──────────────┘
        .
        .
        .
    NEXT

(b) QUERY = 'Y'                                    When WHILE condition is false,
    WHILE QUERY = 'Y' OR QUERY = 'y'◄───────       continue to statement following
        .                                          the NEXT.
        .
        .
        INPUT 'Do you wish to continue'; QUERY
    NEXT

(c) CNT = 0
    WHILE CNT < 10 ◄──────── Counted loop: execute 10 times.
        .
        .
        .
        CNT = CNT + 1
    NEXT
```

Figure 8-1 Loop control methods.

These have been relatively simple examples of the loop concept. In examples of the preceding chapters, we have used the WHILE statement for all three of the techniques shown in Figure 8-1. As we recall, execution of a WHILE continues so long as a particular condition remains true.

The UNTIL Statement

We know that the test *condition* may be any valid relational or logical expression. It is very important to remember that the condition is tested *before* entering the loop. This means that it is possible for the body of the loop never to be executed at all (that is, for the number of repetitions to be zero). For instance, in both the second and third examples of Figure 8-1, the variable that is to control execution of the loop is given an initial value. The need for this in the third example is obvious; the counter must be set to zero. However, in the second example, the need to initialize QUERY is more subtle. If it is not initialized, when execution progresses to the WHILE, the result will be unpredictable. If QUERY was used before, then the test result will depend upon whether or not it contained the letter *Y*. If it has not been used before, then it would contain null. If it contained other than *Y* or *y*, then the condition would immediately be false and control will be transferred to the first executable statement after the NEXT statement. Hence the body of the loop will never be executed.

Although the WHILE is quite adequate for operations of the type illustrated in Figure 8-1, VAX Basic includes another looping structure that is virtually identical to the WHILE: the UNTIL. The UNTIL has a form identical to that of the WHILE. We know that the WHILE causes execution of a block *while* a stated condition is true. As the name suggests, the UNTIL causes execution of a block *until* a stated condition becomes true. Use of the UNTIL is illustrated by the examples of Figure 8-2, which correspond exactly to those of Figure 8-1. In this respect, WHILE and UNTIL are somewhat redundant, in that they are merely two different ways of implementing the same logic. However, there are instances when one of the forms might be either misleading or simply very

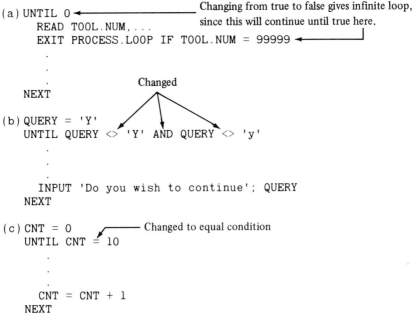

Figure 8-2 Using the UNTIL.

clumsy and the other is more straightfoward. You will notice this as you write more and more loop-control applications.

Exercise

8-1. Modify the program in Figure 7-14 so that looping is controlled with an UNTIL rather than with a WHILE.

The ITERATE Statement

We have found the EXIT statement to be convenient to break out of a loop when the need occurs. Execution of the EXIT causes processing to continue with the statement following the NEXT statement. In loop processing, the situation commonly occurs in which the remaining statements of a loop are to be skipped for this pass, but the loop is not to be terminated. Thus, we must jump to the NEXT statement. The distinction between the effect of the EXIT and this need is illustrated in Figure 8-3. We should be aware of the fact that we already can perform the action of Figure 8-3 using two different methods.

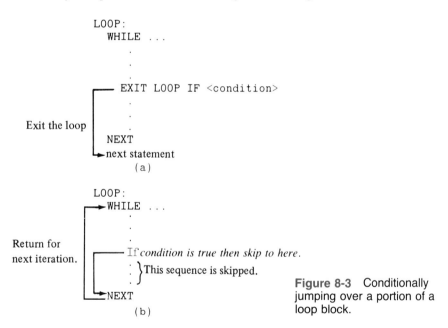

Figure 8-3 Conditionally jumping over a portion of a loop block.

One way is to make the statements to be skipped part of an IF block that is executed conditionally. The other is to use a GOTO that transfers control to the NEXT statement if the particular condition becomes true. In general, it is best to avoid the GOTO and the associated line-number reference. However, there is a special statement called the ITERATE that performs the required task.

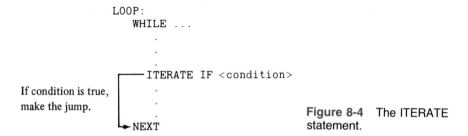

Figure 8-4   The ITERATE statement.

Using the ITERATE is illustrated in Figure 8-4. Here the ITERATE statement transfers control to the loop's NEXT statement exactly as illustrated in Figure 8-3(b). It is functionally equivalent to using a GOTO in this case but, like the EXIT, it is preferable because it is designed specifically for this single use. Again note that EXIT transfers control to the first statement *following* the loop, whereas ITERATE allows a portion of the body of the loop to be skipped, but it *continues the iteration*. The following example is a further illustration of the ITERATE statement:

Example 8-1

A table of the square roots of positive values of the following function is to be printed:

$$y = x^3 - 3x^2 + 7x - 1$$

For values of x that result in negative y, a message to that effect should be displayed. The values of x are to be entered interactively. The user is to end the terminal session by entering the value of 0 for x.

The program in Figure 8-5 computes and prints the table entries. Note how the ITERATE is used to skip the remainder of the loop body if the value of Y is negative.

```
100  PRINT 'X', 'SQR(Y)'
105  X = 1
110  WHILE X <> 0
120     INPUT  X
130     Y = X**3 - 3*X**2 + 7*X - 1
140     IF Y < 0
        THEN
            PRINT "Y is negative"
            ITERATE
        ELSE
            Z = SQR(Y)
        END IF
150     PRINT X, Z
160  NEXT
32767 END
```

Figure 8-5   Using the ITERATE statement.

Counted Loops Using the FOR–NEXT

Counted Loops

Loops executed a specified number of times are commonly called *counted loops*. As an illustration, the program segment of Figure 5-20 has been modified slightly and repeated here as Figure 8-6. Note that this loop is executed exactly ten times. The following commentary on this example reviews how such a counter loop works:

1. The variable CNT is used as a counter (commonly called the *control variable*) to control the loop. Its value is initialized to 1 prior to entering the loop (statement 2200).
2. The test for loop continuation is made by statement 2210, in which CNT is compared to 10. When the condition is no longer satisfied, execution of the WHILE is terminated, and execution continues to the statement following 2250.
3. The *body* of the loop consists of statements 2220–2240. These will be repeatedly executed.
4. Upon completion of each pass through the loop, the control variable CNT is increased by 1.

```
1000   DECLARE INTEGER CNT
   .
   .
   .
2200   CNT = 1
2210   WHILE CNT <= 10
2220      INPUT "What is the next pair of numbers"; A,B
2230      PRINT "Their product is: "; A*B
2240      CNT = CNT + 1
2250   NEXT
```

Figure 8-6   A counted loop.

Exercise

8-2. What would occur in the sequence of Figure 8-6 if each of the following conditions occurred?

a. The loop control variable CNT is initialized to 10 instead of 1.
b. The test for CNT (statement 2210) is CNT < 10 instead of CNT <= 10.
c. A value of 1 is subtracted from CNT rather than added in statement 2240.
d. Statement 2200 is numbered 2215 instead of 2200.

The FOR–NEXT Statement Combination

Counted loops are so common in programming that Basic includes a special pair of statements that provides automatic control of the loop. The loop of

```
1000   DECLARE INTEGER CNT
  .
  .
  .
2210   FOR CNT = 1 TO 10
2220      INPUT "What is the next pair of numbers"; A,B
2230      PRINT "Their product is: "; A*B
2250   NEXT CNT
```

Figure 8-7 A counted loop using the FOR-NEXT.

Figure 8-6 is rewritten in Figure 8-7 using a FOR–NEXT construct. This loop functions in exactly the same way as that of Figure 8-6 and produces the same results. Details of how the FOR–NEXT works are given in Figure 8-8. Upon entering the loop (the FOR statement at line 2210), the control variable CNT is set to the initial value. Upon encountering the NEXT statement, it is automatically increased by the increment of the STEP value. If the increment is 1, then the STEP may be omitted, as in statement 2210 of Figure 8-7. The test value (10 in this case) is the maximum allowable value for which the loop will be executed. When this value is exceeded, execution automatically continues at the statement following the NEXT.

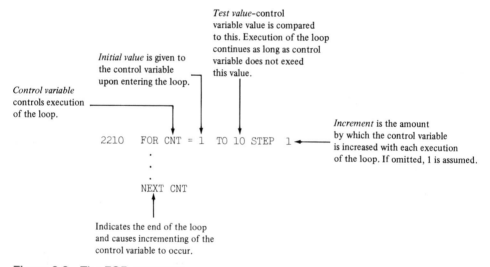

Figure 8-8 The FOR statement.

The general form of the FOR statement is

FOR *var* = *expr* TO *expr* [STEP *expr*]

The following examples further illustrate the characteristics of the FOR statement:

```
FOR J = 5 TO X+3
```

Note that the initial value need not be 1. Furthermore, the initial value, the test value, and the increment can all be expressions. If X contains 4, then this loop is executed for values of 5, 6, and 7, or three times.

```
FOR I = 0 TO 13 STEP 2
```

In this case, the loop is executed for values of 0,2,4,6,8,10, and 12. Note that the control variable need not end up equal to the test value. The rule is that when the step size is positive, the loop will be executed as long as the control variable does *not* exceed the test value.

```
FOR A = -1.5 TO 2.4 STEP 0.1
```

Fractional quantities are allowable in the FOR statement. This loop executes 40 times.

```
FOR C = 0 TO -5 STEP -1
```

It is possible to use a negative increment. Here the loop is executed for values of C of 0, -1, -2, -3, -4, and -5 (six times). For negative step size, the looping continues as long as the control variable is *not less* than the test value.

Exercises

8-3. How many times would the loops controlled by each of the following FOR statements be executed, and what values would J take on before each loop terminates?

a. FOR J = 7 TO 13
b. FOR J = 3 TO 13 STEP 3
c. FOR J = 5 TO -5 STEP -1
d. FOR J = 0 TO 3*X-1   (assume X = 4)

8-4. In Exercise 5-12, we examined how the three essential operations on a counter are done when the counter is used for loop control with the WHILE statement. We saw that the loop-control variable in that case must be initialized and incremented in separate assignment statements. How are these three operations done in the FOR–NEXT structure?

If you find that flowcharts provide you with valuable insight in understanding the logic of a problem, then you might wish to consider a special flowchart form for the FOR–NEXT. Remember that the initialization, counting, and testing functions are performed automatically by the FOR–NEXT. Hence they should not be explicitly shown as part of the program logic. To this end, an alternative flowchart form for representing a FOR–NEXT loop is shown in

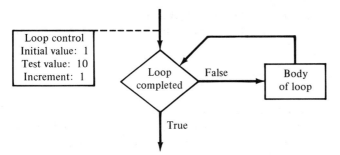

Figure 8-9 Flowchart representation of FOR-NEXT.

Figure 8-9. Here we see that the control details pertaining to the loop are included in a separate description box. This carries all the detailed information necessary to write the FOR statement.

Principles of Nested Loops

Calculating Tables

Inflation and the decreasing purchasing power of the dollar are prime problems today. We continually read how $10 worth of goods today will cost us $11 or $12 next year, $13 or $14 the year after, and so on. Predictions such as these are based on the expected annual rate of inflation. To illustrate, let us assume that economists predict a 7 percent annual inflation rate. Then the cost of purchasing $10 worth of goods in one, two, and three years would be calculated as follows:

The general form for the calculation is

$$\text{Cost next year} = \text{Cost this year} \times (1 + \text{inflation rate})$$

Current year: $10 purchases $10 worth of goods.

$$
\begin{aligned}
\text{Cost after 1 year} &= 10 \times (1 + 0.07)\\
&= 10.70
\end{aligned}
$$

$$
\begin{aligned}
\text{Cost after 2 years} &= \text{Cost after 1 year} \times (1 + 0.07)\\
&= 10.70 \times 1.07\\
&= 11.45
\end{aligned}
$$

$$
\begin{aligned}
\text{Cost after 3 years} &= \text{Cost after 2 years} \times (1 + 0.07)\\
&= 11.45 \times 1.07\\
&= 12.25
\end{aligned}
$$

The preceding example illustrates performance of the calculation for an interest rate of 7 percent. If we needed tables for 8 percent, 9 percent, and 10 percent, then we would repeat this sequence of operations for each of the interest rates.

Now let us consider for a moment what is happening here. The operation of calculating the table for one rate involves a process to be repeated a desired number of times: a counted loop. If we assume that an eight-year table is to be prepared, then the preceding process involves the following:

For 8 times, repeat the following
New cost = Old cost times factor (factor = 1 + interest rate)
Print results

We can see that this fits right into our FOR–NEXT loop scope. Let us now address the next step: calculating series of tables for a range of interest rates. Here let us assume that the rates to be used start with a beginning value and are increased by 1 to some ending value. Now our logic becomes

For interest from beginning to ending values, repeat the following
For 8 times, repeat the following
New cost = Old cost times factor
Print results

Nested Loops

This calculation of a series of values (costs for several years) for *each* of a series of *other* values (interest rates) illustrates a new programming concept: one loop completely within another loop. An *inner* loop contained *entirely* within an *outer* loop, as is the case here, is called a *nested loop*. The value of the outer-loop control variable remains temporarily fixed while the inner loop is repeatedly performed. Each time the inner-loop control variable completes the steps through its allowed values, the outer-loop control variable changes by its step size, the inner control variable is reinitialized, and the process repeats. Example 8-2 illustrates nested FOR–NEXT loops.

Example 8-2

Design and code a program that will calculate a series of inflation tables as just described. Input is to be the beginning and ending annual inflation rates to control processing. Eight-year tables are to be calculated in increments of 1 percent for each interest rate, starting and ending with the input values. The program must print appropriate headings and a termination message.

Example 8-2 is typical of many that are encountered in programming; that is, a series of tables must be computed and printed. To help us in planning how the printed output is to appear, a print layout form is shown in Figure 8-10(a). A single table sample output using an inflation rate of 7 percent is included in Figure 8-10(b).

1-10										11-20										21-30									
1	2	3	4	5	6	7	8	9	0	1	2	3	4	5	6	7	8	9	0	1	2	3	4	5	6	7	8	9	0
	I	N	F	L	A	T	I	O	N		T	A	B	L	E								D	A	T	E	:		
	C	O	S	T		O	F		$	1	0		W	O	R	T	H		O	F		G	O	O	D	S			
	I	N	F	L	A	T	I	O	N		R	A	T	E		=		X	X		P	E	R	C	E	N	T		
			Y	E	A	R									C	O	S	T											
			X	X										X	X	.	X	X											

(a)

```
INFLATION TABLE         DATE: 13-Jan-86
COST OF $10 WORTH OF GOODS

INFLATION RATE =  7 PERCENT

    YEAR        COST
     1         10.70
     2         11.45
     3         12.25
     4         13.11
     5         14.03
     6         15.01
     7         16.06
     8         17.18
              (b)
```

Figure 8-10 Output for Example 8-2. (a) A printer layout form. (b) Sample output.

Operations to be performed in this program involve

1. Initialize as needed.
2. Accept inflation rates.
3. Print headings.
4. Compute and print table values.
5. Print termination message.

Note that in this example, a new set of headings is printed for each table. Thus, printing of headings will not be done in the initialization module. A hierarchy chart illustrating the modules for this program is shown in Figure 8-11. The preceding steps 1 and 2 are both initialization operations.

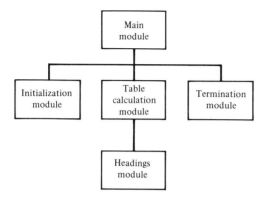

Figure 8-11 Hierarchy chart for Example 8-2.

Once the needs of this program are broken down into modules, the logic of the table-calculation module is relatively simple. We need only expand the earlier pseudocode description as follows:

For interest from beginning to ending values, repeat the following
    Print headings
    Initialize cost to 10
    For 8 times, repeat the following
        New cost = Old cost times factor
        Print results

A Program Using Nested FOR Loops

After all of this development, the program of Figure 8-12 is relatively straightforward. This program will require an *outer* loop that will execute for values of inflation rate ranging from some beginning value to an ending value (for instance, 6 to 12). From the use of indentation, the inner and outer loops are readily apparent. Each pass through the outer loop will cause entry into the inner loop (statement 3070), which will produce a complete table, including headings, for the current value of RATE. We should note that each pass through the inner loop causes the variable COST to be changed (this is the object of

```
 !      Figure 8-12   Program for Example 8-2.
 !
 !
100    ! INFLATION RATE - EXAMPLE 8-2
110    ! THIS PROGRAM CALCULATES A SERIES OF INFLATION RATE
120    ! TABLES.   SUCCESSIVE TABLES ARE CALCULATED STARTING
130    ! WITH A BEGINNING RATE AND ENDING WITH AN ENDING
140    ! RATE.   THE USER ENTERS THESE QUANTITIES INTO THE
150    ! VARIABLES "INIT" AND "FINAL".
160    !
1000   ! Main Program
1010      GOSUB   INITIALIZE
1020      GOSUB   PROC.TABLE
1030      GOSUB   TERMINATE
1040      STOP
1050   ! End of main program
1060   !
          INITIALIZE:
          DECLARE INTEGER RATE, INIT, FINAL, Y
2010      H1$ = "INFLATION TABLE        DATE: "
2020      H2$ = "COST OF $10 WORTH OF GOODS"
2030      H3$ = "INFLATION RATE = ## PERCENT"
2040      H4$ = "  YEAR         COST"
2050      D$  = "  ##          ##.##"
2060      INPUT "Enter the beginning and ending inflation rates"; INIT,FINAL
2070      RETURN
2080   ! End of initial routine
2090   ! Outer loop - controls inflation rate increments
          PROC.TABLE:
          FOR RATE = INIT TO FINAL
3030         FACTOR = 1 + RATE/100   !  For use in calculations
3040         COST = 10     !   Set cost back to initial value
3050         GOSUB HEADINGS
3060   !     Table processing (inner) loop
3070         FOR Y = 1 TO 8
3080            COST = COST * FACTOR
3090            PRINT USING D$, Y, COST
3100         NEXT Y
3110   ! End of inner loop
3120      PRINT   PRINT   PRINT
3130      NEXT RATE
3140   ! End of outer loop
3150      RETURN
3160   ! End of processing routine
3170   !
          TERMINATE:
          PRINT
4020      PRINT "PROCESSING COMPLETE"
4030      RETURN
4040   ! End of termination routine
4050   !
5000      HEADINGS:
          PRINT H1$; DATE$(0)
5020      PRINT H2$
5030      PRINT
5040      PRINT USING H3$, RATE
5050      PRINT
5060      PRINT H4$
5070      RETURN
5080   ! End of heading routine
5090   !
32767  END
```

Figure 8-12   Calculating tables—Example 8-2.

the program). However, for each new table, it must be initialized back to a value of 10 (see line 3040). By contrast, the rate remains constant within the inner loop. Thus, prior to entering the inner loop, an "inflation factor" (FACTOR) is calculated. This avoids the identical calculation for each pass through the inner loop. If using flowcharts helps you clarify the logic of a program, then you might study that of Figure 8-13. Note that the nature of each loop is carefully documented.

Nested loops are commonly encountered in programming. This example illustrated the concept using the FOR–NEXT structure. As might be expected, exactly the same nesting techniques can be programmed using the WHILE and UNTIL.

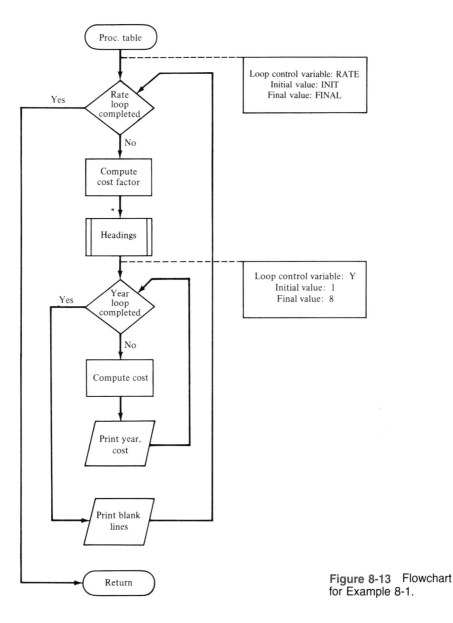

Figure 8-13 Flowchart for Example 8-1.

Exercises

8-5. Control of the loop in Figure 8-12 is contained within the processing loop (the FOR statement on line 2090). Make the changes necessary to place the control in the main program. In other words, loop control should relate to the GOSUB at line 1020.

8-6. How many tables would be prepared (that is, how many passes through the outer loop) if the initial and final values entered were the same? What if the final value were smaller than the initial value?

Summarizing the FOR–NEXT

The FOR–NEXT provides a powerful tool. However, as with any of the other features of the language, we must be careful to use this construct within a prescribed set of rules; in this case, the following limitations apply:

1. The control variable is used by the Basic system to control the loop. It is automatically incremented after each pass. It should not be changed by statements within the loop. However, it can be used inside the loop just as any other variable as long as it is not changed.
2. When the loop runs to completion, the value of the control variable should be regarded as undefined.
3. If execution of the loop is terminated by an EXIT (without going to completion), then the control variable remains at its value when the exit occurred.
4. For positive STEP values, a loop is terminated when the control variable is incremented to a value that *exceeds* the upper limit defined in the FOR statement. If the STEP value is negative, then the loop is terminated when incrementing produces a value *less than* the limit value.
5. FOR loops can be nested up to a maximum of 12 levels.
6. The ranges of two loops may not overlap. That is, an inner loop must be completely contained within the outer loop.
7. If two loops are nested, they must not use the same control variable.
8. Entry into a FOR–NEXT loop is only through the FOR statement. *Do not branch into the body of the loop from outside the loop.*

These points are illustrated in Figure 8-14.

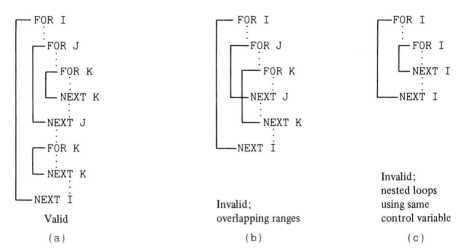

Figure 8-14   (a) Three-level nesting—Valid (b) Overlapped loops—Invalid
(c) Same control variables for inner and outer loops—Invalid.

Exercise

8-7. What will be the value for the variable A at the end of each of the
following sets of nested loops, assuming all loops run to completion?

```
a. A = 0
   FOR I = 1 TO 10
   .
   .
   .
   FOR J = 1 TO 10
   A = A + 1
   NEXT J
   .
   .
   .
   NEXT I
```

```
c. A = 0
   FOR I = 7 TO -2 STEP -1
   .
   .
   .
   FOR J = 0 TO 5
   .
   .
   .
   NEXT J
   A = A + 1
   NEXT I
```

```
b. A = 0
   FOR I = 1 TO 10 STEP 2
   .
   .
   .
   FOR J = 7 TO 13
   A = A + 1
   NEXT J
   .
   .
   .
   NEXT I
```

```
d. A = 0
   FOR I = 1 TO A
   .
   .
   .
   FOR J = 1 TO 9
   A = A + 1
   NEXT J
   .
   .
   .
   NEXT I
```

Looping Statements as Statement Modifiers

About Statement Modifiers

We have already learned about using the IF as a statement modifier in Chapter 5, for instance:

```
EXIT PROCESS.LOOP IF VALUE$ = 'EOF'
```

Similarly, it is possible to use the WHILE, UNTIL, and the FOR to modify a statement. The use of these as statement modifiers is equivalent in effect to corresponding WHILE–NEXT, UNTIL–NEXT, and FOR–NEXT loops in which the body of the loop consists of one line. The modifier form is simply a convenient way of writing such one-line loops. Let us consider examples illustrating each.

The WHILE and UNTIL as Statement Modifiers

The general form of the WHILE and UNTIL used as statement modifiers is

$$statement \begin{bmatrix} \text{WHILE} \\ \text{UNTIL} \end{bmatrix} condition$$

The nature of this form is illustrated by the examples of Figure 8-15, which include a loop form and an equivalent statement-modifier form. Note that all four of the program segments are functionally equivalent.

Explicit Loop   **Statement Modifier**

```
100  X = XMIN           100 X = XMIN
110 UNTIL X > XMAX      110 X = X**2 UNTIL X >XMAX
120   X = X**2          120 PRINT X
130 NEXT
140 PRINT X


100 X = XMIN            100 X = XMIN
110 WHILE X <= XMAX     110 X = X**2 WHILE X <= XMAX
120   X = X**2          120 PRINT X
130 NEXT
140 PRINT X
```

Figure 8-15 The WHILE and UNTIL as statement modifiers.

The FOR as a Statement Modifier

Occasionally, the programmer encounters a situation in which a single statement must be repeatedly executed a predetermined number of times. For instance, let us assume that we must print a row of asterisk characters five times in order to allow a user to align paper in the printer. A FOR–NEXT is shown in Figure 8-16(a) to perform this operation. However, this single statement can be executed repeatedly more conveniently by using the form of Figure 8-16(b). Used this way, the FOR is called an *unconditional statement modifier*. In effect, it creates a single-line loop. (A statement modifier affects *only* the statement immediately preceding it. Therefore, it cannot be used with statement blocks.)

```
500   DECLARE INTEGER LINES
  .
  .
  .
1000  FOR LINES = 1 TO 5
1010    PRINT "********************"
1020  NEXT LINES
```

(a)


```
1010    PRINT "********************" FOR LINES = 1 TO 5
```

Figure 8-16 The FOR as
a statement modifier.

(b)

Another situation in which the FOR as a statement modifier is useful is for the purpose of closing all open files before terminating processing. The error routine of Figure 7-15 includes program termination if the occurring error is not one of several for which a test is made; it also includes closing the one channel that was opened. The action of closing all open files before terminating is shown in the segment of Figure 8-17. Note that this operation causes all 12 channels to be closed. Usually they will not all be open, but no error results if an unopened channel is directed to be closed. This technique ensures that any open files will be closed.

```
ELSE
  PRINT "UNEXPECTED ERROR"
  PRINT "ERROR = "; ERR
  PRINT "ERROR LINE = "; ERL
  PRINT "TERMINATING PROCESSING"
  CLOSE I FOR I = 1 TO 12
  STOP
```

Figure 8-17 Closing all files.

Statement Modifier on the FOR Statement

The statement being modified by a WHILE or an UNTIL modifier can itself be the FOR statement of a FOR–NEXT loop. This is shown in the sequence given in Figure 8-18. This is a convenient form because it gives the loop-control feature of the UNTIL (or WHILE) yet provides the automatic incrementing-of-a-variable feature of the FOR.

```
FOR N = 1  UNTIL X < 0.0001
  X = 0.5**N
  PRINT N,X
NEXT N
```

Figure 8-18 Using the UNTIL as a
statement modifier on the FOR.

Exercise

8-8. Use calculator mode to generate a table of square roots for the integers 1 through 10.

UNLESS Modifier

There is also an UNLESS modifier, which is functionally equivalent to an IF NOT modifier. (As we learned in Chapter 5, NOT is a logical operator that reverses the sense of the condition test.) Thus,

```
PRINT  A UNLESS A = B
```

is functionally equivalent to

```
PRINT  A IF NOT A = B
```

and also to

```
PRINT  A IF A <> B
```

More than one modifier can be appended to a statement. VAX Basic evaluates such compound modifiers from *right to left*; control passes to the next statement (*not* to the preceding modifier on the same line) when a given modifier test fails. Because *all* the conditions must be satisfied for the modified statement to be executed, the compound modifier is effectively equivalent to simple conditions connected by a logical AND. For example, in the statement

```
100  PRINT  A IF A = 5 UNLESS B = 10
```

the value of A is printed only if B is not equal to 10 *and* A is equal to 5.

Interrupting Execution

With all of these looping capabilities, we have some powerful tools at hand. In fact, we can now proceed to write programs with very complex logic. As we learned in Chapter 5, we can use immediate mode to debug a program that terminates at a STOP statement or on an error condition. Occasionally, bad program logic will cause a program to lock into an infinite loop. VAX Basic allows you to stop program execution *from the keyboard*, make inquiries, change variable values if desired, and then continue. To illustrate such a debugging session, we consider the following example:

Example 8-3

An investment earns interest at a specified rate compounded annually. A program is to determine the number of years it takes for the initial investment to double in value. We shall calculate compound interest using the following formula.

$$A = P(1 + r)^n$$

where

P denotes the principal.

r denotes the interest rate in decimal per payment period.

n denotes the number of periods.

A denotes the value after *n* periods.

A loop is required that uses calculation of the interest for increasing values of *n* to control the loop. That is, *n* is to begin with a value of 1 and increase by 1 for each pass through the loop. Execution of the loop is to be terminated for the first value of the accumulated amount *A* that exceeds twice the original principal *P*. Assume there will be no input or output operations by other statements within the loop.

```
830   PERIOD = 1
840   FACTOR = (1 + RATE/100)
850   WHILE AMOUNT <= 2*PRINC
860     AMOUNT = PRINC*FACTOR**PERIOD
870     .
        .
        .
      NEXT
900   PRINT 'Number of iterations ';PERIOD
```

Figure 8-19 Loop control.

In this example, we have to calculate *A* repeatedly (loop) until *A* is greater than two times *P*. The program segment in Figure 8-19 is intended to carry out the operations. Presumably, the value of the variable PERIOD is incremented within the loop. However, let us assume that the programmer accidentally omitted the incrementing statement. (Unlike the FOR loop, UNTIL and WHILE do not automatically increment a counter; that is, the counter does *not* serve as a loop-control variable.) Thus, the value of AMOUNT will never change, and we will have an infinite loop.

Because the loop involves no input or output, we will not see anything on the screen that might provide a clue as to what is taking place. Eventually we will realize that something is wrong, terminate execution, and try to debug the program.

Following is a typical sequence of steps in a debugging session.

1. To stop program execution from the keyboard, we hold down the Control key and depress the letter C (with Control still down). This is called a *control* C; it immediately terminates program execution and returns the system to command mode. (This is a particular example of the use of *control characters*, which are discussed more fully in Chapter 11.)

2. Enter the immediate-mode statement

   ```
   PRINT LINE
   ```

   The predefined variable LINE contains the line number at which execution was interrupted. In this case, the displayed line number will be 850 or greater but less than 900 (execution will remain within the loop).

3. We can then refer to a program listing to determine just where we are in the program. Furthermore, we can use the LIST command to list all or part of the program without disturbing the state of the program.

4. Since this loop is controlled at line 850 by AMOUNT and PRINC, and PRINC depends upon PERIOD, it is reasonable to assume that their values are related to the source of the error. At this point, we would like to use immediate mode to look at the values of AMOUNT and PERIOD. However, with a *control* C we cannot direct *where* the program will terminate execution. We need the program to stop when AMOUNT and PERIOD have

the values we suspect are causing the difficulty. Hence we insert the statement

      855 STOP

in the program inside the WHILE–NEXT loop and execute the program again. Upon encountering this statement, the computer will print

      STOP AT LINE 855

and suspend execution.

5. We then type the immediate-mode statement

      PRINT 'AMOUNT = '; AMOUNT, 'PERIOD = '; PERIOD

This will print at the terminal the values of these variables assigned in the program. The output (for P = 10000, R = 8.1) will be

      AMOUNT = 10810 PERIOD = 1

This is not particularly informative.

6. We continue program execution where it was terminated by the STOP statement by typing

      CONTINUE

7. After repeating steps 5 and 6 a few times, we realize that AMOUNT and PERIOD are not changing. At this point, we should be able to recognize the source of the difficulty and correct the error by deleting the STOP statement and inserting the following statement (with its appropriate statement number, in this case 855).

      PERIOD = PERIOD + 1

Additional Control Structures

By now we have a plethora of looping structures at our disposal. However, our selection-structure arsenal is rather slim, consisting only of the IF, which allows a choice of one of only two courses of action. As we shall see, there are situations in which one of several choices is called for, depending on conditions. In this portion of the chapter, we shall learn about two such multiple-selection structures that are part of VAX Basic. In both, the choice of the statement to which control transfers is based on the value of an expression. By its nature, the test in an IF statement is boolean (that is, two-valued). As we shall learn, the test in multiple-selection structures is not boolean.

SELECT–CASE Structure

The SELECT–CASE construct allows the program to execute any one of a number of statement blocks, depending on the value of the test expression. The

```
2000 !
2010 ! FILE OPEN ERROR TRAP
2020     IF ERR = 2
            THEN PRINT F$;" Is a bad filename."
        ELSE
            IF ERR = 5
                THEN PRINT "File ";F$;" does not exist."
            ELSE
                IF ERR = 10
                    THEN PRINT "You are not authorized to use ";F$
                ELSE
                    PRINT "Unexpected error"
                    PRINT "Error code = ";ERR
                    PRINT "Error line = ";ERL
                    PRINT "Terminating processing."
                    CLOSE I% FOR I% = 1 TO 12
                    STOP
                END IF
            END IF
        END IF
```

Figure 8-20 Multiple selection.

error-correction routine of Example 7-5 (Figure 7-15) is a perfect illustration of a need of this type. The appropriate portion of this example is repeated here as Figure 8-20. In this example, nested IFs are structured to cause one of four actions to take place. The multiple-selection representation of such a structure is shown in Figure 8-21.

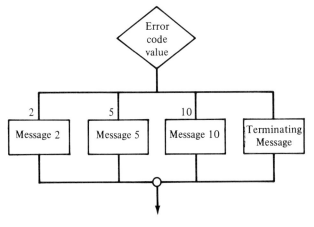

Figure 8-21 Flowchart representation of the multiple selection logic.

```
      2000 !
      2010 ! FILE OPEN ERROR TRAP
      2020       SELECT ERR ◄──────── Variable to be tested          If test variable contains
Equivalent to ──── CASE = 2 ◄────────────────────────────────────── this value, then take
ERR = 2            PRINT F$;" Is a bad filename."◄───────────────── this action.
                   CASE = 5
                   PRINT "File ";F$;" does not exist."
                   CASE = 10
                   PRINT "You are not authorized to use ";F$
                   CASE   ELSE
                   PRINT "Unexpected error"
                   PRINT "Error code = ";ERR       ⎫  If none of the above,
                   PRINT "Error line = ";ERL       ⎬  then do this.
                   PRINT "Terminating processing." ⎭
                   CLOSE I% FOR I% = 1 TO 12
                   STOP
              END SELECT
```

Figure 8-22   The SELECT-CASE statement.

Exactly the same function is performed by the SELECT–CASE used in Figure 8-22. Note that this form includes the two keywords SELECT and CASE. The SELECT includes the variable or expression to be tested (ERR) in this example. Each of the CASE options indicates the test condition and test value; for instance, the first CASE corresponds to the following value of the test variable:

```
      ERR = 2
```

Following the keyword CASE is the action to be taken if the condition is true.

The example of Figure 8-22 gives us basic insight into the SELECT–CASE. Let us consider the more general illustration shown in Figure 8-23. The following comments elaborate on this example:

```
SELECT   A%+B%          Expression to be tested.
  CASE = 10             Relational operator
          .                  Statement block to be executed
          .                  if value of test expression is 10.
          .
  CASE   1 TO 9          Range of values.
          .                  Statement block to be executed if
          .                  test expression lies between
          .                  1 and 9 inclusive.
  CASE ...
          .                             .
          .                             .
          .
  CASE ELSE
          .                  Statement block to be executed
          .                  if no match is found in
          .                  previous CASE statements.
END SELECT
```

Figure 8-23   Description of the SELECT-CASE.

1. The test expression is specified following the keyword SELECT.

2. The SELECT–CASE construct must be terminated by the END SELECT keywords. The code between SELECT and END SELECT is called a SELECT *block*.

3. Each statement in a SELECT block can have a line number. This is especially important in connection with error trapping, where an error might occur at a statement within the SELECT–CASE. In such a case, a separate line number must be assigned for each statement that may generate an error. If the error recovery uses a RESUME to return control to the line at which the error occurred, execution begins at the start of the line. In the case of a multistatement line, this may not be at the statement that generated the error. By numbering every statement in the SELECT block, the RESUME will always transfer control to the statement that caused the error.

4. The CASE statements specify a possible value or set of values for the test expression. The block of statements between CASE statements is called a CASE block. The CASE block to be executed for a given set of values follows the CASE statement that specifies this set. It is terminated by either another CASE or an END SELECT.

5. The keyword CASE is followed by either a relational expression or a range of values whose limits are connected by the keyword TO.

6. Only one of the CASE blocks in a SELECT–CASE structure is executed. After a CASE block is executed, control passes to the statement immediately following END SELECT.

7. Only one CASE ELSE block is allowed, and it is optional. It is executed if no match is found in any of the preceding CASE statements. If no ELSE clause is given and no match is found, control passes to the statement following END CASE without any action being taken.

8. SELECT blocks can be nested within a CASE or CASE ELSE block.

9. The logic of the SELECT–CASE construct can be implemented by multiple IF statements. However, even with suitable indenting, multiple IFs can be confusing to the reader. The SELECT statement greatly simplifies the code of multiple selection, and it should be used instead of multiple IFs whenever possible.

As a final illustration of the SELECT–CASE, let us consider the following example to perform grade processing:

Example 8-4

Write a program segment to assign letter grades to test scores and count the number of each of the letter grades.

```
100  DECLARE BYTE TEST.SCORE, COUNT.A, COUNT.B, &
                    COUNT.C, COUNT.D, COUNT.F
110  DECLARE STRING GRADE
  .
  .
  .
1000 SELECT TEST.SCORE
1010    CASE >= 90
1020       GRADE = 'A'
1030       COUNT.A = COUNT.A + 1
1040    CASE  80 TO 89
1050       GRADE = 'B'
1060       COUNT.B = COUNT.B + 1
1070    CASE  70 TO 79
1080       GRADE = 'C'
1090       COUNT.C = COUNT.C + 1
1100    CASE  60 TO 69
1110       GRADE = 'D'
1120       COUNT.D = COUNT.D + 1
1130    CASE  < 60
1140       GRADE = 'F'
1150       COUNT.F = COUNT.F + 1
1160    CASE    ELSE
1170       PRINT 'INCORRECT TEST SCORE '; TEST.SCORE
1180 END SELECT
```

Figure 8-24 Processing grades with the SELECT-CASE.

The program segment for this example shown in Figure 8-24 is reasonably self-explanatory.

Exercise

8-9. Rewrite the following nested IF–THEN–ELSE structure using the SELECT–CASE structure.

```
IF CLASS >= 1 AND CLASS <= 3
   THEN RATE = 0.02
ELSE
   IF CLASS = 4
      THEN RATE = 0.03
   ELSE
      IF CLASS = 5
         THEN RATE = 0.05
      END IF
   END IF
END IF
```

Menu Control

The SELECT–CASE statement is ideal for implementing *menus*. A menu is a list of options, in an interactive prompt-driven program, from which the user can make a desired selection. In order for program execution to continue from the point where the list of selection is printed, you must type in your choice at the keyboard. To illustrate this, let us consider the following example:

Example 8-5

A special program is to be written to perform a variety of processing operations on files; the modules include the following:

1. Create a new file.
2. Kill an existing file.
3. Add records to an existing file.
4. Delete records from an existing file.
5. Modify records of an existing file.

This example involves preparing a menu module to allow the user to select whichever option is desired.

A menu approach to this problem is illustrated in Figure 8-25, which also includes a sample dialog. Note that labels rather than line numbers are used to identify the modules to be executed.

```
    .     Open files and perform
    .     other operations common
    .     to all functions.
100   DECLARE STRING Q, OPTION
110   DECLARE BYTE OPTION
    .
    .
    .
300  ! MENU SCHEDULE
310   Q = 'Y'
320   UNTIL Q = 'N'
330     PRINT "This is a file maintenance program."
340     INPUT "Do you wish to continue (Y/N)"; Q
350     PRINT "The options available to you are:"
360     PRINT " C - Create a new file"
370     PRINT " K - Kill an existing file"
380     PRINT " A - Add records to a file"
390     PRINT " D - Delete records from a file"
400     PRINT " M - Modify an existing record"
405     INPUT "Which option do you want (C,K,...)"; OPTION
410     SELECT OPTION
420       CASE = "C"
430         GOSUB C.FILE
440       CASE = "K"
450         GOSUB K.FILE
460       CASE = "A"
470         GOSUB ADD.REC
480       CASE = "D"
490         GOSUB DEL.REC
500       CASE = "M"
510         GOSUB MOD.REC
520     CASE ELSE
530         PRINT "Option must be C, K, A, D or M."
540     END SELECT
550   NEXT
560   CLOSE ...
570   STOP
    .
    .
    .
```

Figure 8-25   A menu program for Example 8-5. (The program listing is continued on the next page.)

```
15000 ! File create routine
  .
  .
  .
15980   PRINT "File creation completed"
15990 RETURN
  .
  .
  .
16000 ! File kill routine
  .
  .
  .
16990 RETURN
  .
  .
  .
32767 END
```

```
This is the file maintenance program.
Do you wish to continue (Y/N) ? Y
The options available to you are:
 C - Create a new file
 K - Kill an existing file
 A - Add records to a file
 D - Delete records from a file
 M - Modify an existing record
Which option do you want C, K, A, D or M?   C
       .
       .           (Creation dialog)
       .
File creation completed
Do you wish to continue?
```

Figure 8-25　(cont.)

Menu control of access to various components of a program is a commonly used technique. It is a convenient method for providing easy-to-remember access to numerous operations and is often used to control and/or limit access among users to particular operations. Menu-driven programs fit well within structured programs. They may contain a main menu and other menus that are subordinate to it. Such *nested menus* require suitable messages to inform the user at what level of the hierarchy the program is operating.

Exercise

8-10. What would occur in Figure 8-25 if the CASE ELSE were omitted and a user entered ''X'' at line 400?

The ON–GOSUB–OTHERWISE Statement

The menu-control sequence of Figure 8-25 is a useful tool. However, in some cases, where all of the options involve GOSUBS, there is another way to handle

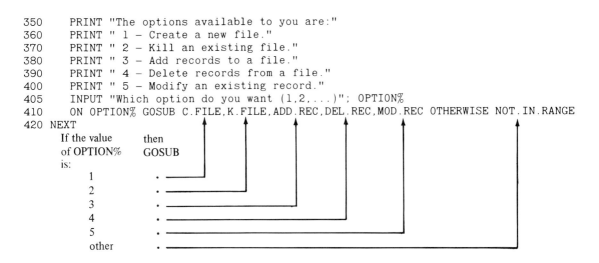

```
350      PRINT "The options available to you are:"
360      PRINT " 1 - Create a new file."
370      PRINT " 2 - Kill an existing file."
380      PRINT " 3 - Add records to a file."
390      PRINT " 4 - Delete records from a file."
400      PRINT " 5 - Modify an existing record."
405      INPUT "Which option do you want (1,2,...)"; OPTION%
410      ON OPTION% GOSUB C.FILE,K.FILE,ADD.REC,DEL.REC,MOD.REC OTHERWISE NOT.IN.RANGE
420 NEXT
```

Alternate form 410   ON OPTION% GOSUB 15000,16000,17000,18000,19000 OTHERWISE 20000

Statement numbers or labels can be used.

Figure 8-26 The ON-GOSUB-OTHERWISE statement.

this. Rather than giving the user options "C," "K," and so on, assume that the options are the numbers 1 through 5. Furthermore, if a number not in this range is entered, then the module name NOT.IN.RANGE is to be executed.

Again, nested IFs can in general be used to implement such a multiselection structure. But for special cases in which the test condition depends on consecutive whole-number values beginning with 1, it is simpler and preferable to use a special multiselection statement, the ON–GOSUB, provided by VAX Basic. It transfers control to *one of several* subroutines. Each subroutine must be terminated by a RETURN statement, which returns control to the first statement after the calling ON–GOSUB. It is illustrated in Figure 8-26. As we see here, the target can be either a line number or a label. The set of values of the test expression for which control transfers to one of the subroutines is called the *range* of the expression; it starts with 1 and goes through the whole numbers up to the number of targets. If the test expression is real, it will be truncated to yield an integer. Here we see that if OPTION% is 1, then the first target is selected; if it is 2, then the second target is selected, and so on. On execution of the subroutine, the RETURN statement will cause execution to continue at line 420.

The OTHERWISE clause is optional; note that a comma cannot appear between the last target and this clause. If the test expression's value is outside its range, Basic transfers control to the target specified in this clause if there is an OTHERWISE clause. However, without the OTHERWISE, an error condition occurs (code ERR = 58). If no ON ERROR has been set, then the error terminates the program and the following message is displayed:

```
% ON STATEMENT OUT OF RANGE AT LINE 410
```

Exercise

8-11. Write an ON–GOSUB statement (and whatever else is necessary) to select the subroutine to be executed based on the variable A as follows:

Value of A	Line
1	1000
2	1700
4	2500
6	3000
7	4000
8	3000

In Retrospect

VAX Basic provides a great variety of capabilities with its control structures. Table 8-1 attempts to put them into perspective by summarizing and contrasting their overlapping capabilities.

Table 8-1 Summary of Various Capabilities of Some Control Structures in VAX Basic

Structure	Comments
There are three types of program loops:	Passage through a loop can be controlled as follows:
FOR–NEXT	By specifying starting and ending values and a step size for a loop-control variable.
WHILE–NEXT UNTIL–NEXT	By specifying a condition in the first statement of the loop.
For all three preceding forms	Testing a condition within the loop block allows either early exit from the loop (with the EXIT statement) or direct transfer to the loop's NEXT statement (with the ITERATE statement).
There are five modifiers:	Statement modifiers are keywords that allow:
IF UNLESS	Execution of a statement conditionally.
WHILE UNTIL FOR	Execution of a statement repeatedly; that is, creation of an implied loop.
There are three selection structures:	These provide for options as the result of a test:
IF	Allows for the execution of either of two alternatives as the result of a test.
SELECT–CASE	Allows for the execution of any one of multiple alternatives as the result of a test.
ON–GOSUB	Transfer of temporary control to one of *several* locations, depending on condition.

The following comments are intended as guidelines in choosing the appropriate control structure. (In many cases, it will not matter which one you choose.)

1. The FOR–NEXT structure must include a counter, which also serves as the loop-control variable. The loop-control variable in FOR–NEXT is changed automatically by a specified, fixed step size. If the body of the loop is to be executed a predetermined number of times and the step size of the loop-control variable is fixed, the FOR loop should be used. If the number of passages through the loop depends on a condition whose value (true or false) may change in the body of the loop, it is in general preferable to use a WHILE or UNTIL loop.
2. The WHILE and UNTIL loops do not involve a loop-control variable; if a counter is included in either of these structures, it must be incremented explicitly in the body of the loop.

Answers to Preceding Exercises

8-1. Make the following changes:

```
510     LOOP = 0
        ASK:
        UNTIL LOOP
570     LOOP = - 1 IF LEFT$(Q$,1) <> 'Y' AND LEFT$(Q$,1) <> 'y'
```

Note the changes from = to <> and from OR to AND on line 570.

8-2. a. The body of the loop will be executed once.
  b. The body of the loop will be executed nine times.
  c. The control value will never reach the test value, and the computer will enter an infinite loop.
  d. The control value will be reinitialized to 1 on every pass through the loop body, resulting in an infinite loop. Counters must be initialized *before* entering the loop body in order to serve as loop-control variables.

8-3. a. 7; J = 7,8,9,10,11,12,13
  b. 4; J = 3,6,9,12
  c. 11; J = 5,4,3,2,1,0,-1,-2,-3,-4,-5
  d. 12; J = 0,1,2,3,4,5,6,7,8,9,10,11

8-4. It is important to recognize that none of the three fundamental counter operations is done by a separate statement in the FOR–NEXT structure. The counter is initialized explicitly in the FOR statement itself. The incrementation and test are implicit, being built into the structure. Note also that because there is no counter associated with the WHILE (or UNTIL) loop, NEXT is not followed by a variable in these loops, as it is in the FOR loop.

8-5. Delete the text line with the FOR statement on line 2090 and line 3130 (NEXT RATE) from the routine PROC.TABLE. Insert the following two lines in the main program:

```
1018    FOR RATE = INIT TO FINAL
1022    NEXT RATE
```

8-6. The loop would be executed once if they are the same. When the step size is positive, if the initial value exceeds the test (final) value, the termination condition is already met, so the loop will not be executed at all.

8-7. a. 10 x 10 = 100
b. 7 x 5 = 35
c. 10; the inner loop does not change the value of A.
d. 0; the outer loop will never be executed.

8-8. Remember that calculator-mode (and immediate-mode) statements must fit on a single line and must start in column 1.

```
PRINT I, SQR(I) FOR I = 1 TO 10
```

8-9.
```
SELECT CLASS
    CASE 1 TO 3
        RATE = 0.02
    CASE = 4
        RATE = 0.03
    CASE = 5
        RATE = 0.05
END SELECT
```

8-10. No match will be found, and control will transfer to the statement following the END SELECT statement.

8-11.
```
 500   ON A% GOSUB 1000, 1700, 9999, 2500, 9999, 3000, 4000, 3000
 :
 :
9999   !  Dummy Subroutine
10001 RETURN
```

Programming Problems

8-1. Write a program to compute the average of a group of values. The *number of values* to be averaged, as well as the values themselves, is to be entered from the keyboard. Output should include the number of values and the average, both suitably identified.

8-2. Expand problem 8-1 as follows: All the values must now lie within a specified range, also to be entered from the keyboard. If any input value lies outside of the specified range, it is *not* to be included in the computation, and a suitable message is to be printed. Additional output should include a count of the out-of-range values.

8-3. One objective of inventory control for a manufacturing company is to minimize the overall cost resulting from carrying inventory and setting up for new production runs. The term *economic order quantity* refers to the most economical quantity of a given item to produce in a single run for specified cost conditions; more explicitly, the economic order quantity is computed according to the expression

$$Q = \sqrt{\frac{2rs}{C}}$$

where Q = economic order quantity.

R = annual number of units required.

S = setup cost per order.

C = inventory cost to carry one unit for one year.

A manager would like a program that will calculate tables such as the following:

```
ECONOMIC ORDER QUANTITY
UNITS REQUIRED: 200,000
INVENTORY COST: 0.030

SETUP COST          QUANTITY
    12.00             12649
    12.50             12910
    13.00             13166
    13.50             13416
    14.00             13663
```

Input to the program will be

Example Values	
R	200000
C	0.030
Beginning value of S	12
Ending value of S	14
Increment of S	0.5

Upon completing the table, the program should ask the manager whether or not another table is desired.

8-4. Modify problem 8-3 to allow a range to be entered for both S and R and print a series of tables. Nested FOR–NEXT loops will be required for this.

8-5. Modify problem 8-4 to print the results in a single table, with the columns representing increasing values of S and the rows, increasing values of C.

8-6. Expand problem 7-5 to print each examination-group average as a bar graph, as shown by the following example output:

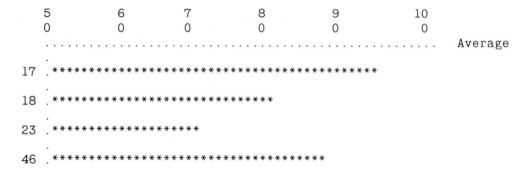

```
   5       6       7       8       9        10
   0       0       0       0       0        0
 . . . . . . . . . . . . . . . . . . . . . . . . . . . . . . . . . . . . . . . . . . . .   Average
       .
17  .***********************************************
       .
18  .****************************
       .
23  .*******************
       .
46  .**************************************
```

8-7. Write a program to compute an amortization schedule for a fixed-payment loan. The program to be written must

a. Accept from the keyboard the amount to be borrowed, the annual interest rate in percent, and the number of months over which the loan is to be paid.
b. Calculate the monthly payment.
c. For each month, calculate and print how much was applied to interest and how much to the loan.
d. At the end of the report, print the total interest paid.

To calculate the monthly payment at the beginning of the program, use the following formula:

$$\text{Monthly payment} = \frac{i \times (\text{loan amount})}{1 - (1 + i)^{-n}}$$
$$\text{(for all except the last month)}$$

where i = monthly interest rate expressed as a decimal fraction. For instance, an annual rate of 18 percent would give

$$i = (18/100)/12 = 0.18/12 = 0.015$$

n = number of monthly payments

To calculate interest relating to each monthly payment, use

$$\text{Monthly interest charge} = \text{previous month's balance} \times i$$

$$\text{New principal} = \text{Previous principal} - \text{payment}$$
$$+ \text{ monthly interest charge}$$
$$\text{(for all except the last month)}$$

The output should appear as follows:

```
LOAN SUMMARY
  AMOUNT OF THE PURCHASE: 100.00
  ANNUAL RATE OF INTEREST: 21
  NUMBER OF MONTHS:  12

MONTHLY PAYMENT BASED ON ABOVE:  $9.32

  PAYMENT    PREVIOUS    AMOUNT OF    AMOUNT APPLIED       NEW
  NUMBER     PRINCIPAL   INTEREST     TO PRINCIPAL      PRINCIPAL

     1        100.00       1.75           7.57            92.43
     2         92.43       1.62           7.70            84.73
     .            .           .              .               .
     .            .           .              .               .
     .            .           .              .               .


  TOTAL INTEREST PAID ON 100.00 LOAN = 11.73
```

For the last month, the payment should be the previous principal together with the interest on that principal. This will ensure that the new principal is zero for the last month.

Because of the way the computer handles numbers, you will find that the sum of the monthly interest and monthly principal differs sometimes from the monthly payment by 1 cent.

When processing is complete, the program should ask the user if another table is to be calculated.

8-8. The value of e, the base of the natural logarithm, is given by the infinite series

$$e = 1 + \frac{1}{1} + \frac{1}{1 \times 2} + \frac{1}{1 \times 2 \times 3} + \frac{1}{1 \times 2 \times 3 \times 4} + \cdots$$

The preceding expression can be simplified for computational purposes by factoring any number of finite terms in the series. If we keep only the terms written explicitly in the expression just given, we get the approximation

$$e_4 = 1 + \frac{1}{1}\left(1 + \frac{1}{2}\left(1 + \frac{1}{3}\left(1 + \frac{1}{4}\right)\right)\right)$$

Write a program to compute e_{10}, that is, the approximation in which the last term in the factored form is $(1 + 1/10)$. The correct value of e to ten decimal places is 2.7182818284. The printed value of e_{10} should contain *exactly* the number of decimal places to which this approximation is good. (Compare the computed and correct values, digit by digit, until you find a difference.)

8-9. Write a program to compute the value of π, using 100 terms in the following series:

$$\frac{\pi}{4} = \frac{\sin(1)}{1} + \frac{\sin(3)}{3} + \cdots + \frac{\sin(2n-1)}{2n-1} + \cdots$$

As in problem 8-8, print exactly the number of decimal places to which the approximation is good. The correct value of π to 15 decimal places is 3.141592653589793.

8-10. Modify problem 4-3 as follows: The customer deposits $100.00 every month, the yearly interest rate is 8.5 percent, and the interest is compounded quarterly (see problem 4.5). Output should be in the form of a table, showing the interest paid during the year and the total capital at the end of each year for ten years, as in the following example:

Monthly deposit: $100.00.

Yearly interest: 8.5%.

Compounded quarterly.

Year	Interest for year	Total capital
1	105.30	1,305.30
2	219.83	2,725.13
3	344.42	4,269.55
.	.	.
.	.	.
.	.	.
10	1,582.68	19,619.40

Note that the program will have to *compute* all relevant quantities for *each* conversion period, even though it will *print* them only for every fourth conversion period.

9

Arrays and Array Processing

CHAPTER OUTLINE

Preview

Examples and techniques up until now have all involved the notion of reading a set of data values, operating on them, printing results, and then reading the next set of data values and so on. In other words, each data record is read, processed, and then discarded in favor of the next one. However, some applications require that related data values be read and saved *for later processing. The subject of this chapter is arrays, with which it is possible to handle large numbers of quantities by using a simple notation. From this chapter, you will learn about the following:*

1. The concept of subscripting and using subscripted variables in Basic.

2. *The DIM statement, which declares that a* **variable name** *consists of a* **group of related variables.** *The result is commonly called an* **array**; *individual variables in the array are referred to as* **subscripted variables** *or* **array elements.**
3. *Arrays consisting of rows and columns—that is, two-dimensional arrays.*
4. *Performing the following operations on arrays:*

   a. *Loading data into an array.*
   b. *Searching an array.*
   c. *Printing the values of the array elements.*
   d. *Modifying values of the elements of an array.*

The Rationale for Arrays

Calculation of the Mean

The mean (also called the *arithmetic average*) of a set of values is defined as the sum of the values divided by the number of values in the set. For example, the mean of the five numbers 11, 4, 27, 54, 19 is

$$\text{Mean} = (11 + 4 + 27 + 54 + 19)/5$$

We can actually write a program to compute the mean using only a single variable to hold the sum of the quantities being averaged. The program segment for such a computation is given in Figure 9-1. The reason we do not need five

```
       .
       .
       .
900    LAST = 5
1000   SUM = 0
1010   FOR CNTR = 1 TO LAST
1020     READ VALUE
1030     SUM = SUM + VALUE
1040   NEXT CNTR
1050   AVE = SUM/LAST
       .
       .
       .
5000   DATA 11,4,27,54,19
```

Figure 9-1 Calculating the average of five numbers.

variables for the five values to be averaged is that, once we have accumulated a given value, that value is no longer needed for the rest of the calculation. The only remnant of the value required at the end of each pass through the loop is in the accumulated sum. This is shown in Table 9-1.

This is perfect for calculating the mean. However, let us consider the operation of determining the median, a task that will require using more than a single variable.

TABLE 9-1 Values of the Variables in the Program of Figure 9-1 After Each Pass Through the Body of the Loop

CNTR	AMOUNT	SUM
1	11	11
2	4	15
3	27	42
4	54	96
5	19	115

Calculation of the Median

Roughly speaking, the *median* of a set of numbers is the middle value of those numbers. As we shall see from the following, the precise definition depends on whether the number of values is odd or even. The median of the set of five numbers from Table 9-1 is 19. Note that half of the numbers in the set are smaller than 19 (4 and 11), and half of them are larger (27 and 54). This is illustrated in Figure 9-2(a). Thus, if the number of values is odd, the median is the middle value of the set. However, what if the set consists of an even number of values? Then the median is the average of the *two* middle values, as illustrated in Figure 9-2(b).

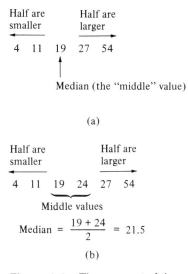

Figure 9-2   The concept of the median.

The circumstances here are fundamentally different from the calculation of the mean in several respects.

1. All the values must be in memory at the same time.
2. These values must be *arranged in sequence*.
3. There must be a way to identify the middle value(s), for example, by numbering their positions. We did this part "by eye" in the preceding example. But we could not do it this way if we had a very large set. In either case, the computer is not capable of such reasoning, regardless of how simple it may be.

In order to write the program to compute the median, we see that we need to hold *all* of the data values in the set in memory *at the same time*. One way of doing this is to define as many different variables as there are values in the data set. However, this is not an acceptable approach for at least three reasons: (1) It is completely impractical to code for large sets of numbers (imagine writing assignment statements with 1000 variables); (2) it obscures the logic of the problem; and (3) it requires appreciable changes in the code when the number of variables changes. In addition, there are also applications for which much more efficient code can be written with all related variables in memory at the same time, even though this is not necessary.

Exercise

9-1. Find the median of each of the following data sets:

    a. 13   9 27 5 18
    b. 103 29 56 7 35 12

Principles of Arrays

The Concept of Subscripting

Let us consider an engineer who has a data set consisting of 20 test values that she must process. In order to identify each one, she might call them "values 1 through 20." Using mathematical terminology, she might refer to respective values as "v one," "v two," and so on. The commonly used mathematical representation is $v_1, v_2, \ldots v_{20}$, where the numbers are called *subscripts*. Note that the group has a name (v), and each element has a unique identifying number. (This is much less cumbersome than giving individual names such as $a, b, c, \ldots, t$.)

With this, we can speak of the data set v consisting of 20 elements. If we wish to get technical, we can refer to the data set v_i, where the subscript i ranges from 1 through 20:

    v_i where $i = 1$ to 20

A final very important point is that this notation can be much more readily generalized to an arbitrary number of elements n simply by allowing the subscript to range from 1 to n, as follows:

$$v_i \quad \text{where } i = 1 \text{ to } n$$

Note that the preceding range representation for n looks very much like the form of the FOR statement in Basic. Indeed, subscripting in computer languages and the Basic FOR are patterned after methods of mathematics. Even the following mathematical form of the mean formula virtually tells us how to write the corresponding Basic code to perform the task:

$$\text{Mean} = \frac{\text{The sum of the } v_i \text{ for } i = 1 \text{ to } n}{n}$$

Subscripted Variables in Basic—Arrays

All variables named in a program reserve space for the storage of one value; this may be numeric or string. Thus, for example, the variables HOLD, WORK, and NAME\$ would provide us with three memory areas for data. These are commonly referred to as *simple variables*. Basic also allows us to use *subscripted variables*, which correspond to the notions of subscripting described in the preceding section. The data set v that represents the collection of all of the subscripted elements is called an *array*. This name is used in both mathematics and programming languages.

Recall that a variable name in a computer language represents the address of a particular memory location and the number of bytes required by that variable (for instance, two for integer and four for floating point). On the other hand, associated with an array name is the beginning position in memory of the array, the number of bytes associated with the data type, and the number of elements in the array.

When we need a particular variable in a program, we simply use its name. If we need a particular element of an array, we must use the array name *and* the appropriate number or subscript. The combination of array name and subscript uniquely specifies a single variable, called an *array element*. An array element is an ordinary variable and can be used in a program much as any other simple variable.

Note that whereas up to now we have used the terms *variable* and *variable name* synonymously, this is not possible for arrays. The *array name* stands for an *entire group of related variables* (locations); the *subscript points* to a *particular* location within the collection; the two combined identify a *single variable*, the *array element*. The array notation and related concepts are shown in Figure 9-3. We shall learn later in this chapter why the numbering starts with 0 rather than with 1. Note also that *each* of the elements in the array, no matter how many there may be, is now described uniquely by *two* variable names: the array name and the subscript name. As we shall see next, this method of dealing with a group of related variables will allow us to increase their number with trivially simple modifications to the program.

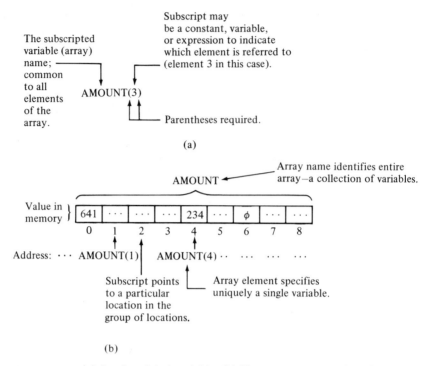

Figure 9-3   (a) A subscripted variable. (b) Memory representation of an array.

Arrays as Data Structures

Backing off for a moment, we see that we have dealt with three broad types of data: floating-point, integer, and string. We have also used *records,* which are made up of component *fields* that can be any of the three broad types. We see that a record is a more complex structure than a simple variable because it is made up of variables in some organized way. In this sense, an array is similar to a record because it is an organized collection of data items. However, the array differs from the record in that all the elements of the array are of a single type, that is, floating-point, integer, or string. In a broad sense, we are dealing with the concept of *data structures.* A data structure is a collection of related data items governed by a set of rules for grouping and manipulating these items. We shall learn more about data structures in chapters that follow.

Defining an Array in a Program

As we learned earlier, when a simple variable is introduced in a program, the system reserves a memory area for that variable. The situation is somewhat more complicated for arrays because an area must be reserved for the many elements comprising the array. In order to give us flexibility in program design, Basic allows us to specify the number of elements for which we need space reserved. This is done with the DIM statement, illustrated in Figure 9-4. The number inside the parentheses following the array name specifies the maximum allowed subscript value, called the *upper bound.* The value used for the upper

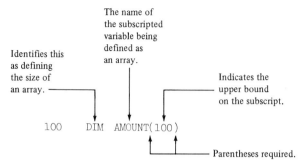

Figure 9-4　The DIM statement.

bound can be as large as needed by the program, although in practice it is limited by the amount of memory available in the program. The DIM statement, like the DATA statement, is nonexecutable; it is usually placed at the beginning of the program.

Determining the Median of a Data Set

Example Definition

As our first illustration of using arrays, let us consider the following example to determine the median of a data set:

Example 9-1

> The file TEST.DAT contains test values that range from 0 to 500, stored one value per record. The maximum number of values that will ever be stored is 100. The last data value will be followed by a trailer with a value of − 1. Note that this is not part of the data set; it is only a flag to indicate the end of the data. A program is required to determine the median of the data set.

Let us consider this example in two phases. For the first phase, we will assume that the data values are stored in the file in ascending sequence (the smallest first and the largest last). For the second, we will make no assumptions about the data, and it will be necessary to perform a sort.

Program Planning—First Phase

From the example definition, we see that an array with an upper bound of 100 is required. The first action is to read the values from the file into an array. Even though the example statement indicates that there will be no more then 100 values in the file, the program should perform a check. For this we must decide what to do if there are more than 100 values in the input file. Upon examining the circumstances, let us assume that we have decided to handle this by displaying a message on the screen and continuing processing using only the first 100 values.

In general, whenever a data set is stored in an array, it is important to know how many elements have been assigned values. The count of array elements containing meaningful data is called the *actual* array size. This is to be contrasted with the *potential* array size, which is the number of locations reserved when the group is created. The simplest way to establish the actual array size is to use a counter. For instance, let us assume the we have stored 47 values in the array AMOUNT. Then they will be stored as elements AMOUNT(1) through AMOUNT(47), and the value stored in the counter will be 47. In some instances, it is convenient to store the count as element 0 of the array. In this illustration, this number of elements in the array might be stored as AMOUNT(0). This is especially useful when working with functions or subroutines that involve arrays.

Regarding the median example, once the values have been read, it is only necessary to select the element(s) representing the median. Remember that its value depends upon whether there is an odd or an even number of data values. The examples of Figure 9-5 illustrate finding the value. Note the use of integer arithmetic in the case where the number of values is odd.

(a)   4 , 11 , 19 , 27 , 54

        (1) (2) (3) (4) (5)

                  ↑

                 └────── Median element

Figure 9-5   Determining the median of a data set.

Odd number of elements:
    The subscript of the median element
    can be calculated as

$$\text{Subscript} = \frac{\text{Number of elements}}{2} + 1$$

$$= \frac{5}{2} + 1$$

$$= 2 + 1$$
$$= 3$$

$$\text{Median} = \text{Element } 3$$
$$= 19$$

(b)   4 , 11 , 19 , 24 , 27 , 54

        (1) (2) (3) (4) (5) (6)

               ↑   ↑

             └───┴── Used to calculate the median

Even number of elements:
    The two desired subscripts can be
    calculated as follow:

$$\text{Subscript } 1 = \frac{\text{Number of elements}}{2}$$

$$= \frac{6}{2}$$

$$= 3$$

$$\text{Subscript } 2 = \text{Subscript } 1 + 1$$
$$= 4$$

$$\text{Median} = \frac{\text{Element } 3 + \text{element } 4}{2}$$

$$= \frac{19 + 24}{2} = 21.5$$

```
100      DIM AMOUNT(100)
110      DECLARE INTEGER CHECK.POINT, POINT, CNT
200   !
1000     GOSUB SETUP
1020     GOSUB READ.ARRAY
1040     GOSUB FIND.MEDIAN
1060     GOSUB FINISH.UP
1080     STOP
1110  !
         SETUP:
           OPEN 'TEST.DAT' FOR INPUT AS FILE #1
2050
         READ.ARRAY:
           CNT = 0
           INPUT #1, POINT
           WHILE CNT < 100 AND POINT > -1
             CNT = CNT + 1
3010         AMOUNT(CNT) = POINT
             INPUT #1, POINT
           NEXT
           IF POINT > -1
             THEN PRINT 'Number of values in the input file exceeds 100.'
             PRINT 'Only the first 100 values are being used.'
           END IF
           RETURN
3120  !
         FIND.MEDIAN:
           CHECK.POINT = CNT/2
4010       IF 2*CHECK.POINT <> CNT
             THEN MEDIAN = AMOUNT(CHECK.POINT + 1)
           ELSE
             MEDIAN = (AMOUNT(CHECK.POINT) + AMOUNT(CHECK.POINT + 1))/2.0
           END IF
4100       RETURN
4110  !
         FINISH.UP:
           PRINT 'Number of values processed: '; CNT
           PRINT 'Value of the median is:    '; MEDIAN
5030       CLOSE #1
5040       RETURN
32767    END
```

Figure 9-6 Finding a Median—Phase 1 of Example 9-1.

The logic of the first-phase solution is very simple. A loop for reading the data from the file is required, followed by a selection action to obtain the median. The complete program solution is shown in Figure 9-6. There are several important things to notice about this program.

1. The first value is read from the file by a separate INPUT statement outside the loop. Since the value read will be used to control termination of the loop, this provides a "look-ahead" capability in controlling the loop.
2. Because two different criteria are used for controlling this loop, a WHILE statement with an explictly incremented counter (CNT) is used. In this instance, it is more convenient than a FOR.
3. Regarding the logic of this loop, note that the loop will be entered after the first data value has been read. In general, the value of CNT will be incremented to be in step with the data read only when the loop is repeated.

4. If, for example, there are two data values and the trailer, the following sequence will occur:

   a. The first value will be read outside the loop.
   b. CNT will be incremented to 1 and this value stored in VALUE(1).
   c. The second data value will be read by the last statement of the loop.
   d. The loop will be repeated since the conditions are true.
   e. CNT will be incremented to 2 and the second value stored in VALUE(2).
   f. The third value (the trailer) will be read.
   g. Since POINT equals -1, the loop will be terminated.
   h. Two data values were read, and the value of CNT is 2.

5. If the data set consists of 100 values plus the trailer, the preceding process would be repeated with 100 values being loaded and the value of CNT set to 100.

6. If the data set consists of 101 values (or more) plus the trailer, the program would read 101 values before exiting. (You should carefully check this logic to be certain that you agree.) Upon terminating, the value of POINT will not be -1, and the excessive-values message will be displayed.

7. In the IF statement of line 4010, the determination is made regarding whether CNT is odd or even. If it is odd, then integer arithmetic in the preceding line will cause the remainder to be discarded. Hence the test

   ```
   2*CHECK.POINT <> CNT
   ```

   will be true; refer to the example in Figure 9-5(a).

8. A single expression involves two different elements of the array:

   ```
   MEDIAN = (VALUE(CHECK.POINT) + VALUE(CHECK.POINT+1))/2.0
   ```

   Here we see, for instance, that if the value of CHECK.POINT is 6, then the value of CHECK.POINT + 1 is 7. This gives the two middle values for the even-data-count case.

The program in Figure 9-6 illustrates the real power of an array when it is combined with a looping structure. Note that the variable CNT serves a *dual* purpose: *as loop counter in the control structure and also as subscript in the data structure.* As CNT is incremented in its role as loop counter, the body of the loop processes successive array elements, that is, CNT points to successive locations in the array in its role as subscript.

Sorting the Values in an Array—Example 9-1, Second Phase

If the data values are not in sequence when they are read into memory, then they must be sorted before the median can be determined. The topic of sorting data is an extremely important one in the computing field; in fact, there are entire books on the subject. For this example, we shall use a method that corresponds to the way in which we might sort a short list of numbers manually. It is not very efficient for computer use, but it will illustrate the process of evolving a program solution through a pseudocode approach. (Note that an alternative sorting method is the subject of one of the programming problems at the end of this chapter.)

	Original Set					Sorted Set				
(a)	87	13	64	27	6					
(b)	87	13	64	27	6̶	6				
(c)	87	1̶3̶	64	27	6̶	6	13			
(d)	87	1̶3̶	64	2̶7̶	6̶	6	13	27		
(e)	87	1̶3̶	6̶4̶	2̶7̶	6̶	6	13	27	64	
(f)	8̶7̶	1̶3̶	6̶4̶	2̶7̶	6̶	6	13	27	64	87

Figure 9-7 Steps in sorting a data set.

Assume that we have the list of five numbers of Figure 9-7(a) to sort into an ascending sequence. A simple approach is to look over the entire data set, find the smallest value, cross it out, then write it down as the first number in a new list. This is illustrated in Figure 9-7(b). We then scan the list again, searching for the smallest one remaining (ignoring the one that is crossed out). After the second search, we have the result shown in Figure 9-7(c). This process must be repeated as many times as there are elements in the list. The final result is a new list with the elements in ascending sequence, as shown in Figure 9-7(f).

This process is readily adapted to arrays using the FOR to handle the looping operations. However, it is important to understand that the solution requires a second array to hold the sorted set of values. We see this in the following pseudocode solution:

For "New array subscript" from 1 to number of elements
    Find smallest remaining value from old array and place in new array

Here we see that a main loop will be required to repeat the search for the smallest remaining value. This loop will be executed a number of times equal to the number of elements in the array. This rough cut at our problem represents the broad steps in progressing from (a) to (b) to (c) and so on in the illustration of Figure 9-7. Now we have two things to recognize. First, another loop will be required, one to search for the smallest remaining value. The strategy for this part involves several steps.

1. The first value in the data set is assumed to be the smallest; it is placed in a memory location set aside to hold the value assumed to be the smallest at any stage of program execution.
2. The next value is compared to the smallest one. If this next value is smaller than the assumed smallest, then the assumed smallest is replaced by this next value, and we "mark the spot" in the original data set that held the value placed in the assumed-smallest location; otherwise, the assumed smallest value is left alone.
3. Step 2 is repeated for each succeeding value. When all values in the data set have been processed in this manner, the assumed smallest is the actual smallest of the remaining ones, and the current "marked spot" identifies

	Assumed smallest		Smallest value so far
Element	Value		↓
1	87		87 13 64 27 6

| 2 | 13 | 87 13 64 27 6 |

Note that 13 is still the "smallest."

| 2 | 13 | 87 13 64 27 6 |

| 2 | 13 | 87 13 64 27 6 |

Entire set has now been scanned. The smallest element is the fifth one, with a value of 6.

| 5 | 6 | 87 13 64 27 6 |

Figure 9-8 Searching for a smallest value.

its position in the original data set. These first three steps are shown in Figure 9-8.
4. Place the smallest remaining one into its proper location in the sorted set and "cross it out" from the original set.
5. Repeat steps 1 through 4 until all values in the original data set have been placed in their proper locations in the sorted data set.

The second thing to recognize is that some means will be necessary to "cross out" each value from the original array as it is selected (refer to Figure 9-7). One simple way to do this is to replace it by a value that is larger than any possible data value. This concept is illustrated in Figure 9-9. With this, the pseudocode is as shown at the top of the next page.

Original Set					Sorted Set
87	13	64	27	6	
87	13	64	27	9999	6
87	9999	64	27	9999	6 13

and so on

Figure 9-9 The effect of replacing in sorting.

FOR "New array subscript" from 1 to number of elements
    Set HOLD to largest possible value
    FOR "Old array subscript" from 1 to number of elements
       IF old array element is less than value in HOLD
          THEN Copy value from old array element to HOLD
               Save element number
       END IF
    NEXT
    Copy value in HOLD to new array
    Replace array element in old array with largest possible value
NEXT

Additional code required by Figure 9-6 to do this job is shown in Figure 9-10. Although this method of sorting is not very elegant, it does work and is very intuitive. As we can see, the code corresponds closely to the preceding pseudocode. Note that, in contrast to the program of Figure 9-6, this one uses FOR loops to control the looping. In fact, the variable INNER, which is used to control the inner loop, is also used as the subscript in referencing elements of the array. It is important to understand that this dual role for the variable INNER is not forced on us by Basic syntax; it is *chosen* because it is convenient in carrying out the desired operations.

There is one additional change that still has to be made to the *existing* code in Figure 9-6 to mesh with the code in Figure 9-10. This is left as an exercise.

```
100  DIM AMOUNT(100)
105  DIM IN.VALUE(100)
110  DECLARE INTEGER  CHECK.POINT, POINT, CNT,                    &
                      INNER, OUTER, HOLD, HOLD.PNTR

200  !
1000 GOSUB SETUP
1020 GOSUB READ.ARRAY
1030 GOSUB SORT.ARRAY
1040 GOSUB FIND.MEDIAN
1060 GOSUB FINISH.UP
1080 STOP
       .
       .
       .
```

```
    SORT.ARRAY:
       FOR OUTER = 1 TO CNT
          HOLD = 32767  ◄─────────────── This ensures that the first compare of the
          FOR INNER = 1 TO CNT            inner loop causes a replacement.
             IF IN.VALUE(INNER) < HOLD   If next element of old array is smaller
                HOLD = IN.VALUE(INNER) }  than the previous smallest value, then
                HOLD.PNTR = INNER      }  replace it and save its element number.
             ENDIF
          NEXT INNER
          AMOUNT(OUTER) = HOLD  ◄──────── Put smallest remaining value into the new array.
          IN.VALUE(HOLD.PNTR) = 32767◄─── Set this corresponding element of
       NEXT OUTER                         the old array to a "large" value.
       RETURN
```

Figure 9-10   Sorting the elements of an array.

Exercises

9-2. Change the code in Figure 9-6 so that the combined program of Figures 9-6 and 9-10 functions properly.

9-3. What would be the effect on the logic of the program in Figure 9-6 if the sequence of statements inside the WHILE loop in READ.ARRAY were changed to

```
AMOUNT(CNT) = POINT
CNT = CNT + 1
INPUT #1, POINT
```

and CNT were initialized to CNT = 1 instead of CNT = 0?

More About the DIM Statement and Arrays

Characteristics of the DIM

From Example 9-1 we have seen that the DIM statement is used to reserve the necessary memory for elements of an array. Although our focus at the moment is on the DIM statement, VAX Basic provides four statements for performing this operation. The DIM statement described here is the standard one. Later in this chapter we shall learn how to use the familiar DECLARE for this task. The two remaining, COMMON and MAP, are described in later chapters. The following comments that elaborate on the principles of the DIM statement apply equally to DECLARE, except as noted:

1. More than one DIM statement is allowed in a program; we see this in the program of Figure 9-10.
2. More than one array may be listed in a single DIM statement; the array names must be separated by commas. Thus, the two DIM statements of Figure 9-10 could be combined into

    ```
    100  DIM AMOUNT(100), IN.VALUE(100)
    ```

3. Arrays can be any of the data types allowed in VAX Basic; that is, floating-point, integer, or string. The data types of the arrays may be specified by the appropriate suffix (dollar sign for string, percent sign for integer) or lack of it (floating point). (This does *not* apply to DECLARE.)
4. The same name can be used for a simple variable and a subscripted variable. That is, within a given program, A and A(I%) could both be used and would be every bit as different as A and B(I%) would be. But this is poor programming practice and should be avoided.
5. The upper bound on the value of each subscript is listed explicitly inside the parentheses following the array name in the DIM statement. In addition, VAX Basic provides a *default lower bound* of 0 for each subscript. The number of allowed subscript values is therefore one larger than the upper bound. As a rule, the element numbered 0 is not used because a counting sequence beginning at 1 is less confusing than one beginning at 0.

6. The bounds in all arrays on lines 100 and 105 are constants. DIM statements in which *all* bounds are constants are called *nonexecutable* or *declarative* DIMs. With such statements, memory is allocated when the Basic program is translated into machine language, rather than when the program is executed. An array name in a nonexecutable DIM statement cannot appear in any other DIM statement. A nonexecutable DIM statement must precede the program statement in which the declared array is first referenced. It is good programming practice to place all nonexecutable DIMs together at the beginning of the program, before any executable statements.

7. The use of the DIM statement to allocate memory for an array is sometimes referred to as "dimensioning the array." (DIM is actually an abreviation for DIMENSION, and either form may be used.) This is a different use of the word *dimension* then in "the dimension of an array." One refers to reserving memory locations; the other, to the *number of subscripts*. (The latter arises in connection with *multidimensional arrays,* which are described later in this chapter.) This double usage is sometimes confusing for beginning students. Use of the word *dimension* in this book refers to the number of subscripts.

8. When referencing an array declared in a nonexecutable DIM, you must be certain not to use a subscript value that exceeds the declared upper bound; otherwise, the system will signal the error message

Subscript out of range (ERR = 55)

Exercises

9-4. Identify the errors in each of the following program segments:

```
a. 500   X = A(35)
    .
    .
    .
   600   DIM A(40)
b. 500   DIM A(35)
    .
    .
    .
   600   X = A(40)
c. 500   DIM A(35)
    .
    .
    .
   600   DIM A(40)
```

9-5. What would happen if the condition test

CNT < 100

were omitted in the program of Figure 9-6?

Implicit Memory Allocation

Actually, if the value of a subscript will not exceed 10 [for instance, AMOUNT(10) is the element with the largest subscript], then the array need not be defined in a DIM. Consider the following statement, which might be included as part of a program:

```
AMOUNT(4) = 0
```

Furthermore, assume that AMOUNT has not been dimensioned in a DIM statement and that this is the first time it is encountered in the program. When the Basic interpreter first encounters it, the system will automatically allocate space as if the following DIM had been included in the program:

```
DIM AMOUNT(10)
```

This is called *implicit memory allocation*. In general, it is considered poor programming practice and should be avoided. All arrays in a program should be allocated memory explicitly, regardless of their sizes.

The only reason implicit allocation is mentioned in this text is that it is possible to get the subscript-out-of-range error message under seemingly strange conditions. For instance, let us assume that we include the following statement in our program to calculate the square root of A:

```
HOLD = SQRT(A)
```

Unfortunately, the name of the desired function is SQR, not SQRT. The interpreter will consider SQRT as an implicitly defined array. Hence, if the value A exceeds 10, the out-of-range error occurs.

Executable DIM; Dynamic Memory Allocation

The nonexecutable DIM statement creates *static* arrays. A static array is one whose size (number of elements) does not change during execution. This works well in applications in which a given array is very nearly the same size each time the program is run. But static arrays have some disadvantages. One disadvantage is that each array occupies its portion of memory during the entire execution of the program. This is a distinct disadvantage if a program will not fit into memory. To illustrate how dynamic arrays can be useful, let us assume that we have a program that includes the following arrays:

RATES   Real array consisting of 10,000 elements.
          Used only in the PREP.DATA module.
POINTS%   Integer array consisting of 15,000 elements.
          Used only in the COMPENSATE module.

VAX Basic provides a mechanism, the *executable* DIM statement, for *dynamic memory allocation* for arrays. Executable DIM creates arrays during execution time. Such arrays are called *dynamic* arrays. Using the executable DIM, the

```
DECLARE INTEGER ARRAY.SIZE
   .
   .
   .
PREP.DATA:
   ARRAY.SIZE = 10000
   DIM RATES(ARRAY.SIZE)
      .⎫
      .⎬ Module statements
      .⎭

   ARRAY.SIZE = 1
   DIM RATES(ARRAY.SIZE)
   RETURN
COMPENSATE:
   ARRAY.SIZE = 15000
   DIM POINTS%(ARRAY.SIZE)
      .⎫
      .⎬ Module statements
      .⎭

   ARRAY.SIZE = 1
   DIM POINTS%(ARRAY.SIZE)
   RETURN
```

Figure 9-11 Using the executable DIM.

arrays can be set to their required sizes when needed and reduced to virtually nothing when not needed. This is illustrated in the program segment of Figure 9-11. The following additional comments relate to the executable DIM:

1. If an array named in an executable DIM statement is referred to in the program before the DIM itself executes, the system will signal an out-of-range error.
2. An array name can appear in more than one executable DIM. Contrast this with the corresponding situation for a nonexecutable DIM, as described in the preceding section, item 6.
3. An executable DIM statement reinitializes the array to zero for numeric arrays or the null string for string arrays. Thus, if the values of an array are to be used at the very beginning of a program and then again at the end, an executable DIM should not be placed between these two uses.

Exercises

9-6. An array defined with 100 elements contains 30 values sorted in ascending sequence, starting with ARR(1) and ending with ARR(30). Write the code required to accept a value from the keyboard and insert it in proper sequence in the array ARR. Assume that the array has been loaded in another part of the program.

9-7. The following interactive program allows the user to enter a set of ten examination scores from the keyboard, calculate their mean and the number of scores that exceed the mean, and print the relevant values.

```
1000  ! Main program
1010     GOSUB INITIALIZE
1020     GOSUB PROCESS.ARRAY
1030     GOSUB COUNT.LARGE
1040     GOSUB PRINT.VALUES
1100     STOP
2000  !
       INITIALIZE:
2010     DECLARE INTEGER CNT, TOTAL, SCORE(10)
2020     DECLARE INTEGER CONSTANT NUMSCORES=10
2030     CNT=0
2040     TOTAL=0
2100     RETURN
3000  !
       PROCESS. ARRAY:
              .
              .
              .
32767   END
```

Change the main program and the subroutine INITIALIZE to allow the user the option of repeating the loop for additional data sets. Each data set is to be preceded by an entry from the keyboard of the number of data values in the set. Memory is to be allocated dynamically with an executable DIM.

Allocating Memory with DECLARE

We have already used the DECLARE statement in Chapter 6 to assign data types and names to variables. One convenient feature of this statement is that it can be used to declare the type of an array and *also* to allocate memory to it. For instance, if we wished to use the integer array SCORE in a program, the upper bound could be specified by either of the following:

```
DIM SCORE%(200)
```

or

```
DECLARE INTEGER SCORE(200)
```

When creating arrays with DECLARE, it is necessary to specify a data-type keyword (explicit typing). Arrays created by the DECLARE statement are static; in other words, their size is fixed and the bounds must be constants. Basic initializes arrays to zero or the null string; but, as with other variables, we should initialize arrays explicitly for good programming practice.

Searching an Array

Example Definition

The operation of searching a data set for a given value is one of the most common actions encountered in programming. For instance, a payroll program might be designed so that each employee record includes a pay code. Corresponding pay rates might be included in an entirely separate file. The operation of computing gross pay would involve reading the employee record and pay code, then searching a table for the pay code in order to find the corresponding rate. There is a myriad of such applications, including the one illustrated by Example 9-2.

Example 9-2

An on-line processing system requires that the value of a code field (named PREFIX.VALUE$) entered by the user be monitored to ensure that it is allowable. The program includes a table of allowable values stored in the string array PREFIX (it has been DECLAREd in the main portion of the program to be string). A count of the number of elements in the array is stored in the integer variable PREFIX.CNT. A routine named VERIFY is required to do the following:

IF the array PREFIX contains the value entered for PREFIX.VALUE$
  THEN the integer variable FOUND% must be set to true (− 1)
  ELSE it should be set to false (0)

The examples in Figure 9-12 illustrate the needs of this routine. An important perspective on this routine is obtained by looking at it from the point of view

PREFIX Table Value in PREFIX.CNT = 7

PVS
RBP
IRI
CPT
ECZ
WIE
PNR

Figure 9-12 Typical table values.

If PREFIX.VALUE$ is	then FOUND% is set to
CPT	− 1 (true)
ABC	0 (false)

of its input and output. That is, certain data values must be available to the routine so that they can be used in the processing. This is the input to the routine. Similarly, the results of that processing will be data that represent the output of the routine. This is shown schematically in the diagram of Figure 9-13.

| Input | VERIFY | Output |

PREFIX.VALUE$
PREFIX
PREFIX.CNT
                                 FOUND%

Figure 9-13 Input to and output from the VERIFY routine.

A Program Solution

Without a doubt, the most important thing about this solution is to think it through very carefully. Actually, if properly planned, the solution is nearly trivial. One approach to take is to set the value of FOUND% to false (0) upon entering the routine. This is reasonable because the value will never have been found prior to searching the table. Then the next step is the search loop. Putting our thoughts in the form of pseudocode gives the following:

> Set FOUND% to false
> Repeat the following until the end of the table or FOUND% is true
>   IF next table entry equals input value, set FOUND% to true

The program module of Figure 9-14 is every bit as compact as the preceding pseudocode. Notice that, through the use of appropriate looping structures, everything is controlled by the condition of the FOR statement. Furthermore, incrementing of the array subscript is controlled automatically by the FOR.

```
VERIFY:
  FOUND% = 0
  FOR I% = 1 UNTIL I%= PREFIX.CNT OR FOUND%
    FOUND% = -1 IF PREFIX.VALUE$ = PREFIX(I%)
  NEXT I%
  RETURN
```

Figure 9-14 A table search routine for Example 9-2.

Exercise

9-8. What would happen in the program segment of Figure 9-14 if the OR in the FOR statement were accidentally entered as an AND?

Two-Dimensional Arrays

Rows and Columns of Data

Many applications, both business and scientific, deal with tables that have rows and columns. To illustrate this concept, let us assume that we work for a water resources management company that is considering computerizing some of their

TABLE 9-2 Annual Precipitation Summary
(Measured in Millimeters)

Month	Station				
	1	2	3	4	5
January	132	155	93	111	132
February	106	112	75	105	125
March	91	114	84	96	108
April	59	71	52	63	73
May	45	69	48	58	68
June	36	35	28	23	33
July	22	17	17	20	21
August	15	13	6	8	12
September	23	19	11	16	21
October	48	45	25	27	30
November	90	117	77	84	102
December	120	141	92	102	110

data. To aid their water forecasting for one drainage basin, they maintain records of monthly precipitation at five different measuring stations. A typical annual summary is shown in Table 9-2.

Here we see that the table consists of twelve rows (month) and five columns (station) arranged in a convenient, easy-to-use form. For instance, we can immediately see that station-3 measured 52 millimeters of precipitation during the month of April. In other words, we locate any item by its row and column. These and many other operations are commonly performed on two-dimensional arrays. Let us examine how these are done in Basic.

Two-Dimensional Arrays in Basic

Up until now, each of the arrays that we have used required a single subscript to specify one of the elements of the array. For example, WORK(7) refers to a unique array element of the array WORK. In most programming languages, arrays may be defined with one subscript or with two or more. It is possible to describe the entire collection of data values in Table 9-2 by an array that uses two subscripts for identifying elements. For instance, if the array PRECIP has been defined to hold this table, then the April/station-3 precipitation element could be identified a shown in Figure 9-15.

The number of different subscripts required to specify an array element is called the *dimension* of the array. Thus far we have used only *one-dimensional* arrays. (A one-dimensional array is often also called a *list* or a *vector*). The subscripts for multidimensional arrays are placed inside the parentheses following the array, just as for one-dimensional arrays, and are separated by commas.

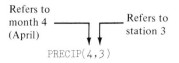

Figure 9-15 Using two subscripts.

Thus, the dimension of an array is the number of subscripts inside the parentheses. Arrays in VAX Basic can have up to 32 dimensions. The array illustrated in Figure 9-15 is a *two-dimensional* array.

Facts About Two-Dimensional Arrays. In general, the same rules apply to declaring and using multidimensional arrays as to one-dimensional arrays; only the number of upper bounds (one for each subscript) that have to be specified is different. For instance, the array for Table 9-1 could be declared by either of the following statements:

```
DIM PRECIP%(12,5)
DECLARE  INTEGER PRECIP(12,5)
```

Following are some additional points that can be added to our previous summary about arrays.

1. The DIM statement provides two independent pieces of information for each declared array: the dimension of the array (number of subscripts) and the number of allowed values for each subscript. These two together determine the number of locations reserved for the array. Thus, the DIM statement

   ```
   DIM ARR(100), CHARA$(50)
   ```

   reserves 101 memory locations for the array ARR and 51 locations for the array CHARA$. For multidimensional arrays, *each* subscript can take on all of its allowed values for each allowed value of any of the other subscripts. For example, consider the following two arrays:

   ```
   DIM BIG(5,8), BIGGER(9,19,4)
   ```

   In the case of BIG, the first subscript can take on any of the six values in the range 0–5 for every one of the nine values in the range 0–8 of the second subscript. The total number of reserved locations for the array BIG is therefore $6 \times 9 = 54$. Similarly, the total number of locations allowed to the array BIGGER is $(9 + 1) \times (19 + 1) \times (4 + 1) = 1000$.
2. Regarding the executable DIM statement, some of the bounds may be constants, but at least one bound must be a variable. For example,

   ```
   DIM  ARR(X,Y)
   DIM  ARR(10,Y)
   ```

   are both executable, but

   ```
   DIM  ARR(10,5)
   ```

   is nonexecutable. The variable bounds can be either simple or subscripted variables, but they cannot be expressions.
3. The executable DIM can change the *bounds* of the array (size of allocated memory), but it cannot change its *dimension* (number of subscripts).
4. In referencing an array element, the number of subscripts used must be the same as the number of subscripts used when defining the array. In other words, the dimension of the array in the defining statement must agree with its dimension in the rest of the program.

Exercises

9-9. What is the dimensionality of each of the following arrays, and how many elements does each have?

a. A(7,1,1,11,13)
b. B(5,7,9,10)
c. C(4,3,2,1,6,7)

9-10. Write a program segment that displays the elements of a one-dimensional array A(50) in two-dimensional tabular form. Each line of output should have five elements in consecutive print zones, as shown here.

A(1)   A(2)   A(3)   A(4)   A(5)
  .
  .
  .
A(46)   A(47)   A(48)   A(49)   A(50)

Multidimensional Array Processing

Loading Data into a Two-Dimensional Array

Actually, processing data stored in multidimensional arrays differs little from processing with single-dimensional arrays. Perhaps the thing to keep in mind is that it is very easy to become confused between the different subscripts. In fact, precisely this problem is illustrated by the following examples:

Example 9-3

The file PRECIP.DAT contains the annual precipation data illustrated by Table 9-2. Information is stored one data value per record of the file, with all of the values for station 1 followed by all for station 2 and so on. That is, the first record of the file contains the value for January, station 1; the second contains the value for February, station 1, and so on. A module is required to read this file into the array defined by the following statement:

```
DECLARE INTEGER PRECIP(12,5)
```

Assume that the data file contains the exact number of values required for this array.

In mathematics, the conventional notation is that the first subscript refers to the row and the second to the column. This fits with the preceding DECLARE statement because there are 12 rows and 5 columns (refer to Table 9-2). However, this viewpoint is often very misleading because of the versatility afforded by the computer. For instance, when the data values are stored in the array, it is every bit as easy to print them as shown in Table 9-2, with stations across the top, as it is to print them with the months across the top. Furthermore, the row–column concept loses its significance when one is dealing with arrays that have three or more dimensions. The best way to view things is in terms of "first subscript, second subscript" (from left to right). Hence, in this example, the first subscript represents the month number, and the second represents the station number. In order to read the data for station 1, we must set the second subscript to 1 and allow the first subscript to range from 1 to 12. Then the operation of reading for station 1 is as shown in Figure 9-16(a). Similarly, the corresponding operation for station 2 is as shown in Figure 9-16(b).

```
DECLARE INTEGER PRECIP(12,5)
OPEN 'PRECIP.DAT' FOR INPUT AS FILE #1
 .
 .
 .
FOR MONTH = 1 TO 12
  INPUT #1, PRECIP(MONTH,1)
NEXT MONTH

(a)

FOR MONTH = 1 TO 12
  INPUT #1, PRECIP(MONTH,2)
NEXT MONTH

(b)
```

Figure 9-16   Inputting for individual stations.

The two loops of Figure 9-16 (and the three others required for the other stations) can be implemented equally well with nested FOR loops, as shown in Figure 9-17. Here the outer-loop subscript (STATION) will remain fixed for each of the 12 passes through the inner loop. Thus, the sequence in which the respective values of PRECIP will be loaded is

$$(1,1)\ (2,1).\ .\ .(12,1)\ (1,2)\ (2,2).\ .\ .(12,2).\ .\ .(11,5)\ (12,5)$$

In this sequence, the first subscript is said to *vary most rapidly*.

As a minor variation, let us assume that the data set has been stored in the file grouped by station rather than month: That is, the first value is for January/station 1, the second for January/station 2, and so on. Using the same

```
DECLARE INTEGER PRECIP(12,5)
OPEN 'PRECIP.DAT' FOR INPUT AS FILE #1
 .
 .
 .
FOR STATION = 1 TO 5
  FOR MONTH = 1 TO 12
    INPUT #1, PRECIP(MONTH,STATION)
  NEXT MONTH
NEXT STATION
```

Figure 9-17   Loading a two-dimensional array.

```
DECLARE INTEGER PRECIP(12,5)
OPEN 'PRECIP.DAT' FOR INPUT AS FILE #1
  .
  .
  .
FOR MONTH = 1 TO 12
  FOR STATION = 1 TO 5
    INPUT #1, PRECIP(MONTH,STATION)
  NEXT STATION
NEXT MONTH
```

Figure 9-18 Loading a two-dimensional array.

array as in Example 9-3, it is only necessary to recognize that we must now vary the second subscript (STATION) most rapidly. The program segment to do this is shown in Figure 9-18.

Printing the Values Stored in an Array

Printing the contents of a two-dimensional array is much like loading one. That is, either the first or second subscipt can be varied most rapidly to achieve the desired output form.

Example 9-4

A routine is required to print the elements of the array PRECIP in a table form identical to that of Table 9-2.

The primary difference between loading and printing is that pains must be taken on output to ensure that headings and columns are properly aligned. This is readily done with PRINT USING, whereby everything can be aligned in the mask fields. This is illustrated in the program segment of Figure 9-19. One

```
H1$ = '                         Station
H2$ = '               ------------------------'
H3$ = 'Month          1    2    3    4    5'
H4$ = '----------------------------------------'
M$  = '\          \    ###  ###  ###  ###  ###'
PRINT H1$
PRINT H2$
PRINT H3$
PRINT H4$
  .
  .
  .
FOR MONTH = 1 TO 12
  READ MONTH$
  PRINT USING M$, MONTH$,PRECIP(MONTH,1),PRECIP(MONTH,2), &
                  PRECIP(MONTH,3),PRECIP(MONTH,4),PRECIP(MONTH,5)
NEXT MONTH
  .
  .
  .
DATA 'January','February','March','April','May','June'
DATA 'July','August','September','October','November','December'
```

Figure 9-19 Printing a table—Example 9-4.

problem with this form is that element names must be listed individually in the PRINT statement for each of the five stations. This is an inconvenience that would become very clumsy if, for instance, there were 16 stations. An alternate solution is described in Chapter 10.

Exercises

9-11. What would be the result if the following change were made in the FOR statement in Figure 9-19?

```
FOR MONTH = 12 TO 1 STEP -1
```

9-12. A two-dimensional array A(I,J) has memory allocated by the statement

```
DIM A(6,8)
```

Write the code necessary to calculate a new array B(I,J), defined for all allowed values of J as follows:

```
B(0,J) = A(1,J)
B(1,J) = A(2,J)
       .
       .
       .
B(5,J) = A(6,J)
B(6,J) = A(0,J)
```

Searching a Two-Dimensional Array

The action of searching a two-dimensional array is virtually identical to that of searching a one-dimensional array, as illustrated by the following example:

Example 9-5

The array PRECIP is to be searched to find the largest and smallest precipitation values.

The nested loops of Figure 9-20 perform this operation. Note that LARGEST is initialized to 0, and SMALLEST, to 32767. These choices are based on the assumption that the data set will contain a value larger than 0 and a value smaller than 32767, reasonable assumptions considering the nature of the example. These values ensure that replacements will occur in the IF statements during loop execution.

```
LARGEST = 0
SMALLEST = 32767
FOR STATION = 1 TO 5
  FOR MONTH = 1 TO 12
    IF PRECIP(MONTH,STATION) > LARGEST THEN LARGEST = PRECIP(MONTH,STATION)
    IF PRECIP(MONTH,STATION) < SMALLEST THEN SMALLEST = PRECIP(MONTH,STATION)
  NEXT MONTH
NEXT STATION
```

Figure 9-20   Searching an array—Example 9-5.

Arithmetic Operations on
Elements of a Two-Dimensional Array

All of the preceding examples have involved processing the data in an array without modifying the values. Let us consider two examples that involve changing these values.

Example 9-6

> For a particular runoff study, each of the values of the array PRECIP is to be multiplied by the variable FACTOR.

Actually, this is merely more of the same, as we see by inspecting the nested FORs of Figure 9-21. Each entry in the array will be changed by multiplication of the value stored in the variable FACTOR.

```
FOR STATION = 1 TO 5
  FOR MONTH = 1 TO 12
    PRECIP(MONTH,STATION) = FACTOR*PRECIP(MONTH,STATION)
  NEXT MONTH
NEXT STATION
```

Figure 9-21   Multiplying each element in an array by a constant—Example 9-6.

The next example involves summarizing the data from the array PRECIP and creating two new one-dimensional arrays, ST.PRECIP and MO.PRECIP.

Example 9-7

> Two new summary arrays (one-dimensional) are to be created. The first is ST.PRECIP (consisting of five elements) and is to contain the annual totals for each of the five stations. The second is MO.PRECIP (consisting of 12 elements) and is to contain the monthly average of each of the five stations.

By inspecting the program segment of Figure 9-22, we see again that the operations are controlled by nested loops. The new wrinkle here is in using

```
DIM PRECIP(12,5), ST.PRECIP(5), MO.PRECIP(12)
  .
  .
  .
FOR STATION = 1 TO 5
  ST.PRECIP(STATION) = 0
  FOR MONTH = 1 TO 12
    ST.PRECIP(STATION) = ST.PRECIP(STATION) + PRECIP(MONTH,STATION)
  NEXT MONTH
NEXT STATION
FOR MONTH = 1 TO 12
  MO.PRECIP(MONTH) = 0
  FOR STATION = 1 TO 5
    MO.PRECIP(MONTH) = MO.PRECIP(MONTH) + PRECIP(MONTH,STATION)
  NEXT STATION
  MO.PRECIP(MONTH) = MO.PRECIP(MONTH)/5
NEXT MONTH
```

Figure 9-22   Summing elements of an array—Example 9-7.

arrays of accumulators (ST.PRECIP and MO.PRECIP). Since they are indeed accumulators, they must be initialized. Note that each individual accumulator is initialized as the first statement of the outer loop.

Another type of operation that is commonly encountered in array processing is that of adding the elements of two different arrays and forming a third.

Example 9-8

Two consecutive years of precipitation data are stored in the arrays PRECIP.1 and PRECIP.2. Values for these two arrays are to be added and placed in the array PRECIP.

Compared to Example 9-7, this example is quite simple. As we see in Figure 9-23, it is identical in form to the operation of loading the array (Figure 9-17).

```
DIM PRECIP(12,5), PRECIP.1(12,5), PRECIP.2(12,5)
.
.
.
FOR STATION = 1 TO 5
  FOR MONTH = 1 TO 12
    PRECIP(MONTH,STATION) = PRECIP.1(MONTH,STATION) + PRECIP.2(MONTH,STATION)
  NEXT MONTH
NEXT STATION
```

Figure 9-23   Summing two arrays—Example 9-8.

Using a Three-Dimensional Array

The use of two separate arrays to store the data of two consecutive years in Example 9-8 is one way of handling the need. However, what if five or ten years of data were required? Then using five or ten different two-dimensional arrays would be clumsy. The solution to this problem is to use a three-dimensional array, as illustrated by the next example.

Example 9-9

The array Y.PRECIP includes three dimensions with subscript assignments as follows:

First subscript: year (first, second, third, and so on).
Second subscript: month.
Third subscript: station.

A routine similar to that of Example 9-7, which will total the annual precipitations for each month/station and store the results in the two-dimensional array PRECIP, is required.

This example actually combines the operations of Examples 9-7 and 9-8. In Example 9-7, values from an array were accumulated in another array; in this example, the contents of a three-dimensional array are summarized in a

```
DIM Y.PRECIP(10,12,5), PRECIP(12,5)
.
.
.
FOR STATION = 1 TO 5
  FOR MONTH = 1 TO 12
    PRECIP(MONTH,STATION) = 0
    FOR YEAR = 1 TO 10
      PRECIP(MONTH,STATION) = PRECIP(MONTH,STATION) + Y.PRECIP(YEAR,MONTH,STATION)
    NEXT YEAR
  NEXT MONTH
NEXT STATION
```

Figure 9-24   Using an array as an accumulator—Example 9-9.

two-dimensional array. In Example 9-8, corresponding elements of two arrays were added together. This example expands this concept one step further. A program segment to perform these operations is shown in Figure 9-24. Note that, prior to beginning the accumulation process in the innermost loop, the element of PRECIP into which the accumulated value is to be placed is set to zero.

In Retrospect

The array provides the programmer with a powerful tool for manipulation of data. Through use of subscripting, it is possible for a program to process data sets consisting of thousands of values as easily as sets consisting of only a handful of values.

Answers to Preceding Exercises

9-1. a. Sorted data: 5 9 13 18 27
         Median = 13
      b. Sorted data: 7 12 29 35 56 103
         Median = (1/2)(29 + 35) = 32

9-2. As we learned previously, if the data values are not in sequence when read into memory, we need to introduce a second array to hold the sorted set of values. In the program segment in Figure 9-10, the array IN.VALUE holds the unsorted data, and the array AMOUNT holds the sorted data. But in the program of Figure 9-6, we used only a single array, AMOUNT, since the input values were supposed to have been presorted. Clearly, the routine READ.ARRAY in Figure 9-10 refers to the input (unsorted) values, whereas the routine FIND.MEDIAN refers to the sorted values. Hence, line 3020 in Figure 9-6 must be changed to

```
3020   IN.VALUE(CNT) = POINT
```

9-3. The first value will still be stored in AMOUNT(1), and so on. If the data set contains 99 or fewer values, the program will function correctly. But if the data set has 100 or more values, only the first 99 will be loaded into the array AMOUNT because the loop will terminate at CNT = 100 before loading AMOUNT(100). Moreover, when the loop terminates at CNT = 100, the value of POINT will not be −1, and the excessive-value message will be displayed (incorrectly, if there are exactly 100 data values).

9-4. a. A declarative DIM statement must precede any reference to the array for which it allocates memory.
b. It is not possible to reference an array element whose subscript is larger than the upper bound specified in a declarative DIM.
c. A given array cannot appear in more than one declarative DIM.

9-5. When CNT exceeds the value 100, it will exceed the declared upper bound in its role as a subscript on line 3010. An out-of-range error will therefore be generated.

9-6.

```
1000 DIM ARR(100)
1010 DECLARE INTEGER I,J
   .
   .
   .
2000 INPUT 'Input any number'; NUMBER
     POINT = 1
     NOT.FOUND = -1
     WHILE NOT.FOUND AND POINT <= 30
       IF NUMBER > ARR(POINT)
         THEN POINT = POINT + 1
         ELSE NOT.FOUND = 0
       ENDIF
     NEXT
2100 ! Open up space for new value
2110   ARR(J + 1) = ARR(J) FOR J = 30 TO POINT STEP -1
2120 ! Place new value in its proper sequence
2130   ARR(POINT) = NUMBER
```

9-7. The following modifications have to be made:

```
1014 CONTINUE$ = 'YES'
1018 WHILE CONTINUE$ = 'YES'
     .
     .
     .
1050 INPUT 'Do you wish to process another data set ';&
          '<YES/NO>';CONTINUE$
1060 NEXT
     .
     .
     .
2010 DECLARE INTEGER CNT, NUMSCORES, TOTAL
2015 INPUT 'Number of scores'; NUMSCORES
2020 DIM INTEGER SCORE(NUMSCORES)
```

9-8. The program will produce the correct output only if the array PREFIX contains the value stored in PREFIX.VALUE$ *and* this value is the last one in this array. If this value is not present in the array or if it is present but is not the last element in the array, the compound condition in the FOR statement will never be satisfied, the loop-control variable will continue incrementing until it references a subscript larger than the declared upper bound, and an out-of-range error will be generated.

9-9. a. Five-dimensional; $8 \times 2 \times 2 \times 12 \times 14$ elements.
b. Four-dimensional; $6 \times 8 \times 10 \times 11$ elements.
c. Six-dimensional; $5 \times 4 \times 3 \times 2 \times 7 \times 8$ elements.

9-10.
```
1000 FOR I% = 1 TO 50
        PRINT A(I%),
        PRINT IF I% = (I%/5)*5
     NEXT I
```

9-11. The entries in the table would be labeled incorrectly. The sequence in which the *names* of the months would be entered into MONTH$ by READ would still be the same because this sequence is determined by the order of the months' names in the data pool. However, the precipitation data would be printed in reverse order, starting with PRECIP(12,STATION) and ending with PRECIP(1,STATION). Hence the December data would be labeled "January," and so on.

9-12. 1000 DIM A(6,8), B(6,8)
.
.
.
```
FOR I = 0 TO 5
    B(I,J) = A(I+1,J) FOR J = 0 TO 8
NEXT I
B(6,J) = A(0,J) FOR J = 0 TO 8
```

Programming Problems

9-1. The following file is used as input for several programming problems. A data file consists of integer data stored one value per record (line). There will never be more than 100 data values in the file.

  The data file is to be read into an array and printed as it is read. Then reverse the contents of the array elements. For instance, if 37 data values were read, then the array contents would be switched such that

$X(1)$ is replaced by $X(37)$
$X(2)$ is replaced by $X(36)$
.
.
.
$X(37)$ is replaced by $X(1)$

Print the array contents after the switch and check the results.

9-2. Two quantities commonly used to characterize statistical data are the *mean* and the *standard deviation*. The mean, $\bar{x}$, of a set x_i of n values is simply the arithmetic average of these values. However, it does not give the complete picture of a data set. For example, the two sets of

10, 50, 90   50, 50, 50

both have means of 50, but there is a significant difference in the two. The standard deviation, SD, is used to give an indication of the data spread. It is conveniently defined by the formula

$$SD = \sqrt{VAR}$$

where VAR is the variance, which is represented by the formula

$$VAR = \sum_{i=1}^{n} \frac{(x_i - \bar{x})^2}{n - 1} \qquad i = 1, \ldots, n$$

For the data points 10, 50, and 90, the variance is

$$VAR = \frac{(10 - 50)^2 + (50 - 50)^2 + (90 - 50)^2}{3 - 1}$$

$$= \frac{1600 + 0 + 1600}{2}$$

so that the standard deviation is

$$SD = 40$$

Using the data file of problem 9-1, calculate and print the number of data values, the mean, and the standard deviation. Note that other forms of the expression for the standard deviation are sometimes given. However, use the form given here.

9-3. Modify problem 3-5 to use an array to store the Fibonacci numbers.

9-4. The input file for this problem consists of a data set with a 9999 trailer (call this the A set), followed by another data set with its 9999 trailer (call this the B set). Assume that A and B will each consist of no more than 50 data values and that each is arranged in ascending sequence. Write a program to read these values and merge the two sets into the single array C (which may therefore consist of up to 100 elements). The elements in C are to be in ascending sequence.

9-5. Assume that the data values in the file of problem 9-1 fall in the range 0–99. Write a program to read this file and determine how many values fall in each of the following categories:

0–9	50–59
10–19	60–69
20–29	70–79
30–39	80–89
40–49	90–99

Use a ten-element array as counters for the preceding ten categories. Do not use a series of IF statements. Rather, form the quantity $(S/10) + 1$, where S is the value read, and truncate this quantity. For instance:

$60/10 = 6.0$, which yields 6 when truncated.

$63/10 = 6.3$, which yields 6 when truncated.

$69/10 = 6.9$, which yields 6 when truncated.

The truncated result gives the subscript of the appropriate counter.

9-6. A technique for reducing the effect of random errors in experimental data involves averaging sets of neighboring data points. An array A(I) contains a set of 100 experimental values. Write a program to replace each element of A except the first and the last by

$$B(I) = (1/3)(A(I - 1) + A(I) + A(I + 1))$$

9-7. This is a modification of problem 6-7. The square enclosure is now enlarged to nine positions in both directions (a 9×9 square). Use a two-dimensional array, MAZE(ROW,COL), to track the rat's movement. The program is to read and print, in sequence, the squares that the rat traversed to reach the door. Note that, on any given walk, the rat may partially retrace his steps. Also print the number of random steps it took the rat to locate the door.

9-8. A manufacturer's inventory of six types of tools is distributed over four warehouses. These data values are to be stored in an array with the following format:

			Tool			
Warehouse	1	2	3	4	5	6
1						
2						
3						
4						

The first subscript refers to warehouse, the second, to tool type. The table entries are the number of tools of a given type stored in a given warehouse. The dollar values of the individual tools are

$$PRICE(1) = 7.50$$
$$PRICE(2) = 2.30$$
$$PRICE(3) = 6.95$$
$$PRICE(4) = 12.20$$
$$PRICE(5) = 11.59$$
$$PRICE(6) = 8.79$$

Write a program to read the first 24 records from the data file of problem 9-1 into the inventory array, input the tool prices from the keyboard, and compute

1. Total number of each tool.
2. Dollar value of each tool.
3. Dollar value in each warehouse.
4. Total dollar value.

Information is stored with all of the values for tool 1 followed by all for tool 2, tool 3, and so on. Output is to include a heading that contains the values of the individual tools. The inventory itself and the computed quantities are to be printed in the following tabular form:

Warehouse	Tool						Warehouse $ value
	1	2	3	4	5	6	
1	1	1	1	2	2	2	81.91
2	3	3	3	4	4	4	180.57
3	5	5	5	5	6	7	275.82
4	6	7	0	7	8	2	256.80
Number of tools	15	16	9	18	20	15	93
Tool $ value	112.50	36.80	62.55	219.60	231.80	131.85	795.10

9-9. A common problem in information processing is *sorting* a list of items, that is, arranging them in either ascending or descending order. There are many sorting methods, most of which involve use of arrays. We have already learned one such method. This problem is concerned with the method known as the *bubble sort*.

The bubble-sort algorithm for an array with N elements involves at most $N-1$ *passes*. A pass comprises a sequence of comparisons of adjacent elements, with an exchange of the two elements if they are out of sequence with respect to each other. At the end of any pass that involves exchanges, at least one additional element is guaranteed to have been placed in its correct final position. We will consider a bubble sort in *ascending* sequence.

The first pass starts by comparing A(1) and A(2) and exchanging their contents if A(1) > A(2). (Here it is important to distinguish between the *locations*, that is, the *names* of the array elements, and their *contents*, that is, their *values*. The locations remain fixed; the values get shuffled around.) You should use a subroutine to exchange any two elements, as needed. Continue this procedure with A(2) and A(3), and so on, through A(N − 1) and A(N). This completes the first pass, and A(N) is guaranteed to contain the largest value.

Each consecutive pass starts with A(1) and A(2), but the ending pair changes from pass to pass. The second pass ends with A(N − 2) and A(N − 1), because A(N) is already known to contain the largest value. In general, at the end of a given pass through I elements, A(I) will contain the largest values in A(1), . . ., A(I). After N − 1 passes, the array is guaranteed to be sorted in ascending sequence.

The following diagram illustrates the procedure to sort a set of five sample values. Comparisons that involve a swap are identified by arrows. In principle, this set might require 5 − 1 = 4 passes. In practice, because of the particular initial distribution, the array is sorted after two passes, and only three passes are required to confirm this.

Locations	Contents				
	Initial	*2*	*3*	*4*	*5*
A(1)	11	11	11	11	11
A(2)	45	27	27	27	27
A(3)	27	45	45	32	32
A(4)	65	65	32	45	45
A(5)	32	32	65	65	65
		End of pass 1	End of pass 2	End of pass 3	

Largest value is last.

We see that the smaller values "bubble" their way up, one location at a time. Let us consider a slight improvement of the standard bubble sort. It relies on the fact that if a pass is completed without any exchanges, the array is known to be sorted and sorting can terminate.

The program calls for nested loops: an outer loop to cycle through the passes and an inner loop to cycle through the comparisons and possible exchanges within each pass. The outer loop is to continue as long as the *preceding* pass involved at least one swap. A logical variable whose value changes when a pass is completed without any exchanges can be used to control the outer loop. Be sure to initialize this variable properly to force the body of the outer loop to execute at least once. The inner loop can be a FOR–NEXT whose stopping point decreases by one with each succeeding pass.

For your first stub program, check your overall logic by verifying that each subroutine was reached, and do *one exchange* in *the first pass*. Print the initial and final arrays to verify that this stub is functioning correctly. For your second stub, do *one complete pass*. Then put in the outer loop to finish the sort.

10

Matrix Operations

Preview

In mathematics, one- and two-dimensional arrays are called matrices. *Whereas examples in Chapter 9 deal with operations on individual elements of arrays, mathematicians are commonly interested in operations dealing with entire arrays. A good illustration of this is the program segment of Figure 9-20, in which each element of the array is multiplied by the value in FACTOR. It would be much simpler to code something like*

PRECIP = FACTOR*PRECIP

and have each element of the entire array multiplied by FACTOR.
In many applications, operations like this are so common that Basic includes capabilities of this type. These are the MAT operations, which operate on one- and two-dimensional arrays. Some of the MAT operations involve specialized mathematical concepts; but others are generally applicable, are relatively simple to use, and provide the user

with powerful programming capabilities. This chapter presents some of the MAT operations that are available in Basic.

1. The ability to read an entire array into memory with the execution of a single MAT statement and to set the size of the array automatically.

> MAT READ   *Obtain data from DATA statements.*
> MAT INPUT   *Obtain data from keyboard.*
> MAT INPUT#   *Obtain data from a file.*

2. The ability to print the entire contents of an array with the execution of a single MAT PRINT statement.

3. The concept of operating on entire arrays almost as if they were simple variables. In mathemetics, this is called **matrix manipulation.** *This includes*

> *a. Multiplying elements of an array by a single value.*
> *b. Adding and subtracting corresponding elements of two arrays.*
> *c. Multiplying two arrays.*

4. The mathematical operations of finding the transpose, inverse, and determinant of a matrix.

MAT Input and Output Operations

Principles of the MAT READ Statement

Example 9-4 (Figure 9-18) involves printing the precipitation/station data in Table 9-2. In order to print month names (rather than numbers), the list of month names is included in two DATA statements. As each line is to be printed, the next month name is READ from the data pool. Although this was sufficient for some applications, others might require that this list of names be read into a string array in order to be available in random sequence. This is easily done with the sequence of statements Figure 10-1(a). However, exactly the same

```
DECLARE STRING MONTH.NAME(12)
  .
  .
  .
FOR MONTH = 1 TO 12
  READ MONTH.NAME(MONTH)
NEXT MONTH
(a)
```

Figure 10-1   Loading an array from the data pool. (a) Using a FOR/NEXT loop. (b) Using MAT.

```
DECLARE STRING MONTH.NAME(12)
  .
  .
  .
MAT READ MONTH.NAME

(b)
```

operations are carried out by the MAT READ of Figure 10-1(b). That is, this statement causes the read operation to be executed repeatedly until a value has been read for all elements. One important item to notice is that the MAT READ, as do other MAT statements, ignores the zero element; that is, MONTH.NAME(0) remains unused. This example highlights the value of MAT statements: They manipulate entire arrays with single statements. Note that if the DECLARE statement had been left out in Figure 10-1(b), the upper bound on the array would have been specified implicitly by the MAT statement itself. However, we shall continue the practice of creating arrays and specifying their upper bounds explicitly.

The power of MAT READ is further enhanced by its ability to change the array size dynamically. For instance, an array can be statically defined as consisting of 12 elements and changed to 6 when the MAT READ is executed. This is illustrated by the following example:

Example 10-1

The number of months to be read into the array MONTH.NAME can vary from 2 to 12. The data pool will include one numeric entry indicating the number of months to be read, followed by the month names. A program segment is required to read the month names into the MONTH.NAME array and change the array bound to reflect the number of entries.

In the program segment of Figure 10-2 we see that the array is bounded in the DECLARE statement to handle the largest number of values that will be

```
DECLARE STRING MONTH.NAME(12)
DECLARE BYTE MONTH.CNT
  .
  .
  .
READ MONTH.CNT
MAT READ MONTH.NAME(MONTH.CNT)
  .
  .
  .
DATA 5
DATA 'January','February','March','April','May'
```

Figure 10-2 Changing the array bound with the MAT READ— Example 10-1.

used. It is important to recognize that the array bounds specified in a DECLARE must be constants. The number of elements to be loaded is first read into the variable MONTH.CNT. Then this value is included in the MAT READ to specify the new size of the array. Execution of this statement would read the five month names *and* change the size of the array to 6. (The number of allowed subscript values is always one larger than the upper bound because of the zero position.) All subsequent processing will be as if the size value in the DECLARE statement for MONTH.NAME were originally 5. Note the difference between the forms of the MAT READ of Figure 10-1(b) and that of Figure 10-2. In Figure 10-1(b), the matrix name appears without subscripts because the size of the array is *not* being changed; in Figure 10-2, it contains a bound because its size *is* being changed. It is important to understand that the size of an array can only be decreased using this method; it cannot be increased.

Reading Two-Dimensional Arrays

Exactly the same techniques can be used with arrays of two dimensions; it is only important to be aware of the order in which the subscripts are varied. This is illustrated by the next example.

Example 10-2

The precipitation data set of Table 9-2 (or desired portion thereof) is included in DATA statements within a program. Each DATA statement contains the data values for one month. They are preceded by a DATA statement with two numbers, representing the number of months (rows) and the number of stations (columns). Following is a typical set of DATA statements.

```
DATA 4,3
DATA 112,  98, 105
DATA 116, 100, 105
DATA  97,  89,  93
DATA  82,  71,  80
```

These represent the data for three stations over a four-month period. Read these values into the array PRECIP and size the array bounds downward according to the number of values read.

For the purpose of comparison, these data values are read with nested FOR loops in Figure 10-3(a). If we think in terms of rows and columns, they are loaded by row (month). To accomplish this, the second subscript is varied most rapidly. That is, when the outer loop is entered, the value of the first

```
DECLARE INTEGER PRECIP(12,5)
DECLARE BYTE MONTHS, STATIONS
DATA 4,3
DATA 112,  98, 105
DATA 116, 100, 105
DATA  97,  89,  93
DATA  82,  71,  80
  .
  .
  .
READ MONTHS, STATIONS
FOR MONTH = 1 TO MONTHS
  FOR STATION = 1 TO STATIONS
    READ PRECIP(MONTH,STATION)
  NEXT STATION
NEXT MONTHSTATION
(a)

READ MONTHS, STATIONS
MAT READ PRECIP(MONTHS,STATIONS)
(b)
```

Figure 10-3 (a) Reading a two-dimensional array. (b) Reading and changing bounds.

subscript MONTH is set to 1. Then in the inner loop, the value of the second subscript STATION ranges from 1 to 3, while the first subscript remains at 1. Then the outer loop increments the first subscript by 1 (to 2), and the inner loop is repeated. This is important because it is exactly the order in which subscripts are varied by the MAT READ statement of Figure 10-3(b). In this case, the values are read in the same way they are read in Figure 10-3(a), *and* the array size is changed according to the values in the variables MONTHS and STATIONS.

The MAT INPUT Statement

The values of a matrix can be entered interactively by the MAT INPUT statement. This statement works in exactly the same way as MAT READ (except for the source of the data). Like MAT READ, MAT INPUT allows for input of integer, floating-point, or string matrices. Like the INPUT statement, MAT INPUT displays a question-mark system prompt, then awaits the values to be entered. If a user prompt is desired, then it must be displayed by a separate PRINT statement, since a string prompt cannot be included with the MAT INPUT in the same way it can be included with the INPUT. To illustrate the MAT INPUT, let us assume that the statements of Figure 10-4 are included in a program.

```
DECLARE BYTE A(10,15)
  .
  .
  .
PRINT "Enter 54 numbers separated by commas: "
MAT INPUT A(6,9)
```

Figure 10-4   The MAT INPUT statement.

Execution of the MAT INPUT statement will reduce the size of matrix A to 7 × 10 elements. After the system prompt is displayed, the computer will await entry of the values, separated by commas, from the keyboard. Data values will be stored in consecutive elements, with the second subscript varying most rapidly (as with the MAT READ). Thus, the sequence in which information is stored will be

(1,1), (1,2). . .(1,9). . .(2,1), (2,2). . .(6,8), (6,9)

It is important to recognize that striking the Return key normally terminates input of data. Since a total of 54 values is to be entered, the cursor would reach the end of the screen and cause a *screen wrap* before all of the values have been entered. (If the cursor reaches the end of the screen and there is more information to be displayed, it automatically moves, or *wraps*, to the next line.) If it is desired to start a new screen line as values are being entered (for instance, after each group of nine data points), then the ampersand symbol (&) must be used. For instance, the data could be entered as follows:

?25, 122, 2, 23, 100, 89, 30, 21, 88, & cr

65, 0, 13, 113, 101, 42, 85, 11, 39 & cr

and so on

If the Return key is depressed prior to entering the full number of values (without using the &), then the entire array will not be filled.

All of these principles regarding the MAT INPUT apply equally to input from a file. The important thing to keep in mind is that the data file must have been created with no end-of-line characters. In other words, it must consist of one record with a number of fields corresponding to the number of elements to be read. Thus, the file of Example 9-3 could not have been read using the MAT INPUT# because it consists of one field per record.

In some applications, a situation might occur in which a MAT READ or INPUT reads fewer than enough elements to fill the entire array. In such a case, how do we know exactly how many values have been read? The answer is that Basic provides two system functions, NUM and NUM2, that return the number of values transferred by MAT READ and INPUT operations. Following the input of a matrix, NUM contains the number of rows that have been input (or, for a one-dimensional array, the number of elements entered). NUM2 contains the number of elements in the last row that have received values (or 0 for a one-dimensional array). For instance, if, in response to the MAT INPUT of Figure 10-4, 30 data values were entered, then NUM would contain 4 (four rows) and NUM2 would contain 3 (three values in the last row). These functions can be invoked as any others in a program, for example, in an assignment statement such as

```
ROW.COUNT = NUM
```

Exercise

10-1. If the MAT statement in Figure 10-4 were replaced by the following and the user entered 26 numbers in response to the MAT statement, what would be the contents of ROW.COUNT and COLUMN.COUNT?

```
MAT INPUT (5,7)
ROW.COUNT = NUM
COLUMN.COUNT = NUM2
```

The MAT PRINT Statement

Much is made of the fact that the MAT READ and MAT INPUT of the preceding section can cause the size of the array to be reduced. This is important because most of the MAT statements operate on the entire array, whether all elements have been loaded with data or not. Perhaps the simplest illustration is the MAT PRINT, which can be used for printing all or a portion of an array, excluding row and column 0. If only the array name is given (without subscripts), the entire array is printed. Hence, if the array size has been changed, only those elements corresponding to the new size are printed. For instance, consider the following:

```
MAT PRINT PRECIP
```

If this statement is executed following the sequence of Figure 10-3(a), then a full 60 values will be printed, since the array size remains 12 by 5. On the other hand, if it is executed following execution of the Figure 10-3(b) statements, then only the actual data values loaded (12 of them) will be printed.

Actually, the MAT PRINT does provide some additional flexibility in the case of the array in Figure 10-3(a). That is, it is possible to include subscripts together with the array name in the MAT PRINT. Then Basic will print all the elements whose subscripts are not larger than the specified ones. Thus, the following MAT PRINT will work properly with the array loaded by Figure 10-3(a):

```
MAT PRINT PRECIP(4,3)
```

However, MAT PRINT does *not* change the number of elements in the array; that is, it does not change the bounds specified in the statement that created the array.

A measure of control over the output format can be exercised by a choice of punctuation at the end of the MAT PRINT array list. If a comma is chosen, each array element on a line will print in a new print zone. If a semicolon is chosen, compact printing will result, in which each array element on a line will be separated by one space. With either zone or compact printing, each row of a two-dimensional array will start on a new line. If there is neither a comma nor a semicolon, each array element will print on a separate line. Four additional examples of MAT PRINT are shown in Figure 10-5.

```
100   DECLARE BYTE A(15)
   .
   .
   .
200   MAT PRINT A        Prints all 15 elements in a single column (one per
                         line).

300   MAT PRINT A,       Prints across the page using the print zones;
                         yields as many elements per line as allowed by the
                         device

400   MAT PRINT A;       Prints on one or more lines in compact fashion.

500   MAT PRINT A(12)    Prints only the first 12 elements of A in a single
                         column. Does *not* change bound specified in line
                         100.
```

Figure 10-5 Examples of the MAT PRINT statement.

Exercise

10-2. The statement DECLARE BYTE X(100) is included in a program. Write a sequence of statements that will perform the following:

a. Ask the user how many values (up to 100) are to be entered.

b. Accept the required number of values from the keyboard, load them into the array, and size the array downward as appropriate.

c. Give the user an appropriate message if the number of values actually entered is unequal to the number specified in response to how many values are to be entered.

Enter your routine into the computer to make certain it works.

Manipulation of Matrices

The algebra of matrices is composed of many powerful operations for manipulating matrices. VAX Basic includes some of the common matrix operations. Although these operations do not include the zero elements, some of them do destroy the previous contents of these elements.

Initialization Statements

The matrix initialization statements provide for intializing all elements of an array (except the zero elements) and for changing the bounds downward. These

```
100   DIM A(25), B(15,10), C(20,20), D$(10)
  .
  .
  .
300   MAT A = ZER            Sets elements A(1) through A(25) to 0.

400   MAT A = ZER(15)        Sets elements A(1) through A(15) to 0 and
                             reduces upper bound of A to 15.

500   MAT B = CON            Sets elements B(1,1) through B(15,10) to 1.

600   MAT B = CON(10,10)     Sets elements B(1,1) through B(10,10) to 1 and
                             reduces upper bounds of B to (10,10).

700   MAT C = IDN            Creates an identity matrix; that is, sets all
                             elements to 0 except C(1,1), C(2,2),
                             C(3,3),...,C(20,20), which are set to 1.

800   MAT D$ = NUL$          Sets elements D$(1) through D$(10) to a null
                             string.
```

Figure 10-6   MAT initialization statements.

statements, which are illustrated in Figure 10-6, provide for setting all elements of a matrix as follows:

ZER   Set all elements of a numeric array to 0.
NUL$ Set all elements of a string array to null.
CON   Set all elements of a numeric array to 1.
IDN   Set the elements of a square numeric array as follows:
       $A(I,J) = 0$ for I not equal J
       $A(I,J) = 1$ for I equal J
       This is called an identity matrix.

Scalar Multiplication

Example 9-7 (Figure 9-21) involves the multiplication of each element of the array PRECIP by a single value in the variable FACTOR. In mathematics, a single value is called a *scalar*; this is in contrast to an array, which consists of many values. The multiplication of an array by a single value is called *scalar multiplication*. Basic allows us to perform this as a MAT operation. In general, in scalar multiplication, each element of a matrix càn be multiplied by a constant, variable, or expression, as illustrated in Figure 10-7. Note that the scalar quantity must be enclosed in parentheses.

```
100   DIM A(15,12), B(15,12)
    .
    .
    .
200   MAT A = (150)*B        Duplicates each element in B into A and
                             multiplies each element in A by 150.

300   MAT A = (X+5)*A        Multiplies each element in A by the value
                             from X + 5.

400   MAT A = B             Copies each element of B into A.
```

Figure 10-7   Scalar multiplication.

With this capability, the nested FOR loops of Figure 9-21 are not necessary, as the entire operation can be done with the following statement:

```
MAT PRECIP = (FACTOR)*PRECIP
```

Exercise

10-3. Write a program segment to produce a 3×5 matrix A whose elements are

$$A(I,J) = 7$$

for all I and J.

Matrix Arithmetic—Addition and Subtraction

The three arithmetic operations of addition $(+)$, subtraction $(-)$, and multiplication $(*)$ can be performed on matrices. (The operation of division is not defined in matrix algebra.)

For addition or subtraction, the matrices must have the same numbers of rows and columns. These operations are defined mathematically as addition and subtraction of the individual elements:

$$A(I,J) = B(I,J) + C(I,J) \quad \text{Addition}$$
$$A(I,J) = B(I,J) - C(I,J) \quad \text{Subtraction}$$

```
100   DIM A(20),B(20),C(15),D(15),E(15)
  .
  .
  .
500   MAT C = D + E        Valid operation.

600   MAT A = D + E        Valid operation; decreases upper bound of A to 15.

700   MAT C = A + B        Invalid since C is too small to hold the result.

800   MAT A = B + C        Invalid since B and C are different sizes.
```

Figure 10-8   Addition and subtraction of matrices.

Examples of both correct and incorrect addition of matrices are given in Figure 10-8. Note that in statement 600, the size of the matrix A will be reduced to be consistent with matrices D and E.

Example 9-8, which requires that the elements of the arrays PRECIP.1 and PRECIP.2 be added, becomes almost trivial when MAT addition is used, that is

```
MAT PRECIP = PRECIP.1 + PRECIP.2
```

Matrix Arithmetic—Multiplication

The operation of matrix multiplication is more complicated than addition or subtraction. In fact, a nonmathematician can appreciate the value of adding corresponding elements of two arrays, but a mathematical background is necessary to understand fully the operation and value of multiplication. So if you have a limited mathematical background, do not be too concerned if the following is difficult to comprehend.

The product of two matrices, A × B, is defined only if the number of columns of A is equal to the number of rows of B; we denote this number by N. The matrix product is then defined mathematically for each element of the resultant matrix by

$$C(I,J) = \sum_{K=1}^{N} A(I,K)*B(K,J)$$

```
100   DIM A(12,9), B(9,6), C(9), D(15,20), X(15,15), Y(20)
  .
  .
  .
500   MAT X = A*B        Valid operation; X reduced in upper bounds to (12,6).

600   MAT X = B*A        Invalid since the number of columns in B is unequal
                         to the number of rows in A.

700   MAT A = X*D        Invalid since A is not large enough.

800   MAT Y = A*C        Valid operation; Y reduced in upper bound to 12.
```

Figure 10-9   Matrix multiplication.

The product inside the summation symbol is ordinary multiplication of two numbers. The resultant matrix C has the same number of rows as A and the same number of columns as B. If both A and B are square matrices, then both matrix products A*B and B*A are defined; however, in general, they are not equal to each other. For instance, in statement 500 of Figure 10-9, the number of columns in A and the number of rows in B are both 9. The resulting matrix will have the same number of rows as A and columns as B—12 × 6 in this case. The receiving matrix must be large enough to hold the resulting product. Note that statement 800 involves multiplying a two- and a one-dimensional matrix, producing a one-dimensional result.

Matrix Transposition, Inversion, and the Determinant

As with multiplication, the topics of this section require a knowledge of the mathematics of matrices to be really appreciated. VAX Basic provides functions for the three matrix operations of transposition, inversion, and taking the determinant. The transpose B of a matrix A is defined in matrix algebra by

$$B(I,J) = A(J,I)$$

In other words, to transpose a matrix, its rows and columns must be interchanged. This is done using the transpose Basic function TRN.

Inversion is defined only for square matrices. The inverse B of a matrix A is defined mathematically by

$$A \times B = B \times A = 1$$

where the multiplication is matrix multiplication and **1** is the identity matrix. The Basic function that computes the inverse is INV. Not all matrices have inverses. When the inverse does not exist, an attempt to compute it will cause an error message. When Basic calculates the inverse of a matrix, it also computes its determinant, which is placed in DET. Hence, DET contains the value of the determinant of the last matrix inverted with INV. These operators are illustrated in Figure 10-10.

```
100   DIM A(12,9), B(15,15), C(15,15)
   .
   .
   .
300   MAT B = TRN(A)     Copies the rows of A into the columns of B and
                         changes size of B to (9,12).

400   MAT A = TRN(B)     Invalid; A is not large enough.

500   MAT C = INV(B)     Inverts the matrix B, places it in C and calculates
                         the determinant of B and stores it in DET.

501   D = DET            Places the value of the determinant of B in the
                         simple variable D.

600   MAT B = INV(A)     Invalid; A must be a square matrix.

700   MAT B = INV(B)     Invalid; VAX Basic does not allow the inverse to
                         be stored back into the original matrix.
```

Figure 10-10   Matrix transposition, inversion and the determinant.

Exercises

10-4. Write a program segment that accepts from the keyboard a matrix (use a MAT INPUT), calculates its transpose, and prints both the matrix and its transpose. Each row of the array is to print on a separate line, and printing is to be compact.

10-5. Write a program segment to compute the inverse B of a 6×6 matrix A. (Assume that the matrix A has been loaded.) Verify that B is in the inverse by computing the product A*B and comparing it to the identity matrix. Print a message to indicate whether or not B is indeed the inverse.

10-6. For a 2×2 matrix, the determinant is simply the difference between the two products formed from the elements on the two diagonals. That is, if A is a 2×2 matrix, then the determinant of A is given by

$$\det A = A(1,1)*A(2,2) - A(1,2)*A(2,1)$$

Write a program segment to accept a 2×2 matrix from the keyboard. Test if its inverse exists by computing the determinant explicitly. If the inverse does not exist, the program should give a message to that effect. Otherwise, it should compute the inverse and print the inverse and the determinant.

In Retrospect

Of all the chapters we have studied thus far, this chapter on MAT operations is the most specialized. It is only in special situations where the use of this feature is of advantage. However, when appropriate, the MAT operations provide the programmer with an extremely powerful tool for manipulating arrays.

Answers to Preceding Exercises

10-1. ROW.COUNT = 4
COLUMN.COUNT = 5

10-2.
```
1000    DECLARE BYTE X(100), NUM.ENT
1100    CONTINUE$ = 'Y'
     ENTER.NUMS:
      WHILE CONTINUE$ = 'Y'
        PRINT 'How many values do you wish'
        INPUT 'to enter (between 1 and 100)'; NUM.ENT
        IF NUM.ENT < 1 OR NUM.ENT > 100
          THEN
            PRINT 'Must be between 1 and 100'
            PRINT 'Please try again'
            ITERATE ENTER.NUMS
          ELSE
            MAT INPUT X(NUM.ENT)
            CONTINUE$ = 'N'
        END IF
      NEXT
      PRINT 'Matrix not filled' IF NUM <> NUM.ENT
```

10-3.
```
1000    DECLARE BYTE A(3,5)
           .
           .
           .
        MAT A = CON
        MAT A = (7)*A
```

10-4.
```
1000    DECLARE BYTE A(4,7), B(7,4)
           .
           .
           .
        PRINT 'Enter 28 numbers separated by commas'
        MAT INPUT A
        MAT B = TRN(A)
        PRINT 'Matrix A'
        PRINT
        MAT PRINT A;
        PRINT \ PRINT
        PRINT 'Matrix B'
        PRINT
        MAT PRINT B;
```

10-5.
```
1000    DECLARE REAL A(6,6),B(6,6),C(6,6),D(6,6),E(6,6)
           .
           .
           .
        MAT B = INV(A)  ! Compute inverse of A
        MAT C = A*B  ! C should be the identity matrix
        MAT D = IDN  ! D is the identity matrix
        MAT E = ZER  ! E is the zero matrix
        IF C - D = E
           THEN PRINT 'B is indeed the inverse of A'
           ELSE PRINT 'A*B is not the identity matrix'
        END IF
```

10-6.

```
1000    DECLARE
             .
             .
             .
        MAT INPUT A
        DETERM = A(1,1)*A(2,2) - A(1,2,)*A(2,1)
        IF DETERM = 0
          THEN PRINT 'The matrix A has no inverse'
          ELSE
            MAT B = INV(A)
            PRINT 'The determinant of A is '; DET
            PRINT 'The inverse of A is '
            MAT PRINT B;
        END IF
```

Programming Problems

10-1. True-false examinations consisting of up to 50 questions each are to be processed by the computer. The input file consists of the following information:

First record	Number of questions in exam.
Second record	Answer key (up to 50 answers).
Following records	ID number.
	Answers (up to 50 answers).

Answers are recorded as 1(true) or 0 (false). For instance, the first three records of an examination consisting of 10 questions might be as follows:

10	Header record (number of questions).
1, 0, 1, 1, 0, 0, 1, 1, 0 , 1	Answer key (10 answers).
2173, 1, 0, 1, 1, 0, 1, 0, 1, 0, 1	(ID number followed by answers).

Write a program to score each examination and print the results. Points of note relating to this program are as follows: (1) The MAT INPUT statement should be used to read the answer key into an answer-key array. The value from the header (number of questions) can be used to size the array downward. (2) Each examination (records following the answer key) includes an ID number (integer) followed by the answers. A MAT INPUT should be used to read each of these into an array. An appropriate adjustment will be required when comparing the answer-key array with the data array. (3) The data file will be terminated with a trailer of 9999 for the ID number.

The program must print the score for each ID together with appropriate headings and descriptive information.

10-2. An important application of matrix algebra is to the solution of simultaneous equations, such as

$$
\begin{array}{r}
3x + 4y - 5z = -11 \\
x - 5y + 2z = -8 \\
-7x - y + 3z = 16
\end{array}
$$

Using the laws of matrix algebra, the equivalent matrix form is

$$
\begin{pmatrix} 3 & 4 & -5 \\ 1 & -5 & 2 \\ -7 & -1 & 3 \end{pmatrix} \begin{pmatrix} x \\ y \\ z \end{pmatrix} = \begin{pmatrix} -11 \\ -8 \\ 16 \end{pmatrix}
$$

where the product on the left-hand side of the equation is matrix multiplication. This is commonly written as

$$ AX = B $$

Here A represents the coeeficient matrix; X, the matrix of the unknowns; and B, the constant matrix. If these quantities were not matrices, we would solve this equation for X by dividing both sides of the equation by A. However, since matrix algebra has no division operation, it is necessary to multiply both sides by the *inverse* of A. Thus, we can solve for X as

$$ X = A^{-1} B $$

where A^{-1} is the inverse of A. Note that it is essential for A^{-1} to multiply B from the left.

   Write a program that will read the coefficient and constant arrays of a linear system and solve for the unknowns using this method. Remember, the array X will contain the desired values for the unknowns (x, y, and z in the earlier example).

10-3. Consider a two-dimensional matrix B with J rows and K columns and a one-dimensional matrix A with J columns. Then A*B (matrix multiplication) is a one-dimensional matrix with K columns. If all elements of A are 1, then each element of A*B is the sum of the columns of B. Use MAT statements to write a program to compute and print the column sums of a matrix.

10-4. This is a generalization of problem 9-8, the warehouse problem. Rewrite the program using MAT statements and the results of problem 10-3 wherever possible. Also, allow for the possibility of percentage changes in the price of a given tool. This problem illustrates the general principle and is a very simple example of a *spreadsheet*: a program whose output is a table and with the capability that changes in the *entries* to the table are *automatically reflected in all computed quantities* based on these entries.

11

Additional String Operations

CHAPTER OUTLINE

Preview

We have used string quantities in our programs since Chapter 2 and have used a limited number of string functions since Chapter 6. The processing of string data is a very important topic in programming. This chapter presents some of the commonly encountered operations in processing string data, including the following topics:

1. Principles of how string information is coded in memory using the ASCII coding method.
2. Manipulating characters by using their ASCII values.
3. The distinction between printable characters and control characters (which cause control actions such as generating an audible alarm).
4. The LINPUT statement, provided especially to input string information, including commas and other special characters.

5. *Converting numeric data to string form and string data consisting of numbers to numeric form. These operations are done with the NUM$ and VAL functions.*
6. *Generating strings of identical characters using the SPACE$ and STRING$ functions.*
7. *The use of the EDIT$ function to operate on a string field, performing editing operations, such as eliminating leading spaces and changing lowercase to uppercase.*
8. *The INSTR statement, which searches a string for any designated substring of characters.*

Concept of ASCII Characters

The Nature of Binary Numbers

Remember from early descriptions that the basic addressable unit of memory in the VAX is the byte, which consists of eight binary digits—*bits*. Since electronic circuits are easily recognized as being on or off, a binary system is used, where *off* represents the binary digit 0 and *on* the binary digit 1. Thus, the eight bits of each byte of memory can be represented as an eight-binary-digit number ranging from 00000000 to 11111111. Although it is not the intent of this book to delve into the nature of the binary number system, an insight into its nature is helpful. Actually, the binary system is much like our conventional decimal system. Where the place values of decimal digits increase by ten times in progressing from the right, place values of binary digits increase by two times in progressing from the right. Thus, the binary number 1101 actually represents the decimal number

$$1 \times 8 + 1 \times 4 + 0 \times 2 + 1 \times 1 = 13$$

Continuing this example would show that the decimal values in the range 00000000 to 11111111 are 0 to 255.

Actually, the preceding is essentially the way that integers are stored in VAX memory, except they occupy more than one byte. Moreover, *all* characters, including alphabetic and punctuation, are stored as sequences of bits.

The ASCII Character Set

In order to store string data, it is necessary to use some type of coding system to convert between a character such as a letter and a sequence of bits such as 1011001. Each character of the character set—letters, special characters, and digits—must be assigned its own unique code. If the full byte is used, then it would be possible to code 256 characters. (There are 256 different combinations of 0s and 1s in an 8-bit number.)

There are two commonly used character-coding methods. The Extended Binary Coded Decimal Interchange Code (EBCDIC) is used by IBM (and IBM-compatible manufacturers) for their mainframe computers. It uses the full 8-bit capacity of the byte, and hence the code consists of 256 characters. The American Standard Code for Information Interchange (ASCII) is used by Digital Equipment Corporation and most other computer manufacturers, as well as by IBM for their microcomputers. ASCII is a 7-bit code and hence can represent only 128 characters. (Note: The expanded ASCII character set is coded in 8 bits and has a set of 256 characters.) In the VAX, characters in ASCII are represented in memory by the rightmost 7 bits of the byte. (The leftmost bit is ignored for character coding.) For instance, Table 11-1 is a partial list of the uppercase letters and their ASCII representations.

TABLE 11-1 ASCII Values for Some Uppercase Letters

Letter	Binary ASCII Value	Decimal ASCII Value
A	1000001	65
B	1000010	66
C	1000011	67
D	1000100	68
E	1000101	69
.		
.		
.		
X	1011000	88
Y	1011001	89
Z	1011010	90

The lowercase letters have a simple relationship to the uppercase letters, in that each lowercase letter differs from its uppercase counterpart by a single bit. We can see this relationship by comparing Table 11-2 to Table 11-1. Here we see that the sixth bit from the right is 1 for the lowercase letters and 0 for the uppercase letters. Since this bit position represents a decimal value of 32, the decimal value of each lowercase letter is 32 greater than that of the corresponding uppercase letter.

TABLE 11-2 ASCII Values for Some Lowercase Letters

Letter	Binary ASCII Value	Decimal ASCII Value
a	1100001	97
b	1100010	98
c	1100011	99
d	1100100	100
e	1100101	101
.		
.		
.		
x	1111000	120
y	1111001	121
z	1111010	122

Whenever a string value is entered into the computer, it is converted character by character into ASCII and placed in memory one character per byte. For example, the name *Bob* is represented as shown here.

String	Decimal ASCII Value	Binary ASCII Value
B	66	1000010
o	111	1101111
b	98	1100010

In Chapter 5, we learned that when string values are used to form a relational expression, the concept of *greater than* and *less than* corresponds to an alphabetic sequence. The binary coding shown in Tables 12-1 and 12-2 illustrates the basis for this. That is, the determination of whether one ASCII character is greater than or less than another is based solely on their ASCII values. From Table 11-1 we see that the letter C (67) is obviously larger than the letter A (65). Furthermore, it should now be evident why the lowercase letters are all larger than any of the uppercase letters. The order of the characters of a character set is called its *collating sequence*. The full ASCII character set is listed in the table in Appendix II.

The ASCII set is used to represent two general types of characters: *printable* and *control*. Printable characters are just what their name implies: the digits, uppercase letters (A, B, C,. . .), lowercase letters (a, b, c,. . .) and special characters (+ , $, %,. . .). When a printable character is entered at the terminal, it is displayed on the screen; the entered character is said to be *echoed* by the system. This action consists of two steps. First, the computer sends the ASCII bit pattern for that character to the terminal. Second, the terminal interprets the bit pattern according to its own set of internal codes and displays it on the screen. Of the printable ASCII characters, there are two that produce different visual effects on the screen than the others. These are the *space* character, ASCII value 32, and the *delete* character, ASCII value 127. Striking the space bar of the terminal causes the computer to *insert* a space character (ASCII 32) into memory and to echo as an empty position on the screen. Striking the delete causes the system to backspace over the last inserted character and *remove it from memory*. On most terminals, it does *not* remove the echoed character from the screen, but a newly typed character will then echo and replace the deleted one on the screen.

The first 32 characters in the ASCII table (decimal values 0 through 31) are control characters. Control characters are used for a variety of system-control operations, such as indicating the end of a file or causing an audible sound. They cause a variety of actions to take place when they are sent to a terminal as output. We shall learn about some of the control characters later in this chapter.

Exercises

11-1. Give the decimal equivalent of each character in the string "VAX 780".

11-2. Translate the following sequence of decimal ASCII values into their corresponding characters:

86 65 88 32 66 97 115 105 99

The CHR$ and ASCII Functions

For certain operations, it is convenient to be able to convert a numeric value to its ASCII character or to obtain the decimal value of an ASCII character. The former is done with the CHR$ function, and the latter, with the ASCII function. As we recall from Chapter 6, a system function operates on its *argument* and returns (provides for use in the program) a result in the form of the function *value*. The argument of the ASCII function is a string. The function returns the decimal ASCII value of the *first* character in the string.

Statement(s) executed	Then the output from PRINT Y would be:
1000 Y = ASCII("A")	65
2000 X$ = "A" 2010 Y = ASCII(X$)	65
3000 X$ = "ABCDE" 3010 Y = ASCII(SEG$(X$,3,3))	67
4000 X$ = "ABCDE" 4010 Y = ASCII(X$)	65

Figure 11-1   The ASCII function.

For instance, Figure 11-1 illustrates the ASCII function. At lines 1000 and 2010, the decimal ASCII value of the letter A (ASCII 65) is stored in Y. At line 3010, the ASCII function uses the SEG$ function as an argument that extracts the letter C for the ASCII function. At line 4010, the argument of the ASCII function has a length of 5. Since this function operates only on the first character of a string, it returns the ASCII value of the first character from X$ (the letter A).

The CHR$ function, which is the reverse of the ASCII function, is illustrated in Figure 11-2. Its argument is a decimal integer, and it returns the

Statement(s) executed	Then the output from PRINT X$ would be:
1000 X$ = CHR$(65)	A
2000 X$ = CHR$(77) + CHR$(61) + CHR$(55)	M=7
3000 X$ = "" 3010 X$ = X$ + CHR$(J) FOR J = 97 TO 104	abcdefgh

Figure 11-2   The CHR$ function.

corresponding ASCII character. Line 1000 creates a single character whose ASCII value is 65 (the letter A), then stores it in the string variable X$. The result of printing X$ is shown at the right. The other two examples involve concatenating characters one at a time, with the results shown. Each of these should be studied carefully to ensure a good understanding.

Exercise

11-3. What will be stored in Z$ after execution of the following statements?

```
X$ = "R"
Z$ = CHR$(ASCII(X$) + 32)
```

Using the CHR$ and ASCII Functions. The CHR$ and ASCII functions provide us with the capability to operate on individual bytes. As a very simple example of character operation, let us consider the following:

Example 11-1

> The variable A$ contains one character. If the character is a lowercase letter, then convert it to uppercase. Otherwise, leave it unchanged.

This is a minor variation of Exercise 11-3, in which the CHR$ and ASCII functions are very convenient for the operation. Remembering that each of the uppercase letters differs from its lowercase counterpart by the amount 32, if we subtract 32 from the ASCII value of a lowercase letter, we have the ASCII value of the corresponding uppercase letter. This method is used in the sample statements of Figure 11-3. At lines 1000 and 1010, the string quantity is converted to its ASCII value and the ASCII value is checked. The conversion takes place by subtracting 32 as needed. Exactly the same action results from each of the tests in statements 2000 and 3000, in which the comparison is made using the string variable A$ directly rather than its ASCII value. Note that in statement 3000, the entire conversion is made by using a function call as the argument of another function.

A bit of ingenuity is required to extend this technique to convert all lowercase letters in a string to uppercase.

```
1000   B = ASCII(A$)
1010   IF B >= 97 AND B <= 122
         THEN A$ = CHR$(B - 32)
       END IF

2000   IF A$ >= "a" AND A$ <= "z"
         THEN B = ASCII(A$)
              A$ = CHR$(B - 32)
       END IF
3000   IF A$ >= "a" AND A$ <= "z"
         THEN A$ = CHR$(ASCII(A$) - 32)
       END IF
```

Figure 11-3 Changing a letter from uppercase to lowercase— Example 11-1.

```
5000   FOR PNTR = 1 TO LEN(ST$)
5010     A$ = SEG$(ST$,PNTR,PNTR)
5020     IF A$ >= "a" AND A$ <= "z" THEN
           ST$ = LEFT$(ST$,PNTR-1) + CHR$(ASCII(A$)-32) + RIGHT$(ST$,PNTR+1)
         END IF
5030   NEXT PNTR
```

Figure 11-4   Changing a string from uppercase to lowercase—Example 11-2.

Example 11-2

A routine is required to convert all lowercase letters in the string ST$ to uppercase. Leave all other characters unchanged.

For this, we require a loop that is executed a number of times corresponding to the length of ST$. (Each character of ST$ must be checked.) The statement sequence of Figure 11-4 uses the technique of statement 3000 in Figure 11-3 to perform the required operation. As an illustration of what takes place, assume that ST$ contains the phrase

Go for it-now.

Furthermore, assume that the loop has been executed such that PNTR now contains a value of 11. Then Figure 11-5 is a schematic representation of what takes place in statements 5010 and 5020 of Figure 11-4.

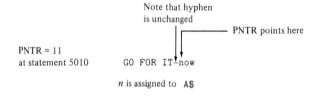

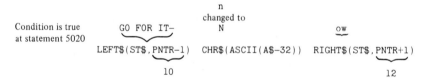

Figure 11-5   Sample execution—Example 11-2.

Exercise

11-4. Assuming that X$ contains the letters A-Z, what will be stored in Z$ after execution of the following statements? Explain what happens.

```
Z$ = ""
Z$ = Z$ + CHR$(ASCII(SEG$(X$,I,I) + 32) FOR I = 1 TO LEN(X$)
```

Control Characters

The BEL Character

Although ASCII includes 32 control characters (values from 0 through 31), we will study only the most commonly used ones. All of them may be entered into memory by use of the CHR$ function. For example, the ASCII value 7 is assigned to the variable NOISE$ by the following statement:

```
NOISE$ = CHR$(7)
```

This is a particularly convenient character. Occasionally, it is desirable to have the program alert the user by some means in addition to visual display on the CRT. The BEL character, which has an ASCII value of 7, provides an audio alarm in the form of a buzzer or bell that is built into most terminals. To gain insight into the handling of control characters by output devices, let us consider the execution of the PRINT statement sequence of Figure 11-6(a). (Assume starting with a clear screen.) When statement 1000 is executed, the ASCII value 65 is transmitted to the terminal. The internal circuitry of the terminal decodes this value and causes a particular operation to take place. This operation is to print (or display) the letter A and move to the next position on the screen (this action is automatic when a character is displayed). Then the next character, which is ASCII 66, is transmitted, the letter B is displayed, and the screen shows AB: See Figure 11-6(a). When statement 1020 is executed, the ASCII value 7 is sent to the terminal. Rather than displaying a letter or some other character, the code 7 is interpreted by the terminal as the code to ring the terminal bell (buzzer). Note that it does *not* move the cursor; that action is caused only by displaying a character (or by a code that explicitly causes cursor movement). Transmission of the last character then causes the letter C to be displayed.

Exactly the same results will be obtained from the equivalent statements of Figures 11-6(b) and (c). The result of printing SAMPLE$ in Figure 11-6 is

		Output at Terminal	Terminal shows:
1000	PRINT CHR$(65);	A	A
1010	PRINT CHR$(66);	B	AB
1020	PRINT CHR$(7);	Noise	AB (no change)
1030	PRINT CHR$(67);	C	ABC
	(a)		

```
2000  PRINT CHR$(65); CHR$(66); CHR$(7); CHR$(67)
          (b)

3000  SAMPLE$ = CHR$(65) + CHR$(66) + CHR$(7) + CHR$(67)
3010  PRINT SAMPLE$
          (c)
```

Figure 11-6   Sending the BEL character to the terminal.

```
1000   PRINT CHR$(7)
1010   PRINT "You have exeeded the maximum!"
          (a)

2000   PRINT CHR$(7); "You have exeeded the maximum!"
         (b)

100    NOISE$ = CHR$(7)
  .
  .
  .
3000   PRINT NOISE$;
           (c)
```

Figure 11-7   Using the BEL character.

obvious once we understand just how the output devices interpret control characters. Although four characters were transmitted to the terminal, only three characters were printed. One of them (the third) caused the bell to be sounded.

Typical examples of this character to sound a warning are illustrated in Figure 11-7. The form in which the BEL character is defined as a separate variable and used as shown in Figure 11-7(c) is commonly encountered in programming.

The Line-Feed and Carriage-Return Characters

The line-feed (LF) character, ASCII value 10, causes progression to the *next* line. The carriage-return (CR) character, ASCII value 13, causes the cursor to return to the beginning of the *current* line. Thus far, our experience with the carriage-return operation has related to striking the Return key on the terminal keyboard. We strike this key and the printing element (or cursor) returns to the leftmost position and progresses to a new line. Technically speaking, the Return key on a terminal transmits only a CR character. However, the system automatically appends a line-feed *character* when the Return *key* (RETURN) is pressed. This is illustrated in Figure 11-8. On the other hand, the line-feed key (LINEFEED) enters *only* the LF character.

```
                       Strike Return key
This is a short ◄─── here and
line. Press ◄─────── here and
return key. ◄─────── here
        ASCII 13.     ASCII 10
This is a short line. Press return key.
```
Sequence of characters entered into the computer
(43 of them from 40 keystrokes)

Figure 11-8   Using the Return key.

It is important to recognize that the computer does not differentiate *within memory* between a control character and a printable character. When performing string operations, we can operate on control characters exactly as we operate on printable characters. In the string illustrated in Figure 11-8, the LF and CR characters were entered into memory directly from the keyboard by pressing the Return key. If we so desired, we could create an equivalent string by entering these two control characters by the assignment statement of Figure

```
A$ = "This is a short"+CHR$(13)+CHR$(10)+"line. Press"+CHR$(13)+CHR$(10)
     +"return key."+CHR$(13)+CHR$(10)
```

Figure 11-9 Creating a string with imbedded control characters.

11-9. Note that the CHR$ function in an assignment statement provides a direct way of imbedding a control character in a string. In this form, the string consists of 43 characters (its length is 43), six of them being control characters.

If we were to perform string operations on this string, such as obtaining its length or extracting a substring, then the control characters would be treated just as any other characters. For example, consider the following statement:

```
C$ = LEFT$(A$,16)
```

The value returned to C$ would have a length of 16 and would consist of "This is a short" *and* the CR character (ASCII 13). However, what if the value of A$ were displayed by the following statement?

```
PRINT  A$
```

To understand fully the effect on output, it is helpful to know how a serial printing device such as a terminal works. (Terminals are called *serial* because they handle characters one at a time as they are transmitted from the computer.) When the PRINT statement is executed, the characters that make up A$ are transmitted to the terminal one after the other, beginning with the first. When the code 84 (the ASCII value of the letter T) is transmitted, the terminal's internal circuitry causes it to display the character T. As successive characters are transmitted, the circuitry responds accordingly. However, when the CR is transmitted, a carriage-return operation is carried out. This sequence of operations is illustrated in Figure 11-10.

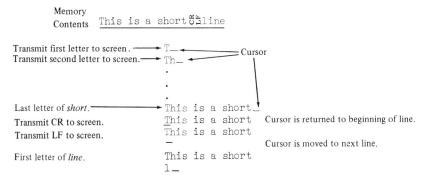

Figure 11-10 Character by character action of displaying a string.

The Form-Feed Character

Each time a PRINT statement is executed, a new line of output is displayed or printed (assuming that the statement is not ended with a semicolon). If the statement is executed 100 times, we get 100 printed lines. If the output device is a printer, then the printed output will be continuous across the perforation separating one page from the other. This is not a very desirable situation; it would be much better if the printer would advance to a new page whenever the current one becomes filled. Fortunately, most hard-copy terminals and printers include a built-in feature that allows for page control. On many of these devices, a selector switch can be set to correspond to the length of the printed form (usually 8.5 or 11 inches). For instance, setting the printer for a form length of 11 inches means that the paper-advancing mechanism has a "home" or *top-of-form* position every 11 inches. If the printer is directed to reposition to the top of form, then it will progress to this position regardless of where the form is positioned at the time. Properly positioning the paper within the feed mechanism of the printer will cause the continuous-form paper to be positioned to the top of the next page. The form-feed action can be initiated either by an external action of pressing a button or switch on the printer or by the internal action of receiving an appropriate code from the computer. The latter provides us with the ability to perform paper-positioning operations under program control. For example, we might write a program in which we want to skip to a new page after 54 lines have been printed. Our program logic would then include a counter which, after printing 54 lines, would cause a *form-feed* operation to be performed. This is controlled from within the program by the form-feed character, which has an ASCII value of decimal 12.

A program segment illustrating how this is used in a program is shown in Figure 11-11. When the form-feed character is transmitted, it causes the paper carrier to advance to the top of the next page and then perform the required printing operation. If this code is transmitted to a CRT or a printer that does not include form-control capability, the result will depend upon the particular machine. Usually a few lines are skipped.

```
        .
        .
        .
2020  LINE.CNT = LINE.CNT + 1
      PRINT #4, ...(output line)
2030  IF LINE.CNT > 54
      THEN
         PAGE.CNT = PAGE.CNT + 1
         PRINT #4, CHR$(12); TAB(20); "Summary Report #4"; TAB(50);     &
                              "Page"; PAGE.CNT
         LINE.CNT = 0
      ENDIF
```

Figure 11-11 Page control using the form feed.

Control Characters as Predefined Constants

In many string-manipulation applications, it is necessary to work with control as well as printable characters. The action of building strings using the CHR$ function and ASCII values, as in Figure 11-9, tends to be somewhat clumsy. To simplify this, VAX Basic uses reserved names to designate several of the commonly used control characters as well as two of the other ASCII characters. They are called *predefined constants*. (We have already created our own named

TABLE 11-3 Some Predefined Constants

Constant Name	ASCII Value	Function of Character
BEL	7	Sounds the terminal bell.
BS	8	Varies; see example in Figure 11-12.
HT	9	Moves the cursor to the next tab stop.
LF	10	Moves the cursor to the next line.
FF	12	Used to control the printer. It causes the printer to reposition the paper to the top of the next page.
CR	13	Moves the cursor to the beginning of the current line.
SP	32	Inserts a space.
DEL	127	Backspaces over the preceding character; on most terminals, it does not remove the echoed character from the screen.

constants with the DECLARE CONSTANT statement in Chapter 6.) Some of the most commonly used predefined constants are listed in Table 11-3.

Predefined constants provide us with an alternative way to build a string containing control characters. Their use can make source code easier to understand. For example, let us consider the statements in Figure 11-12. Statement 200 will create exactly the same string as the statement of Figure 11-9. If the display of statement 300 is to a hard-copy device, it will cause the output of Figure 11-12(c). In this example, the printer will first print LIST:, one character at a time. Then the print element will be backed up one position for each BS character. The underscores will then be ''overprinted,'' producing the result shown in Figure 11-12(c). If the output device is a CRT, the underscores will replace the printed letters, and the final screen result will be five underscores.

```
          .
          .
          .
(a)   200 A$ = "This is a short"+CR+LF+"line. Press"+CR+LF+"return key."+CR+LF

(b)   300 PRINT "LIST:"+BS+BS+BS+BS+BS+"_____"
(c)   LIST:
```

Figure 11-12   Using predefined constants.

Exercises

11-5. Rewrite the expression in line 300 of Figure 11-12(b) using the CHR$ function instead of the predefined constant. It should be clear which version makes the source code easier to understand.

11-6. Show what the output would be if the following X$ were printed on a terminal.

```
X$ = CHR$(49) + CHR$(50) + LF + BS + CHR$(51) + CHR$(52)
```

11-7. Rewrite the expressions in Figure 11-7 using a predefined constant instead of the CHR$ function.

Keyboard-Entered Control Characters

Many of the control characters may be entered by holding down the control key (CTRL) and striking a printable character key. This combination is commonly indicated by CTRL/x, where x is a printable character. For instance, we have already used the key combination of Control and the letter C to terminate execution of a program. As we know, the CRTL/C echoes on the terminal as $^\wedge$C. Table 11-4 summarizes the properties of several of the most useful CTRL combinations.

TABLE 11-4 Properties of Some Double-Key-Entry Control Statements

Keys Used to Enter	ASCII Character	ASCII Value	Purpose	Visible Effect on Output Device
CTRL/C	ETX	3	Cancels program execution, output, system command, or any other operation; returns system to Basic command mode (to user).	Echoes as $^\wedge$C; return of control to user is indicated by "Ready."
CTRL/S	DC3	19	Suspends display of output on terminal until CTRL/Q is pressed.*	Scrolling stops.
CTRL/Q	DC1	17	Resumes output suspended by CTRL/S.*	Scrolling resumes.
CTRL/U	NAK	21	Cancels current program line and performs a carriage return/line feed.	Echoes as $^\wedge$U.
CTRL/L	FF	12	Form feed.	Advances to top of next page.
CTRL/G	BEL	7	Sounds the terminal bell.	None.

* This description applies to suitably set devices.

Entering Text Information

The Problem of Delimiters

To illustrate one of the very important considerations in writing an interactive program, let us consider the following example:

Example 11-3

A data-entry program requires that name and address information be entered for each student registered at a college. The name is to be entered and stored in the variable in the following form:

Last name, comma, First name, Middle initial

A typical name entry would be

Alvarez, Jose A

For this task, consider the following statement:

```
INPUT "Enter student name (Last, First MI)"; FULL.NAME$
```

If the screen dialogue is as shown in Figure 11-13(a), then we have a serious problem. That is, the comma following the last name will be treated as a delimiter by the input statement, which will see *Alvarez* as one field and *Jose A* as another. Since there is only one variable in the INPUT list, only the last name is accepted and the remainder is discarded. If we wish to force the issue and restrain the INPUT from interpreting the comma as a delimiter, then the input must be enclosed in quotes, as illustrated by the example of Figure 11-13(b). Although this is adequate to do the job, it is clumsy. Since the quotes are not part of the data, they become an extra pair of characters that the person doing the data entry must watch for carefully. Not only does it slow the data-entry operation, but it introduces another possibility for errors.

```
INPUT "Enter student name (Last, First MI)"; FULL.NAME$

Enter student name (Last, First MI)? Alvarez, Jose A
```

(a)   Only the portion up
                          to the comma is accepted.

```
Enter student name (Last, First MI)? "Alvarez, Jose A"
```
                                                              User enters input
                                                              enclosed in quotes.
(b)   Entered into FULL.NAME$

Figure 11-13   Inputting text information—Example 11-3.

This general problem is further compounded by the input of text information from a file. Although requiring the data-entry person to use quotes might solve the problem for interactive input, there is no equivalent action if the information is to be read from a file and does not include such quotes. The problem becomes impossible if a given field from some records might include a comma and others do not include one.

In order to get around this problem (which presents itself in a variety of forms), VAX Basic includes two special statements for accepting text information: LINPUT and INPUT LINE. The primary focus in this book is on the LINPUT statement, which is described in the next section.

The LINPUT Statement

The LINPUT statement accepts *all* characters in a line input from the keyboard or a file, *including* quotation marks, spaces, and punctuation marks. It then assigns that line to a string variable specified in the statement. (The INPUT LINE does exactly the same thing except it also includes the terminating carriage-return and line-feed characters. For most applications, use of the LINPUT is preferred.) Use of the LINPUT is illustrated in Figure 11-14. The following comments summarize the characteristics of the LINPUT statement:

1. This statement, which may be used with or without a channel number, assigns a string value to a string variable. Without a channel number, it provides for interactive input of a string value from the keyboard. The channel number, if used, must be preceded by a pound sign, for example:

       LINPUT #3, QUOTE$

   Use of a channel number presupposes an opened file.
2. *All* characters up to the CR-LF terminators are included as part of the string. The LINPUT differs in this respect from the INPUT, which interprets characters such as commas, semicolons, and quotation marks as delimiters. The length of the string that is entered includes all special characters.
3. If entry is from the keyboard, a user prompt may be included, exactly as with the INPUT statement. The separator (comma or semicolon) between a user prompt and the string variable works exactly as with the INPUT statement.

```
LINPUT "Enter student name (Last, First MI)"; FULL.NAME$

Enter student name (Last, First MI)? Alvarez, Jose A
                                      ↑
                                      └───────── Everything is accepted.
```

Figure 11-14   Using the LINPUT statement—Example 11-3.

Exercises

11-8. The program of Example 11-3 includes the following LINPUT statement:

```
LINPUT "Enter student name <Last, First MI>"; FULL.NAME$
```

The data-entry person has been instructed simply to strike the Return key if there are no more data entries to be made. When this occurs, the integer variable FINISHED is to be set to true (-1).

Write the appropriate IF statement to do this. It may be necessary to experiment with the statement to determine exactly what happens if the Return is pressed without entering any data.

11-9. In response to each of the following statements, the string ZYXWVU was entered at the terminal. What are the lengths of A$ and B$?

```
1000   LINPUT A$
1010   LINE INPUT B$
```

Manipulation of Numeric Data Stored as String Data

Mixed Numeric and Character Data in a String

In some types of applications, a string field will consist of subfields that include both numeric and string data. This is illustrated by the following example:

Example 11-4

Information has been extracted from a *database management system* (DBMS) and written to an ASCII file for processing by a Basic program. (A DBMS is software designed to manage and manipulate sets of data.) Each output line (record) is exactly 28 bytes in length and includes the following information:

Field	Positions	Typical Data
Name	1–20	
Total units	21–24	048.5
Total grade points	25–28	106.5

The grade-point average is to be calculated for each student as the total grade points divided by the total units.

The process of accessing each record and breaking it into its component fields is relatively simple using the LINPUT statement and SEG$ function, as shown in Figure 11-15. The problem we have here is that the numeric values UNITS$ and POINTS$ are string and not numeric. If we attempted to perform the division operation

```
GPA = POINTS$/UNITS$
```

we would get an error. An arithmetic expression can operate only on numeric quantities. There are two ways in which this can be handled.

```
LINPUT #1, IN.FIELD$
NAME$ = SEG$(IN.FIELD$,1,20)
UNITS$ = SEG$(IN.FIELD$,21,24)
POINTS$ = SEG$(IN.FIELD$,25,28)
```

Figure 11-15 Extracting fields from a fixed-length record—Example 11-4.

String Arithmetic Operations

The first method for performing the desired division operation uses *string arithmetic functions*. These are system functions whose arguments are strings that contain numeric values. These functions perform arithmetic operations on their arguments and return the results in the form of function values that are also numeric strings. The properties of string arithmetic functions are summarized in Table 11-5.

TABLE 11-5 Properties of String Arithmetic Functions

Format of Function	Description	Number of Digits After the Decimal Point
SUM$(A$,B$)	B$ is added to A$	Same as argument with most digits after decimal.
DIF$(A$,B$)	B$ is subtracted from A$	Same as SUM.
PROD$(A$,B$,P%)	A$ is multiplied by B$	Expressed explicity by value of the parameter P%.
QUO$(A$,B$,P%)	A$ is divided by B$	Expressed explicitly by value of the parameter P%.

String arithmetic functions offer two advantages over corresponding arithmetic operations performed on numeric data types. One is that many more significant digits can be stored and involved in arithmetic operations. The other, which is critical in many accounting applications, is that string arithmetic is not prone to the round-off error that is a characteristic of the nature of binary floating-point numbers. However, arithmetic string operations take considerably longer to execute than ordinary operations performed on numeric data types.

The needed grade-point average calculation for Example 11-4 can be done with the following statement:

```
GPA$ = QUO$(POINTS$,UNITS$,2)
```

Note that, because the value of P% in this expression is *positive* 2, the result will be rounded two digits to the *right* of the decimal point (the number is rounded to the nearest hundredth). A typical output value would be 2.78.

Because of the slow speed of string arithmetic and the fact that it is clumsy if many operations are involved, it is not used unless the particular application needs require it. The more common approach is to perform appropriate type-conversion operations, as described by the next section.

The VAL and NUM1$ Functions

The other way of handling arithmetic with numeric strings involves converting the string value to the numeric data type. This is accomplished with the VAL function. Its argument is a numeric string, which may contain a leading sign, digits, an uppercase E, and a decimal point. The returned result is the floating-point value of that string. The solution to GPA calculation of Example 11-4

```
LINPUT #1, IN.FIELD$
NAME$ = SEG$(IN.FIELD$,1,20)
UNITS = VAL(SEG$(IN.FIELD$,21,24))
POINTS = VAL(SEG$(IN.FIELD$,25,28))
GPA = POINTS/UNITS
```

Figure 11-16   Using the VAL function.

using this capability is shown in Figure 11-16. As a rule, use of this function should be accompanied by an appropriate error-recovery routine. If the string to be converted is not a valid numeric form, then an error occurs; for example, an attempt to convert any of the following strings will produce an error:

$$25.67.1 \qquad 782+ \qquad A65.1$$

When this occurs, the program will terminate if the ON ERROR has not been activated.

The NUM1$ function performs the opposite conversion: numeric to string. Its argument is a numeric expression (either floating-point or integer format), and it returns a string of numeric characters. It is illustrated in Figure 11-17. The first two examples are reasonably straightforward; the third is more complex. Frequently, in building an output line to be written as a fixed-format record (such as Example 11-4), leading zeros must be included to fill out the field. That is the purpose of the technique in this third example.

```
A% = 2107
A$ = NUM1$(A%)
```
Integer quantity in A%. converted to string with length of 4 and assigned to A$.

```
B = -157.683
B$ = NUM1$(B)
```
Floating-point quantity in B converted to string with length of 8 (includes - and .) and assigned to B$.

```
C% = 32%
C$ = RIGHT(NUM1$(1000%+C%),2%)
```
Two-digit integer in C% converted to string with a leading zero (032), length of 3; assigned to C$.

Figure 11-17   Using the NUM1$ function.

Other String Functions

Strings of Identical Characters

The programmer often encounters situations in which a long string composed of a given character is required (for example, a string of hyphens). The SPACE$ and STRING$ functions both create strings made up of identical characters. The SPACE$ function returns a string of blank spaces. It has one argument that specifies the number of spaces to be generated. The STRING$ function has two arguments. The first one specifies the length of the generated string, and the second one specifies the ASCII value of the character that makes up the string.

```
M$ = "###                                   ##.##"
M$ = "###" + SPACE$(40) + "###.##"
```

Figure 11-18 Using the
SPACE$ function.

As an illustration of the SPACE$ function, consider an image mask for a PRINT-USING that requires a large number of spaces. Figure 11-18 includes the definition of a typical image defined in the conventional way and an equivalent definition using the SPACE$ function. Here the argument of the SPACE$ function specifies that 40 spaces are to be generated. The concatenation operations build exactly the same result as that achieved by the first form.

Often a string of characters other than the space is desired. For instance, let us assume that we would like an entire line of asterisks (65 of them) printed across the page to separate the headings from the detail output. For this we can use the following form of the STRING$ function:

```
H$ = STRING$(65,ASCII("*"))
```

The details of this expression are explained in Figure 11-19.

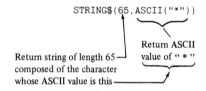

Figure 11-19   The nature of the STRING$ function.

Exercise

11-10. What will be stored in L$ for each of the following, with A$ defined as shown?

```
A$ = "X"
a. L$ = A$ + SPACE$(6) + A$
b. L$ = STRING$(5,"-") + A$ + STRING$(5,"-")
c. X$ = SPACE$(4)
   Y$ = STRING$(6,"=")
   L$ = Y$ + X$ + "A"
```

The EDIT$ Function

To illustrate the next topic, let us consider another example, one that is typical of those encountered in manipulating string data.

Example 11-5

An interactive quizzing system displays a question on the screen and requests an answer from the student with the following LINPUT statement:

```
LINPUT "The answer to the above question is"; RESPONSE$
```

The correct answer is stored in the variable ANS$ in uppercase, for example:

```
RANDOM ACCESS
```

The value in RESPONSE$ must be compared to the value in ANS$ to determine if the student response is correct.

Correct answer

```
RANDOM ACCESS
```

Correct answers but not equal when comparing

RANDOM ACCESS	Three spaces between words
RANDOM ACCESS	Space in front of first word
Random Access	Lower case letters

Figure 11-20 Typical input values for Example 11-5.

At first consideration, this might appear to require nothing more than a simple IF statement. However, consider the nature of the input; the student response might be any one of those illustrated in Figure 11-20. Clearly, in an environment where the testing is for knowledge of concepts, all four of these example responses should be considered correct. However, using the test

```
IF RESPONSE$ = ANS$ THEN . . .
```

only the first would be correct. Prior to making the comparison, it is essential that the following editing actions take place:

1. Reduce multiple spaces between words to one space.
2. Eliminate leading spaces (and trailing spaces).
3. Convert lowercase to uppercase.

With the programming skills that we now have at our disposal, we can perform all of these operations. For instance, the first editing operation requires inspecting characters of the string one at a time, searching for a space. (A FOR loop will handle this.) If one is detected, and the next position is also a space, then the second space must be deleted from the string and so on. This is a tricky operation.

To simplify operations such as this, VAX Basic includes the EDIT$ function, which provides a wide variety of powerful string-editing capabilities. It requires two arguments:

1. The string expression to be edited.
2. An integer expression that specifies the editing function(s) to be performed.

Execution of this statement produces a new string as the function value. For example,

```
A$ = EDIT$(S$,K)
```

TABLE 11-6 The EDIT$ Function

Value	Action
1	Discard the parity bit.*
2	Discard all spaces and tabs.
4	Discard all carriage returns, line feeds, form feeds, deletes, escapes, and nulls.
8	Discard leading spaces and tabs.
16	Reduce spaces and tabs to one space.
32	Convert lowercase to uppercase.
64	Convert [to (and] to).
128	Discard trailing spaces and tabs.
256	Suppress all editing for characters inside quotes.

* The parity bit is a bit used to check for internal hardware errors in data handling.

converts the source string S$ to a new string and assigns it to A$. The conversion is performed according to the value of the integer represented by K, as specified in Table 11-6.

In Figure 11-21(a), we see a sequence of statements that successively perform the needed operations on RESPONSE$. The result of this sequence will convert each of the "different" forms of Figure 11-20 to a form that is identical to the value stored in ANS$.

```
RESPONSE$ = EDIT$(RESPONSE$,16)      Discard excess spaces between words
RESPONSE$ = EDIT$(RESPONSE$,8)       Discard leading spaces
RESPONSE$ = EDIT$(RESPONSE$,128)     Discard trailing spaces
RESPONSE$ = EDIT$(RESPONSE$,32)      Convert to uppercase
```

(a)

```
RESPONSE$ = EDIT$(RESPONSE$,8+16+32+128)  ⎫ Equivalent forms
RESPONSE$ = EDIT$(RESPONSE$,184)          ⎭
```

(b)

Figure 11-21   Using the EDIT$ function—Example 11-5.

One of the convenient features of this function is that the argument specifying the editing functions is additive. That is, the individual codes in Table 11-6 can be added to carry out multiple editing operations. Because each code is a power of 2, any combination of two or more codes will give a unique result. This is illustrated by the two forms of Figure 11-21(b). In the first, each code is indicated and the system is allowed to perform the arithmetic. This is preferable to the second form, as it reduces the possibility for error and provides better documentation.

Searching a String

In string processing, a common operation is to search a string for a particular substring. To illustrate this, let us consider the following example:

Example 11-6

Within a program, the variable MEMBER$ contains a person's name (last name first):

Johnson Linda A.

A routine is required that will perform the following operations:

1. Extract the last name and place it in the variable L.NAME$.
2. Switch the last name and remainder of the name to put it in full-name order and place it in the variable F.NAME$. The preceding name would be

Linda A. Johnson

At first consideration, we see that we must search for the first space in the string. (This assumes that names such as *McGee* will not include a space following the *Mc*—this is a standard practice in computer storage of names.) The UNTIL modifier makes this very simple, that is:

```
PNTR% = 1
PNTR% = PNTR%+1 UNTIL MID$(MEMBER$,PNTR%,1) = ' '
```

Inspecting this brings up a potential problem. That is, if the name is preceded by one or more spaces, then the condition will immediately be true and PNTR% will remain at 1. Giving a little more thought to this, we would see that the following operations are involved:

1. Discard leading and trailing spaces.
2. Convert multiple spaces to one space.
3. Find the first space (terminating the last name).
4. Extract the last name and place it in F.NAME$.
5. Build the F.NAME$ field.

A routine to do this is shown in Figure 11-22. Note that before the search is performed, the string is cleaned up. When the full name field is formed, a space must be added preceding the last name.

```
HOLD$ = EDIT$(MEMBER$,8+16+128)
PNTR% = 1
PNTR% = PNTR%+1 UNTIL MID$(HOLD$,PNTR%,1) = ' '
L.NAME$ = LEFT$(HOLD$,PNTR%-1)
F.NAME$ = RIGHT$(HOLD$,PNTR%+1) + ' ' + L.NAME$
```

Figure 11-22   Manipulating a string field—Example 11-6.

The INSTR Function

One thing to note about the search in Figure 11-22 is that trouble is lurking in the background if the field being searched does not contain the search value. For instance, if the field MEMBER$ contained the seven letters

Johnson

and nothing more, the MID$ function would progress beyond the end of the string. However, this is easily remedied by using another test condition on the UNTIL. Searching a string for a given substring is such a common operation that Basic includes the powerful INSTR function for exactly this purpose. Its arguments are the string to be searched, the beginning position in that string where the search is to start, and the substring for which the search is to be carried out. If the function finds the substring, it returns the position of the substring's first character relative to the *beginning* of the string. This is exactly as is done by the UNTIL modifier form of Figure 11-22. If the desired substring is not found, the function returns zero. An expanded version of the search procedure of Figure 11-22 is included with the equivalent form of the INSTR function in Figure 11-23. Note that, in both examples, the value of PNTR% is set to 0 if the substring is not found. In the case of the INSTR statement, this is done automatically by execution of the statement.

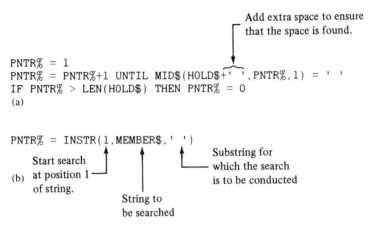

Figure 11-23   Using the INSTR function.

As another example of how the INSTR function is used, let us consider the following example. It is characteristic of the search-and-replace function found in word-processing programs.

Example 11-7

The string TEXT$ includes embedded occurrences of three consecutive pound signs, as illustrated by the following sample:

```
This is###an example###of embedded###codes.
```

Each such occurrence is to be replaced with a single space; thus, the preceding example would become

```
This is an example of embedded codes.
```

Here we have a situation in which the search and other operations are to be repeated until all occurrences have been found and corrected. A program segment to perform this operation is shown in Figure 11-24(a). If the first execution of the INSTR function returns a value of 0 (the embedded code is not found), then the WHILE loop does not execute at all. Using the sample data, the first search will stop as illustrated in Figure 11-24(b).

```
PNTR% = INSTR(1,TEXT$,'###')
WHILE PNTR% > 0
  TEXT$ = LEFT$(TEXT$,PNTR%-1) + ' ' + RIGHT$(TEXT$,PNTR%+3)
  PNTR% = INSTR(1,TEXT$,'###')
END WHILE
```

(a)

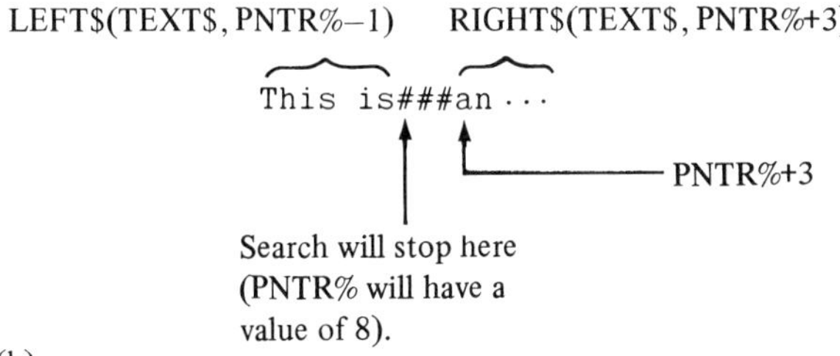

LEFT$(TEXT$,PNTR%−1)   RIGHT$(TEXT$,PNTR%+3)

```
This is###an···
```

PNTR%+3

Search will stop here
(PNTR% will have a
value of 8).

(b)

Figure 11-24 Repeated searching of a string.

One thing about this solution is that the search always begins at the first character of the string, even though preceding executions of the INSTR have already searched part of it. This can be inefficient if long strings are to be searched and the search string occurs frequently. Even worse, beginning the search at the first position will result in an infinite loop if the string being searched is not changed as it is in this example. For instance, let us assume that TEXT$ is to remain unchanged and the new string is to be built in HOLD$. Now each successive search must begin following the position at which the previous value was found in the string. A program segment to perform this search is included in Figure 11-25. Evaluation of this example is left as exercises.


```
HOLD$ = ''
PNTR% = INSTR(1,TEXT$,'###')
IF PNTR% = 0
  HOLD$ = TEXT$   ! If no ###s, print entire string
ELSE
  BEGINNING% = 1
  WHILE PNTR% > 0
    HOLD$ = HOLD$ + SEG$(TEXT$,BEGINNING%,PNTR%-1) + ' '
    BEGINNING% = PNTR% + 3
    IF BEGINNING% < LEN(TEXT$)
    THEN
      PNTR% = INSTR(BEGINNING%,TEXT$,'###')
    ELSE
      HOLD$ = HOLD$ + RIGHT$(TEXT$,BEGINNING%-3)
      PNTR% = 0
    END IF
  END WHILE
END IF
```

Figure 11-25 Starting at other than position 1 with the INSTR.

Exercises

11-11. In the example of Figure 11-25, what changes would be required in the program if the search were for five consecutive # signs rather than three?

11-12. In the example of Figure 11-25, what will happen if the string ends with three consecutive # signs?

11-13. A substring of B$, beginning with the first character and terminated by the first space character, is to be placed in C$. If there is not a space in B$, then place all of B$ into C$. Assume that the first character of B$ will not be a space. Write a program segment to do this.

In Retrospect

The properties of the string functions we have studied and used thus far are summarized in Table 11-7.

TABLE 11-7 Commonly Used String Functions

Function	Value Returned
ASCII(A$)	Decimal ASCII value of first character in A$.
CHR$(K)	ASCII character corresponding to decimal value K.
DATE$	Date in the form *dd-mm-yy*.
EDIT$(A$,K)	String A$ edited according to the code K; see Table 11-6.
INSTR(P,A$,B$)	Beginning position of substring B$ in A$, specified relative to beginning of A$; if search for B$ in A$ is unsuccessful, returns a value of 0; search starts at position P of A$.
LEFT$(A$,K)	Leftmost K characters of A$.
LEN(A$)	Length of A$.
MID$(A$,K,L)	Substring of A$ beginning at position K of A$ and containing a total of L characters.
NUM1$(K)	Numeric string that corresponds to the value of K.
RIGHT$(A$,K)	Rightmost characters of A$ beginning with position K.
SEG$(A$,K,L)	Substring of A$ beginning at position K of A$ and ending in position L, inclusive.
SPACE$(K)	String containing K spaces.
STRING$(K,L)	String containing K occurrences of the character whose decimal ASCII value is L.
TIME$	Time of day in the form *hh:mm* AM or *hh:mm* PM.
VAL(A$)	Floating-point value of the numeric string A$.

Answers to Preceding Exercises

11-1. 86 65 88 32 55 56 48

11-2. VAX Basic.

11-3. *R* in X$ is converted to *r* in Z$.

11-4. The uppercase letters that comprise X$ will be converted to lower-case in Z$. The SEG$ function pulls out one character at a time from X$, beginning with the first (I = 1) and ending with the last (I = LEN(X$)). The ASCII function converts each of these characters into its ASCII value, addition of 32 gives the corresponding lowercase value, and the CHR$ function then returns the corresponding lowercase letter.

11-5. Note that the last literal in the PRINT statement consists of five underscore characters.
```
300   PRINT "LIST:" + CHR$(8) + CHR$(8) + CHR$(8) &
                    + CHR$(8) + CHR$(8) + "_____"
```

11-6. The line feed moves the cursor to the next line, and the backspace causes it to back up one space before continuing the output.
```
12
 34
```

11-7. a. 1000 PRINT BEL
b. 2000 PRINT BEL;'You have exceeded the maximum!'
c. 1000 NOISE$ = BEL

11-8.
```
    FINISHED = -1 IF FULL.NAME$ = ""
or  IF FULL.NAME$ = ""
        THEN FINISHED = -1
    END IF
or  FINISHED = -1 IF LEN(FULL.NAME$) = 0
```

11-9. The length of A$ is 6; that of B$ is 8. B$ includes the CR and LF characters.

11-10. a. X   X
b. -----X-----
c. ======   A

11-11. In two places: PNTR% = INSTR(1,TEXT$,'#####')
Inside the WHILE loop: BEGINNING% = PNTR% + 5
                        IF BEGINNING% + 4 < LEN(TEXT$)

11-12. When the ending # signs are located, the logical value of the relational expression

```
BEGINNING% + 2 < LEN(TEXT$)
```

will become false and the ELSE block will be executed. At this point, the RIGHT$ function will cause the three trailing # characters to be truncated. Then the value of PNTR% will be set to zero, causing the relational expression

```
PNTR% > 0
```

in the WHILE to become false. The loop will be terminated.

11-13.
```
1000   PNTR = INSTR(1,B$," ")
       PNTR = LEN(B$) IF PNTR = 0
       C$ = LEFT(B$,I)
```

Programming Problems

11-1. Write a program to replace each character in a message by another character. This process is called *encryption*, and the scrambled message is called a *cryptogram*. The encryption will be based on the addition of a specified number to the ASCII value of each character in the original message. The program is to do the following:

a. Accept a message from the keyboard.
b. Generate a random digit between 0 and 9. Subtract this digit from 31. The result is the encryption number to be added to each character of the message.
c. Convert the message into its encrypted form.
d. Print the original and encrypted messages and the encryption number, suitably identified.

11-2. Keyboard entry of a line of data (with INPUT LINE) is normally signaled to the computer by depressing the RETURN key. However, the LINE FEED and ESCAPE keys can also be used. Where the RETURN key causes the two characters carriage return (13) and line feed (10) to be appended to the line, the other keys involve different characters to be appended. For the first portion of this program, you are to write a short program that will show you what these appended characters are.

Then write a program to accept text from the keyboard and write it to an output file. One or more lines from keyboard input are to form one line of output, as controlled by terminating an input line with the appropriate key, as follows:

RETURN   To this line it will be necessary to concatenate the next line entered.

> LINE FEED   Concatenate this input line to previous lines (if any) and write to the output file.
>
> ESCAPE   Concatenate this input line to previous lines (if any), write to the output file, and then write a form feed.
>
> CONTROL Z   Terminate input (this is the end-of-file indicator for keyboard entry—ERR 11).

The following input and corresponding output illustrate what is to be done:

Input:
```
THIS TEST (cr)
LINE IS (cr)
SHORT.(lf)
BUT IT (cr)
ILLUSTRATES THE POINT.(cr)
OKAY?(esc)
NEXT PAGE.(lf)
control Z
```

Output:
```
THIS TEST LINE IS SHORT.
BUT IT ILLUSTRATES THE POINT. OKAY?
```

(Skip to new page.)
```
NEXT PAGE.
```

11-3. This problem involves writing a subroutine to allow changes to be made to a name-and-address file. Input to the routine is to be via the following program string variables:

NAMES—person's name (maximum length: 20).

ADDR—street address (maximum length: 20).

CITY—city (maximum length: 14).

STATE—state (length: 2).

ZIP—Zip code (length: 5).

```
1) Name:      Alfred Jones
2) Address:   123 Okay St.
3) City:      Oakland
4) State:     CA
5) Zip:       94123
Line to be corrected (enter 0 if no more corrections)?
```

At this point, user enters 2 and hits RETURN

```
1) Name:      Alfred Jones
2) Address:   _____
3) City:      Oakland
4) State:     CA
5) Zip:       94123
```

At this point, user enters new address and hits RETURN

```
1) Name:
2) Address:   6251 Better Ave.
3) City:      Oakland
4) State:     CA
5) Zip:       94123
Line to be corrected (enter 0 if no more corrections)?
```

At this point, user corrects another line or enters 0 to terminate this sequence.

Figure 11-26 Sample screen displays.

The routine is to display the values and ask if corrections are desired, as illustrated by the example screen frames shown in Figure 11-26. This program is intended to use direct cursor control. The only change to the screen display is to be the requested line change. In that case, delete the previous value, fill the line with the underscore character equal in number to the allowable field length, and position the cursor at the beginning.

Output from the subroutine is the same as the input, including corrections made within the subroutine. For any corrections made in NAMES, ADDR, or CITY, the lengths of 20, 20, and 14, respectively, should be checked. For any that are less than the required length, pad to the right with spaces in order to make them the maximum length; for any that are longer, truncate.

Codes used for cursor positioning are terminal dependent. You will need to look up the code characters that are specific to your terminal in order to write this program as stated.

11-4. Each record of an address data file contains a person's name, street address, city and state, and Zip code. For instance, the following is a typical record:

```
AL JONES/4762 WINDY WAY/SAN FRANCISCO CA/99123
```

Notice that fields are separated by the slash character and that the city and state are treated as a single field. The objective of the program is to print mailing labels. For each record, the program must

a. Access each field from the record.
b. With the exception of the first letter in each word, convert letters to lowercase. The state is to remain uppercase.
c. Print an address label for each person; for instance, the preceding would print as follows:

Al Jones
4762 Windy Way
San Francisco, CA   99123

Note that the Zip code is separated from the state by two spaces. Assume that the labels on which the addresses are printed are six lines in height.

12

User-Defined Functions and Subprograms

CHAPTER OUTLINE

Preview

In Chapter 6, we learned about library functions that perform a variety of operations for us. For instance, if we need the square root of a quantity, we might use

```
ROOT = SQR(AMOUNT + 5)
```

Here we call or invoke the function merely by including its name in an expression. It is important to understand that the SQR function is not something that is built directly into the hardware of the computer; rather, it is a routine that has been prepared by the providers of the Basic interpreter. The functions described in Chapters 6 and 11 provide us with a wide range of commonly needed operations. The Basic language is further enhanced by the provision for the user to define functions and separate subprograms to perform operations as required by the user. From this chapter you will learn about the following concepts:

1. *The two broad categories of user-defined functions: those consisting of only one line and those consisting of multiple lines.*
2. *How to make data available to the function.*
3. *The distinction between variable names that are limited to use within a function (called* local *variables) and those that are meaningful throughout the program and functions (called* global *variables).*
4. *Principles of recursive functions, whereby a function can repeatedly call itself to perform a desired operation.*
5. *The technique of preparing a function as an entirely independent program and calling it from another program.*
6. *Principles of separately prepared subprograms, which include much more versatility than functions with regard to data passed between the subprogram and the program that calls it.*

User-Defined Functions

When working with user-defined functions, it is important to distinguish between *defining* the function and *invoking* the function. User-defined functions are invoked in exactly the same way as system functions. Defining the function is something that we have not encountered with system functions, since they are included with the overall Basic system. To avoid becoming confused between defining a function and invoking it, we will need to keep in mind the different roles played by these two operations. In example programs of this chapter, we shall see the function defined and the function invoked.

Single-Line Functions

As we learned in Chapter 2, the assignment statement allows us to define a set of operations (in the form of an expression) that, when executed, calculates a value and assigns it to a variable. Some typical forms are shown in Figure 12-1. In each of these, a single set of calculations is performed to produce a

Formula	Basic statement	Operation	Data quantity operated on (Input data)	Result (Output)
$F = \dfrac{9C}{5} + 32$	F = 9*C/5 + 32	Centigrade to Fahrenheit.	C	F
$y = x^3 + 2x^2 - 6x + 13$	Y = X**3+2*X*X-6*X+13	Evaluate polynomial.	X	Y
$P = 2(l + w)$	P = 2*(L+W)	Perimenter of rectangle.	L and W	P
$A = P(1 + r)^t$	A = P*(1+R)**T	Compound interest.	P, R and T	A

Figure 12-1   A variety of formulas.

single result. In the first two, the "input" consists of a single quantity (C in the first and X in the second). However, the third and fourth examples involve more than one input quantity.

In these examples, we see the essential features of the Basic single-line function:

1. The operations to be performed can be defined as a single expression.
2. Even though more than two data values might be operated upon (serve as input), only one result is returned. This is, in fact, the essence of the function concept.

Let us assume that, in a particular program, we must convert Centigrade temperature to Fahrenheit in many different places, as illustrated in the assignment statements in Figure 12-2(a). Note that each time a temperature must be converted, the identical set of operations must be specified in each of the corresponding expressions. If a function were defined to perform this overall sequence of arithmetic operations, then a form, as illustrated in Figure 12-2(b), could be used.

	Using an expression	Using a function
1080	CHECK.TEMP = 20 + (9*CENT/5 + 32)	CHECK.TEMP = 20 + FAHR(CENT)
1670	HOLD = 9*IN.TEMP/5 + 32	HOLD = FAHR(IN.TEMP)
2210	IF 9*C.LIMIT/5 + 32 > F.LIMIT THEN . . .	IF FAHR(C.LIMIT) > F.LIMIT THEN . . . .
	(a)	(b)

Figure 12-2 Temperature conversion.

The definition for a function such as this must provide the following pieces of information:

1. The function name (FAHR in the example of Figure 12-2).
2. The data type of the result returned by the function. In the temperature example, this is floating-point. This is said to be the data type of the function itself.
3. The number and data types of the parameters used to evaluate the function. FAHR involves one such input quantity: the Centigrade temperature, which is also floating-point. A function definition for the interest calculation of Figure 12-1 would presumably involve three parameters: P, R, and T.
4. The set of operations to be carried out. For FAHR this is the expression itself, which is defined in Figure 12-1.

In older versions of Basic, all these tasks are done with the DEF statement. Since VAX Basic still supports this approach, let us consider it first.

Every user-defined function can be defined with the DEF statement, as illustrated by the two examples of Figure 12-3. Here we see that the definition of a single-line function requires, in order:

1. The keyword DEF (define function).
2. The name of the function.
3. A list of variables to be operated on and their data types (enclosed in parentheses); this is not required if there is no input to the function. These variables are called the *formal parameters*.

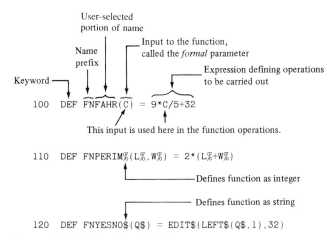

Figure 12-3   Function definitions.

4. An equal sign.
5. The expression that defines the operations to be performed.

In these examples, we see that the function type is defined implicitly. For instance, the function FNFAHR is floating-point; FNPERIM% is integer, as denoted by the %; and FNYESNO$ is string, as denoted by the $. If desired, a data-type keyword can precede the function name for the purpose of explicitly typing the function. If the function is not typed explicitly, the function name should be prefixed by the letters FN, even though this is necessary only under special circumstances.

Once again, it is important to recognize that the definitions of Figure 12-3 only specify the operations to be performed *when the function is invoked*. By itself, *the function definition does not cause any calculations to occur*. A function is invoked when its name is used in an expression outside of the DEF statement. In this role, it behaves just as a system function, such as SQR.

For instance, let us assume that, in two different places in a program, we must perform the temperature conversion, as shown in Figure 12-4. In the call

```
! Define the functions

100  DEF FNYESNO$(Q$) = EDIT$(LEFT$(Q$,1),32)
110  DEF FNPERIM%(L%,W%) = 2*(L%+W%)
120  DEF FNFAHR(C) = 9*C/5+32

! Invoke the functions
1310 CHECK.TEMP = 20 + FNFAHR(CENT)
1500 IF FNFAHR(C.LIMIT) > F.LIMIT THEN ...
1890 FENCING% = FNPERIM%(LENGTH%,WIDTH%)
2010 INPUT "Do you wish to continue <Y/N>"; RESPONSE$
2020 IF FNYESNO$(RESPONSE$) = "Y" THEN ...
```

The value of CENT from here is substituted here when the function is invoked. The value of FNFAHR is then computed and used to evaluate CHECK.TEMP.

Figure 12-4   User-defined functions.

of line 1310, the input variable is CENT. This is called the *actual parameter*. When the function is called (used in an executable statement), the value of the actual parameter is used in place of the formal parameter C in the definition at line 120, and the calculation is carried out. In the case of line 1890, where there are two parameters (corresponding to the definition in line 110), values of the actual parameters are assigned, from left to right, to the corresponding formal parameters.

Exercises

12-1. The volume of a right-circular cylinder of base radius *r* and height *h* is given by

$$\text{Volume} = \pi r^2 h$$

Assume that the corresponding function definition is

```
500   DECLARE SINGLE CONSTANT PI = 3.14159
510   DEF VOL(R,H) = PI*R**2*H
```

In using this function, a programmer became confused about the order of the arguments and wrote

```
1500   VOLUME = VOL(HEIGHT,RADIUS)
```

Note that the radius and length are interchanged. Would this result in an error condition? What would happen?

12-2. The current values of LENGTH% and WIDTH% on line 1890 in Figure 12-4 are 60 and 24, respectively. Give the value returned by FNPERIM% on line 1890 and describe how this value came to be calculated.

12-3. Define a function that converts hours, minutes, and seconds to seconds. Use integer values throughout. Then write an example program statement to calculate the number of seconds in 4 hours, TIME.MIN% minutes, and TIME.SEC% seconds.

Local and Global Variables

One of the first things we learned about was the role of the variable in a programming language. That is, for each simple variable we define, one memory area is reserved to hold the value assigned to that variable. For instance, let us assume that the following statement appears at the very beginning of a program:

```
INPUT "What is the starting value"; START
```

Execution of this statement, followed by entry from the keyboard, will cause a value to be placed into the memory area reserved for START. Then the value will be available from anywhere in the program, whether in some other module or the same module, simply by referring to the name START. In this sense, the variable START is said to be a *global variable:* It has meaning everywhere in the program.

In function definitions, we have quite a different situation. For example, in the definition of line 120 (Figure 12-4), the variable C is used as the formal parameter. It is that variable that is used in constructing the defining expression. An extremely important point here is that this parameter is *not* global to the entire program. In fact, it has meaning only within the function definition itself. It is *local* to the function definition. This means that a program using FNFAHR could use the variable C for something completely unrelated to the temperature. This variable would refer to a *different memory location* than that allocated to the parameter of the function definition. This concept is central to external modules, which we shall learn about later in the chapter.

On the other hand, variables that are used in the function definition but that do *not* appear in the formal-parameter list (enclosed in parentheses) are *global* variables. That is, such a variable refers to the *same* memory location as one with the same name that appears outside of the function definition.

To expand on the role of formal parameters, let us examine the sequence of steps that takes place when a user-defined function is first defined and then invoked. As an illustration of these steps, let us consider the perimeter calculation call in Figure 12-4. Furthermore, we shall assume that the values for LENGTH% and WIDTH% are 75 and 30, respectively. (Note: The exact operations performed by the system might not be exactly as described in the following, but they can be perceived to be so.)

1. When the Basic processor encounters the DEF statement, it reserves separate memory locations for the function itself and for the formal parameters. The location for the function is accessible to the entire program module; those for the formal parameters are accessible only to the function. That is, when line 110 is encountered, three memory locations are reserved: FNPERIM%, L%, and W%.
2. When the function is invoked, the values of the actual parameters of the function are substituted for their counterpart formal parameters in the defining expression of the function. In this example, when line 1890 is executed, the values 75 from LENGTH% and 30 from WIDTH% are assigned to the local variables L% and W% in the defining expression (line 110). This is referred to as *passing values* to the function.
3. The local variables L% and W% are then used to evaluate the defining expression, and the result is assigned to the function name itself. In our example, the function is assigned the value

$$2*(75 + 30) = 210$$

4. The statement that invoked the function is executed, using the value of the function. That is, at line 1890, the value 210 of the function is assigned to the variable FENCING%.

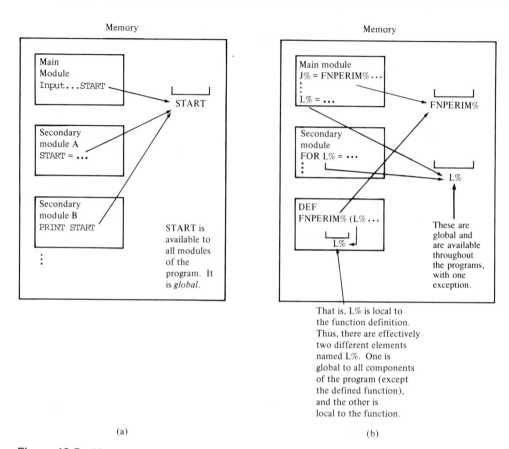

Figure 12-5   Memory allocation for local and global variables.

```
100   DEF FNA(X) = EXP(X + 4) + 1 !Valid; user-defined functions can be
                                      defined in terms of system functions
200   DEF FNB(X) = (X + Y)**2      !Valid; Y is global to the program
                                      module because it does not appear in
                                      the formal parameter list.
300   DEF FNC(X) = SQR(FNA(X))     !Valid; one user-defined function can
                                      be defined in terms of another.
400   DEF FND(X) = X * FND(X - 1)  !Invalid for single-line functions;
                                      The defining expression for a
                                      single-line function cannot
                                      reference the function being
                                      defined.
500   DEF ADD(A,B,C) = A + B + C   !Valid; the FN prefix can be
                                      omitted provided the function is not
                                      referenced in the program before it
                                      is defined.
600   DEF INTRND = INT(10 * RND)   !Valid; a function can be defined
                                      without any formal parameters if no
                                      values are passed to it.
```

Figure 12-6   Additional examples of functions.

A schematic representation of memory allocation for local and global variables is shown in Figure 12-5.

Figure 12-6 includes some additional examples to illustrate various other features of the DEF statement.

Exercise

12-4. Describe what happens when the function defined on line 100, Figure 12-4, is invoked on line 2020.

Multiline Functions

Although single-line functions are sufficient for some purposes, most function-oriented operations require several lines of code. For instance, if any operation is to be done on a conditional basis, then a single-line function cannot be used. To illustrate this, let us consider Example 12-1.

Example 12-1

An integer function is required to calculate the perimeter of a rectangle, given the length and width. The quantity returned is to be the calculated perimeter if it is greater than 200; otherwise, the value 200 is to be returned.

The desired function definition is shown in Figure 12-7, which illustrates the following important points:

1. The DEF statement has the same form as the single-line function except that it does not include the defining expression.
2. The function definition is ended by the END DEF statement.
3. The function operations are defined between the DEF and the END DEF.
4. The result is returned by assigning the value to the function name. Note that in doing so, the function name is used as if it were simply another variable.

This portion of DEF statement
is the same as that of the
single-line function.

```
DEF FNPERIM%(L%,W%)          Note that the DEF does not
   TEMP% = 2*(L% + W%)       include the defining expressions.
   IF TEMP% > 200
   THEN                      Function block contains the
      FNPERIM% = TEMP%       statements that comprise the
   ELSE                      function definition.
      FNPERIM% = 200
   END IF
END DEF    ◄────── Identifies the end of the function definition.
```

Figure 12-7 A multiline function for Example 12-1.

5. The variable TEMP% that is used in the function is global, since it is not declared as a parameter in the function call. This actually illustrates one of the weaknesses of the Basic function. That is, if the variable TEMP% is used in another part of the program, its value will be changed when the function is executed. For example, assume that the variable TEMP% is used as follows at the beginning of the program:

```
INPUT "How many values are to be processed"; TEMP%
```

If the function is called after this statement, then the value in TEMP% will be lost. This is called a *side effect* and is obviously undesirable. One way to avoid side effects is to adopt a standard for selecting variable names. For instance, all variable names to be used locally in functions might be preceded with the letters FL, to indicate *F*unction *L*ocal. Then those two letters would never be used as the first two letters of a variable name in the main program.

Calling a multiline function is identical to calling a single-line function. For instance, the call of line 1890 in Figure 12-4 could refer to the single-line function of Figure 12-4 or the multiline function of Figure 12-7.

One of the convenient features of functions is that we can do virtually anything in a multiline function that we can do in a program. The next example expands on Example 12-1.

Example 12-2

A function is required to calculate either the perimeter or the area of a rectangle. The DEF statement for this function is to be as follows:

```
DEF FNRECT%(C$,L%,W%)
```

The parameters are as follows:

L%   Length; must be between 100 and 200.
W%   Width; must be between 50 and 150.
C$ If "P," then calculate and return the perimeter; otherwise, calculate and return the area.

If the length is not within the allowable values then return a value of 0; if the width is not within the allowable values, then return a value of −1.

Note that in this example, the parameters are not all of the same type: one of them is string. In general, parameters may be whatever types are needed for a particular application. We see the function definition in Figure 12-8. Another important feature of this example is that it uses the EXIT DEF statement, which allows early exit from the function. It transfers control to END DEF, which, in turn, exits the function and returns control to the main calling program. In this respect, it is similar to the EXIT statement that we have seen used in many of the programming examples.

```
DEF FNRECT%(C$,L%,W%)
  IF L% < 100 OR L% > 200
  THEN
    FNRECT% = 0
    EXIT DEF ←——————— Exit from the function
  END IF
  IF W% < 50 OR W% > 150
  THEN
    FNRECT% = -1
    EXIT DEF ←——————— Exit from the function
  END IF
  IF C$ = "P"
  THEN
    FNRECT% = 2*(L%+W%)
  ELSE
    FNRECT% = L%*W%
  ENDIF
END DEF
```

Figure 12-8 A multiline function for Example 12-2.

Exercise

12-5. Modify the function of Figure 12-7 to eliminate use of the temporary variable TEMP%.

12-6. A utility bills on the basis of usage and type of customer. Types A and B are charged a flat $20. All others are charged as follows:

1. .80 × units used if units used are less than 10.

2. .12 × units used if units used are equal to or greater than 10.

Write a function that uses customer type and units used as arguments and returns the charge.

Placement of Function

Where should a function definition be physically placed in a program, at the beginning or the end? The answer to this is that it can be placed anywhere. Whenever a DEF statement is encountered during execution of a program, the Basic system automatically skips ahead until it finds the corresponding END DEF statement. Because of this, the function can actually be defined right in the middle of a program without causing the system any problem. However, this is bad practice and accomplishes little except adding confusion to the program. Some computer facilities standardize and use set statement number ranges for different operations. For example, statement numbers in the 26000 to 29999 range might be used for error-recovery routines, and numbers from 22000 to 25999, for function definitions. Another facility might use a standard whereby all functions are defined at the beginning of the program.

The important item regarding placement really relates to whether the function definition appears in the program before or after the call for the function. Either is permissible. However, if a function is called before it is defined, then there are some restrictions regarding typing. That is, either implicit typing must be used or the DECLARE FUNCTION statement must be included. (The

DECLARE FUNCTION statement is not described in this book.) If the function is defined at the beginning of the program (before it is called), then explicit typing can be used, and the FN is not required preceding the function name.

Explicit Typing

Explicit typing is used in the function definition of Figure 12-9, where the clumsy $ and % have been eliminated from the function name and parameters. Note that both the function and the parameter types are preceded by type definitions. When a type is given, all parameters that follow will be of that type until another type is listed. Thus, W as well as L will be of type INTEGER in Figure 12-9.

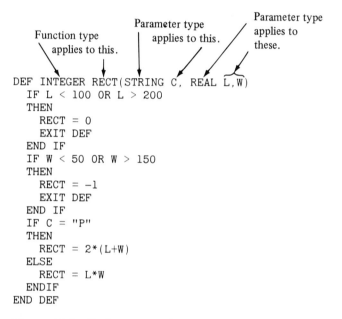

```
DEF INTEGER RECT(STRING C, REAL L,W)
  IF L < 100 OR L > 200
  THEN
    RECT = 0
    EXIT DEF
  END IF
  IF W < 50 OR W > 150
  THEN
    RECT = -1
    EXIT DEF
  END IF
  IF C = "P"
  THEN
    RECT = 2*(L+W)
  ELSE
    RECT = L*W
  ENDIF
END DEF
```

Figure 12-9 Explicit typing of a function.

Some example calls of this function are shown in Figure 12-10. Here we see that the actual parameters in the call correspond in number and type to the formal parameters of the function definition. Again, it is important to remember that the typing technique used here is only possible when the function is defined before it is called in the program.

```
DECLARE INTEGER AREA, LEN, MEAS.1, MEAS.2
.
.
.
DEF INTEGER RECT(C,L,W)
.
.
.
END DEF
.
.
.
AREA = 2*RECT("A",LEN+20,60)
.
.
.
IF RECT("P",MEAS.1,MEAS.2) > P.LIMIT THEN ...
```

Figure 12-10 Functions calls.

Summarizing User-Defined Functions

In the preceding sections, we have learned much about user-defined functions. However, there remain a number of loose ends that have not been covered by the preceding examples. The following summarizes characteristics that we have already learned and describes some other very important points.

1. Both single-line and multiline functions defined by the DEF statement return exactly one value to the statement that called the function.
2. VAX Basic allows 0 to 8 parameters in a DEF statement. The actual parameters should agree in number, type, and sequence with those in the formal parameter list. If the data type is not specified explicitly, the parameters are of the implicit or default type and size.
3. The function definition can be placed anywhere in the program. If a function is called before it is defined, then implicit typing is required, and the name must be preceded with the letters FN.
4. Formal parameters (C$, L%, and W% in Example 12-2) are local to the function definition. There are two aspects to locality in this context. One is that if any of the formal parameters are modified in the function block, the corresponding actual parameters are unaffected. For instance, if the value of L were changed in the function block of Figure 12-9, it would not change the value of MEAS.1 in the function call of Figure 12-10. Thus, the function does not change the value of the parameter passed to it; only the function value is returned. The second aspect is that a local variable is distinct from any global variable with the same name used outside of the function definition. That is, they represent different memory locations. Thus, the variable L could be used in the calling program of Figure 12-10 and would be totally independent of the local variable L defined as a parameter of the function.
5. Any variable used in the defining function block but not included in the formal-parameter list of the DEF is *not local* to the function. Rather, it is *global* to the program module in which the function is defined. Any change to such a global variable inside the function definition is the same as making the same change in the main program.

6. The result of a function is returned to the main program by assigning the value to the function name (using it as if it were an ordinary variable).
7. Functions that are explicitly typed *cannot* end with a percent or dollar sign. For implicitly typed functions, integer-function names must end with a percent sign and string-function names must end with a dollar sign.
8. During program execution, when the Basic processor encounters a DEF statement, control of the program passes to the next executable statement following the end of the function definition. Execution of a function is *only* through a function call.

Exercise

12-7. Write a function to perform a validity check on a Social Security number to ensure the following:
a. Length is 9.
b. Contains only digits.
If both of these tests are satisfied, the function should return the value 0; otherwise, it should return the value -1.

Then write a program segment that does the following:
a. Inputs a Social Security number (SSN) from the keyboard.
b. Invokes the function to check the SSN for validity.
c. Rings a bell, prints a message, and loops to input again when the SSN is invalid.

Recursive Functions

The Concept of the Factorial

Many applications of mathematics require use of a special entity called a *factorial*. Loosely speaking, the factorial of a number is the product of all the whole numbers from 1 to the number itself. For example, the factorial of 5, which is called 5 factorial and written as 5!, is

$$5! = 1 \times 2 \times 3 \times 4 \times 5$$
$$= 120$$

In general, the factorial is commonly defined as

$$N! = \begin{cases} 1 \text{ if } N = 1 \\ 1 \times 2 \times 3 \times \ldots \times N \quad \text{if } N >= 1 \end{cases}$$

Example 12-3

Prepare a routine whose input is an integer value and whose output is the factorial of the input. If the input is 0, return a value of 1; if it is negative, return a value of 0.

Without a doubt, the simplest programming approach to calculating a factorial is to use a FOR loop, as illustrated in Figure 12-11. Use of a FOR–NEXT

```
FACT = 1                          FACT = 1
FOR X = 1 TO N                    FACT= X*FACT FOR X = 1 TO N
  FACT = X*FACT
NEXT X

(a)                               (b)
```

Figure 12-11   Calculating a factorial using a FOR.

sequence is illustrated in (a); a very concise form using a FOR statement modifier is shown in (b). If we desired this to be a function, it would only be necessary to add the required defining statements.

Fundamental Principles of Recursion

In an earlier part of this chapter, the observation was made that the defining block of a function can include almost anything that can comprise a program. For instance, in the function segment of Figure 12-12(a), the function block includes a call for the SQR function. It is possible to include a call to a system function or to another user-defined function. This is a convenient feature.

```
DEF OPERATE(A,B)
  C = SQR(A+B)
  .
  .
  .
END DEF

(a)


DEF OPERATE(A,B)
  .
  .
  .
  C = OPERATE(...
END DEF

(b)
```

Figure 12-12   (a) A function definition calling another function. (b) A recursive call.

We might wonder now what happens if the defining block includes a call to itself: that is, the function being defined, as illustrated in Figure 12-12(b). Interestingly, there are cases in which this is useful. A function that can invoke itself is said to be *recursive*. In VAX Basic, it is possible to define recursive multiline functions. (Recursive single-line functions are not allowed.)

The use of recursion to solve a problem is not confined to programming; it is a standard and powerful method of mathematics. The fundamental idea underlying recursion is to solve a problem in terms of a simplified version of itself. This process is continued repeatedly, with each recursive call nested in the preceding one. (The nesting is implicit in the function call itself, not explicit in the program.) In order for a recursive procedure to terminate, it must reach a stage at which the problem can be solved without any further use of recursion. Otherwise, the recursive function calls will continue indefinitely. (This is effectively an infinite loop.) There are thus two essential parts to any recursive procedure.

1. A step in which a simple value of the function is computed directly without recursion. Although this is the *first* step in *defining* the function mathematically, it is the *last recursive call*. It is called the *anchor* or *stopping* step.
2. A step in which the problem refers to a simpler version of itself. This is called the *inductive* or *recursive* step.

Let us now see how this principle of recursion can be used to calculate the factorial.

Calculating a Factorial by Recursion

Let us consider 5! again, which can be written as

$$5! = 5 \times 4 \times 3 \times 2 \times 1$$

But we can separate the 5 multiplier from the rest and represent it as

$$5! = 5 \times 4!$$

So we see that the factorial is defined in terms of itself but at a lower level. This is a very clever way of looking at it. Carrying this to completion would eventually lead us to 1 factorial, which we know is defined as 1. Using this approach to the problem, the factorial can be defined in recursive form as

$$1! = 1 \qquad \text{(stopping step)}$$
$$N! = N \times (N - 1)! \quad \text{if } N > 1 \quad \text{(inductive step)}$$

Next let us consider how to write this as a recursive function in Basic. Recursion is one of those topics for which finding a simple example is difficult. If the example is simple enough to use for illustrating the technique, it is usually one that can be programmed more easily by other methods. This is the case with recursion. Thus, the recursive function for finding the factorial of a number is more cumbersome than the simple loops of Figure 12-11. However, it does illustrate the principle of recursion, which is invaluable for some types of applications. (See programming problem 12-4 at the end of the chapter.)

The basic definition of recursion leads directly to the program counterpart shown in Figure 12-13. Recursion is possible because *new local variables are*

```
DEF INTEGER FACTRL(INTEGER N)
  IF N < 0
  THEN
    FACTRL = 0
  ELSE
    IF N = 0 OR N = 1
    THEN
      FACTRL = 1
    ELSE
      FACTRL = N*FACTRL(N-1)
    END IF
  END IF
END DEF
```

Figure 12-13 A recursive function to calculate factorial.

generated at each recursive call. The following comments elaborate on the characteristics of recursive function calls in general and on this example in particular:

1. The first step is to ensure that the number to be operated on is not negative. If it is, then a value of 0 is returned.
2. Then a test is made to determine if the number is equal to the stopping value:

   ```
   IF N = 1
   ```

3. If the condition is false (N is greater than 1), the function reduces the computation to a simpler one by invoking itself again.

   ```
   FACTRL = N * FACTRL(N - 1)
   ```

4. The nested function calls required to evaluate a recursively defined function effectively substitute for the explicit loop in the iterative version of Figure 12-11. Some of the program complexity is therefore hidden because the iteration is explicit, while the repeated function calls are implicit.
5. Recursive calls generate new local variables every time the function calls itself. Because of this, a recursive function uses more memory than the corresponding iterative code. It also tends to be slower because of the additional function calls.

Certain problems can be coded much more concisely using recursion instead of the iterative alternative. In such situations, the machine inefficiencies that accompany recursion are more than offset by substantial ease of programming and greater program clarity. Use of recursion should be confined to such applications. These are generally of a more advanced nature.

   Execution of this function is illustrated in Table 12-1 for calculating the factorial of the value 3.

TABLE 12-1 Steps in the Evaluation of a Recursively Computed Factorial Function

Step	Function Reference	Value Passed to Current Local Variable	Returned Function Value	Values Stored in Additional Local Variables
1	Function is called.	3	–	–
2	Function is called recursively.	2	–	3
3	Function is again called recursively.	1	1	3, 2
4	Control is returned to preceding function reference.	–	2	3
5	Control is returned to preceding function reference.	–	6	–

Exercise

12-8. The mathematical operation of exponentiation can be defined recursively by

$$x^0 = 1 \qquad \text{(stopping step)}$$
$$x^n = x * x^{n-1} \quad \text{for } n > 1 \quad \text{(recursive step)}$$

Define a recursive function to be used in performing exponentiation. If the input value is negative (considered an error condition), return a value of 0 so that the program can test for such an occurrence.

External Modules

Terminal Session Reexamined

Let us review the procedure we have been following in preparing and running a program. After logging in, the following sequence has ensued:

```
$ BASIC
Ready
```

The dollar sign ($) is a VMS (operating-system) prompt, to which we responded with the BASIC command. In the very beginning, we learned the difference between Basic statements and system commands, between VMS-level and Basic-subsystem-level commands. That is, the VMS-level commands, identified by V in the command summary in Chapter 2, are technically referred to as DCL (Digital Command Language) commands. The preceding BASIC command is a DCL command. When this command is entered, the operating system places the system at the Basic-subsystem level. This is referred to as the Basic *environment*. The system prompt at this level is "Ready." The commands at this level, identified by B in the command summary in Chapter 2, are technically referred to as compiler commands.

After placing a program in memory either by entering new text or by loading an old program, we execute it with the RUN command and/or save it on auxiliary storage with the SAVE command. Both RUN and SAVE are compiler commands. Examples of entering the Basic environment, placing a program in memory, and executing it are described in Chapter 1; this procedure is summarized in Figure 12-14. The important notion here is that we are dealing with a single program, even though we might have it divided into modules. None of our examples has involved bringing two separate programs together and running them almost as if they were one. There are advantages to this capability.

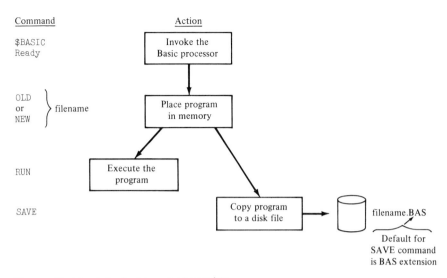

Figure 12-14 A typical terminal session.

The Concept of External Modules

In Chapter 3, we saw how modularity can be achieved by the use of GOSUB-type subroutines. User-defined functions add to this capability. However, neither subroutines nor user-defined functions provide the degree of module independence that is important for many programming applications. With the exception of variables declared as parameters, all variables in a program are global. This can create real problems with large programs where a variable name used in one part of a program can be accidentally duplicated in another. Situations in which final output is incorrect because some intermediate variable was accidentally changed are usually extremely difficult to find. The problem is further compounded when several programmers are working independently on different modules of the program. Although we have viewed our programs as consisting of relatively independent modules, this represents a *logical* organization. From a physical point of view, the computer sees our program as a single block of statements.

The topic of the remainder of this chapter is the concept of *external modules*. These are sections of code that are entered, compiled, and saved totally independently of one another but that can be combined to form a program. VAX Basic provides two types of external modules: *subprograms* and *external functions*. These are powerful extensions of the modules we have been using to this point. They achieve a much higher level of module independence by providing tighter control over the communication of variable values between modules. *All* variables except those we expressly choose to exchange between modules will be local to a given module.

External modules are enhanced by the following useful characteristics:

1. They can call and be called by any separately compiled program module. This includes programs written in languages other than Basic on the VAX.
2. They allow up to 255 parameters.

3. They allow *entire arrays* to be passed as parameters.
4. VAX Basic has several parameter-passing mechanisms. For some of these, a change in the parameter value in the called module also changes that parameter value in the calling module; these are called *modifiable parameters*. The default is that variables and arrays are modifiable, but constants and expressions are not. An external module can therefore return more than one value to the module by which it was invoked.

Before beginning our study of external modules, let us first expand on the simple procedure for creating and executing programs illustrated in Figure 12-14.

Creating and Running External Modules

The overall procedure of running a program that includes an external module is illustrated in Figure 12-15.* Note that there are several additional steps beyond simply loading and running, as we have done to this point. To understand fully this set of operations, it might be useful to review some terminology.

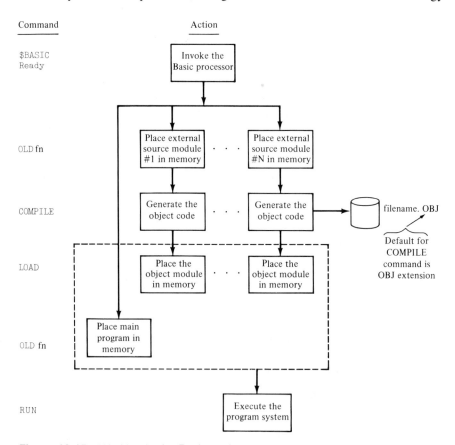

Figure 12-15   Working in the Basic environment with external modules.

---

* VAX Basic allows the use of external modules at the Basic level, as illustrated in this example, and also at the DCL level. Implementation at the DCL level is not covered in this book.

Source code is code written in a high-level language (Basic in our case). *Compilation* is the process of translating source code into machine language; the result is called *object code*. The COMPILE command creates an object module from a source module in memory and writes it to disk. The object file has the same file name as the source file but a file type (extension) of OBJ. The LOAD command loads an object module into memory and makes it available for execution with the RUN command.

To summarize, running a multimodule program in the Basic environment requires the following steps:

1. Compile the external modules with the COMPILE command.
2. Load the resulting object module(s) into memory with the LOAD command.
3. Load the main program into memory with the OLD command.
4. Bring the whole system together and execute it with the RUN command.

We shall consider an example of a terminal session to execute a multimodule program after learning about the Basic statements necessary to create an external function.

External Functions

An external function is a separately compiled program module. This is in contrast to user-defined functions created by the DEF statement, which are not compiled separately. An external function is created by the FUNCTION statement. Its end is signalled by the END FUNCTION statement, and EXIT FUNCTION allows early exit from the function (transfers control to END FUNCTION). These three statements replace, respectively, DEF, END DEF, and EXIT DEF of functions created by the DEF statement. The FUNCTION statement must be the first statement in the module, apart from comments. The END FUNCTION statement, which must be the last statement, returns the function value and transfers control to the statement that invoked the function. The function name can consist of from 1 to 30 characters, the first one of which must be alphabetic. The external function corresponding to the example of the DEF function in Figure 12-9 is shown in Figure 12-16.

```
FUNCTION INTEGER RECT(STRING C, INTEGER,L,W)
  IF L < 100 OR L > 200
  THEN
    RECT = 0
    EXIT FUNCTION
  END IF
  IF W < 50 OR W > 150
  THEN
    RECT = -1
    EXIT FUNCTION
  END IF
  IF C = "P"
  THEN
    RECT = 2*(L+W)
  ELSE
    RECT = L*W
  END IF
END FUNCTION
```

Figure 12-16 Definition of an external function.

The EXTERNAL Statement

Although the sequence of Figure 12-15 causes the object module for the compiled code of an external procedure to be loaded into memory, the Basic system has one further need. That is, if our program is to make a call to a module that is external to it, then a special EXTERNAL statement is required. This effectively causes the Basic system to make a linkup between the calling program and the external called module. After the external function is declared, it can be invoked *in the program in which it has been declared* exactly as if it were a DEF function. The EXTERNAL statement is not executable; it must precede any reference in the calling module to the function declared in the statement. An example of its form is shown in Figure 12-17. This corresponds to the equivalent form of Figure 12-10, in which the DEF statement is used to include the function internally.

Function type required

List of parameter types required; must correspond one for one to parameters in FUNCTION statement

```
EXTERNAL INTEGER RECT(STRING,INTEGER,INTEGER)
DECLARE INTEGER AREA, LEN, MEAS.1, MEAS.2
 .
 .
 .
AREA = 2*RECT("A",LEN+20,60)
 .
 .
 .
IF RECT("P",MEAS.1,MEAS.2) > P.LIMIT THEN ...
```

Figure 12-17 The EXTERNAL statement.

To illustrate the command sequence in running the program in Figure 12-17, let us assume that the main program has the filename MAIN1 and that the Basic version of the external function has the filename RECT. Then the sequence of commands to be entered in preparing and executing this program is given in Figure 12-18. This sample terminal session is a specific implementation of the general procedure shown in the schematic of Figure 12-15.

It is important to understand that the preceding example only illustrates the very simplest (default) options available with external functions. There are additional powerful features that will not be covered in this book.

```
OLD RECT

Ready

COMPILE

Ready

LOAD RECT

Ready

OLD MAIN1

Ready

RUN
```

Figure 12-18 Commands to run the two-module program shown in Figure 12-17.

More About Local and Global Variables

Now that we are using external modules, it becomes important to clarify some terminology. One of the words is *module*. Since our first program, we have thought in terms of program modules. Each task to be programmed has been broken down into logical parts, each part performing some particular task. These have been called *modules*. It is very important to recognize that this modular structure is meaningful only to us; the Basic system sees our collection of modules as a single program. Thus, as mentioned earlier, the modular structure is only logical in nature, being a result of the logic of our organization of parts. On the other hand, external modules are physically separate components that are brought together to form the whole. That is the reason for the EX-TERNAL statement. We can see that the distinction between *module* as used in preceding chapters and *external module* as used in this chapter is quite significant.

This distinction brings us back to the topic of local and global variables. Here again we need to sharpen our interpretation of these terms. In general, we consider a variable as being local to some program segment if it cannot be accessed from outside that segment. Our earlier discussion was confined to a *single separately processed module*. Within that framework, the term *global* was used to distinguish quantities that were accessible to the entire module from those that were accessible only to the DEF function defined within that module (that is, were local to that function). When we divide a program into *several separately compiled modules*, we must further distinguish quantities that are accessible to one or more of these different modules. A situation can therefore arise where a variable is local in one respect and global in another. For example, let us consider a specific variable that is accessible outside a DEF function; it is global in the sense in which we used the term earlier. However, this same variable may still be accessible only within the module in which the DEF function is compiled, in which case it is local with respect to other separately compiled modules. On the other hand, it is sometimes desirable that it be accessible to other externally compiled modules, in which case it is global with respect to these other modules. This is illustrated in Figure 12-19. Clearly, when there is a possibility of ambiguity, it becomes important to specify the

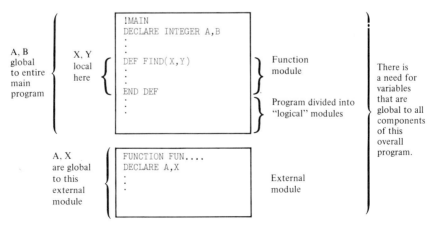

Figure 12-19   Local and global concepts.

program segments that can access the quantity in question and not simply use the terms *global* and *local*.

It must be emphasized again that separately compiled modules provide us with a very powerful program-organization tool: the strict control achieved over information flow between modules. The only way variables can be shared between separately compiled modules is by explicitly chosen program constructs: parameters and files (which we have already used) and MAP blocks and COMMON blocks (which we shall learn about). It is therefore much more difficult for separately compiled modules to cause unwarranted side effects among one another. As we have learned, program variables within DEF and GOSUB blocks can inadvertently be made accessible outside the blocks to the module in which they are defined. Consequently, information flow between such blocks is much less strictly controllable.

Exercise

12-9. Rewrite the program segment of Figure 12-7, using an external function instead of the DEF function.

Subprograms

Fundamental Principles

VAX Basic supports another type of separately compiled module—the *subprogram*. It is called by the CALL statement. In this sense, it is similar to the internal subroutine called by the GOSUB, as illustrated in Figure 12-20. Here we see that both are called by an independent statement, and both return control to the statement following the call. In the subprogram, the SUB statement must be the first statement, and the END SUB statement, the last. The END SUB (in addition to signaling the end of the subprogram) returns control to the calling program in the same way as the RETURN of the internal subroutine returns control to the calling module. In another sense, the subprogram is similar to

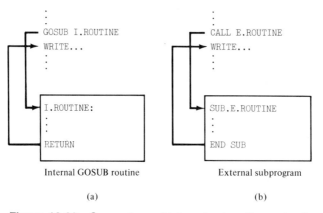

```
    :                              :
    :                              :
 ┌─ GOSUB I.ROUTINE             ┌─ CALL E.ROUTINE
 └► WRITE...                    └► WRITE...
    :                              :
    :                              :
    :                              :

 ┌─ I.ROUTINE:                  ┌─ SUB.E.ROUTINE
 │  :                           │  :
 │  :                           │  :
 └─ RETURN                      └─ END SUB

   Internal GOSUB routine          External subprogram

          (a)                            (b)
```

Figure 12-20   Comparison of internal subroutine and external subprogram.

the external function, in that it is compiled completely separately from the main program.

One of the important differences between the subprogram and the external function relates to the manner in which information is returned to the calling program. With a function, exactly one result must be returned via the function name. Because the function itself receives a value, it is technically a data type. However, with a subprogram, *one or more results* (or none at all) *are returned via parameters only,* the same device used for transmitting data *from* the calling program *to* the subprogram. The subprogram itself does not receive a value; hence it is not classified as a data structure. A function is usually simpler to use than a subprogram if the single returned value is to be used in the evaluation of an expression. The function itself can then serve this purpose; the subprogram itself cannot. The properties of the two types of external modules are compared in Figure 12-21.

	External Function	Subprogram
First statement (apart from commentary)	FUNCTION	SUB
Last statement	END FUNCTION	END SUB
Name takes on a value itself	Yes	No
Declaration by EXTERNAL	Required	Optional
Calling method	Invoke by name from preexisting statement (Same as system function)	By a separate statement; the CALL (Similar to the GOSUB)
Arrays allowed as arguments	Yes	Yes
Modifiable parameters	Yes	Yes
Recursive calls allowed	Yes	Yes
Control returned to	Statement that invoked function (Same as system function)	Statement *after* the one that called subprogram (Same as GOSUB)

Figure 12-21 Comparison of main properties of external functions and subprograms.

```
1000 ! Calling Program
1010 EXTERNAL SUB RECT(STRING,INTEGER,INTEGER,INTEGER)
1020 DECLARE INTEGER LEN, WIDTH, AREA
          .
          .
          .
2040 INPUT "What are the length and width"; LEN,WIDTH
     CALL RECT("A",LEN,WIDTH,AREA)

     PRINT "The area is:"; AREA
```

Input to the subprogram

Output from the subprogram

```
1000 SUB  RECT(STRING C, INTEGER L,W,R)
          IF L < 100 OR L > 200
          THEN
             R = 0
             EXIT SUB
          END IF
          IF W < 50 OR W > 150
          THEN
             R = -1
             EXIT SUB
          END IF
          IF C = "P"
          THEN
             R = 2*(L+W)
          ELSE
             R = L*W
          ENDIF
     END SUB
```

Result is returned via this parameter

Used in calculations

Figure 12-22   Calling a subprogram.

To illustrate the external subprogram, let us consider a simple example. In Figure 12-22, we see a subprogram that corresponds to the example of the DEF function in Figure 12-9 and the external function in Figure 12-16. Here we see four parameters in the list, the first three being identical to those of the corresponding internal function. As with the function, each of the actual parameters in the call can be a constant, a variable (including an array *element*), an expression, or a function. One of the most important features illustrated here is the concept of the *modifiable parameter*. This is a parameter modified by the subprogram and used to return a result to the main program. *Any* of the subprogram parameters can serve in this role. Modifiable parameters serve as two-way streets; they can serve as either input or output or both. However, for each parameter that is to be used to return a result, the actual parameter in the call *must be a variable* (that is, it cannot be a constant, expression, or function call). We see that the fourth parameter in the list in the subprogram of Figure 12-22 is a modifiable parameter.

The operation of including an external subprogram during a run is virtually identical to that for including an external function. For this, refer to Figure 12-18.

Using an Array as a Parameter

Another of the powerful features of external subroutines is that it is possible to pass an entire array as a parameter. When passing an array, it is necessary to specify the array name followed by commas enclosed in parentheses. The number of commas must be one less than the array dimension. For a one-dimensional array, the array name must be followed by the open and close parentheses, with no included comma. The example of Figure 12-23 illustrates passing arrays as parameters. This example creates a two-dimensional array with equal upper bounds for the two subscripts, loads the array with values, and passes the array to a subprogram as a parameter. (In matrix terminology, the array created on line 1010 is a *square matrix,* that is, a matrix with equal number of rows and columns.) The subprogram sets the elements of the matrix along both diagonals to 0. These changes are then returned to the calling program. It would be much more cumbersome if the two-module program were to reproduce the same result with the array elements being passed back and forth individually.

```
1000   ! Main Program
1010   DECLARE LONG I,J,SQR.MAT(10,10)
1020   FOR I = 0 TO 10
           FOR J = 0 TO 10
             SQR.MAT(I,J) = I * J
           NEXT J
       NEXT I
1030   CALL DIAG(SQR.MAT(,))
1090   END
2010   SUB DIAG(LONG X(,))
2020       FOR L = 0 TO 10
               IF K = L OR K = 10 - L + 1
               THEN                              Set diagonal
                   X(L,K) = 0                    elements to 0
               END IF
           NEXT L
2030   END SUB
```

Figure 12-23   Passing an entire array.

Exercise

> **12-10.** Rewrite the program of Figure 12-7, using a subprogram instead of a DEF function.

Example of a Multimodule Program

The following example illustrates a multimodule program:

Example 12-4

> Write a program to find the largest of three integers entered from the keyboard. The main program should accept the input numbers, call a

subprogram that finds the largest one, and print the result. This subprogram is to find the largest integer by calling another subprogram that finds the larger of two integers.

The program for this example is shown in Figure 12-24. The following commentary describes important aspects of this example:

1. The main program calls the subprogram MAX3. The subprogram MAX3 in turn calls another subprogram MAX2.
2. The subprogram MAX3 calls the subprogram MAX2 twice: the first time to assign the larger of its first two parameters to BIGGER, and the second time to assign the larger of its third parameter and BIGGER to QUANT (the fourth parameter in its list). The result is returned to the main program through the modifiable parameter QUANT.
3. The subprogram to find the larger of two numbers compares the two values and assigns the larger one to the third parameter in its list. This value is returned to the calling subprogram through the modifiable parameter LARGER.
4. Main programs and subprograms can use the same variable names and line numbers. For example, the variables UNO, DUO, on line 3010 could have been named FRST, SCND; since each set of FRST, SCND would be local to its subprogram, this would not cause problems with the program.

```
1000  ! Main program
1010  DECLARE BYTE NUM.1, NUM.2, NUM.3, LARGEST
1020  INPUT 'Enter three integers'; NUM.1, NUM.2, NUM.3
1030  CALL MAX3(NUM.1,NUM.2,NUM.3,LARGEST)
1040  PRINT 'The largest is '; LARGEST
1090  END

1010  SUB MAX3(BYTE FRST,SCND,THRD,QUANT)
1020     CALL MAX2(FRST,SCND,BIGGER)
1030     CALL MAX2(THRD,BIGGER,QUANT)
1090  END SUB

1010  SUB MAX2(BYTE UNO,DUO,LARGER)
1020     IF UNO > DUO
         THEN
            LARGER = UNO
         ELSE
            LARGER = DUO
         END IF
1090  END SUB
```

Figure 12-24 A subprogram calling another subprogram.

Exercise

12-11. Rewrite the program of Figure 12-24 so that the subprogram to find the larger of two numbers is replaced by an external function.

The COMMON Statement

Thus far, we have learned two ways in which separately compiled modules can communicate with one another. For functions, a single result is returned to the calling program through the name of the function. For subprograms, results are returned through modifiable parameters. There is yet another method by which external modules can communicate, the COMMON statement. This statement assigns variables in different modules to the *same* memory locations within the computer. It is important to understand that the variables in question belong to separately compiled modules and can have different names. The COMMON statement defines an area in memory that can be shared by separately compiled modules. This area is called a COMMON *block*. Different modules can share such an area by specifying the same block *name*. The COMMON statement also declares the variables that can access the locations in that block. Its form is illustrated in Figure 12-25. The following commentary describes important aspects of COMMON:

1. The name in parentheses following the keyword COMMON is the name of the block. Multiple COMMON blocks with the same name *in different modules are overlaid.* (That is how the area is shared.)
2. Variables declared in COMMON blocks with the same name in different modules share locations. Corresponding variables in shared blocks must be of the same type and occupy the same area. Thus, A and X in Figure 12-25 must be of the same type and size, and similarly, B and Y, C and Z.
3. Multiple COMMON blocks with the same name *in the same module* are *concatenated* (laid end to end).
4. Subprogram SUBNAME in Figure 12-25 has no parameters; all communication between the main program and subprogram is through the COMMON block. This need not be the case. Modules may communicate by a combination of COMMON and parameters.

```
1000   ! Main program
1010   COMMON(COMAREA) LONG A, STRING B = 20, C(30) = 10
  .
  .
  .

1010   SUB SUBNAME
1020      COMMON(COMAREA) LONG X, STRING Y = 20, Z(30) = 10
  .
  .
  .
```

Figure 12-25 The COMMON statement.

Earlier in the chapter, the point was made that a variety of problems can be avoided by communicating through the argument list (and the function value). Some experienced programmers argue that external modules should communicate with one another *only* through arguments. Nonetheless, there are cases where use of COMMON is desirable.

Exercise

12-12. Rewrite the program of Figure 12-24 so that the value of the largest integer is returned to the main program through a COMMON area.

In Retrospect

In this chapter, we learned techniques that considerably enhance our ability to modularize our programs. We can use both single-line and multiline functions defined by the DEF statement within the program to return exactly one value. During program execution, when the Basic processor encounters a DEF statement, control of the program passes to the next executable statement following the end of the function definition. Execution of a function is *only* through a function call.

In addition, multiline functions can be defined as separately compiled program modules and included in the program by appropriate commands.

The subprogram gives the programmer significant ability to define separately defined program modules that are accessed with the CALL statement. The subprogram is much more versatile with respect to the way that it can be used. To this end, all of the data types, including arrays, may be passed as parameters. Furthermore, there is greater flexibility regarding values returned to the calling program: It can be none at all, or one, or more.

Answers to Preceding Exercises

12-1. The computer would substitute the value of the first argument, the height of the cylinder, for the radius in the formula on line 510, and the radius would be substituted for the height. There would be no computer error, but the results would be incorrect (unless the values for HEIGHT and RADIUS happened to be the same).

12-2. FENCING% = 2*(60 + 24) = 168
When line 1890 executes, the values 60 and 24 are substituted for L% and W%, respectively, in the defining expression for FNPERIM% on line 110. This expression is evaluated, and the result is assigned to the function FNPERIM%. This value of the function is then transmitted back to line 1890, where it is assigned to the variable FENCING%.

12-3.
```
100 DEF TIME.SEC%(HRS%,MIN%,SEC%) = 3600**2*HRS% + 60*MIN% + SEC%
     .
     .
     .
1000 TOTAL.SEC% = TIME.SEC%(4,TIME.MIN%,TIME.SEC%)
```

12-4. The value of the string RESPONSE$ is substituted for Q$ in the argument of LEFT(Q$,1) on line 100, which pulls out the first character of RESPONSE\$. If this first character is a lowercase letter, the EDIT\$ function converts it to uppercase. The result of the EDIT\$ operation is assigned to the function FNYESNO\$. The value of this function is then tested on line 2020. This procedure ensures that if the user responds with ''y'', ''YES'', ''yes'', or ''Yes'' instead of with ''Y'', the proper action is still taken.

12-5.
```
DEF FNPERIM%(L%,W%)
    IF 2*(L% + W%) > 200
    THEN
        FNPERIM% = 2*(L% + W%)
    ELSE
        FNPERIM% = 200
    END IF
END DEF
```

12-6.
```
DEF FNBILL(TYPE$,UNITS)
    IF TYPE$ = 'A' OR TYPE$ = 'B'
    THEN
        FNBILL = 20.00
    ELSE
        IF UNITS < 10
        THEN
            FNBILL = 1.80*UNITS
        ELSE
            FNBILL = 2.12*UNITS
        END IF
    END IF
END DEF
```

12-7.
```
1000   DECLARE INTEGER CNT, WRONG, STRING ISS
1010   DEF INTEGER SSN.ERR(STRING SSN)
       WRONG = 0   !Initialize error to false
       IF LEN(SSN) <> 9
          THEN   WRONG = -1
          ELSE
             CHECK.SSN:
                FOR CNT = 1 TO 9
                   ISS = MID$(SSN,CNT,1)
                   IF ISS < '0' OR ISS > '9'
                      THEN
                         WRONG = -1
                         EXIT CHECK.SSN
                   END IF
                NEXT CNT
       END IF
       SSN.ERR = WRONG
       END DEF
          .
          .
          .
2000   CONTINUE = -1
       WHILE CONTINUE
         INPUT 'Social Security number'; SSN
         CONTINUE = SSN.ERR(SSN)
         PRINT BEL; 'Invalid SS number D try again' IF SSN.ERR(SSN)
       NEXT
```

12-8.
```
1000 DEF REAL POWER(REAL X, INTEGER N)
         IF N < 0
           THEN
             X = 0
           ELSE
             IF N = 0
               THEN
                 POWER = 1
               ELSE
                 POWER = POWER(X,N - 1)*X
             END IF
         END IF
     END DEF
```

12-9.
```
1000     FUNCTION INTEGER PERIM(INTEGER L,W)
           DECLARE INTEGER TEMP
           TEMP = 2*(L + W)
           IF TEMP > 200
             THEN P = TEMP
             ELSE P = 200
           END IF
         END FUNCTION
```

12-10.
```
1000     SUB PERIM(INTEGER L,W,P)
           DECLARE INTEGER TEMP
           TEMP = 2*(L + W)
           IF TEMP > 200
             THEN P = TEMP
             ELSE P = 200
           END IF
         END SUB
```

12-11. Replace lines 1020 and 1030 of SUB MAX3 by

```
1020   BIGGER = LARGER(X,Y)
1030   QUANT  = LARGER(Z,BIGGER)
```

Replace lines 1010 and 1090 of SUB MAX2 by

```
1010   FUNCTION BYTE LARGER(BYTE,P,Q)
1090   END FUNCTION
```

12-12. In the main program, add line 1005 and change line 1030:

```
1005   COMMON(COMAREA) BYTE LARGEST
1030   CALL MAX3(NUM.1,NUM.2,NUM.3)
```

In SUB MAX3, change line 1010 and add line 1015:

```
1010   SUB MAX3(BYTE X,Y,Z)
1015   COMMON(COMAREA) BYTE QUANT
```

Programming Problems

12-1. In interactive programs, it is quite common to request a user to enter some numeric response in answer to a question. For instance, a menu program might require a numeric entry from 1 to 10; a quizzing program might ask for a question number from 1 to 75, and so on. In such instances, two different error conditions commonly arise. First, the quantity entered may not be numeric, and second, the quantity entered may not be within the allowable range. Write an integer function to check that the number entered is

1. Numeric.
2. Within the allowable range (as a function option).

Use of the function is illustrated by the following sequence of code:

```
300  INPUT "PLEASE SELECT AN OPTION BETWEEN 1 AND 9"; N$
310  NUM = NUM.CHECK(N$,1,9,"Y")
320  IF NUM = -32768
        THEN ITERATE
        ELSE CONTINUE$ = 'NO'
     END IF
```

With reference to the sample call of statement 310, the arguments of the function call are

First argument (N$)—numeric quantity to be tested.

Second argument (1)—smallest allowable value for the number.

Third argument (9)—largest allowable value for the number.

Fourth argument ("Y")—"Y" if the range check is to be performed,
"N" if the range check is not to be performed.

If the number is valid and within the range (if required in the particular test), then return its numeric value. If it is invalid, the function should print an appropriate error message and return a value of -32768.

12-2. Write a program to evaluate the function

$$f(x) = a\sqrt{1 + x^2} + \sin x$$

by defining a user-defined function in terms of system functions. Use nested FOR–NEXT loops to step through all combinations of

$x : 0.1, 0.2, \ldots , 2.0$ (step size 0.1)

$a : 0.01, 0.02, \ldots , 0.1$ (step size 0.01)

Output should be in the form of a suitably identified table with columns corresponding to different values of a and rows corresponding to different values of x.

12-3. The formula for computing the value of an investment compounded quarterly for a given number of quarters is

$$A = P * (1 + I/4)^N$$

where P is the initial investment, I is the *annual* rate of interest, and N is the number of conversion periods (4 * years). This problem requires calculating the number of conversion periods it takes to double the initial investment, that is, to have $A = 2P$.

The preceding formula can be solved for the number of conversion periods.

$$N = \log(A/P)/\log(1 + I/4)$$

Hence, the expression for the number of conversion periods to double the investment becomes

$$N_2 = \log(2)/\log(1 + I/4)$$

Write a program to produce a two-column table for doubling an investment for quarterly conversion. Use the system function LOG and a user-defined function to compute N_2. The function should be general enough to work for *any* number of (finite) conversion periods per year. The number of yearly conversion periods is to be input from the keyboard. The first column should have the *yearly* interest rate, in percent, from 7.0 to 11.0 in steps of 0.5. These limits and the step size should also be input from the keyboard. The second column should give the number of *years*. Terminate execution after the first conversion period for which $A >= 2P$. If, for example, it takes 29 quarters, the answer should be in the form 7.25. Then ask the user if another set of parameters is to be processed. If yes, enter the new set; otherwise, terminate.

12-4. The number of combinations of N distinct objects taken K at a time (for example, the number of different hands, each containing K playing cards, out of a deck of N different cards) is given by the *binomial coefficient*.

$$C(N,K) = N!/((N - K)!K!), \quad \text{for } N >= K$$

As N gets very large, the factorial function can get too large for the computer to store, even though the binomial coefficient itself is not too large. The difficulty therefore lies in computing $C(N,K)$ directly in terms of the factorials. However, a little manipulation shows that $C(N,K)$ can be defined recursively.

$$C(N,O) = 1$$
$$C(N,K) = (N - K + 1)C(N,K - 1)/K \quad \text{for } K >= 1$$

The recursive form bypasses the previously mentioned difficulty. This is thus an example where recursion allows us to extend the range of solution of a problem beyond what can be done by brute force.

Write a program to compute the binomial coefficient for any positive integer N and K such that $N > K$, using a recursively defined function. Note that $C(N,K)$ is always an integer. Output should be a table with values of N from 1 to 25 (rows) and values of K from 1 to 8. Bear in mind that the table will have some blanks because of the condition $N >= K$. Note also that the largest value of $C(N,K)$ you will be calculating is approximately 10^6, whereas $25!$ is of the order 10^{25}. This is *sixteen orders of magnitude* larger than the largest integer that can be stored in a LONG variable, which is of the order of 10^9.

12-5. This problem involves calculating the square root of a number using the Newton method of successive approximation. The method starts with an initial guess of the answer and then iterates to refine this answer. The *iteration formula* for finding an answer more accurate than the preceding one is

next approx = (preceding approx + N/preceding approx)/2

where N is the number whose square root is sought. To illustrate, let us assume that we want the square root of 10. There are various ways of computing the starting value. Let us use the following method, in order to illustrate external functions. We know that this square root is bounded by 3 and 4 ($3^2 < 10 < 4^2$). We take 3.5 as the initial guess. The next approximation is then

$$(3.5 + 10/3.5)/2 = 3.18$$

This answer becomes the preceding approximation for the next iteration

$$(3.18 + 10/3.18)/2 = 3.162$$

The iterations can be repeated as many times as needed to get an answer within some specified accuracy.

Write a program that will accept a value from the keyboard and call a *user-defined* function to compute the next approximation. Use the functional form

$$f(x) = (x + N/x)/2$$

Use an *external* function to find the integer bounds, x and $x + 1$, and return $x + 0.5$ for the starting point of the Newton iteration. Continue the iteration process until the new approximation differs from the preceding one in absolute value by less than 0.0001. Print the number, its square root, and the number of iterations required. The user should have the opportunity to enter another number. Terminate by entering 0.

12-6. It is often necessary to find the value of a variable x for which a given function of x, $f(x)$, is equal to zero. We are then looking for what is called a *zero* or a *root* of the function $f(x)$; that is, a value $x = b$ such that $f(b) = 0$. Students of algebra are familiar with the fact that there is a general formula for the two roots of the quadratic function $f(x) = ax^2 + bx + c$. However, we often need to find the roots of a function for which no general formula exists.

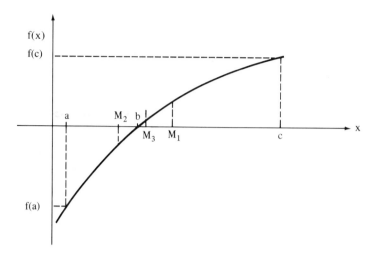

Figure 12-26   Finding the root of a function.

Geometrically, we are looking for a point b at which the graph of $f(x)$ crosses the x axis, as shown in Figure 12-26. We assume that we are given two values of x, a and c, for which $f(a)$ and $f(c)$ are of opposite sign. We then see from the graph that $f(x)$ must have at least one root, b, between $x = a$ and $x = c$.

One method for finding an approximate root is called the *bisection* or *interval-halving* method. It consists of repeatedly dividing in half the interval in which the root lies, determining in which half the function changes sign (by evaluating the function at the new midpoint), and identifying the end points of the new interval. The first midpoint is labeled M_1 on the graph; the second, M_2, and so on. This procedure gives a sequence of decreasing intervals of x that bracket the root. The process is terminated when a specified criterion is met.

We shall take as our criterion the condition that the difference in the absolute values of the function at consecutive midpoints be less than some prescribed value. The value of the function at the i point is denoted by $f(M_i)$, that at the next consecutive point, by $f(M_{i+1})$. Then the magnitude of the difference of the absolute values of $f(M_i)$ and $f(M_{i+1})$ is to be less than a specified constant EPS. (This difference is often denoted in mathematics by the Greek letter epsilon.)

Write a program to find the root of

$$f(x) = x - \cos(x)$$

in the interval $[0, \pi/2]$. Note that these end points do bracket a root: $f(0) = -1, f(\pi/2) = \pi/2$. Use an *external function* to evaluate $f(x)$ and a *subprogram* to compute the midpoint of the interval and the function value at midpoint. The subprogram should return to the program the end points of the new interval. The main program should

1. Accept input from the keyboard of
   a. Initial end points of the interval.
   b. Value of EPS.
2. Use a subroutine to check that each interval brackets a root of the function (function has opposite signs at the ends of the interval); give error message if it does not.
3. Call subprogram.
4. Terminate execution if either the convergence criterion has been met or the function value at the midpoint is a root.

Your first stub program should test the interconnection of the various modules and item (1) of the preceding list. The second stub should verify item (2) and do one full calculation (no looping). For the final version, add the loop.

13

Advanced File Processing

CHAPTER OUTLINE

Preview

In Chapter 7, we had our first exposure to using data files. Until now, our use of files has been very limited in scope; the examples have used files as a relatively simple extension of techniques we have studied using the keyboard INPUT and the READ–DATA pair. This chapter delves into the topic of files and file processing much more extensively. Important topics covered in the chapter are the following:

1. The three file structures: sequential, relative, and indexed. This relates to the way in which data are organized in the file.

2. *The two file-access methods: sequential and direct. This relates to the way in which records are read from and written to the disk files.*

3. *The concept of a key field, which is a field in a record that can uniquely identify each record in the file. It is through the key-field concept that it is possible to access any desired record in a file independent of the others (this is direct access).*

4. *Use of the MAP statement to define the exact layout of fields in a record.*

5. *Features of the OPEN statement that allow the programmer to specify both the type of file organization and the file access to be used.*

6. *The GET statement, which is used for input of records in place of the INPUT statement.*

7. *Sequential-file processing, including the operations of adding records to an existing file and changing information in existing records.*

8. *Relative-file processing, including the operations of creating a relative file, accessing a selected record, adding records to an existing file, and changing information in existing records.*

9. *Indexed-file processing, including the operations of creating an indexed file, sequential accessing of records, direct accessing of records, adding records to an existing file, and changing information in existing records.*

Concepts of File Management

Introduction

One characteristic of files to which we paid no attention in the preceding chapters relates to the length of various records in the file. Records were whatever length was required for the particular set of fields to be read. For example, consider the following two sample records that might be read from a disk file using the principles of Chapter 7 or from a DATA statement:

First record has a
length of 22 bytes.

```
"Jack Olson",48.0,3.20
"Scott Baldwin",125.5,3.15
```

Second record has a
length of 26 bytes.

Note that the first record consists of 22 bytes, and the second, 26 bytes; obviously, each record will have a length as determined by the data stored in it.

Although it may be intuitively apparent to us that this "is the way to do it," it is not. More commonly, files are structured so that each record has exactly the same length as every other record. Such a file is commonly called a *fixed-length record* file. A file in which each record may have a different length is called a *variable-length record* file. Because of the relative ease of introducing file-processing concepts with terminal-format files, we relied on this type of file in our initial exposure in Chapter 7 to file processing. Terminal-format files are sequential files of variable-length records. As we have clearly learned, they can only be accessed sequentially, which limits their practical use severely. Most file processing involves fixed-length records because of greater versatility of file organizations based on such records. The focus in this chapter is therefore on the fixed-length format.

In using files beginning in Chapter 7, we gave little thought to what goes on when we input information from the disk. If you have assumed that information is brought into the program one character at a time as with the keyboard, you have been quite incorrect. Where information in main memory can be accessed by the individual byte, information stored on disk is accessible only by large blocks. We have not seen this at the Basic level because there is a portion of the VAX operating system devoted exclusively to managing information on disk. It is called the *Record Management System (RMS)* and gives us a wide range of features for easily handling data files. When we use the INPUT# statement, RMS goes into action and does everything for us, from getting the data from disk to making it available in the variables that we have defined.

File Access

To illustrate the broad methods of file processing, let us consider a simple example.

Example 13-1

> An organization maintains a file of all of its members. Each record of the file contains the name, address, dues amount, and other important information for one member.

It is easy to imagine two ways in which this file might be processed. First, a membership bill for each member might be generated by starting with the first record in the file and progressing to the last. This is the concept of *sequential processing* with which we are familiar from Chapter 7. It is so called because records are processed in sequence one after the other by proceeding from the first record of the file to the last. Note that the entire file is processed during a single processing run.

On the other hand, consider the type of processing involved when dues payments are received and the payment information is entered into the appropriate member records. As each check is received, the information is to be entered into the record for that member. This is quite a different way of processing the file. For example, on a very slow day, perhaps only one payment might be received and entered into the file. It might be for the first record in the file,

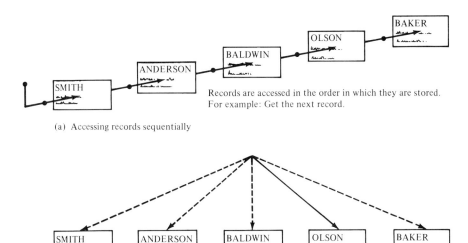

(a) Accessing records sequentially

Any record can be accessed as needed.
For example: Get the record of OLSON

(b) Accessing records directly

Figure 13-1 File processing.

or for the last, or for any in between. This type of processing calls for *direct access* to any record in the file; consequently, it is called *direct-access processing* or simply *direct processing*.

Let us contrast the two. In sequential processing, the next record to be processed is the next one in the file. In direct processing, the next record to be processed is whichever one is desired from the file. These concepts are illustrated in Figure 13-1. Obviously, we need some way of getting to a specific record rather than simply the "next" one. To cover a broad range of needs, RMS includes three file structures: sequential, relative, and indexed. All three can be used for sequential processing; the second and third are well suited to direct processing as well.

Exercises

13-1. What is the main difference in the way data can be accessed in internal memory and on disk?

13-2. What is the difference between sequential processing and direct processing?

Sequential File Structure

Sequential organization is the oldest and simplest in computing. A sequential file contains the records in the order in which they were written. That is, the first record written is the first in the file, the second written is the second in

⟶   Records are stored in the order in which they were written to the file.

SMITH	ANDERSON	BALDWIN	OLSON	BAKER	
First record written	Second record written	Third record written	Fourth record written	Fifth record written	Next record will be written here.

Figure 13-2   Sequential file structure.

the file, and so on. This concept is illustrated in Figure 13-2. If a given record of the file is desired, then all of the records preceding it must be read until the desired record is found (see Figure 13-1(a)). This is much the same as the method we might use in attempting to find a particular piece of music on a tape. If it is in the middle of the tape, the tape must be moved past all pieces preceding it. Obviously, files with the sequential structure are well suited to sequential processing.

The sequential file structure can be used with either fixed- or variable-length records.

The Concept of a Key

It is easy to visualize how the system must operate for sequential processing; each time a record is required, it simply gets the next one in line. However, what about direct processing? In the example of Figure 13-1(b), the record for OLSON is to be processed. Some means is clearly needed by which the program can identify that particular record. In the simple example of Figure 13-1, reference to a record is via the name, one of the fields of the record. The example illustrates getting the record with a name field value of OLSON. Using names might be adequate for a small system that is handled manually. However, it leaves much to be desired for an automated system; the major problem is duplication. There may be several people named OLSON. More commonly, an institution uses some type of numbering system. For instance, we are all familiar with the Social Security number or the driver's license number. In the case of the membership system of Example 13-1, the organization might assign each member a member number. Then the program would request the desired record by the member number. Direct access could then be through this number, which is commonly called the *key,* since it represents the "key" to accessing individual records.

Relative File Structure

The use of magnetic disk for auxiliary storage gives real versatility for file processing. For instance, any desired record of a disk file can be accessed by referring to its disk address. In other words, it is possible to say "Get record 4" without looking at the three records preceding it, as would be required with sequential structure. This concept is illustrated in Figure 13-1(b). Needless to say, in order to do this, the file management system would require some method of knowing the exact location of each record in the file. One way of doing this is to divide the file area into a series of fixed-length *record cells,* as illustrated in Figure 13-3(a). For the fixed-length record structure, the cell length is the

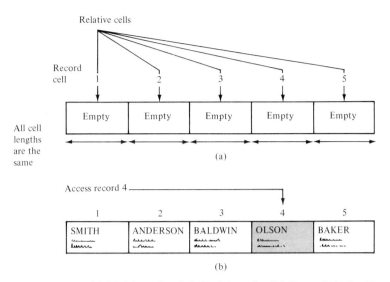

Figure 13-3 (a) Division of a disk file into cells. (b) Records in the file.

same as the length of the record. For the variable-length structure, the cell length is the length of the longest record that is expected in the file. This can be very wasteful of disk space.

As we see in Figure 13-3(a), each record cell is identified by its number. The term *relative* is used because the location of each cell is determined by its relative position in the file. In a program, we can say "Get the record from record cell 24" or "Put a new record into record cell number 13." This is an extremely important feature, for we can now access records by their record cell numbers. If our file has been loaded as shown in Figure 13-3(b), then in order to get the record of OLSON, we simply say "Get record 4."

The important thing here is that we must know that OLSON has been stored in record cell 4. This is where the record-key concept enters. The solution is to assign member numbers as consecutive numbers beginning with 1. If OLSON were assigned as member 4, then we would store his record in record cell 4. With this type of arrangement, the first record entered need not be the first record in the file. For instance, if in first entering the records into the file, OLSON were the first one entered, the file would appear as shown in Figure 13-4.

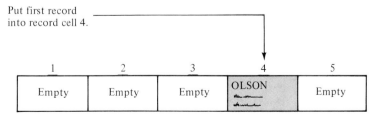

Figure 13-4 Loading a relative file.

The notion of assigning membership numbers so that they correspond to the record cell in which the record is to be placed is a fairly simple concept. Here we know each member's number by the cell in which the information is stored. However, there is an inherent danger in this procedure. What if the data-entry person accidentally directs the program to enter OLSON into record cell 44 when the file is first created? Then, as far as the computer is concerned, OLSON has a membership number of 44, not 4, even though we continue to believe it to be 4. Hence, when we request record 4 during processing, we will not get the desired information. Moreover, we will have no idea where to find OLSON.

Since the member number is an important part of the record information for OLSON, a field would normally be allocated within the record for the membership number. The file might then appear as illustrated in Figure 13-5.

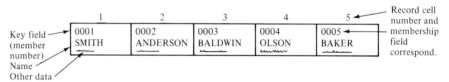

Figure 13-5 Including the membership field in the record.

The program would be designed so that each time a record is accessed, it checks to ensure that the record read is indeed the correct record.

Obviously, this field is the key to accessing information in the file; hence it is called the *key field*. Most of the record processing about which we shall learn in the chapter relates to using files with a key field.

In general, the method of using a key field that corresponds to the record cell number works if we can assign key values that begin with 1 and do not jump around over a large range. For example, let us assume that there are 160 members in the organization. Furthermore, the member numbers have already been assigned and range from 0001 to 1600 (which the membership clerk is not about to change). It is important to understand that the entire storage area of 1600 cells would actually be reserved on disk. Thus, the entire membership of 160 would occupy only 10 percent of the reserved space. As a general rule, there is no way around wasting space under such conditions when using the relative organization. Figure 13-6 illustrates how the records for five typical

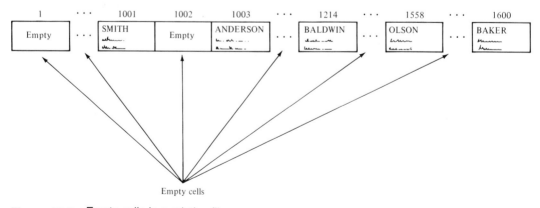

Figure 13-6 Empty cells in a relative file.

members would appear. The indexed structure described next is much more versatile and resolves this dilemma.

As we have learned, the relative file structure is well suited to direct processing, since any record can be accessed by its record cell number. In addition, relative files can be processed sequentially in exactly the same way as sequential files.

Indexed File Structure

We are all familiar with the concept of an index. For example, the directory in a large building is an index. To find the office of, for instance, Dr. Lukenbill, we would look the name up in the directory (index) and read the corresponding office number. (The idea of scanning a logically sequenced table is preferable to searching door by door for the particular name.) Similarly, if we wished to read the section in this book about *functions*, we would

- Turn to the index.
- Find the word *function*.
- Note the page number.
- Turn directly to that page.

Exactly the same thing can be done with computer files. For example, let us consider the case of the "spread-out" member numbers illustrated in Figure 13-6. In building this file system, we might assign the records to consecutive record cells, as in Figure 13-3(a) but make a notation of where each member's record is stored, such as the following table:

Member Number	Record Cell
1001	1
1003	2
1214	3
1558	4
1600	5

Whenever access to a given record is required, the table will be searched to find the member number, and then the record can be read using the corresponding record cell number. This is illustrated in Figure 13-7, in which the table is searched for member number 1558, and then record cell 4 is read.

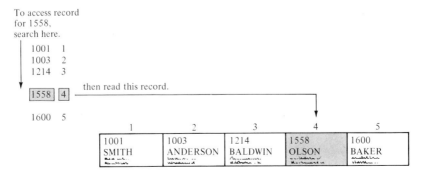

Figure 13-7   Using an index table to find a file entry.

This is exactly the principle employed with computer file-processing systems. The table of the record key values and corresponding record numbers is maintained in a separate portion of the file, called the *file index*. This file structure is called the *indexed file structure* and provides the programmer with a great deal of versatility. Thus, if we stored our membership file as an indexed file, it would contain a corresponding index. The index is created by RMS as part of the file. With such a system, if a program requires the record for member 1558, RMS finds the actual record location from the index, then reads that record from the data portion of the file, exactly as illustrated in Figure 13-7. This is superior to searching the file itself because the index is usually much smaller than the data portion of the file, can be brought into primary memory more quickly, and is much more quickly searched.

One of the advantages of indexed files under RMS is that RMS does all of the work for us. For instance, let us assume that the membership file has been created with the member-number field in the record as the key field. If we need to write a new record, RMS puts it in the data file *and* makes an appropriate entry in the index. If we need a particular record, we give RMS the value of the key, and RMS returns the record. When processing, we can access records of the file either sequentially or directly. That is, for sequential processing, we can process the file by beginning with the first record in the file and proceeding to the last. In such a case, we would say "Get the next record" each time a record is desired for processing. For direct processing, we can say "Get the record with the following key field value."

Another of the important features of indexed files is that RMS maintains the index in a sorted sequence, with the smallest entry first and the largest last. The nature of the index and its relationship to the data portion of the file is shown in Figure 13-8. Here we see that entries in the index, which include the key value and corresponding record number, are in sequence based on the value of the key field. In performing sequential processing on an indexed file, the actual order of the records in the file has absolutely no meaning to us, since our access is via the index. Hence, to us as programmers, the "first" record in the file is the one pointed to by the first entry in the index, 1001 in this

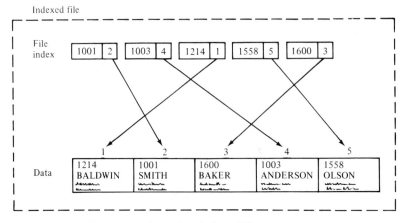

Figure 13-8   Representation of an indexed file.

case. It makes no difference that record 1001 is physically the second record in the file. Similarly, the "next" record is the one pointed to by the second index entry, and so on. When using an index, the term *next logical record* is commonly used. A logical record is the data record as seen from the viewpoint of the program. (We shall learn later in the chapter about a related concept, the *physical record.*) Thus the first logical record in the file is record 1001, the next logical record is record 1003, and so on. This has nothing to do with the physical placement of records in the file; it only relates to sequencing indicated by the index.

The fact that the index is sorted allows table-searching methods to be used that are much faster than if the table entries were in random order. Whenever a new record is added, RMS places it "somewhere" in the data portion of the file, then inserts the key into the directory in the proper position to maintain its sequence. Thus, sequential processing of an indexed file actually involves accessing the records in the order of the index entries. Since the index is in a sorted sequence on the key value, the file management system simply accesses the data records in the order of the index values. Thus, indexed files provide sequential access, even though the file management system is accessing the data records in a physically random order.

One other valuable feature of the indexing technique is that an index can be built on any field in the record. For instance, the file of Figure 13-8 could have a second index using the person's name. Thus, direct access into the file could be either by the member number or by the name. In this instance, member number is the *primary key*; the person's name is a *secondary key*. RMS allows only a single primary key, but it allows the designation of more than one secondary key for given file. Combining all of these features with the fact that the key field can be either string or numeric provides a powerful tool to the programmer. We shall learn more about the indexed-file structure after first studying sequential files and relative files.

Exercises

13-3. The Department of Motor Vehicles (or some such agency) in every state maintains a record on every registered driver in the state. What would probably be used for a key field in such a system? Why not use the person's name as the key field?

13-4. What is the main problem in performing direct processing on a sequentially ordered file?

13-5. To get an idea of how much faster it is to do computations in primary memory than it is to transfer data between memory and auxiliary storage, we need to know the characteristic times of these operations. Internal operation speeds of modern computers are measured in times ranging from microseconds (10^{-6} sec) to nanoseconds (10^{-9} sec). A typical time required to locate and access a record on disk is on the order of 10 to 100 milliseconds (1 millisec $= 10^{-3}$ second). Thus, the ratio of the time it takes to do a disk read or write to the time it takes to do a simple internal operation ranges from 10^5 to 10^8. To get a feel for the ratio of the two physical times, it is helpful to think of these limiting values as ratios of human time scales: 10^5 seconds to 1 second, and 10^8 seconds to 1 second. Convert 10^5 seconds and 10^8 seconds into approximate numbers of days and years, respectively.

Processing Fields in a Record

Numeric Data

From the beginning, we have known that integers occupy two bytes and are stored in special binary form. Likewise, floating-point numeric quantities are stored in memory in a special four-byte binary floating-point format. Whenever a numeric quantity is entered from the keyboard or read from a terminal-format file, it is automatically converted from its ASCII form to the appropriate binary numeric form. In fact, we learned how to do this conversion using the VAL function in Chapter 11. Although the ASCII form is simple and convenient for terminal-format files, it is not very efficient for general file-processing activities. For example, assume that a file contains a field for the amount owed on a customer account. When a payment is received, the actions required to update the file (if the amount owed is in ASCII) would be as follows:

1. Convert the amount owed to floating point.
2. Subtract the amount paid from the amount owed.
3. Convert the new amount owed from floating point to string.

Unless there is some very good reason for storing the amount owed in ASCII (there usually is not), the preceding conversion operations are a needless waste of time. If the numeric quantities in the records of a file were stored in numeric format, then conversion back and forth would be unnecessary. VAX Basic provides this capability through the MAP statement, which (among other things) provides for the definitions of variables and their types.

Record Definition—the MAP Statement

To illustrate how the MAP statement is used in a program, let us consider some of the fields that might be included in the record of Example 13-1.

Example 13-2

Each record of an input file includes the following information:

Field	Type	Length	Variable Name
Member type	String	1	MEMB.TYPE
Member number	Integer	2	MEMB.NUM
Member name	String	30	MEMBER
Membership status	String	3	STATUS
Membership year	Integer	2	YEAR
Dues paid	Floating point	4	DUES

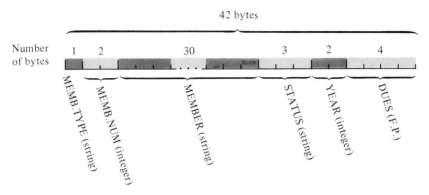

Figure 13-9 Record layout in memory.

In the preceding definition, note that lengths of numeric fields are determined by their types. That is, integers occupy two bytes, and floating-point quantities occupy four bytes. Of course, string fields are defined with whatever length is appropriate to the needs of the application. Figure 13-9 represents a memory layout of how this record would appear on disk (or as read into memory).

Within a program, in order to create a file with a record of this type or read a record from an existing file, this exact format must be defined. This is done with the MAP statement, which allocates a *static* (fixed) area in memory and describes the contents of this area. Various features of the MAP statement are illustrated in Figure 13-10(a), which is the required MAP for Example 13-2. The name of the area of memory reserved for this record is MEMB.REC,

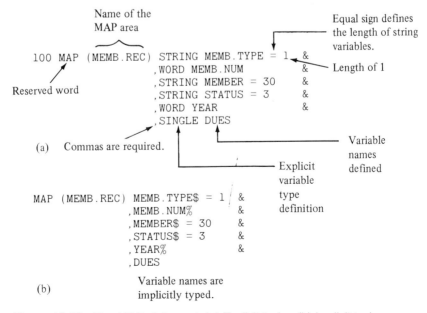

Figure 13-10 The MAP statement. (a) Explicit typing (b) Implicit typing.

the name enclosed in parentheses following the reserved word MAP. This statement will cause an area of memory to be reserved that is defined by the list of variables that follow the MAP name. In this example, data types are declared explicitly. Furthermore, the length of each string field is explicitly indicated following the equal sign. The resulting memory area reserved by this statement will correspond exactly to the layout illustrated in Figure 13-9. If we add up the lengths in Figure 13-10 (both explicit for strings and implicit for numeric variables), we see that the total is 42 bytes.

Regarding the explicit definition of the variable types, note that the form used in the MAP statement is the same as that in the DECLARE statement. As with the DECLARE, string and integer variables do not include a type suffix ($ and %) because explicitly declared variables cannot end in a dollar or percent sign. The form in Figure 13-10(b), which contains implicitly typed variables, should be contrasted with that of 13-10(a), in which they are explicitly declared.

Observe that the physical form of this MAP uses continuation lines. Remember, the & allows us to write a single statement over several lines. Actually, the MAP could be written on a single line, as follows:

```
MAP (MEMB.REC) STRING MEMB.TYPE=1, INTEGER MEMB.NUM,...
```

The forms of Figure 13-10 provides a far superior documentation level. Note also in this example that the separating commas are included at the beginning of each new line, as opposed to the end of the preceding line, as follows:

```
MAP (MEMB.REC) STRING MEMB.TYPE = 1,    &
               INTEGER MEMB.NUM,        &
               STRING MEMBER = 30,      &
               STRING STATUS = 3,       &
               INTEGER YEAR,            &
               SINGLE DUES
```

There are two reasons for this, both for convenience. First, if a comma is forgotten, it is much easier to detect its absence if all commas are positioned at the beginning of the line rather than at the end. Second, if a definition is later modified by adding another field after the last one, it is easy to forget to add the comma after this last field before adding the new one, for example:

```
MAP (MEMB.REC) STRING MEMB.TYPE = 1,    &
               INTEGER MEMB.NUM,        &
               STRING MEMBER = 30,      &
               STRING STATUS = 3,       &
               INTEGER YEAR,            &
               SINGLE DUES              &
               STRING CODE = 5
```

Although this is an error that is detected by the compiler, its avoidance is helpful in speeding up the programming process. The positioning of the comma is really a matter of personal preference.

A single program can include as many MAP statements as is required. Interestingly, a program can have more than one MAP statement with the same

```
300   MAP(BUDGET)        CODE$ = 3                 &
                         ,LOCATION$ = 4            &
                         ,DIVISION$ = 4            &
                         ,ACTIVITY$ = 5            &
                         ,BUDGETD$ = 8             &
                         ,EXPENDIT$ = 8            &
                         ,ENCUMBR$ = 8


310   MAP(BUDGET)        IDENTIFICATION$ = 11  &
                         ,ACTIVITY$ = 5        &
                         ,COSTS$ = 24
```

Figure 13-11   Examples of the MAP
statement.

```
320   MAP(BUDGET)        PAYABLE$ = 40
```

MAP name. This is illustrated in Figure 13-11, where the three MAP statements in lines 300, 310, and 320 have the same name and reference the same 40 bytes of memory. The memory allocated by these three MAP statements is said to be *overlaid*. By mapping an area of memory, BUDGET in this case, in more than one way, we can access this area in different ways, as needed. The mapping defined in line 300 defines individual fields of the record. In statement 310, the identification information contained in the first three fields is treated as a single field (IDENTIFICATION$). This multiple mapping would simplify programming if these fields are to be treated as a single field in some instances and as three individual fields in others. For example, the statement

```
IF HOLD$ = IDENTIFICATION$ THEN ...
```

would be less clumsy and serve as better documentation than

```
IF HOLD$ = CODE$+LOCATION$+DIVISION$ THEN ...
```

The MAP statement of line 320 would allow us to treat the entire record as a single field.

Characteristics of the MAP Statement. The following are some of the more important characteristics of the MAP statement:

1. The MAP statement creates an area of memory called a *program section* (PSECT). This is an area of *static memory*, that is, an area whose size or position in memory does not change during program execution.
2. A MAP statement must *name* the created area. In effect, the MAP name defines an area of memory in much the same way as a variable name defines a memory location. However, the MAP-named area can contain more than one variable. The name appears in parentheses immediately after the word MAP, follows the usual rules for variable names, and cannot be used as a variable name elsewhere in the program except in an OPEN or another MAP statement. Different MAP names define different reserved areas. Multiple

MAPs with the same name reference the *same* reserved area; the area is said to be *overlaid*. Variables with the same name can appear in different overlaid MAP statements only if the positions and data types match exactly.

3. The MAP statement can be used to declare data types explicitly. All variables following a given data-type keyword are of that type until another type is specified. Variables declared in a MAP statement cannot be declared elsewhere in the program. Variables that are not explicitly declared have their default type.

4. The MAP statement also *describes* the created area by listing the variable names. Because the reserved area is static, all string variables described in MAP have fixed length. The length of string variables is specified by using an equal sign followed by the desired number of characters. If no length is explicitly declared, then default string length of 16 bytes is used. All examples in this chapter use explicit length declaration.

5. Variables in the MAP statement are *not* initialized in VAX Basic.

6. The MAP statement is not executable; it simply *allocates* and *describes* the mapped area. In this sense, it is similar to the DATA statement, which defines data values to be used in a program.

7. The MAP statement must precede any reference in the program to the area it names or to the variables defined in this statement.

Exercise

13-6. Identify the errors in consistency of the following sequence of MAP statements, assuming that these statements are to be included in a program:

```
100 MAP(CHECKMAP)  LONG X,Y
200 MAP(CHECKMAP)  LONG X,Z
300 MAP(CHECKMAP)  LONG Y,X
400 MAP(CHECKMAP)  WORD X,Y
```

Reading Records from a Sequential File Using the MAP

Review of File-Processing Concepts

From Chapter 7, we know that in order to process information from a file, we must first use an OPEN statement. The purpose of the OPEN is to identify the file as INPUT or OUTPUT and to associate the external filename with the internal channel number. Following is a typical OPEN.

```
OPEN "MEMBER.DAT" FOR INPUT AS FILE #1
```

This is quite adequate for the simple terminal-format files that we have used, but it only represents the tip of the iceberg regarding its complete form for handling RMS files. Indeed, following the channel number, VAX Basic allows 26 clauses that can be appended to this statement in order to describe fully the nature of the file. As we shall learn, one of them identifies the memory buffer area defined by a MAP statement into which the record will be placed when the file is read.

To read records from terminal-format files, we used INPUT# statements such as the following:

```
INPUT #1, MEMB.TYPE$,MEMB.NUM%,MEMBER$,STATUS$,YEAR%,DUES
```

Input from files that are processed in conjunction with a MAP is somewhat different. Since the variable names and the input statement are defined by the MAP, you might guess (and correctly so) that the input statement does not involve a list of variables.

Let us consider first the basic nature of the OPEN, then the statement to transfer data from storage into memory, and finally an example of sequential processing. We will begin with the following example:

Example 13-3

A printed listing of selected records of the file of Example 13-2 (named MEMBER.DAT) is required. For each record (member) for which the value of DUES is not zero, print an output line containing each field of the record.

The OPEN Statement

In addition to the standard information provided by OPEN that we know about from Chapter 7, we will need to include the following for this example:

1. Designation that the file structure is sequential (as opposed to terminal format, which is what we get if we do not say otherwise).
2. The name of the MAP area that defines the record format for this file.
3. An indication of whether we will read, write, or do both with this file.

The last point is important and should not be confused with the FOR-INPUT or FOR-OUTPUT clause in the OPEN. Remember from Chapter 7 that the only purpose of this clause is to tell the system whether to look for an existing file (INPUT) or to create a new one (OUTPUT). It has nothing whatsoever to do with whether the file is used for input or output. However, in general, RMS requires the latter information for the program to *use* the file.

The OPEN statement of Figure 13-12 provides all of the needed infor-

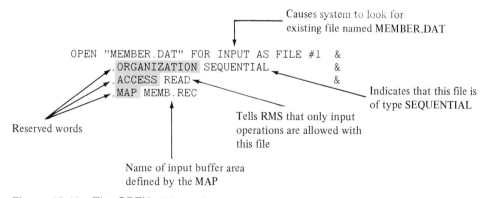

Figure 13-12   The OPEN statement.

mation. This example illustrates many of the important features of the additional OPEN clauses.

1. Additional clauses describing the file are listed following the "conventional" form of the OPEN that we have been using. Note that each clause is separated from the next by a comma. Although the entire statement can be entered on a single line, the continuation form shown here is preferred because of its documentation value.
2. The ORGANIZATION clause defines the file organization. Remember from our earlier studies in this chapter that we shall be learning about SEQUENTIAL, RELATIVE, and INDEXED. The ORGANIZATION clause must precede all other clauses in this portion of the OPEN.
3. The ACCESS clause indicates the type of access to the file that is desired— that is, whether there will be, for example, READ access or WRITE access. In this case, READ is specified, so writing to the file will not be allowed by RMS.
4. The MAP clause identifies the name of the record buffer that has been defined by a MAP statement within the program.

Exercises

13-7. A student remarks about a program: "Since the file was opened FOR INPUT, I cannot write to it." Comment.

13-8. Which clause in the OPEN statement specifies how you can *use* the file?

Input Operations—the GET Statement

For terminal-type input (including input from terminal-format files) the INPUT statement is used. Input for other file types is performed by the GET statement. Since the GET is used in conjunction with the MAP, a list of variables (as required with the INPUT) is not used. With sequential processing of sequential files, the GET causes RMS to read the next record into the designated memory area. As we shall learn later, RMS keeps track of which is the next record by use of a *record pointer*. A record pointer is a memory area maintained by RMS whose contents are the location (address) in memory of a record. Hence, it "points" to that record.

The overall concept of the GET and its relationship to the OPEN and MAP are illustrated in Figure 13-13. Note that for sequential access the GET need only specify the channel number from which the record is to be read. As with the INPUT#, successive executions of the GET causes successive records to be read from the file.

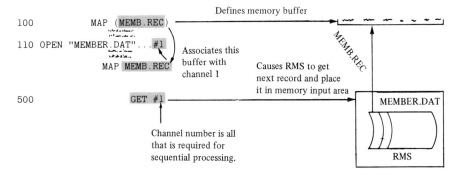

Figure 13-13   Using the GET in a program.

Exercise

13-9. What is the difference between the INPUT# and GET statements?

A Sample Program—Example 13-3

The program itself for Example 13-3 is virtually post-climactic, as we can see by inspecting Figure 13-14. We see that sequential processing of the records in this file is virtually identical to processing a terminal-format file. Repeated execution of the of the GET and PRINT is controlled by the WHILE, which is set up as an infinite loop. The loop is terminated by reading beyond the end of the file; that is, the ON-ERROR causes execution to jump to statement 500 when there are no more records to be processed. Here, the only word of caution

```
100 MAP (MEMB.REC) STRING MEMB.TYPE = 1   &
                  ,WORD MEMB.NUM          &
                  ,STRING MEMBER = 30     &
                  ,STRING STATUS = 3      &
                  ,WORD YEAR              &
                  ,SINGLE DUES
110 MASK$ = "'  ####  'LLLLLLLLLLLLLLLLLLLLLLLLLLL  'LL  ##  ###.##"
200 OPEN "MEMBER.DAT" FOR INPUT AS FILE #1   &
        ,ORGANIZATION SEQUENTIAL             &
        ,ACCESS READ                         &
        ,MAP MEMB.REC
300 ON ERROR GOTO 500
310 WHILE -1
      GET #1
      IF DUES <> 0 THEN   &
        PRINT USING MASK, MEMB.TYPE,MEMB.NUM,MEMBER,STATUS,YEAR,DUES
    NEXT
500 ! Error Routine
510 IF ERR <> 11 ON ERROR GOTO 0
520 PRINT
    PRINT "Processing complete"
32767 END
```

Figure 13-14   A program for Example 13-3.

is to recognize that the MAP statement must precede any reference in the program to the area it names or to the variables defined in it. Hence it is included prior to the OPEN. Regarding the variables defined in the MAP, note that they can be used as any other variables in the program. All of them are included in the list of the PRINT statement, and DUES is used to form the test expression in the IF statement.

Typical File-Processing Operations—Sequential Files

The program of Example 13-3 processes an already existing file. The question now is "Where did the file come from in the first place?" The answer is "From a program that used a MAP and OPEN clauses such as those in the program of Figure 13-14 to create it." It is important to understand that in an actual programming environment, a set of file-processing programs and their related files are closely integrated. Considerable planning is involved in determining the exact information to be included in the file (or files), as well as the various processing operations to be performed. For instance, the membership system would include one or more programs to do at least the following:

1. Create the file. Obviously this is a one-time job.
2. Add records to the file.
3. Print reports (such as that of Example 13-3).
4. Allow for information in individual records to be changed.

File Creation

The program of Figure 13-15 creates a file that corresponds to the one processed by the program of Figure 13-14. Note that this program includes the following checking features to assist the user in creating a new file. This is done by attempting to open for input the filename entered by the user.

1. If a file already exists with the name entered by the user, a warning is issued. If the user wishes to replace the existing one, it is killed and the query-loop control variable FINISHED is set to true (-1). This is done with the KILL statement, which effectively deletes a disk file: You cannot open or access the file after KILLing it.
2. If an error condition occurs during the OPEN, then execution jumps to line 500.

   a. If the error code is 5 (file not found), then the loop control variable is set to true. With the return to the main program, the loop will be terminated.
   b. For any other error code, a message is displayed, and control is returned to the main program. Since FINISHED remains false, the user will be queried again.

In this program, notice that the MAP statement is identical to that of Figure 13-14. Actually, for the creation process, this is overkill, since a record-buffer area is not required unless output operations are to be performed. We might

```
100 MAP (MEMB.REC) STRING MEMB.TYPE = 1    &
                   ,WORD MEMB.NUM          &
                   ,STRING MEMBER = 30     &
                   ,STRING STATUS = 3      &
                   ,WORD YEAR              &
                   ,SINGLE DUES
200 DECLARE INTEGER FINISHED
300 ON ERROR GOTO 500
310 FINISHED = 0
320 PRINT "Ready to create new membership file."
330 WHILE NOT FINISHED
        INPUT "Filename & extension of the new file";F$
        OPEN F$ FOR INPUT AS FILE #1
        CLOSE #1
        PRINT "File already exists."
        INPUT "Do you wish to delete it <Y/N>";Q$
        IF LEFT$(EDIT$(Q$,32),1) = "Y"  OR LEFT$(EDIT$(Q$,32),1) = "y"
        THEN
            KILL F$
            FINISHED = -1
        ENDIF
   CONTINUE.FROM.ERROR.CHECK:
     NEXT
400 OPEN F$ FOR OUTPUT AS FILE #1     &
            ,ORGANIZATION SEQUENTIAL  &
            ,ACCESS WRITE             &
            ,MAP MEMB.REC
410 PRINT "File ";F$;" has been created."
420 CLOSE #1
430 STOP
500 ! Error Routine
510 IF ERR = 5
    THEN
        FINISHED = -1
    ELSE
        PRINT "Bad filename or protected file--try again."
    ENDIF
520 RESUME CONTINUE.FROM.ERROR.CHECK
32767 END
```

Figure 13-15   Creating a file.

wonder what the contents of a newly created file are before any records are written to it. It may seem that, since it contains no records, it must be empty. However, this is incorrect, because every RMS file includes within the file itself descriptive information about the file. Thus, whenever we open a file without writing records, it already occupies disk storage. It is very important to recognize that the characteristics of the file are defined when the file is first created. The amount of information stored depends upon the file structure (SEQUENTIAL, RELATIVE, or INDEXED). All three types include *file-header* and *file-attributes* areas. RELATIVE and INDEXED files include additional parts. In this book, this "preliminary" information will collectively be referred to as the *header* information. For us, the two most important items stored are the file structure (SEQUENTIAL, RELATIVE, or INDEXED) and the record length. Note that the record format (breakdown of fields within the record) is *not* stored in the header area. Thus, when a file is first created, the program does *not* need to furnish a record-format description as provided by the MAP statement. Remember, the MAP serves the purpose of providing a memory area into which RMS can place the accessed record for our program to use. If a program is to create the file without writing any data records, then the MAP is not needed. (As we shall learn, this is not true of indexed files.)

On the other hand, when a file is first created, RMS *does* need to know the record length in order to write it to the header area. To that end, the MAP statement and the MAP clause of the OPEN statement could both be deleted from this file-creation program. However, it would be necessary to include the RECORDSIZE clause in the OPEN in order to furnish RMS with the record length necessary for the header area of the file. Thus, in the program of Figure 13-15, the MAP statement could be omitted and the OPEN statement changed to that of Figure 13-16.

```
400 OPEN "MEMBER.DAT" FOR OUTPUT AS FILE #1 &
          ,ORGANIZATION SEQUENTIAL          &
          ,ACCESS WRITE                     &
          ,RECORDSIZE 42
```

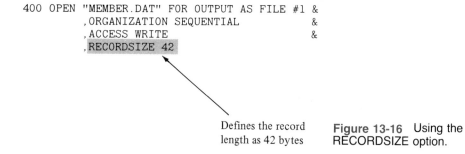

Defines the record length as 42 bytes

Figure 13-16 Using the RECORDSIZE option.

It should be clear that, if a file is to be created *and* records are to be written to the file (both in the same program), then the MAP statement will be necessary. Although it is possible to include both a MAP and a RECORDSIZE clause in an OPEN, there will be no reason to do so in examples of this book. Furthermore, once the file is created, the recordsize is stored in the header part of the file. Hence if an existing file is opened, the RECORDSIZE clause should not be included in the OPEN.

Exercise

13-10. Delete the DECLARE statement on line 200 in the program of Figure 15-15 and run the program. Explain the result. (There is no solution to this exercise at the end of the chapter.)

Appending Records to a Sequential File

In most file-processing applications, records are entered into a file over a period of time. For example, if the file is very large, it might take several days to enter all of the data into the file. Then, when that operation is complete, records will be added periodically. For instance, with the membership system, a new record will be added to the file each time there is a new member. For sequential files, records are added to the end of the file. Hence we need some means for

```
100 MAP (MEMB.REC) STRING MEMB.TYPE = 1   &
                  ,WORD MEMB.NUM          &
                  ,STRING MEMBER = 30     &
                  ,STRING STATUS = 3      &
                  ,WORD YEAR              &
                  ,SINGLE DUES
300 FINISHED = 0
310 INPUT "Filename & extension of file to process";F$
320 OPEN F$ FOR OUTPUT AS FILE #1    &
         ,ORGANIZATION SEQUENTIAL    &
         ,ACCESS APPEND              &
         ,MAP MEMB.REC
330 WHILE NOT FINISHED
    INPUT "Member type";MEMB.TYPE
    INPUT "Member number";MEMB.NUM
    INPUT "Member name";MEMBER
    INPUT "Membership status";STATUS
    INPUT "Membership year";YEAR
    INPUT "Dues amount paid";DUES
    PUT #1
    INPUT "Do you wish to enter another member";Q$
    REPLY$ = LEFT$(EDIT$(Q$,32),1)
    IF REPLY$ = "Y" THEN FINISHED = -1
    NEXT
340 CLOSE #1
350 PRINT "Record entry complete."
32767 END
```

Figure 13-17   Appending records to a file.

positioning RMS at the end of the file so that new records will not overwrite existing ones. This is done in the OPEN statement by specifying the APPEND mode in the ACCESS clause. This clause is shaded in the program of Figure 13-17. Important points of this program are as follows:

1. When the file is opened with ACCESS APPEND, RMS positions its record pointer just beyond the last record in the file. Then, when a new record is written to the file, it is added following the last record.
2. The new record is assembled simply by placing information into the record variables defined in the MAP. As with the program of Figure 13-14, these variables are treated just as any others in the program.
3. Placing information into the record variables does *not* change the contents of the file itself. Remember, the MAP statement defines a buffer area that is in memory, not on disk storage.
4. The contents of the memory buffer are written to the disk file by the PUT statement. Note that it specifies only the channel. In this case, channel 1 is associated with the file named in F$; the corresponding output area is designated in the OPEN as MEMB.REC. Hence, the action of the PUT causes the contents of MEMB.REC to be written to disk.

Some of the Workings of RMS

The concepts that we shall learn regarding file processing in general and RMS in particular only scratch the surface. Indeed, the DEC publication *Guide to*

VAX/VMS File Applications consists of over 300 pages. Obviously, a first programming book cannot cover in-depth details on this topic. However, a knowledge of some of the workings of RMS will make it easier to understand some of the tools that we are learning to use.

Remember that internal memory consists of individual bytes, each of which can be accessed by its address. Thus, the smallest addressable memory unit is the byte. By contrast, the smallest addressable unit of disk storage is the *block*, which consists of 512 bytes. A block is often also referred to as a *physical record*—the data record as seen from the viewpoint of the storage device. Whenever a disk read occurs, an entire 512-byte block, not merely the record in which we are interested, is read into memory. RMS handles all of the manipulation, so that we are unaware of the detailed operations that occur. Whenever a file is opened using a MAP, RMS creates *two* memory areas for handling the I/O operations. The first is the RMS *I/O buffer*, which is 512 bytes in length. (The user can define a larger buffer to improve efficiency.) The second is the *record buffer*, which is defined by the MAP statement. As we have observed, when working with a program, we see the record buffer, but we do not see the I/O buffer.

To illustrate what occurs when a record is read, let us assume that the MEMBER file has been opened and a GET has been executed for the first time. As illustrated in Figure 13-18, RMS takes the following actions:

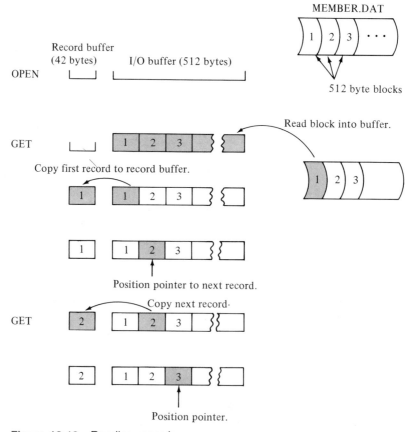

Figure 13-18 Reading records.

1. Read the first block of the file into the I/O buffer.
2. Extract the first record from the I/O buffer and copy it to the record buffer defined by the MAP statement.
3. Move an internal pointer to the next record in order to be ready for the next execution of a GET.
4. Return control to the program.

When the next GET is executed, it will not be necessary for RMS to perform another disk read, since the desired record is already available in the I/O buffer. RMS will simply transfer the second record to the record buffer and return control to the program.

For reading records from a sequential file, the preceding descriptions tell the story. However, RMS actually maintains *two* pointers rather than one: the *current record pointer* and the *next record pointer*. The pointer illustrated in Figure 13-18 is actually the next record pointer. After the second GET of Figure 13-18, the pointer status will be as illustrated in Figure 13-19. The distinction between these two pointers will become significant as we get further into file processing.

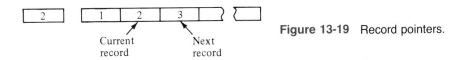

Figure 13-19   Record pointers.

Exercises

13-11. Explain the difference between a logical record and a physical record.

13-12. Explain the difference between a record buffer and an I/O buffer.

Updating an Existing File

Example Definition

In the normal file-processing environment, records are commonly updated directly. For instance, a particular member sends in a dues payment, which must be entered into the record for that member. The entire file need not be accessed, only the single record requiring updating. Although sequential files do allow for direct accessing, it is possible only under very restricted circumstances that are not pursued in this book. However, there are cases in which one or more fields in an entire file must be changed. In such a case, each record must be read, changed if appropriate, and rewritten if changed. Under RMS, it is possible to make a change to a record and rewrite it over the original. This is illustrated by the following example:

Example 13-4

The MEMB.TYPE field of the MEMBER.DAT file can be either of three values, A, B, or P. Type P is to be replaced by one of three subclassifications, to be determined by an operator. An interactive program is required to allow the user to change the member type for each P.

Using the UPDATE Statement—Example 13-4

The new concepts in the program of Figure 13-20 are relatively simple. Note that the ACCESS clause now specifies that the access mode is MODIFY. This allows the program to read and to write this file. (Note: MODIFY is the default mode if the ACCESS clause is omitted.) Within the processing loop, each record is checked to see if it contains a member type of "P." If it does, the user is requested to enter a new value, and the record is written back to the file by the UPDATE statement (shaded in Figure 13-20). Remember, RMS maintains two record pointers: the current-record and next-record pointers. Different I/O statements affect these pointers differently. Thus, the GET causes the following to occur:

1. The current-record pointer is moved to the next-record pointer position.
2. The next-record pointer is moved to the next available record in the file.
3. The current record is copied into the record buffer.

On the other hand, the UPDATE statement simply writes the contents of the record buffer back to the current record. It does *not* change either of the pointers.

```
100 MAP (MEMB.REC) STRING MEMB.TYPE = 1   &
                  ,WORD MEMB.NUM          &
                  ,STRING MEMBER = 30     &
                  ,STRING STATUS = 3      &
                  ,WORD YEAR              &
                  ,SINGLE DUES
200 OPEN "MEMBER.DAT" FOR INPUT AS FILE #1  &
          ,ORGANIZATION SEQUENTIAL          &
          ,ACCESS MODIFY                     &
          ,MAP MEMB.REC
300 ON ERROR GOTO 500                                     Allows the program both
310 WHILE -1                                              to read and to write this file
    GET #1
    IF MEMB.TYPE = "P"
    THEN
        PRINT "Number: ";MEMB.NUM;"    Name: ";MEMBER
        INPUT "New member type"; MEMB.TYPE
        UPDATE #1
    ENDIF
    NEXT                                                  Writes the present form of
500 ! Error Routine                                       the record in memory back
510 IF ERR <> 11 ON ERROR GOTO 0                          to the current record of the
520 PRINT                                                 I/O buffer
    PRINT "Processing complete"
32767 END
```

Figure 13-20 Updating records—Example 13-4.

More About the MAP

In the preceding examples, all of the programs to process the MEMBER.DAT file used the same MAP statement. In fact, in a real programming environment, such record definitions would be stored as separate files and be readily available to programmers to include in new programs. It simply does not make sense to reenter the same MAP statement each time a new program is written. Not only is it a wasted repetition to rekey the same information, but keying is always prone to error. By copying the standard MAP from disk, the programmer can be certain that the format is correctly defined.

Relative File Processing

Creating and Sequentially Reading a Relative File

Let us assume that the decision has been made to use a relative file for the membership file. If the record format is to be unchanged, then the file-creation program of Figure 13-15 requires only one minor modification. That is, the ORGANIZATION clause in the OPEN must be changed to RELATIVE, as shown in Figure 13-21. RMS does the rest.

```
OPEN "MEMBER.DAT" FOR INPUT AS FILE #1  &
     ,ORGANIZATION RELATIVE              &    Figure 13-21   The OPEN for
     ,ACCESS WRITE                       &    a RELATIVE file.
     ,MAP MEMB.REC
```

The same simple change is all that is required of the program to print selected records of the file (Figure 13-14): The ORGANIZATION clause would be changed from SEQUENTIAL to RELATIVE. However, there is more to say about the GET. Remember, the relative structure allows both direct and sequential access. As we shall learn in a later section, to read a record directly, the GET statement must specify the relative record number. If no record number is designated, then the GET operates exactly as if the relative file were a sequential file: The next record is accessed. The handling of the pointers takes into account the fact that a relative file might not contain records in every cell. In Figure 13-22, we see that execution of a GET copies a record from the I/O

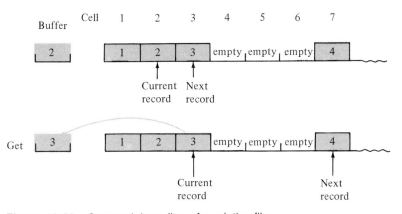

Figure 13-22   Sequential reading of a relative file.

buffer into the record buffer. Since the next cell does not contain a record, RMS moves the next-record pointer to the next cell that does contain data. Hence when we process a relative file sequentially, RMS effectively ignores all empty cells, and we see the data records as if they were coming from a sequential file.

Regarding the MEMB.NUM Field

If we wish to process the relative version of MEMBER.DAT by directly accessing the records, then we must refer to cell numbers. Remember from the previous discussions that the relative structure is most useful in applications where it is possible to use key-field values that correspond to cell numbers. To this end, let us assume that, during the design phase of the file, a decision was made to assign members four-digit membership numbers beginning with 1001. Then cell 1 can be used for member 1001; cell 2, for member 1002, and so on. Within the program, we would use the relationship

$$\text{Cell number} = \text{Member number} - 1000$$

Direct-Access Processing a Relative File

Let us consider the following Example 13-5 to illustrate the principles of direct processing of a relative file.

Example 13-5

As dues are received from members, the operator must update the dues field. A program is required that will allow the operator to enter the member number and then be allowed to enter a new dues value.

In all of the preceding examples, the GET has taken the form

```
GET #1
```

In order to access a selected record, it is necessary to specify the desired cell number, using the following form:

```
GET #1, RECORD cell number
```

For example, to read the record from cell 30, we would use

```
GET #1, RECORD 30
```

In a similar fashion, if the variable REC% contains the cell number of the desired record, we would use

```
GET #1, RECORD REC%
```

Since the member number is 1000 greater than the corresponding cell containing that member record, our program must subtract 1000 from the member number

```
100 MAP (MEMB.REC) STRING MEMB.TYPE = 1    &
                   ,WORD MEMB.NUM          &
                   ,STRING MEMBER = 30     &
                   ,STRING STATUS = 3      &
                   ,WORD YEAR              &
                   ,SINGLE DUES
110 DECLARE WORD SEARCH.MEMBER, REC.NUMBER
200 OPEN "MEMBER.DAT" FOR INPUT AS FILE #1 &
            ,ORGANIZATION RELATIVE         &
            ,ACCESS MODIFY                 &
            ,MAP MEMB.REC
300 PRINT "To update a member record, enter member number."
310 INPUT "Member number";SEARCH.MEMBER
320 ON ERROR GOTO 500
330 WHILE SEARCH.MEMBER > 0
        REC.NUMBER = SEARCH.MEMBER - 1000
        GET #1, RECORD REC.NUMBER
        PRINT "Number: ";MEMB.NUM;"    Name: ";MEMBER
        INPUT "Dues amount"; DUES
        UPDATE #1
        INPUT "Next member (0 if finished)";SEARCH.MEMBER
    CONTINUE.FROM.ERROR.CHECK:
    NEXT
350 PRINT "Processing complete"
360 CLOSE #1
370 STOP
500 ! Error Routine
510 PRINT BELL; "Record not found--try again."
520 INPUT "Next member (0 if finished)";SEARCH.MEMBER
530 RESUME CONTINUE.FROM.ERROR.CHECK
32767 END
```

Get a selected record . . .

. . . then write the record back that was last read.

Figure 13-23 Direct processing a relative file—Example 13-5.

entered by the user. The program of Figure 13-23 performs this operation prior to executing the GET.

Basically, there are two ways in which an error can occur: (1) The member number entered corresponds to an empty cell, and (2) the member number entered corresponds to a cell that is beyond the end of the file. Both of these are handled by the error-recovery routine at line 500.

If the desired record is found, then the member number and name stored in the record are displayed, and the user is allowed to enter the new dues amount. Note that the GET specifies the record number to be read, but the UPDATE does not. The reason is that the UPDATE always writes to the record designated by the current record pointer.

Adding Records to a Relative File

Let us assume that new members of our organization are assigned member numbers according to some defined procedure and that the next number to be used will not necessarily correspond to the next available cell number. Then, as each new record is entered, our program must check to ensure that the member number entered is not one that has already been selected. Conveniently, this will be done automatically for us by RMS when an attempt is made to PUT the record. To see how this is done, let us consider the program of

```
100 MAP (MEMB.REC) STRING MEMB.TYPE = 1    &
                   ,WORD MEMB.NUM          &
                   ,STRING MEMBER = 30     &
                   ,STRING STATUS = 3      &
                   ,WORD YEAR              &
                   ,SINGLE DUES
200 DECLARE INTEGER ERROR.CHECK
300 FINISHED = 0
310 OPEN "MEMBER.DAT" AS FILE #1    &
            ,ORGANIZATION RELATIVE   &
            ,ACCESS MODIFY           &
            ,MAP MEMB.REC
320 ON ERROR GOTO 500
325 ERROR.CHECK = 0
330 INPUT "Member number";MEMB.NUM
    ACCEPT.LOOP:
    WHILE MEMB.NUM > 0
340    IF NOT ERROR.CHECK
           THEN
               INPUT "Member type";MEMB.TYPE
               INPUT "Member name";MEMBER
               INPUT "Membership status";STATUS
               INPUT "Membership year";YEAR
               INPUT "Dues amount paid";DUES
       END IF
       ERROR.CHECK = 0
       PUT #1, RECORD MEMB.NUM-1000
       INPUT "Member number (0 if finished)";MEMB.NUM
    NEXT
350 CLOSE #1
360 PRINT "Record entry complete."
500 ! Error Routine
510 PRINT BELL; "Cannot use this number--try again."
520 INPUT "Next member (0 if finished)";MEMB.NUM
530 IF MEMB.NUM > 0
        THEN
            ERROR.CHECK = -1
    ENDIF
    RESUME ACCEPT.LOOP
32767 END
```

Figure 13-24 Adding records to a relative file.

Figure 13-24. In order to illustrate different programming techniques, note that the method of loop control is that of the sequential append program of Figure 13-17. That is, processing is terminated by the user entering a member number of 0. To this end, the first member number is requested prior to the loop. Then, at the last statement of the loop, the next member number is requested.

Regarding error possibilities, there are two conditions that can cause an error when the PUT is executed. First, a nonexisting cell number may be referenced. That is, reference to a member number that exceeds by more than 1000 the largest allowed cell number is obviously incorrect; a value less than 1000 for MEMB.NUM results in a negative cell reference. Second, if the addressed cell already contains a record, RMS will not allow another to overwrite it. (This can be done only with the UPDATE statement.) All of these occurrences cause the error routine beginning at line 500 to be entered. The user is prompted to enter another value for MEMB.NUM. If it is greater than

0, ERROR.CHECK is set to true. When execution RESUMEs at the first statement in ACCEPT.LOOP, it falls directly through to the PUT statement to try again, since NOT ERROR.CHECK is now false. If MEMB.NUM is equal to 0, the condition in the WHILE is now false, and execution falls through to the NEXT statement, which subsequently results in termination of the loop.

Obviously, there are many other methods of implementing the actions performed by the program of Figure 13-24. In considering other approaches, remember to keep the program user friendly. For instance, the logic should be structured so that the user need not reenter all of the fields for an invalid member number.

Record Pointers with Relative Files

When one is performing direct processing on a relative file, there is not much need to be concerned with the record pointers. However, in some cases, it is useful to perform both direct and sequential processing on a file. For instance, a particular program might require that the records for all member numbers greater than a particular value be updated. This would involve direct access to the desired record, then sequential access to those that follow. For operations such as this, we must be aware of the effect of the GET and PUT on the record pointers.

TABLE 13-1 Record Pointers for Processing Relative Files

	Processing	Current Record	Next Record
GET	Sequential	Previous next record	Next nonempty cell in file
	Direct	Designated record	Next nonempty cell in file
PUT	Sequential	Pointer value destroyed	Next nonempty cell in file
	Direct	Pointer value destroyed	Not changed

Thus, in the preceding example, it would be possible to use a direct GET to process the first record, then sequential GETs to process those that follow. Note that the current-record pointer is meaningless after a PUT operation, whether it is sequential or direct.

Exercise

13-13. A program requires that records in a file be read, updated, and rewritten. Processing of the file is to be sequential, so a programmer decides to omit the RECORD qualifier and includes the following in the processing loop. What will happen?

```
GET #1   ! Get next record from disk
    .
    .
    .
PUT #1   ! Write corrected record back to disk
```

Indexed Files

The Need for Indexed Files

The relative file structure is a big improvement over the sequential structure, since it is readily adaptable to both sequential and direct processing. However, it is lacking in two very important respects.

1. The key field must correspond to the cell numbers. This means that if the field to be used for the key is some preexisting value, it probably will not work. For instance, if the Social Security number, driver's license number, or any string field is to be used, relative organization is not very expedient.
2. It is not practical to use two or more fields as different keys. For instance, assume that the membership system is used by a nationwide organization and includes mailing addresses. Normal access might be based on the member number. However, access to the records may be required via the member's last name. Furthermore, mass mailings might require that address labels be printed in ZIP code sequence.

As we learned in the early portion of this chapter, the indexed file provides the solutions to these needs.

Creating an Indexed File

When creating a sequential or a relative file, it is possible to use either the MAP or the RECORDSIZE clause to tell RMS the length of the record. When creating an indexed file, the MAP must be used because the OPEN statement designates which field is to be used as the key; that is, the key must be a field in the data record. Otherwise, indexed-file creation is virtually identical to that of a sequential file, as illustrated in Figure 13-15. The difference is in the OPEN, as shown in Figure 13-25. As with the sequential and relative structures, RMS stores the record length and other information in the file-header area. In addition, it stores the position of the key field (MEMB.NUM) in the record. The portion of the information stored is illustrated in Figure 13-26. Even though the OPEN refers to a field name, that name is *not* stored in the header area; only the key field's relative position and length are stored. This makes the

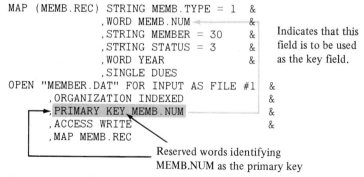

Figure 13-25   Creating an indexed file.

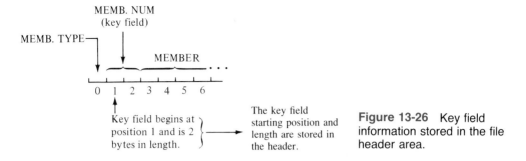

Figure 13-26 Key field information stored in the file header area.

information stored in the header independent of any names that might be selected for a given MAP statement used with an indexed file.

Exercise

13-14. What is the essential difference between the key in a relative file and the key in an indexed file?

Sequential Reading with Indexed Files

One of the advantages of the way in which RMS implements the indexed structure relates to its simplicity of use. For example, an indexed file can be read sequentially in exactly the same way as a sequential file. For instance, Example 13-3 requires that a printed list be generated of all members with a dues value greater than 0. The file in the program for Example 13-3 in Figure 13-14 was organized (and therefore processed) sequentially. The program shown in Figure 13-27 is identical to that for sequential files (Figure 13-14)

```
100 MAP (MEMB.REC) STRING MEMB.TYPE = 1    &
                  ,WORD MEMB.NUM           &
                  ,STRING MEMBER = 30      &
                  ,STRING STATUS = 3       &
                  ,WORD YEAR               &
                  ,SINGLE DUES
110 MASK = "\\   ####   \                      \  \  \  ##  ###.##"
200 OPEN "MEMBER.DAT" FOR INPUT AS FILE #1  &
        ,ORGANIZATION INDEXED              &
        ,ACCESS READ                       &
        ,MAP MEMB.REC
300 ON ERROR GOTO 500                   This is the only change
310 WHILE -1                            over the corresponding
     GET #1                             sequential file program.
     IF DUES <> 0 THEN  &
       PRINT USING MASK$, MEMB.TYPE,MEMB.NUM,MEMBER,STATUS,YEAR,DUES
    NEXT
500 ! Error Routine
510 IF ERR <> 11 ON ERROR GOTO 0
520 PRINT
    PRINT "Processing complete"
32767 END
```

Figure 13-27 Reading an indexed file sequentially.

except for the OPEN statement. Here the ORGANIZATION clause specifies INDEXED. Note that there is no information on the key (MEMB.NUM) in the OPEN; it is not needed because the key information is stored in the header area of the file. In other words, an *existing* indexed file can be opened without specifying a key clause.

With RMS, we get a bonus with our generated list, resulting from the fact that the index is maintained in sorted sequence (with the smallest number first and the largest last). That is, the printed list will be in sequence by member number. Remember from our earlier discussion that the order of indexed files is seen as the order of the index and has nothing to do with the physical placement of records in the file. Each execution of the sequential GET gives us the next logical record.

Sequential Writing with Indexed Files

Adding records to an indexed file is almost as simple as writing to a sequential file. As with the sequential example of Figure 13-17, we simply collect the information and PUT it to the file. RMS automatically adds the record ''somewhere'' in the file (we care not where), then automatically enters the new key into its proper position of the index. However, what if the key field value is one that is already used? The answer is that when the file was first created (by the OPEN of Figure 13-25), a code was entered into the header area of the file indicating that duplicate keys would not be allowed in the file. This is the default. Thus, as in the case of the relative file, the key values must be unique under default; that is, no two records may have the same key-field value. (RMS allows us to create index files that allow two or more records with the same key if we so desire. However, this must be specified at file creation time. We shall learn how to do this in a later section of this chapter.)

As a result of the unique key-value requirement, the program shown in Figure 13-28 includes the error-checking capabilities of the corresponding relative file program (Figure 13-24). We see that there are only two significant differences between this program and that of Figure 13-24. First, the ORGANIZATION clause has been changed to reflect the fact that the file is indexed. Second, the RECORD clause has been deleted from the PUT statement. In this sense, writing sequentially to the indexed file is more like writing to a sequential file. RMS does the hard part for us.

```
100 MAP (MEMB.REC) STRING MEMB.TYPE = 1    &
                   ,WORD MEMB.NUM           &
                   ,STRING MEMBER = 30      &
                   ,STRING STATUS = 3       &
                   ,WORD YEAR               &
                   ,SINGLE DUES
300 FINISHED = 0
310 OPEN "MEMBER.DAT" AS FILE #1     &
         ,ORGANIZATION INDEXED       &
         ,ACCESS WRITE               &
         ,MAP MEMB.REC
320 ON ERROR GOTO 500
330 INPUT "Member number";MEMB.NUM
340 WHILE MEMB.NUM > 0
        INPUT "Member type";MEMB.TYPE
        INPUT "Member name";MEMBER
        INPUT "Membership status";STATUS
        INPUT "Membership year";YEAR
        INPUT "Dues amount paid";DUES
     CONTINUE.FROM.ERROR.CHECK:
        PUT #1
        INPUT "Member number (0 if finished)";MEMB.NUM
     EXIT.FROM.ERROR.CHECK:
     NEXT
340 CLOSE #1
350 PRINT "Record entry complete."
500 ! Error Routine
510 PRINT BELL; "Member number already used--try again."
520 INPUT "Next member (0 if finished)";MEMB.NUM
530 IF MEMB.NUM > 0
    THEN
        RESUME CONTINUE.FROM.ERROR.CHECK
    ELSE
        RESUME EXIT.FROM.ERROR.CHECK
    ENDIF
32767 END
```

File organization is indexed.

Note that no record number is allowed on PUT to an indexed file.

Figure 13-28 Writing to an indexed file sequentially.

Direct Access of an Indexed File

In Example 13-5, records of the relative form of the member file are accessed
and updated on a direct basis. That is, the operator enters a member number,
the program accesses the desired record, the operator enters a new value for
the dues field, and the record is updated. The program of Figure 13-29(a) is
almost identical to that of Figure 13-23 for updating a relative file. The primary

```
100 MAP (MEMB.REC) STRING MEMB.TYPE = 1    &
                  ,WORD MEMB.NUM           &
                  ,STRING MEMBER = 30      &
                  ,STRING STATUS = 3       &
                  ,WORD YEAR               &
                  ,SINGLE DUES

110 DECLARE WORD SEARCH.MEMBER

200 OPEN "MEMBER.DAT" FOR INPUT AS FILE #1  &
         ,ORGANIZATION INDEXED              &
         ,ACCESS MODIFY                     &
         ,MAP MEMB.REC

300 PRINT "To update a member record, enter member number."
310 INPUT "Member number";SEARCH.MEMBER
320 ON ERROR GOTO 500
330 WHILE SEARCH.MEMBER > 0
        GET #1, KEY #0 EQ SEARCH.MEMBER
        PRINT "Number: ";MEMB.NUM;"    Name: ";MEMBER
        INPUT "Dues amount"; DUES
        UPDATE #1
        INPUT "Next member (0 if finished)";SEARCH.MEMBER
    CONTINUE.FROM.ERROR.CHECK:
    NEXT

350 PRINT "Processing complete"
360 CLOSE #1
370 STOP


500 ! Error Routine
510 PRINT BELL; "Record not found--try again."
520 INPUT "Next member (0 if finished)";SEARCH.MEMBER
530 RESUME CONTINUE.FROM.ERROR.CHECK
32767 END
```
(a)

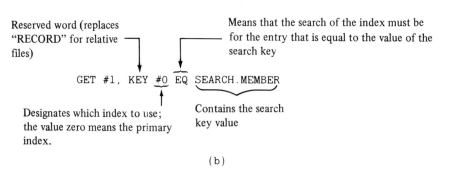

(b)

Figure 13-29 Direct processing an indexed file.

difference relates to the form of the GET statement, which is explained in Figure 13-29(b). In this example, the index will be searched for the index entry that is equal to the search-key value contained in the variable SEARCH.MEMBER. If the value is found, then the desired record is retrieved, and the GET will be successful. If it is not found, then an error will occur, and the error routine beginning on line 500 will be executed.

There is a very important (and subtle) point relating to designating the search-key value. To illustrate it, let us consider the extreme and assume that the requested search-key value is entered into the string variable SEARCH.MEMBER$. Then if the GET is

```
GET #1, KEY #0 EQ SEARCH.MEMBER$
```

we have a conflict problem. That is, the search argument is string, but the index entry is word (integer). This is analogous to, for instance, writing an IF statement as follows:

```
IF AMOUNT% = LIMIT$ THEN ...
```

We clearly have an error of mixing modes. The same problem occurs with the preceding form of the GET; the search key and the index entry must be of the same type.

Actually, this extreme case is not particularly subtle; the subtle part relates to the distinction that RMS makes between different numeric types when it relates to indexes. Note in this program that both MEMB.NUM in the MAP and SEARCH.MEMBER in the DECLARE are explicitly declared as WORD. What if the DECLARE were omitted and the search variable were defined as SEARCH.MEMBER%, an implicitly typed integer? If the system default for integers is LONG (four bytes), then the search variable SEARCH.MEMBER% will be of type LONG. The result is that a type mismatch will occur for the following GET:

```
GET #1, KEY #0 EQ SEARCH.MEMBER%
```

That is, the index entry will be type WORD, and the search argument, type LONG. The type match here must be exact.

Furthermore, if member record 1516 is required, the statement:

```
GET #1, KEY #0 EQ 1516
```

is incorrect, if the system default for integers is different from the declared key type. The best thing to do is always to *use a declared variable as the search argument*. This is illustrated by the next exercise.

Exercise

13-15. A programmer is using a system in which the default integer is LONG. The declared key type is WORD. Write the statement(s) needed to get member record 2166.

More Advanced Operations with Indexed Files

Expansion of the MEMBER.DAT File

To illustrate some of the additional things that can be done with indexed files, let us consider the following expansion of the MEMBER.DAT file structure. (This example involves secondary keys, a topic described in the section immediately preceding Exercise 13-3.)

Example 13-6

The member file is to be expanded to the following format:

Field	Type	Length
Member type	String	1
Member number	String	4
Member last name	String	15
Member first name	String	15
Membership status	String	3
Membership year	Integer	2
Dues paid	Floating	4

This file will include a primary key and two secondary keys, as follows:

Primary: Member number.

Secondary: Member last name.
            Member type + member number.

Note that the member-number field (the primary key field) has been changed from word to string. Also, the name has been broken into two parts: the last name and the first name.

About Key Fields

As we can see, this example requires three different indexes; these will provide significant versatility in processing the file. It is only necessary to designate all required key fields when the file is created, and RMS takes care of the rest. All keys must be variables that are declared in a MAP statement referenced in the MAP clause of the OPEN statement. The MAP and OPEN statements required for creation of this file are shown in Figure 13-30. Here we see three index keys specified for this file. The first is defined as the PRIMARY key, and the others as ALTERNATE keys. The two alternate keys demonstrate new principles.

Since member numbers are assigned by the organization and uniquely identify a member, duplicates must not be permitted. However, a name field

```
                    MAP (MEMB.REC) STRING MEMB.TYPE = 1    &
                                  ,STRING MEMB.NUM =4      &
                                  ,STRING LAST.NAME = 15   &
                                  ,STRING FIRST.NAME = 15  &
                                  ,STRING STATUS = 3       &
                                  ,WORD YEAR               &
Three keys                        ,SINGLE DUES
for this file:  OPEN "MEMBER.DAT" FOR INPUT AS FILE #1     &
                                  ,ORGANIZATION INDEXED              &
Key #0 ───────────►,PRIMARY KEY MEMB.NUM                            &
Key #1 ───────────►,ALTERNATE KEY LAST.NAME DUPLICATES             &
Key #2 ───────────►,ALTERNATE KEY (MEMB.TYPE, MEMB.NUM)            &
                                  ,ACCESS WRITE                     &
                                  ,MAP MEMB.REC        Two fields
                                                       combined
                                                       as a key
```

Figure 13-30 MAP and OPEN for creating a multi-key indexed file—Example 13-6.

is quite a different story, for there will likely be more than one person named Smith. Hence the ALTERNATE KEY clause defining this index field includes the DUPLICATES clause. This fact is recorded in the file header, so that when a new name is entered that duplicates one already in the file (representing a duplicate key), it will not be rejected.

Note that the second ALTERNATE KEY clause creates an index consisting of two fields of the file. This is done by separating the desired fields by commas and including them in parentheses. This is a valuable and commonly used technique. If we assume that the type can be ''P'' for permanent or ''T'' for temporary, then typical values of the combination of these fields would be

    P1556
    P2910
    P3082
    T2004
    T2807
    T4977

Note that the new index is formed by concatenating the two fields in the sequence in which they are listed inside the parentheses in the ALTERNATE KEY clause. Hence if we were to run a report using this index, the report would list all of the type P members in member-number sequence, followed by all of the type T members in member-number sequence. On the other hand, if the report were run on the primary key, the output would be in sequence based solely on the member number.

Reading Records Using Different Keys

Since all of the key information is stored in the file header, subsequent programs that read or write need not designate the keys in the OPEN. Once the file is created, appropriate entries are made in *all* of the indexes for every record added to the file. Furthermore, the file can be accessed sequentially or through

```
CHECK$ = "2106"
GET #1, KEY #0 EQ CHECK$

MEMBER$ = "Javier"
GET #1, KEY #1 EQ MEMBER$

HOLD$ = "P1552"
GET #1, KEY #2 EQ HOLD$

GET #1, KEY #1
```

Figure 13-31   Using different indexes to read a file.

any of the keys. For example, all of the statements of Figure 13-31 could be included in the same program. Note that the required index to search is indicated by #0 for the primary index and #1 and #2 for the alternate indexes (see the number designations in Figure 13-30). The first three examples employ direct access; the last one employs sequential access. If this statement is executed repeatedly in the program, then the records will be read based on the last-name index (they will be in sorted order based on the last name).

The FIND Statement and Record Pointers with Indexed Files

All programming languages include certain elements without which the language would be of limited value and other elements that are not necessary but make programming life much easier. The FIND statement is one such element. In part, it is much like the GET except that it does not read anything into the record buffer. It simply locates the requested record, then allows the program to continue processing. Basically, it affects the record pointers. In some programming applications, it can be used to improve program efficiency. Before we continue to the next example (which utilizes the FIND), let us consider Table 13-2, which summarizes the effect of various indexed-file I/O statements on the record pointers.

TABLE 13-2 Record Pointers for Processing Indexed Files

	Processing	Current Record	Next Record
FIND	Sequential.	Previous next record.	The next logical record (The record specified by the next entry of the currently used index).
	Direct.	Designated record.	No change.
GET (following a FIND operation)	Sequential.	No change.	The next logical record (based on currently used index).
GET (without a previous FIND operation)	Sequential.	Previous next record.	The next logical record (based on currently used index).
GET	Direct.	Designated record.	The next logical record (based on currently used index).
PUT	Sequential.	None.	Not defined.
	Direct.	None.	No change.

A File-Search Example

To illustrate performing both direct and sequential access to a file in a single program, let us consider the following example:

Example 13-7

> An inquiry program is required that will allow the user to enter the last name of the person whose membership record is to be displayed. Since there may be multiple records for a given last name, the program is to display each record that is encountered and allow the user to continue to the next one or quit after the desired record is found.

Actually, the program to perform this function expands upon the logic of the program of Figure 13-24 to add records to a relative file. As each request is made for a name, the program must directly access the desired record, using the last-name index. This forms the main program loop. Since the last-name index is being used, the logical sequence of the file will be based on last name. For instance, a particular portion of the file might contain the following logical sequence of records:

Johansson

Johnson

Johnson

Johnson

Joiner

Jones

Jones

Jordan

Note that, for some names, there may be only one record, but for others, there may be more than one. Let us consider how we might program to handle this by assuming that our program is to find Johnson. The sequence of operations might be as follows:

1. Use the FIND statement to locate the first Johnson record.

   ```
   FIND #1, KEY #1 EQ "Johnson"
   ```

   Note that this is a direct-access operation.
2. Use the GET statement to read the next record.

   ```
   GET #1, KEY #1
   ```

   Note that this is a sequential-access operation.
3. Check to ensure that the record read contains the last name Johnson.
   a. If it does, then display the record and query the user about accessing another record.
   b. If it does not, then quit this part of the program.

Here we see that we will use the FIND for direct access in *locating* the desired name, then GET for sequential access to *read* those of the same name that

```
100 MAP (MEMB.REC) STRING MEMB.TYPE = 1   &
                  ,STRING MEMB.NUM =4      &
                  ,STRING LAST.NAME = 15   &
                  ,STRING FIRST.NAME = 15  &
                  ,STRING STATUS = 3       &
                  ,WORD YEAR               &
                  ,SINGLE DUES
110 DECLARE WORD SEARCH.MEMBER
200 OPEN "MEMBER.DAT" FOR INPUT AS FILE #1  &
         ,ORGANIZATION INDEXED              &
         ,ACCESS READ                       &
         ,MAP MEMB.REC
300 PRINT "To access a record, enter member's last name."
310 INPUT "Last name"; N$
320 ON ERROR GOTO 500
330 WHILE N$ <> ""
340    FIND #1, KEY #1 EQ N$
       LOOK% = -1
     DISPLAY.LOOP:
       WHILE LOOK%
350      GET #1, KEY #1
         IF LEFT$(LAST.NAME$,LEN(N$)) <> N$
         THEN
           PRINT "No more entries for ";N$
           LOOK% = 0
           ITERATE
         ENDIF
         PRINT "Number: ";MEMB.NUM;   &
               "   Name: ";EDIT$(FIRST.NAME,128) + " " + LAST.NAME
         PRINT USING "Status: 'LL... Year: ##   Dues: ###.##", &
                     STATUS, YEAR, DUES
         PRINT
         INPUT "Return for next entry, 'Q' and Return to Quit";Q$
         IF EDIT$(Q$,32) = "Q" THEN LOOK% = 0
       NEXT ! WHILE LOOK%
     NEXT.NAME.FROM.ERROR:
       INPUT "Next name (Return if finished)"; N$
     CONTINUE.FROM.ERROR.CHECK:
     NEXT ! WHILE N$ <> ""
370 PRINT "Processing complete"
    CLOSE #1
    STOP
500 ! Error Routine
510 IF ERL = 340
    THEN
      PRINT BELL; "Following name not in file: "; N$
      RESUME NEXT.NAME.FROM.ERROR
    ENDIF
520 IF ERL = 350
    THEN
      PRINT BELL; "No more entries for: "; N$
      RESUME NEXT.NAME.FROM.ERROR
    ENDIF
530 ON ERROR GOTO 0
32767 END
```

Note: Two error conditions are of interest:
1. FIND does not find requested record (statement 340).
2. GET reads to end of file (statement 350).

} Set up to terminate execution

Figure 13-32   Combining direct and sequential access—Example 13-7.

follow. A program to perform these operations is shown in Figure 13-32. Following the GET at line 350, we see an IF that tests for the name change. As soon as that occurs, the loop-control variable LOOK% is set to false in order to terminate this inner loop. Further consideration of this program is left to exercises that follow.

Exercises

13-16. In the program of Figure 13-32, why is the EDIT$ function used in the PRINT statement (which follows) and what does it do?

```
PRINT "Number: ";MEMB.NUM;  &
"    Name: ";EDIT$(FIRST.NAME,128) + " " + LAST.NAME
```

13-17. In the program of Figure 13-32, the IF statement following the GET sets up for termination of the inner loop if the name read is different from the requested name read in the outer loop. Why then is the error sequence of line 520 needed to do the same thing?

13-18. In using the program of Figure 13-32, the operator is distracted and enters "Carl" instead of "Carlson." Assuming that there is no entry in the file with the last name of Carl, what do you think will occur? Do not bother looking for the answer in the preceding descriptions; it is not there. Give your best "professional" opinion.

More About Direct Accessing—the GE and GT Operators

In the preceding example program, the FIND operation involves finding a record with an index entry equal (EQ) to a given value. In some applications, much looser search requirements may be needed. For example, a search may be desired that will find the specified record *or* the next logical record if the specified record does not exist. For instance, assume that the search is on the member number and that a portion of the file contains the following:

2004

2005

2008

2009

If we request record 2006, the FIND or GET will be unsuccessful. However, if 2006 does not exist (which is the case here), then we might want the next higher one, or 2008. For this, RMS allow us to use the GE operator, which means "*G*reater than or *E*qual to." Hence if our GET is written

```
GET #1, KEY #0 GE "2006"
```

we will always have a successful operation unless the requested number is greater than any in the file.

Similarly, if the first record with a value *larger* than a given value is required, then the GT operator (meaning *"Greater Than"*) can be used. For example, the statement

```
GET #1, KEY #0 GT "2008"
```

will return record 2009.

More About RMS Capabilities

As mentioned at the beginning of this chapter, it would be impractical to present in-depth coverage of RMS file-processing capabilities in a beginning book such as this. However, the preceding examples illustrate a variety of file-processing techniques and provide some powerful principles. The following discussions are designed to let you know that certain other features exist. For more detail, refer to appropriate DEC manuals.

Other Record Operations

In the preceding examples, we have learned to use the GET, PUT, UPDATE, and FIND record operations. In addition to these, the following three statements might be useful:

DELETE Removes the current record from a relative or indexed file.

SCRATCH Deletes all records from a sequential file, beginning with the current record, to the end of the file.

RESTORE Resets the next-record pointer to the first logical record of the file.

Regarding the DELETE statement, note that this action is irreversible. Once executed, the information previously in that record area is no longer available. A new entry can now be written to that area. In many applications, it is desirable to delete the record from active use within the file but to be able to "undelete" (make it available again) at a later time. For instance, in the membership system, it may be desirable to deactivate a member who does not pay the dues and only delete the record if the dues are not paid within, for instance, one year. This is commonly done by programming means whereby a field is included in the record specifically for this purpose. For example, the first field might be STATUS. A value of "A" (for active) might be entered if a member's dues are up to date, or a value of "I" (for inactive) might be entered if they are not. Then programming logic would provide the means for normal processing of only the active members. The file-maintenance program for the membership system might include features to change the status automatically to "I" for any member whose dues are more than 90 days past due and actually to delete the record for any member whose dues are one year past due.

Fixed- and Variable-Length Records

All of the examples of this chapter have used files in which the records are all the same length. These are called *fixed-length record* files. A file in which records are of different length is called a *variable-length record* file. RMS allows variable-length sequential and relative files (but not indexed). Since the relative structure requires that a record length be specified when a file is created, it is necessary to enter a value that is the length of the longest record to be created. Then the cell size is set to this record length. If most of the records are much shorter than the longest one needed, then a significant amount of space will be wasted.

The first thought that should come to mind relates to the MAP statement. That is, if different records may have different lengths, how do we specify the record layout? The answer is that Basic includes features for *dynamic mapping* whereby the MAP can be changed to correspond to the record that has been brought into memory. This concept is not discussed in this book; the reader is referred to appropriate DEC manuals.

Spanning Blocks

Figure 13-18 illustrates the concept of how multiple records are stored in a disk block. (Remember, disk access is by the 512-byte block.) If a record occupies 128 bytes, then a block can contain four records. However, we might wonder what happens to the left-over space if, for instance, the record uses 100 bytes (there is space for five records with 12 bytes remaining.) For sequential files *only,* RMS automatically *spans* blocks. That is, the first 12 bytes of the sixth record would be in the first block, and the next 88, in the second block. RMS takes care of this for us automatically—we need not even be aware that it is taking place.

Since RMS does not span blocks for relative and indexed files, there is the potential for considerable wasted disk space. For instance, if the record length of a relative or indexed file is 260 bytes, then almost 50 percent of the physical space required by the file will be wasted. For a large file, this is a lot of disk area. This problem is resolved by the ability to designate that several blocks be treated as a unit for a particular file. The term used in RMS is the *bucket,* where a bucket can consist of 1 to 31 blocks. For instance, if a file with a bucket size of 6 blocks is desired, then the following clause would be used in the OPEN statement:

```
BUCKETSIZE 6
```

Then in all processing of that file, operations would be as if the block were 3072 bytes rather than 512. For relative and indexed files, in which records are not allowed to span buckets, the wasted space with the sample record length of 260 bytes would be appreciably reduced.

If the BUCKETSIZE clause is not included in the OPEN, then RMS defaults to a size of 1.

In Retrospect

In this chapter, we have learned about the three basic file structures (sequential, relative, and indexed) and a variety of file-processing techniques. With the versatility of indexed files, we might wonder why we should bother using sequential or relative files. After all, indexed files allow almost everything that is possible with the other two forms. (Variable-length records are *not* allowed.)

This is really not the appropriate conclusion because each of the file structures has its strengths and weaknesses. The emphasis in this chapter has been on the basics of file processing. Although illustrated techniques have been selected to show good programming practices, there has been no focus on *optimizing*. Optimizing includes selecting the file structure that is best suited to the particular application and programming environment. For example, if a particular file will always be accessed in the physical order of its records, then there is no reason to use other than a sequential file structure.

Optimizing also involves other considerations. For instance, the selection of a larger bucketsize can both save disk storage and provide for faster processing in some cases. For many applications, it is essential that every effort be made to optimize the file structure and processing. To that end, the DEC manual *Guide to VAX/VMS File Applications* includes over 25 pages on the topic of file-processing performance and *tuning* file processing.

The strengths and weaknesses of the three file structures are summarized in the following tables.

TABLE 13-3 Sequential-File Organization: Advantages and Disadvantages

Advantages	Disadvantages
Simplest organization, adequate for sequential processing.	Direct processing capabilities are limited and not very efficient.
Allows variable-length records.	
Allows block spanning.	Records can be added only to the end of the file.
	Individual records cannot be deleted.

TABLE 13-4 Relative-File Organization: Advantages and Disadvantages

Advantages	Disadvantages
Provides both sequential and direct access with relatively low overhead.	Programmer has no control over nature of the key field, which must correspond to the cell number.
Records can be inserted into any bucket of the file.	Direct access is by the cell number only, which can be clumsy if a key field is used that has no relationship to the cell number.
Allows record deletion.	
	If consecutive numbers are not used (there are large gaps between key numbers), then a large amount of disk space will be wasted with empty cells.

TABLE 13-5 Indexed-File Organization: Advantages and Disadvantages

Advantages	Disadvantages
Key field can be numeric or string.	Highest disk-storage overhead—that is, extra storage is required for indexes.
Logical sequence of records is automatically in sorted sequence based on key.	Highest execution overhead, since RMS has much to do in indexed-file processing — hence accessing records takes longer with indexed files.
Two or more key fields can be specified for a file.	
Duplicate key values are allowed.	
Programmer need not be concerned about physical location of records within the file.	

Answers to Preceding Exercises

13-1. Internal memory can be accessed by the individual byte. Disk storage provides access only by large blocks.

13-2. With sequential processing, records are processed in the order in which they were originally written, beginning with the first one in the file. With direct processing, records are processed in whatever order is desired, for instance, the 462nd, then the 285th, then the 686th, and so on.

13-3. Most likely, the driver's license number, since this is a unique identifier pertinent to the department's business. Names are generally not unique; that is, two or more people might have the same name.

13-4. To access a given record in a sequentially organized file, every record in the file preceding the desired record must be inspected until the desired record is found. This would be extremely slow for a large file.

13-5. 10^5 seconds is approximately 1 day.
10^8 seconds is approximately 3 years.

13-6. 300 Invalid: same two variables as in line 100, but out of position.
400 Invalid: same two variables as in line 100, but different data types.

13-7. FOR INPUT indicates to the system to look for an existing file to be opened. It does *not* control whether input or input operations can be performed.

13-8. The ACCESS clause.

13-9. INPUT# can be used only with terminal-format files, that is, files opened without the ORGANIZATION clause specified in the OPEN statement. It can therefore only access records sequentially. GET can be used only with files opened with the ORGANIZATION clause included. It can access records either sequentially or directly. Both INPUT# and GET transfer records from a storage device into memory.

13-10. Try to identify the illegal operation resulting from the deletion.

13-11. A logical record is the collection of data viewed as a record in the program; its length is defined by the program that created it. A physical record is the collection of data treated as a record in an external storage device; its length is defined by physical characterstics of the hardware and operating system software.

13-12. The record buffer is a section of memory reserved by the *program* and over which the user has control. An I/O buffer is reserved for use by RMS. The I/O buffer is used for transfer of data between memory and external storage. The record buffer is used for transfer of data from memory to memory (between the record buffer and the I/O buffer).

13-13. In the absence of the RECORD clause, GET will access the next record. Then the next access to the specified channel number (PUT, in this case) will be to the *following* record (see, for example, Table 13-1). Hence the updated information will be PUT into the wrong place.

13-14. The key field in a relative file is effectively tied to the cell number, which usually precludes use of the key if the key is an existing field in the record. The key field in an indexed file is independent of any predefined memory location, so that practically any field in the record can serve as the key. For relative files, keys represent logical distances of cells from the beginning of the file. For indexed files, keys are stored in indexes that also contain the physical addresses of the records; the index is maintained by RMS as an integral part of the indexed file.

13-15. Use the following sequence:

```
DECLARE WORD HOLD
HOLD = 2166
GET #1, KEY #0 EQ HOLD
```

13-16. The EDIT$ function deletes trailing spaces from the first name. The purpose is to have the first and last name printed with one space separating the two.

13-17. If the particular name being inspected is the last logical record in the file, then an end-of-file error will occur when an attempt is made to read beyond it.

13-18. In performing the direct GET, if the search-key value is shorter than the index entry, RMS truncates the index entry during the search, so that the length corresponds to the length of the search key value. Hence the first occurrence of a last name with "Carl" as the first four letters will cause a successful FIND. For instance, "Carlson" meets this requirement. This is quite a convenient device, for a name can be located even though the exact spelling is unknown. For example, if the record for "Buchholz" is required, and the person inquiring does not know the exact spelling, then "Buch" or even "Buc" could be entered. Obviously, the fewer letters entered, the more records may require inspection in the inner loop.

   If an exact match is desired for a name that is entered, then the search-key value should be padded with spaces to the full length of the index entry. This would be a simple programming task of doctoring up N$ before executing the FIND of line 340.

Programming Problems

13-1. A company stocks approximately 2000 different items for distribution to its sales representatives. Each part includes a five-position ID code. A decision has been made to computerize the inventory system. The inventory file is to be a relative file. To that end, each item in the inventory will be given a unique four-digit number that will identify the record number of that part in the file. These will be assigned sequentially, beginning with 0002. Record number 0001 will have only one field, the count of the number of records describing different parts. This is illustrated for the first three items in the inventory by the following table:

ID Code	Becomes	Part Number
3792A		3792A0002
771PB		771PB0003
1311C		1311C0004

Thus, the item identified by ID Code 3792A (part number 3792A0002) will be the second logical record in the file, ID Code

771BP will be the third logical record in the file, and so on. Each part record is to include the following fields:

Positions	Description
1–5	Part ID code
6–25	Part description
26–29	Quantity on hand
30–33	Quantity on order
34–37	Reorder level
38–256	Other data

Note that only the ID-code portion of the part number is stored in each record.

This problem involves writing three separate programs for handling this file.

a. *File-creation and record-entry program.* For testing purposes, assume that the maximum number of logical records in the file will be 20. First create the file. Then the program must allow the user to enter up to 20 data records.

b. *File-dump program.* In order to verify file contents, a dump program is required that will print a listing of each record in the file, from the first through the last.

c. *User-inquiry program.* This program will allow the user to enter the full nine-character part number to obtain current information on any item. The logical record whose number is the last four digits of the entered part number should be read. Check the first five characters of the entered part number against the ID code of the record obtained. If they are different, display an error message. If they are the same, then display the individual fields on the screen.

13-2. This problem uses the same data records as problem 13-1, but the inventory file is to be an indexed file. The ID code is to be used as the key field. (The code is *not* extended to become a part number, as it was in problem 13-1.)

13-3. This is an expansion of problem 13-2. A generalized reporting system is required that will print a listing of the file as follows:
a. For every record in the file (same as part b of problem 13-2).
b. For only those records where the quantity on hand plus the quantity on order is less then the reorder level.
For convenience, the user must have the option of having the report printed with the records in any of the following sequences:
a. In file sequence (same as the file dump in part b of problem 13-2).
b. Sorted on the first 10 characters of the part-description field.

13-4. This problem builds on Example 13-7 in the text. Write a program to print mailing labels for all members in MEMBER.DAT whose ZIP codes begin with the four digits 6379, that is, are of the form 6379X, where X is any digit from 0 through 9.

13-5. This problem also builds on Example 13-7. Write a program to print mailing labels for all members with a specific last name. The name is to be entered from the keyboard, and the user is to be queried for possible additional names. Terminate by hitting the Return key.

13-6. In an attempt to avoid bad debts, many companies assign some type of credit rating for each customer, which is based on the customer's ability to pay his or her debts. Write a program that will read an order-control record and verify each customer's credit rating. The customer master file is an indexed file with customer number as the record key. The control file is an RMS sequential file (ORGANIZATION SEQUENTIAL clause in OPEN statement). Record formats are as follows:

Order-Control Record		Customer Master Record	
Record Positions	Field	Record Positions	Field
1–2	Card ID code	1–25	Customer name
3–6	Order number	26–50	Street address
7–12	Date of order	51–75	City, state, ZIP
13–17	Customer number	76–80	Customer number
18–25	Total order amount (dollars and cents)	81	Credit rating code

For each order-control record, read the corresponding master record and check the credit rating as follows:

Order Amount	Credit Rating Must Be
$50,000 or more	A
$20,000–49,999.99	A or B
$ 5,000–19,999.99	A, B, or C
Less than $5,000	A, B, C, or D

Output is required only if the credit rating does not agree with the order amount; if this occurs, output a message on the printer showing the order number, the customer number, and the words INSUFFICIENT CREDIT.

13-7. Budgetary control is a key part of many business operations. One technique often used is to assign each department in the organization a budget and then establish a procedure whereby no expenditure can be made without a certification (by human or computer) that the spender has sufficient funds for that expenditure. Write a program that will read *proposed-expenditure* records, verify that adequate funds exist for the proposed expenditures, and update the budgetary-control records. The budgetary-control file is an indexed file, and the department number is the record key. The expenditures file is a RMS sequential file. Record formats are as follows:

Proposed Expenditures		Budgetary-Control Records	
Record Positions	Field	Record Positions	Field
1–2	Card ID code	1–17	Department name
3–5	Department number	18–20	Department number
6–10	Document number	21–29	Budget
11–18	Amount	30–38	Expenditures this year

For each proposed expenditure record, read the corresponding budgetary-control record. If the proposed expenditure will not cause the expenditures this year to exceed the budget, add the amount to the expenditures-this-year field, and rewrite the budgetary control record. If, however, the proposed expenditure will cause expenditures this year to exceed the budget amount, output a message on the printer showing the department number, document number, and the words INSUFFICIENT FUNDS. (In this event, the budgetary-control record does not need to be rewritten because nothing is changed.)

13-8. Write a program that will update inventory records according to items received and issued. The inventory file is a relative file, with the item ID number providing the relative key. The updating file is called the "activity file"; it contains information on items issued from inventory and received into inventory. Record formats are as follows:

Activity Records		Inventory Records	
Record Positions	Field	Record Positions	Field
1	Document type (R = receipt, I = issue)	1–25	Item description
2–6	Receipt or issue document number	26–28	Item ID number
7–12	Date of receipt or issue	29–32	Item price
13–16	Department to which issued	33–36	Quantity on hand
17–19	Item ID number	37–40	Reorder point
20–23	Quantity issued or received		

For each activity record, update the proper inventory record by adding the quantity received to the quantity on hand or subtracting the quantity issued from the quantity on hand. (Remember that updating includes rewriting.) Printed output should show the document number, document type, item ID number, activity quantity, and new quantity on hand. If the new quantity on hand is less than the reorder point, also print the message TIME TO REORDER.

Appendix I
VAX Basic Reserved Words

Certain words, called *keywords* or *reserved words*, have special meaning in VAX Basic. They include all commands, statement keywords, function names, and operator names. They cannot be used as variable names, array names, or user-defined function names. Following is a complete list of these keywords.

%ABORT	ALLOW	CCPOS	CVTF$
%CDD	ALTERNATE	CHAIN	DAT
%CROSS	AND	CHANGE	DAT$
%ELSE	ANY	CHANGES	DATA
%END	APPEND	CHECKING	DATE$
%FROM	AS	CHR$	DECIMAL
%IDENT	ASC	CLK$	DECLARE
%IF	ASCII	CLOSE	DEF
%INCLUDE	ATN	CLUSTERSIZE	DEFAULTNAME
%LET	ATN2	COM	DEL
%LIST	BACK	COMMON	DELETE
%NOCROSS	BASE	COMP%	DESC
%NOLIST	BEL	CON	DET
%PAGE	BINARY	CONNECT	DIF$
%SBTTL	BIT	CONSTANT	DIM
%THEN	BLOCK	CONTIGUOUS	DIMENSION
%TITLE	BLOCKSIZE	COS	DOUBLE
%VARIANT	BS	COT	DOUBLEBUF
ABORT	BUCKETSIZE	COUNT	DUPLICATES
ABS	BUFFER	CR	DYNAMIC
ABS%	BUFSIZ	CTRLC	ECHO
ACCESS	BY	CVT$$	EDIT$
ACCESS%	BYTE	CVT$%	ELSE
ACTIVE	CALL	CVT$F	END
ALIGNED	CASE	CVT%$	EQ

EQV	IDN	NEXT	RECOUNT
ERL	IF	NOCHANGES	REF
ERN$	IFEND	NODATA	REGARDLESS
ERR	IFMORE	NODUPLICATES	RELATIVE
ERROR	IMAGE	NOECHO	REM
ERT$	IMP	NOEXTEND	REMAP
ESC	INACTIVE	NOMARGIN	RESET
EXIT	INDEXED	NONE	RESTORE
EXP	INPUT	NOPAGE	RESUME
EXPLICIT	INSTR	NOREWIND	RETURN
EXTEND	INT	NOSPAN	RFA
EXTENDSIZE	INTEGER	NOT	RIGHT
EXTERNAL	INV	NUL$	RIGHT$
FF	INVALID	NUM	RND
FIELD	ITERATE	NUM$	ROUNDING
FILE	KEY	NUM1$	RSET
FILESIZE	KILL	NUM2	SCALE
FILL	LEFT	ON	SCRATCH
FILL$	LEFT$	ONECHR	SEG$
FILL%	LEN	ONERROR	SELECT
FIND	LET	OPEN	SEQUENTIAL
FIX	LF	OPTION	SETUP
FIXED	LINE	OR	SGN
FLUSH	LINO	ORGANIZATION	SI
FNAME$	LINPUT	OTHERWISE	SIN
FNEND	LIST	OUTPUT	SINGLE
FNEXIT	LOC	OVERFLOW	SIZE
FOR	LOCKED	PAGE	SLEEP
FORMAT$	LOG	PEEK	SO
FORTRAN	LOG10	PI	SP
FREE	LONG	PLACE$	SPACE$
FROM	LSET	POS	SPAN
FSP$	MAG	POS%	SPEC%
FSS$	MAGTAPE	PPS%	SQR
FUNCTION	MAP	PRIMARY	SQRT
FUNCTIONEND	MAR	PRINT	STATUS
FUNCTIONEXIT	MAR%	PROD$	STEP
GE	MARGIN	PUT	STOP
GET	MAT	QUO$	STR$
GETRFA	MAX	RAD$	STREAM
GFLOAT	MID	RANDOM	STRING
GO	MID$	RANDOMIZE	STRING$
GOBACK	MIN	RCTRLC	SUB
GOSUB	MOD	RCTRLO	SUBEND
GOTO	MOD%	READ	SUBEXIT
GROUP	MODE	REAL	SUBSCRIPT
GT	MODIFY	RECORD	SUM$
HFLOAT	MOVE	RECORDSIZE	SWAP%
HT	NAME	RECORDTYPE	SYS

TAB	TYP	USEROPEN	VPS%
TAN	TYPE	USING	VT
TEMPORARY	TYPE$	USR$	WAIT
TERMINAL	UNALIGNED	VAL	WHILE
THEN	UNDEFINED	VAL%	WINDOWSIZE
TIM	UNLESS	VALUE	WORD
TIME	UNLOCK	VARIABLE	WRITE
TIME$	UNTIL	VARIANT	XLATE
TO	UPDATE	VFC	XOR
TRM$	USAGE$	VIRTUAL	ZER
TRN			

Appendix II
ASCII Characters

This appendix consists of three parts. Part A is a table of the seven-bit ASCII character set and the corresponding decimal equivalent of each character. Part B is a summary of special control characters. Part C is a summary of predefined constants.

II-A The ASCII Character Set

Decimal Value	ASCII Character	Decimal Value	ASCII Character	Decimal Value	ASCII Character	Decimal Value	ASCII Character
0	NUL	32	SP	64	@	96	Grave accent
1	SOH	33	!	65	A	97	a
2	STX	34	"	66	B	98	b
3	ETX	35	#	67	C	99	c
4	EOT	36	$	68	D	100	d
5	ENQ	37	%	69	E	101	e
6	ACK	38	&	70	F	102	f
7	BEL	39	''	71	G	103	g
8	BS	40	(	72	H	104	h
9	HT	41	)	73	I	105	i
10	LF	42	*	74	J	106	j
11	VT	43	+	75	K	107	k
12	FF	44	'	76	L	108	l
13	CR	45	−	77	M	109	m
14	SO	46	.	78	N	110	n
15	SI	47	/	79	O	111	o
16	DLE	48	0	80	P	112	p
17	DC1	49	1	81	Q	113	q
18	DC2	50	2	82	R	114	r
19	DC3	51	3	83	S	115	s
20	DC4	52	4	84	T	116	t
21	NAK	53	5	85	U	117	u
22	SYN	54	6	86	V	118	v
23	ETB	55	7	87	W	119	w
24	CAN	56	8	88	X	120	x
25	EM	57	9	89	Y	121	y
26	SUB	58	:	90	Z	122	z
27	ESC	59	;	91	[	123	{
28	FS	60	<	92	\	124	| Vertical Line
29	GS	61	=	93	]	125	}
30	RS	62	>	94	^ OR ↑	126	˜ Tilde
31	US	63	?	95	— OR ←	127	DEL RUBOUT

II-B Summary of Special Control Characters

Keys Used to Enter	ASCII Character	ASCII Value	Purpose	Visible Effect on Output Device
CTRL/C	ETX	3	Cancels program execution, output, system command, or any other operation; returns system to Basic command mode (to user).	Echoes as ∧C; return of control to user is indicated by "Ready."
CTRL/G	BEL	7	Sounds the terminal bell.	None.
CTRL/L	FF	12	Form feed.	Advances a printer to top of next page.
CTRL/O	SI	15	Suspends or enables screen output. Used as a toggle.	Display of output to the screen is stopped (or restarted). Echoes as ∧O.
CTRL/Q	DC1	17	Resumes output suspended by CTRL/S.	Scrolling resumes.
CTRL/S	DC3	19	Suspends display of output on terminal until CTRL/Q is pressed.	Scrolling stops.
CTRL/U	NAK	21	Cancels current program line and performs a carriage return/line feed.	Echoes as ∧U.
CTRL/Z	SUB	26	End of file.	Echoes as ∧Z.

II-C Summary of Predefined Constants

Constant Name	ASCII Value	Function of Character
BEL	7	Sounds the terminal bell.
BS	8	Varies; see example in Figure 11-11.
HT	9	Moves the cursor to the next tab stop.
LF	10	Moves the cursor to the next line.
FF	12	Used to control the printer. Causes the printer to reposition the paper to the top of the next page.
CR	13	Moves the cursor to the beginning of the current line.
SP	32	Inserts a space.
DEL	127	Backspaces over the preceding character; on most CRT terminals, it does not remove the echoed character from the screen.

Appendix III
Summary of Basic Plus Statements

Conventions Used in This Appendix

In the interest of standardizing, certain conventions are used to represent general statement forms. They are as follows:

1. Items in lowercase are supplied by the programmer. The abbreviations used in this book are as follows:

   arg—argument or arguments used in a function call.

   cond—conditional, which may be true or false.

   const—numeric or string constant.

   expr—arithmetic expression; may be a simple constant or variable.

   int—integer constant

   label—identifies a statement or block of statements.

   list—list of variables, expressions, or constants.

   ln—line number.

   num var—numeric variable

   routine—subprogram name.

   string—string variable or constant (enclosed in quotes).

   string var—string variable.

   type—data type.

   var—numeric or string variable.

2. Items in capital letters (LET, DATA, and so on) must appear exactly as shown, since they represent Basic keywords.

3. Angle brackets <> indicate required elements that are to be supplied by the programmer. For instance,

   LET *<var>* = *<expr>*

   Note: Line numbers on statements, although required, are not shown in angle brackets in the general form.

4. Square brackets [ ] indicate a required choice of one element among two or more possibilities. For example,

$$\text{GOSUB} \begin{bmatrix} ln \\ label \end{bmatrix}$$

5. Braces { } indicate an optional element (or choice of elements, as in rule 4 preceding):

{LET} <var> = <expr>

6. An element followed by ellipses (periods) implies that one or more such elements may be included:

DATA <const>,. . .

Summary of Statements

The following general statement forms include one or more example statements. For simplicity of reference, they are listed alphabetically rather than being grouped by function.

CALL

CALL <routine>
```
CALL BIG.SUB    ! Calls subprogram BIG.SUB
```

CLOSE

CLOSE <expr>,. . .
```
CLOSE #1, #2
CLOSE I%
```

COMMON

COMMON (com-name) {type <var>,. . .}
```
COMMON (BLUE) STRING EMP.CODE = 2, DEP.CODE = 10   !
                        Reserves 2 bytes
                        for EMP.CODE and 10
                        bytes for DEP.CODE
```

DATA

DATA <const>,. . .
```
DATA 25.3, 64, "STRING DATA"
```

DECLARE

DECLARE <type> <var>,. . .
```
DECLARE INTEGER  COUNT, NUM.ITEMS, STRING EMP.NAME
```

DEF

DEF {type}{FN} <var({type}arg,. . .)> = <expr(arg)> single-line function
DEF {type}{FN} <var({type}arg,. . .)>   multiline function
```
DEF FNC(R) = 2.0*3.14*R*R    (single line)
DEF FNCNT$(A,B,C)            (multiple line)
```

DIM

> DIM {*type*} <*var(num var,. . .>),. . .*
> DIM {*type*} <*var(int,. . .)>,. . .*
> ```
> DIM A(20), B%(10, 15), C$(15)
> ```

END

> ```
> END      ! End of program
> ```

END <*block*> where *block* is: DEF
>   IF
>   FUNCTION
>   SELECT
>   SUB

> ```
> END DEF        ! End of multiline function
> END IF         ! End of IF block
> END FUNCTION   ! End of separately compiled function
> END SELECT     ! End of multiple selection
> END SUB        ! End of subprogram
> ```

EXIT <*block*> where *block* is: DEF
>   FUNCTION
>   SUB
>   *label*

> ```
> EXIT   DEF        ! Unconditional transfer to END DEF
> EXIT   FUNCTION   ! Unconditional transfer
>                     to END FUNCTION
> EXIT   SUB        ! Unconditional transfer to END SUB
> EXIT <label>      ! Unconditional transfer to the first
>                     statement following the end
>                     of the specified block
> ```

EXTERNAL

> EXTERNAL <*type*> FUNCTION <*fn-name*>
> ```
> EXTERNAL INTEGER FUNCTION MAXIM    ! Declares MAXIM as a
>                                      separately compiled
>                                      integer function
> ```

FIND

> FIND <*# expr*> {,RECORD <*expr*>}
> ```
> FIND #3 RECORD 15   ! Locates record 15 in file associated
>                       with channel number 3
> ```

FOR

> FOR <*num var*> = <*expr*> TO <*expr*> STEP <*expr*>
> ```
> FOR I = 1 TO 20
> FOR J = N TO 0 STEP -1
> ```

FOR–UNTIL, FOR–WHILE

> FOR <*num var*> = <*expr*> STEP <*expr*> $\begin{bmatrix} \text{UNTIL} \\ \text{WHILE} \end{bmatrix}$ <*cond*>
> ```
> FOR A = 1  WHILE X > 0.0
> FOR B = 3 STEP 4  UNTIL FINISHED%
> ```

FUNCTION

FUNCTION *<type>* *<fn-name>* {*type list*)}
```
FUNCTION REAL VOL.SPHERE(REAL RADIUS)
```

GET

GET *<expr>* {,RECORD *<expr>*}
```
GET #5
GET #6, RECORD N
```

GOSUB

GOSUB $\begin{bmatrix} ln \\ label \end{bmatrix}$
```
GOSUB 750
```

GOTO

GOTO $\begin{bmatrix} ln \\ label \end{bmatrix}$
```
GOTO 260
GO TO 260
```

IF–THEN

IF *<cond>* THEN *<statement block>* END IF
```
IF A=B THEN PRINT "VARIABLES CHECK"
```

IF–THEN–ELSE

IF *<cond>* THEN *<statement block>* ELSE *<statement block>* END IF
```
IF A=B THEN PRINT "CHECK" ELSE PRINT "NO CHECK"
```

INPUT

INPUT {#*<expr>*,} *<list>*
INPUT {*literal,*} *<list>*
```
INPUT #1, A,B,C
INPUT P,Q$
INPUT "WHAT IS THE MAXIMUM", M
```

INPUT LINE

INPUT LINE {#*<expr>*,} *<string>*
```
INPUT LINE Q$
INPUT LINE #4, L$
```

ITERATE

ITERATE {label}
```
ITERATE              ! Unconditional transfer of control
                       to current loop's NEXT statement
ITERATE SEARCH.LOOP  ! Unconditional transfer of control
                       to the NEXT statement in the
                       specified loop
```

KILL

KILL <*string*>

```
KILL "ABC.DAT"    ! Delete the file ABC.DAT
```

LET

{LET} <*var*>,. . . = <*expr*>

```
LET A = B*C + 25.0
A = B*C + 25.0
X%, Y%, Z% = 0    ! Set all 3 variables to zero
```

LINPUT

LINPUT {#<*expr*>,} <*string*>

```
LINPUT Q$
LINPUT #4, L$
```

LSET

LSET <*string var*>,. . . = <*string*>

```
LSET D$ = Q$ + "OVERDUE"
```

MAP

MAP (*map name*) {*type*} <*list*>

```
MAP (LARGE) LONG A,B,  REAL F,G
```

MAT INPUT

MAT INPUT {#<*expr*>,} <*list of matrices*>

```
MAT INPUT #1%, A%, B%
```

MAT PRINT

MAT PRINT {#<*expr*>,} <*matrix name*>

```
MAT PRINT A
```

MAT READ

MAT READ <*list of matrices*>

```
MAT READ A,B
```

MAT ZER

MAT <*matrix name*> = ZER (*int*,. . .)

```
MAT A% = ZER
MAT B% = ZER (15,10)    ! Reduces upper bound of matrix
```

NEXT (used with FOR)

NEXT <*num var*>

```
NEXT J%
```

NEXT (used with UNTIL or WHILE)

NEXT

```
NEXT
```

ON ERROR

$$\text{ON ERROR GOTO} \begin{bmatrix} ln \\ label \end{bmatrix}$$

```
ON ERROR GOTO 30000
```

ON-GOSUB

ON *<expr>* GOSUB *<list of line numbers>*

```
ON N% GOSUB 500, 620, 700, 850
```

OPEN

$$\text{OPEN } \textit{<string>} \begin{Bmatrix} \text{FOR INPUT} \\ \text{FOR OUTPUT} \end{Bmatrix} \text{AS FILE } \#\textit{<expr>}$$

{,RECORDSIZE *<expr>*}

```
OPEN "ABC.XYZ" FOR INPUT AS FILE #1
OPEN F$ FOR OUTPUT AS FILE #2
OPEN "WORK.FLE" AS FILE #3
```

PRINT

PRINT {#*<expr>*,} *<list>*

```
PRINT A,B$,C%
PRINT #1,X,Y,Z
PRINT
```

PRINT-USING

PRINT {#*<expr>*,} USING *<string>* {,*<list>*}

```
PRINT USING M$
PRINT #4, USING "###.##     ###", A,I%
```

PUT

PUT #*<expr>* {,RECORD *<expr>*}

```
PUT #5
PUT #4, RECORD 20%
```

RANDOMIZE

RANDOMIZE

```
RANDOMIZE
```

READ

READ *<var>*,. . .

```
READ A,B$
```

REM

REM *<message>*
! *<message>*
<statement> ! *<message>*

```
REM    EXAMPLE
!      EXAMPLE
I% = 0         !Initialize counter
```

RESTORE

> RESTORE
> ```
> RESTORE
> ```

RESUME

> RESUME *ln*
> ```
> RESUME          !RESUME processing at error line
> RESUME 600      !RESUME at line 600
> ```

RETURN

> RETURN
> ```
> RETURN     !RETURN to statement following GOSUB
> ```

RSET

> RSET <*string var*>,. . . = <*string*>
> ```
> RSET F$ = "FINISHED"
> ```

SELECT

> SELECT <*expr*>
> ```
> SELECT EXAM.SCORES
> ```

SLEEP

> SLEEP <*expr*>
> ```
> SLEEP 20     ! Suspend processing for 20 seconds
> ```

STOP

> STOP
> ```
> STOP
> ```

SUB

> SUB <*routine*> (*type list*)
> ```
> SUB LARGEST(DOUBLE A,B,C)
> ```

UNLESS

> <*statement*> UNLESS <*cond*>
> ```
> PRINT "abc" UNLESS FORGOT = -1
> ```

UNTIL

> UNTIL <*cond*>
> ```
> UNTIL FINISHED = -1
> ```

UPDATE

> UPDATE <*#expr*>
> ```
> UPDATE  #8
> ```

WHILE

> WHILE <*cond*>
> ```
> WHILE FINISHED = 0
> ```

Appendix IV
Summary of VAX Basic Functions

This appendix briefly summarizes VAX Basic functions that are most commonly encountered.

Type	Function	Value Returned
Mathematical	Y = ABS(X)	Absolute value of X.
	Y = ATN(X)	Arctangent (in radians) of X.
	Y = COS(X)	Cosine of X, where X is in radians.
	Y = EXP(X)	Value of e^x, where e = 2.71828 . . .
	Y = FIX(X)	Truncated value of X, SGN(X)*INT(ABS(X)).
	Y = INT(X)	Greatest integer that is less than or equal to X.
	Y = LOG(X)	Natural logarithm of X, $\log_e$ X.
	Y = LOG10(X)	Common logarithm of X, $\log_{10}$ X.
	Y = PI	Constant 3.14159 . . .
	Y = RND	Random number between 0 and 1.
	Y = RND(X)	Random number between 0 and 1.
	Y = SGN(X)	Sign function of X; + 1 if positive, 0 if zero, − 1 if negative.
	Y = SIN(X)	Sine of X, where X is in radians.
	Y = SQR(X)	Square root of X.
	Y = TAN(X)	Tangent of X, where X is in radians.
String	Y% = ASCII(A$)	ASCII value of the first character in the string A$.
	Y$ = CHR$(X)	A single character having the ASCII value of X.
	T$ = EDIT$(S$,M%)	Converts the source character string S$ to the string referenced by the variable T$. The conversion is performed according to the decimal value of the integer represented by M%, as follows. These digits may be summed to produce any combination of these conversions.

1   Trim the parity bit.

2   Discard all spaces and tabs.

4   Discard excess characters: CR, LF, FF, ESC, RUBOUT, and NULL.

8   Discard leading spaces and tabs.

16   Reduce spaces and tabs to one space.

	32	Convert lowercase to uppercase.
	64	Convert [to (and] to).
	128	Discard trailing spaces and tabs.
	256	Do not alter characters inside quotes.

	Y$ = STRING$(N1%,N2%)	Creates string Y$ of length N1%, composed of characters whose ASCII decimal value is N2%.
	Y$ = LEFT$(A$,N%)	A substring of the string A$ from the first character to the Nth character (the leftmost N% characters).
	Y$ = RIGHT$(A$,N%)	A substring of the string A$ from the Nth to the last character (the rightmost characters of the string starting with the Nth character).
	Y$ = MID$(A$,N1%,N2%)	A substring of the string A$ starting with the N1% and being N2% characters long (the characters between and including the N1% to N1% + N2% − 1 characters).
	Y$ = SEG$(A$,N1%,N2%)	A substring of the string A$, starting with the N1% character and ending with the N2% character of A$.
	Y% = INSTR(N1%,A$,B$)	Searches for the substring B$ within the string A$, beginning at character position N1. Returns a value 0 if B$ is not in A$, and returns the character position of B$ if B$ is found to be in A$ (character position is measured from the start of the string).
	Y$ = SPACE$(N%)	A string of N spaces, used to insert spaces within a character string.
	Y$ = NUM$(N)	A string of numeric characters representing the value of N as it would be output by a PRINT statement. For example: NUM$(1.0000) = ƀ1ƀ and NUM$(−1.0000) = −1ƀ.
	Y$ = NUM1$(N)	A string of characters representing the value of N. This is similar to the function NUM$, except that it does not return spaces.
	Y = VAL(A$)	The numeric value of the string of numeric characters A$. If A$ contains any character not acceptable as numeric input with the INPUT statement, an error results. For example: VAL("15") = 15
Matrix	MAT Y = TRN(X)	Transpose of the matrix X.
	MAT Y = INV(X)	Inverse of the matrix X.
	Y = DET	Following an INV(X) function evaluation, the variable DET is equal to the determinant of X.
	Y% = NUM	Following input of a matrix, NUM contains the number of rows entered or, in the case of a one-dimensional matrix, the number of elements entered.
	Y% = NUM2	Following input of a matrix, NUM2 contains the number of elements entered in the last row, or zero in the case of a one-dimensional array.
System	Y$ = DATE$(0)	Current date in the following format: 02-Mar-87
	Y$ = TIME$(0)	Current time of day as a character string, as follows: TIME$(0) = "05:30 PM" or "17:30"

Appendix V
Basic Commands

In addition to the Basic commands summarized here, any VMS-level command may be entered in the Basic environment by preceding the command with a dollar sign ($). Basic passes the command to VMS for execution.

Command	Function
COMPILE	Generates an object module from a BASIC source program. The object module has a default file type of OBJ.
CONTINUE	Resumes execution after a STOP statement or a CTRL/C.
DELETE	Erases a specified line(s) from a BASIC source program.
EXIT	Returns to DCL command level.
HELP	Displays HELP text.
LIST	Displays the current source program on the terminal.
LISTNH	Displays the current source program without header information.
LOAD	Loads an object module into memory.
NEW	Clears memory for the creation of a new program and assigns a new program name.
OLD	Reads a specified BASIC source program into memory.
RENAME	Changes the name of the program currently in memory.
REPLACE	Replaces a stored program with the program currently in memory. In VAX BASIC, REPLACE is identical to SAVE.
RESEQUENCE	Supplies new line numbers for the program currently in memory.
RUN	Executes the program currently in memory or a specified BASIC source program. The program in memory can be (1) a BASIC source program placed in memory with the OLD command, (2) object module(s) placed in memory with the LOAD command, or (3) a combination of 1 and 2.
RUNNH	Identical to RUN but does not display header information.
SAVE	Creates a copy of the current source program on a specified device.
SEQUENCE	Generates line numbers for input text.
UNSAVE	Deletes a specified file.

Appendix VI
Run-Time
Error Messages

Basic returns run-time messages if an error occurs while a program is executing. There are four types of errors with different "severity levels."

I	Informational message
W	Warning message
E	Error message
F	Severe error

Informational and warning messages indicate that something has been detected, but program execution continues. Errors (E and F messages) cause the program to be aborted. It is possible to recover from most errors by including error-handling routines in the program. Recovery routines are not needed for I and W messages. The format of the VAX Basic error message is illustrated by the following example:

```
%BAS-E-INTERR
```

- The letter E indicates the severity level.
- The code INTERR is a code abbreviation identifying the error. This appendix includes an alphabetic list of these abbreviations.
- Following the code will be a message indicating the line number at which the error occurred.

Each of the run-time errors is identified by an error number that can be incorporated into the program error-recovery routines in order to determine which error has occurred.

Part A of this appendix lists the errors by error number and includes an abbreviated description of the meaning. Part B lists the errors in alphabetic order by the code abbreviation. Part C contains an expanded description for commonly encountered errors or those that are not obvious from their abbreviated description.

VI-A Run-time Errors by Error Number

1	BADDIRDEV, bad directory for device
2	ILLFILNAM, illegal file name
4	NO_ROOUSE, no room for user on device
5	CANFINFIL, can't find file or account
7	IO_CHAALR, I/O channel already open
9	IO_CHANOT, I/O channel not open
10	PROVIO, protection violation
11	ENDFILDEV, end of file on device
12	FATSYSIO_, fatal system I/O failure
14	DEVHUNWRI, device hung or write locked
15	KEYWAIEXH, keyboard wait exhausted
16	NAMACCNOW, name or account now exists
18	ILLSYSUSA, illegal SYS() usage
28	PROC_TRA, programmable $^\wedge$C trap
29	CORFILSTR, corrupted file structure
31	ILLBYTCOU, illegal byte count for I/O
35	MEMMANVIO, memory management violation
42	VIRBUFTOO, virtual buffer too large
43	VIRARRDIS, virtual array not on disk
45	VIRARROPE, virtual array not yet open
46	ILLIO_CHA, illegal I/O channel
48	FLOPOIERR, floating-point error or overflow
49	ARGTOOLAR, argument too large in EXP
50	DATFORERR, data format error
51	INTERR, integer error
52	ILLNUM, illegal number
53	ILLARGLOG, illegal argument in LOG
54	IMASQUROO, imaginary square roots
55	SUBOUTRAN, subscript out of range
56	CANINVMAT, can't invert matrix
57	OUTOF_DAT, out of data
58	ON_STAOUT, ON statement out of range
59	NOTENODAT, not enough data in record
61	DIVBY_ZER, division by 0
63	FIEOVEBUF, FIELD overflows buffer
64	NOTRANACC, not a random-access device
66	MISSPEFEA, missing special feature
67	ILLSWIUSA, illegal switch usage
72	RETWITGOS, RETURN without GOSUB
73	FNEWITFUN, FNEND without function call
88	ARGDONMAT, arguments don't match
89	TOOMANARG, too many arguments
97	TOOFEWARG, too few arguments
101	DATTYPERR, data type error
102	ONEOR_TWO, one or two dimensions only
103	PROLOSSOR, program lost—sorry
104	RESNO_ERR, RESUME and no error
105	REDARR, redimensioned array
109	WHA, what?
116	PRIUSIFOR, PRINT–USING format error
122	ILLFIEVAR, illegal FIELD variable
123	STO, stop
124	MATDIMERR, matrix dimension error
126	MAXMEMEXC, maximum memory exceeded
127	SCAFACINT, SCALE factor interlock
128	TAPRECNOT, tape records not ANSI

129	TAPBOTDET, tape BOT detected
130	KEYNOTCHA, key not changeable
131	NO_CURREC, no current record
132	RECHASBEE, record has been deleted
133	ILLUSADEV, illegal usage for device
134	DUPKEYDET, duplicate key detected
136	ILLILLACC, illegal or illogical access
137	ILLKEYATT, illegal key attributes
138	FILIS_LOC, file is locked
139	INVFILOPT, invalid file options
141	ILLOPE, illegal operation
142	ILLRECFIL, illegal record on file
143	BADRECIDE, bad record identifier
144	INVKEYREF, invalid key of reference
145	KEYSIZTOO, key size too large
146	TAPNOTANS, tape not ANSI labeled
147	RECNUMEXC, RECORD number exceeds maximum
148	BADRECVAL, bad RECORDSIZE value on OPEN
149	NOTENDFIL, not at end of file
150	NO_PRIKEY, no primary key specified
151	KEYFIEBEY, key field beyond end of record
152	ILLRECACC, illogical record accessing
153	RECALREXI, record already exists
154	RECBUCLOC, record/bucket locked
155	RECNOTFOU, record not found
156	SIZRECINV, size of record invalid
157	RECFILTOO, record on file too big
158	PRIKEYOUT, primary key out of sequence
159	KEYLARTHA, key larger than record
160	FILATTNOT, file attributes not matched
161	MOVOVEBUF, move overflows buffer
162	CANNOT OPEN FILE
164	TERFORFIL, terminal format file required
166	NEGFILSTR, negative fill or string length
168	ILLALLCLA, illegal ALLOW clause
170	INDNOTFUL, index not fully optimized
171	RRVNOTFUL, RRV not fully updated
173	INVRFAFIE, invalid RFA field
174	FILEXPDAT, file expiration date not yet reached
175	NODNAMERR, node name error
176	NEGTABNOT, negative TAB no allowed
177	TOOMUCDAT, too much data in record
178	ERRFILCOR, error on OPEN—file corrupted
179	UNEFILDAT, unexpired file date
181	DECERR, decimal error or overflow
183	REMOVEBUF, REMAP overflows buffer
227	STRTOOLON, string too long
228	RECATTNOT, record attributes not matched
229	DIFUSELON, differing use of LONG/WORD qualifiers
238	ARRMUSSAM, arrays must be same dimension
239	ARRMUSSQU, arrays must be square
240	CANCHAARR, cannot change array dimensions
245	ILLEXIDEF, illegal exit from DEF*
246	ERRTRANEE, ERROR trap needs RESUME
247	ILLRESSUB, illegal RESUME to subroutine
250	NOTIMP, not implemented
252	FILACPFAI, FILE ACP failure
253	DIRERR, directive error

VI-B Run-time Errors by Error Code

ARGDONMAT, arguments don't match (ERR = 88)
ARGTOOLAR, argument too large in EXP (ERR = 49)
ARRMUSSAM, arrays must be same dimension (ERR = 238)
ARRMUSSQU, arrays must be square (ERR = 239)
BADDIRDEV, bad directory for device (ERR = 1)
BADRECIDE, bad record identifier (ERR = 143)
BADRECVAL, bad RECORDSIZE value on OPEN (ERR = 148)
CANCHAARR, cannot change array dimensions (ERR = 240)
CANFINFIL, can't find file or account (ERR = 5)
CANINVMAT, can't invert matrix (ERR = 56)
CANOPEFIL, cannot open file (ERR = 162)
CORFILSTR, corrupted file structure (ERR = 29)
DATFORERR, data format error (ERR = 50)
DATTYPERR, data type error (ERR = 101)
DECERR, DECIMAL error or overflow (ERR = 181)
DEVHUNWRI, device hung or write locked (ERR = 14)
DIFUSELON, differing use of LONG/WORD or SINGLE/DOUBLE qualifiers
   (ERR = 229)
DIRERR, directive error (ERR = 253)
DIVBY_ZER, division by 0 (ERR = 61)
DUPKEYDET, duplicate key detected (ERR = 134)
ENDFILDEV, end of file on device (ERR = 11)
ERRFILCOR, error on OPEN–file corrupted (ERR = 178)
ERRTRANEE, ERROR trap needs RESUME (ERR = 246)
FATSYSIO_, fatal system I/O failure (ERR = 12)
FIEOVEBUF, FIELD overflows buffer (ERR = 63)
FILACPFAI, FILE ACP failure (ERR = 252)
FILATTNOT, file attributes not matched (ERR = 160)
FILEXPDAT, file expiration date not yet reached (ERR = 174)
FILIS_LOC, file is locked (ERR = 138)
FLOPOIERR, floating-point error or overflow (ERR = 48)
FNEWITFUN, FNEND without function call (ERR = 73)
ILLALLCLA, illegal ALLOW clause (ERR = 168)
ILLARGLOG, illegal argument in LOG (ERR = 53)
ILLBYTCOU, illegal byte count for I/O (ERR = 31)
ILLEXIDEF, illegal exit from DEF* (ERR = 245)
ILLFIEVAR, illegal FIELD variable (ERR = 122)
ILLFILNAM, illegal file name (ERR = 2)
ILLILLACC, illegal or illogical access (ERR = 136)
ILLIO_CHA, illegal I/O channel (ERR = 46)
ILLKEYATT, illegal key attributes (ERR = 137)
ILLNUM, illegal number (ERR = 52)
ILLOPE, illegal operation (ERR = 141)
ILLRECACC, illogical record accessing (ERR = 152)
ILLRECFIL, illegal record on file (ERR = 142)
ILLRECLOC, illegal record locking (ERR = 187)
ILLRESSUB, illegal RESUME to subroutine (ERR = 247)
ILLSWIUSA, illegal switch usage (ERR = 67)
ILLSYSUSA, illegal SYS usage() (ERR = 18)
ILLUSADEV, illegal usage for device (ERR = 133)
IMASQUROO, imaginary square roots (ERR = 54)
IMPERRHAN, improper error handling (ERR = 186)
INDNOTFUL, index not fully optimized (ERR = 170)
INTERR, integer error (ERR = 51)
INVFILOPT, invalid file options (ERR = 139)
INVKEYREF, invalid key of reference (ERR = 144)

INVRFAFIE, invalid RFA field (ERR = 173)
IO_CHAALR, I/O channel already open (ERR = 7)
IO_CHANOT, I/O channel not open (ERR = 9)
KEYFIEBEY, key field beyond end of record (ERR = 151)
KEYLARTHA, key larger than record (ERR = 159)
KEYNOTCHA, key not changeable (ERR = 130)
KEYSIZTOO, key size too large (ERR = 145)
KEYWAIEXH, keyboard wait exhausted (ERR = 15)
MATDIMERR, matrix dimension error (ERR = 124)
MAXMEMEXC, maximum memory exceeded (ERR = 126)
MEMMANVIO, memory management violation (ERR = 35)
MISSPEFEA, missing special feature (ERR = 66)
MOVOVEBUF, move overflows buffer (ERR = 161)
NAMACCNOW, name or account now exists (ERR = 16)
NEGFILSTR, negative fill or string length (ERR = 166)
NEGZERTAB, negative or zero TAB not allowed (ERR = 176)
NETOPERR, network operation error (ERR = 182)
NODNAMERR, node name error (ERR = 175)
NOTENDFIL, not at end of file (ERR = 149)
NOTENODAT, not enough data in record (ERR = 59)
NOTIMP, not implemented (ERR = 250)
NOTRANACC, not a random-access device (ERR = 64)
NO_CURREC, no current record (ERR = 131)
NO_PRIKEY, no primary key specified (ERR = 150)
NO_ROOUSE, no room for user on device (ERR = 4)
ONEOR_TWO, one or two dimensions only (ERR = 102)
ON_STAOUT, ON statement out of range (ERR = 58)
OUTOF_DAT, out of data (ERR = 57)
PRIKEYOUT, primary key out of sequence (ERR = 158)
PRIUSIFOR, PRINT–USING format error (ERR = 116)
PROC_TRA, programmableˆC trap (ERR = 28)
PROLOSSOR, program lost—sorry (ERR = 103)
PROVIO, protection violation (ERR = 10)
RECALREXI, record already exists (ERR = 153)
RECATTNOT, record attributes not matched (ERR = 228)
RECBUCLOC, record/bucket locked (ERR = 154)
RECFILTOO, record on file too big (ERR = 157)
RECHASBEE, record has been deleted (ERR = 132)
RECNOTFOU, record not found (ERR = 155)
RECNUMEXC, RECORD number exceeds maximum (ERR = 147)
RECOVEMAP, RECORDSIZE overflows MAP buffer (ERR = 185)
REDARR, redimensioned array (ERR = 105)
REMOVEBUF, REMAP overflows buffer (ERR = 183)
RESNO_ERR, RESUME and no error (ERR = 104)
RETWITGOS, RETURN without GOSUB (ERR = 72)
RRVNOTFUL, RRV not fully updated (ERR = 171)
SCAFACINT, SCALE factor interlock (ERR = 127)
SIZRECINV, size of record invalid (ERR = 156)
STO, stop (ERR = 123)
STRTOOLON, string too long (ERR = 227)
SUBOUTRAN, subscript out of range (ERR = 55)
SYNERR, syntax error (ERR = 98)
TAPBOTDET, tape BOT detected (ERR = 129)
TAPNOTANS, tape not ANSI labeled (ERR = 146)
TAPRECNOT, tape records not ANSI (ERR = 128)
TERFORFIL, terminal format file required (ERR = 164)
TOOFEWARG, too few arguments (ERR = 97)
TOOLITDAT, too little data in record (ERR = 189)

TOOMANARG, too many arguments (ERR = 89)
TOOMUCDAT, too much data in record (ERR = 177)
UNEFILDAT, unexpired file date (ERR = 179)
VIRARRDIS, virtual array not on disk (ERR = 43)
VIRARROPE, virtual array not yet open (ERR = 45)
VIRBUFTOO, virtual buffer too large (ERR = 42)
WHA, what? (ERR = 109)

VI-C Run-Time Error Descriptions

ARGDONMAT, arguments don't match (ERR = 88)
  Explanation: ERROR—The arguments in a function call do not match the arguments defined for the function, either in number or in type.
BADRECIDE, bad record identifier (ERR = 143)
  Explanation: ERROR—The program attempted a record access that specified a zero or negative record number on a RELATIVE file, or a null key value on an INDEXED file.
CANFINFIL, can't find file or account (ERR = 5)
  Explanation: ERROR—The specified file or directory is not on the device.
DATFORERR, data format error (ERR = 50)
  Explanation: WARNING—The program specifies a data type in an INPUT or READ statement that does not agree with the value supplied.
DEVHUNWRI, device hung or write locked (ERR = 14)
  Explanation: ERROR—The program attempted an operation to a hardware device that is not functioning properly or is protected against writing.
DIFUSELON, differing use of LONG/WORD or SINGLE/DOUBLE qualifiers (ERR = 229)
  Explanation: ERROR—The main and subprograms were compiled with different LONG/WORD modes.
ENDFILDEV, end of file on device (ERR = 11)
  Explanation: ERROR—the program attempted to read data beyond the end of the file.
ERRTRANEE, ERROR trap needs RESUME (ERR = 246)
  Explanation: ERROR—An error handler attempts to execute and END, END SUB, END FUNCTION, SUBEND, FUNCTIONEND, or FNEND statement without first executing a RESUME statement.
FILATTNOT, file attributes not matched (ERR = 160)
  Explanation: ERROR—the attributes in the OPEN statement do not match the corresponding attributes of the target file.
FNEWITFUN, FNEND without function call (ERR = 73)
  Explanation: ERROR—The program executes an END DEF or FNEND statement before executing a function call.
ILLFILNAM, illegal file name (ERR = 2)
  Explanation: ERROR—A file name (1) is too long, (2) is incorrectly formatted, or (3) contains embedded blanks or invalid characters.
ILLIO_CHA illegal I/O channel (ERR = 46)
  Explanation: ERROR—The program specified an I/O channel outside the legal range.
ILLNUM, illegal number (ERR = 52)
  Explanation: ERROR—A value supplied to a numeric variable is incorrect; for example, ''ABC'' and ''1..2'' are illegal numbers.
ILLRECACC, illogical record accessing (ERR = 152)
  Explanation: ERROR—The program attempts to perform an operation that is invalid for the specified file type, for example, a random access on a sequential file.
IMASQUROO, imaginary square roots (ERR = 54)
  Explanation: ERROR—An argument to the SQR function is negative.
INTERR, integer error (ERR = 51)
  Explanation: ERROR—The program contains an integer whose absolute value is greater than 255 in BYTE mode, 32767 in WORD mode, or 2147483647 in LONG mode.
IO_CHAALR, I/O channel already open (ERR = 7)
  Explanation: ERROR—The program attempted to OPEN channel zero (the controlling terminal).
IO_CHANOT, I/O channel not open (ERR = 9)
  Explanation: ERROR—The program attempted to perform an I/O operation before opening the channel.
MATDIMERR, matrix dimension error (ERR = 124)
  Explanation: ERROR—The program attempts to assign more than two dimensions to an array, or reference an array with fewer or more subscripts than there are dimensions in the array, or change the upper bound on an array for which this cannot be done.

NOTENODAT, not enough data in record (ERR = 59)

    Explanation: ERROR—An INPUT statement did not find enough data in one line to satisfy all the specified variable.

NO_CURREC, No current record (ERR = 131)

    Explanation: ERROR—The program attempts a DELETE or UPDATE when the previous GET or FIND failed, or no previous GET or FIND was done.

OUTOF_DAT, Out of data (ERR = 57)

    Explanation: ERROR—A READ statement requested additional data from an exhausted DATA list.

RECOVEMAP, RECORDSIZE overflows MAP buffer (ERR = 185)

    Explanation: ERROR—The OPEN statement specifies a RECORDSIZE value larger than the size of the MAP specified in the MAP clause.

RESNO_ERR, RESUME and no error (ERR = 104)

    Explanation: ERROR—The program executes a RESUME statement outside of the error-handling routine.

STO, Stop (ERR = 123)

    Explanation: INFORMATION—The program executed a STOP statement.

TOOFEWARG, too few arguments (ERR = 97)

    Explanation: ERROR—A function invocation or CALL passed fewer arguments than were defined in the function or subprogram.

Index